Easy Daily Plans

Over 250 Plans for Preschool Teachers

BY SUE FLEISCHMANN

Dedication

This book is dedicated to my wonderful family: My husband, Ron; my children, Ron, Kristin, Jenny, and Kevin; my parents, Bob and Jackie Larsen; and my grandmother, Margaret Anderson. Thank you for your love and support.

Easy Daily Plans

Over 250 Plans for Preschool Teachers

Sue Fleischmann

Illustrations by Marie Ferrante-Doyle

Gryphon House, Inc,

Beltsville, Maryland

Published by Gryphon House, Inc.
10726 Tucker Street, Beltsville, MD 20705
301.595.9500; 301.595.0051 (fax); 800.638.0928 (toll-free)

Visit us on the web at www.ghbooks.com

Library of Congress Cataloging-in-Publication Data

Fleischmann, Sue.
  Easy daily plans for preschool teachers / Sue Fleischmann ; illustrations, Marie Ferrante-Doyle.
     p. cm.
  ISBN-13: 978-0-87659-005-8
  ISBN-10: 0-87659-005-9
 1. Education, Preschool--Activity programs. 2. Education, Preschool--Curricula. 3. Lesson planning. 4. School year. I. Title.
  LB1140.35.C74F537 2007
  372.13'028--dc22

                    2006032357

Gryphon House is a member of the Green Press Initiative, a nonprofit program dedicated to supporting publishers in their efforts to reduce their use of fiber sourced forests. For further information visit www.greenpressinitiative.org.

BULK PURCHASE

Gryphon House books are available for special premiums and sales promotions as well as for fund-raising use. Special editions or book excerpts also can be created to specification. For details, contact the Director of Marketing at Gryphon House.

Table of Contents

May...227

June, July, and August Summer Camp Topics 253

Introduction

Children are active learners who learn by doing. Active learning allows children to explore and solve problems in their own way. This book contains daily plans with developmentally appropriate activities for young children. The activities are open ended so it is possible to adjust them to suit the range of ages and abilities of the children in the classroom. The daily plans are appropriate for many types of programs, including preschools, Head Start programs, cooperatives, home school programs, and family day care programs.

Easy Daily Plans is the perfect book for busy teachers and caregivers to grab and use. The ideas are creative, fun, and easy to implement. The book is organized by month, beginning in September. Listed at the front of each chapter are month-long celebrations (such as National Strawberry Month), week-long celebrations (such as National Pet Week), special days (Thomas Edison's birthday, for example) and holidays (such as Cinco de Mayo), and general daily plans. Simply choose the plans that you wish to do that month, read them, collect the necessary supplies, and get started.

Each daily plan includes a Story Time book list, Group Time activity, and Learning Center Ideas. Additional activities for rhythm and rhyme, small group, projects, outdoor experiences, movement, and games are also included throughout the book. Transition and snack ideas are also included in many plans. All of the activities encourage children to improve listening skills, increase vocabulary, follow directions, develop oral and written language skills, cooperate in a group setting, work on fine and gross motor skills, and develop new skills in the content areas.

Learning takes place all day—from the time the children hang up their coats in the morning to the end of the day when they reconnect with their families. *Easy Daily Plans* offers fun, easy ways to enrich the hours in between.

September

Calendar Time

During Calendar Time, introduce the month of September to the children. Look at the letters in the word *September*. Name each letter, and say the sound and some other words that start with the sound. Whose name begins with the letter *s*? Do this for each letter in the word during calendar time throughout the month.

Monthly Organizer

MONTH-LONG CELEBRATIONS

National Hispanic Heritage Month
Good Manners Month

SPECIAL DAYS AND HOLIDAYS

First Sunday after Labor Day: National Grandparents' Day
September 15: Tomie dePaola's birthday
September 25: Johnny Appleseed's birthday

GENERAL DAILY PLANS

A Bear-y Big Welcome
I Am Special
Names
Squares
School Tools
Animal Friends
Yellow
Numeral 8
Blue
Feelings
Letter *H*
Helpfulness
Circles
Letter *S*
Perseverance

Letter *B*
Elephant Appreciation Day
Fall
Letter *C*
Triangles
Diamonds
Squirrels
Ovals

Note: Please be sure to check for allergies before serving snacks or doing any food-related activities.

National Hispanic Heritage Month

MONTH-LONG CELEBRATION

STORY TIME

Bienvenidos by Cynthia Downs
Fiesta by Ginger Foglesong Guy
Too Many Tamales by Gary Soto
*Tortillas Para Mama and Other
    Nursery Rhymes* by Margot C.
Greigo

SNACK

Make quesadillas. Invite children to sprinkle grated Monterey Jack cheese on a tortilla. Cover it with another tortilla. Put the quesadillas in the microwave for 45 seconds. Cut them in pieces and serve.

Group Time

If possible, invite a parent to come in and talk about the customs and heritage of Spanish-speaking countries. Be aware that customs and even the language vary greatly in Spanish-speaking countries. Talk to the children about the art and textiles that come from Hispanic countries. Some people in Mexico weave baskets and make other art items. Show different works of art, including paintings by Diego Rivera and weavings by other artists.

Learning Center Ideas

Art: Make a mural. The Mexican artist Diego Rivera is known for painting murals. Draw a basic grass and sky background on bulletin board paper. Invite the children to paint the grass and sky. Then encourage them to paint pictures of themselves in the mural.

Art: Paint around a paper cup with glue. Using variegated yarn, wrap it around the whole cup. The Huichol Indians create yarn and beeswax pictures of their stories and legends. Use the Internet to find pictures of the yarn art and tell some of the legends that are told through the art.

Art/Fine Motor: Help children weave placemats (see appendix page 297 for detailed instructions).

Additional Activities

Movement: Play a "Toro" game. Toro means "bull" in Spanish. To play this game, one child is the Toro or the bull. The other children line up on one side of the room. When the children say, "Toro," the bull runs to the other side of the room and tries to tag as many people as he can. Every child he tags becomes another bull and helps tag other children.

Outside: Soccer, called Fútbol, is a very big sport in Mexico. Encourage the children to practice kicking soccer balls through orange cones.

Rhythm and Rhyme: Sing "The Color Song" on appendix page 298.

Good Manners Month

STORY TIME

Remind the children to use good manners during story time.

1. Take turns talking.
2. Listen to others talking.
3. Listen and pay attention.

Everyday Graces (Book of Manners)
    by Karen Garver Santorum
Excuse Me by Karen Katz
OOPS, Sorry by Richard Morgan
Please, Say Please by Margery
    Cuyler
This Little Piggy's Book of Manners
    by Kathryn Madeline Allen

SNACK

Remind children to use good manners as they eat their snack.

1. Put your napkin in your lap.
2. Chew with your mouth closed.
3. Keep your elbows off the table.
4. Ask your neighbor to please pass what you need, rather than reaching.
3. Say, "Excuse me" when leaving the table.

Group Time

Talk about good manners and bad manners. Ask the children for their ideas. Give each child a happy/sad face stick puppet (see Appendix page 296). Tell the children that you are going to give some examples of good manners and bad manners. If the statement describes good manners, they show the happy face. It the statement describes bad manners, they show the sad face. See the Manners Statements on appendix page 297 for some examples.

Learning Center Ideas

Dramatic Play: Invite children to have a pretend tea party. Provide a tea party set and encourage the children to make invitations, pretend to pour tea and serve sandwiches, and thank their guests for coming. Talk about using good manners and practice using them at the tea party.

Literacy: Set out cards and envelopes to write thank-you notes. Print "Thank You" on word cards for the children to copy. Invite children to draw a picture on the front of the card. (Cards can be made by folding white or colored paper in half and cut to fit an envelope.) Children can try to print "thank you" on the inside. Explain to children that sometimes people write a letter also. Help them write a sentence inside of the card.

Math: Set up an estimation station. Put several chewable candy mints in a jar. Invite children to guess how many are in the jar. At the end of the unit, count how many are actually in the container. (Make sure there are enough mints for every child to have one.) Be sure to use the chewable breath mints, not hard candy, to ensure that children do not choke. Explain that when you get up in the morning, you should brush your teeth to keep your teeth healthy and your breath fresh. If you can't possibly brush, some people use breath mints. Invite children to tell you how their mouths feel after they eat the mints.

Additional Activities

Movement: Play "Mother, May I?" The children stand in a line. Take turns calling the children by name and giving them an instruction. Before following the direction, they must ask, "Mother, may I?" You respond, "Yes, you may."

Rhythm and Rhyme: Sing "The Manners Song" with the children (see Appendix page 299).

National Grandparents' Day

National Grandparents' Day is the first Sunday after Labor Day. Invite grandparents to come to school to celebrate the day either the Friday before or the Monday after Grandparents' Day. Keep in mind that not all children may have grandparents, or their grandparents may live too far away to come in for this special celebration. Encourage children to invite another special person to share the day.

STORY TIME

Grandma and Me by Karen Katz
Grandparents by Anne-Laure Fourier LeRay
Just Grandma and Me by Mercer Mayer
My Grandparents and I by Samuel Caraballo (bilingual)
Spot Visits His Grandparents by Eric Hill

TRANSITION

Before moving to a new activity, invite the children to name something they like to do with their grandparents.

SNACK

Invite everyone to share snack time "family style."

Group Time

Encourage the children to introduce their grandparent(s) to the class. Also, invite the grandparents to share something about themselves, their lives, interests, families, and so on. Encourage the children to ask questions.

Learning Center Ideas

Art: Make "loving handprints" art. First, encourage the grandparents to paint their grandchild's hand with washable paint and help them make handprints on one side of a piece of paper. Then, encourage the children to paint their grandparents' hands and make handprints next to theirs (leave about 2" between the handprints). Glue a red heart in between the two handprints that says "I Love You."
Blocks: Encourage the children and their grandparents to create block structures together.
Book Corner: Provide books listed above for the grandparents and children to enjoy.
Math: Encourage grandparents and children to do puzzles together.

Additional Activities

Game: Play Button, Button, Who Has the Button? Place chairs in a circle and ask grandparents to sit. Invite children to sit in a circle in front of their grandparents. One child and grandparent are "IT" together. They sit in the middle of the circle with their eyes closed while the rest of the children and grandparents pass the button around the circle. IT says "Stop," and the child and grandparent open their eyes. They have three guesses to figure out who has the button.
Rhythm and Rhyme: Sing songs that both grandparents and children know. Suggestions include "Twinkle, Twinkle, Little Star," "Mary Had a Little Lamb," and "The ABC Song."
Small Group: Grandparents and grandchildren create a class book (see appendix page 296 for instructions). Using a Polaroid camera, take two pictures of each child and his grandparents. Put one picture in the class book and the other one in a foam frame for the child to decorate and take home.

Happy Birthday, Tomie dePaola

SPECIAL DAYS AND HOLIDAYS

September 15th is Tomie dePaola's birthday. Tomie dePaola is a famous children's book author. Tomie is also an illustrator, so he draws pictures for stories, too. Sometimes he writes his own stories and also draws the pictures. Some examples include *The Art Lesson* and *The Baby Sister*. See www.tomie.com for more information.

STORY TIME

Read *Mice Squeak, We Speak* by Arnold Shapiro. Tomie dePaola drew the pictures. Read the story again, and invite the children to make the animal noises along with the story. Or, choose from these titles:

The Art Lesson
The Cloud Book
The Legend of the Bluebonnet
The Legend of Old Befana
Oliver Button Is a Sissy
Pancakes for Breakfast
Tomie's dePaola's Book of Poems

TRANSITION

Play Pass the Paintbrush. As the children sit in a circle, they pass the paintbrush as the music plays. When the music stops, the child holding the paintbrush moves to the next activity.

SNACK

Read *Pancakes for Breakfast*. Then invite the children to help make pancakes.

Group Time

Before Group Time, copy pictures from the story *Pancakes for Breakfast*. Copy 4-5 pictures of the main events and sequence of the story. At Group Time, tell children that you will read a story without words. The pictures tell the story. Talk about the pictures as you look at the book. Then give the children the copied pictures and encourage them to retell the story by putting the pictures in the proper sequence.

Learning Center Ideas

Tomie dePaola loves art and loves using many different mediums. Offer several different art-related centers for children.

Art: Try different kinds of painting at an easel. Set out the easel with paint and brushes. Add a squeegee, combs, craft sticks, items to make prints in the paint with, and anything else children would like to try. Add glue, sand, or salt to paint and see how it changes the texture.

Art: Encourage the children to use chalk on black construction paper or a dark chalkboard. Invite them to spray the paper with water before they draw for a different effect.

Art: Set out all kinds of construction paper scraps, fabric, yarn, ribbon, thread, other kinds of paper scraps, and other items with which children can experiment making collages.

Blocks: Print with blocks dipped in paint; help the children run cars through paint and then on paper to make tire tracks.

Dramatic Play: Create an Art Studio. Encourage children to take turns being the artist who paints portraits of other children.

Manipulatives: Set out several colors of playdough. Add rolling pins, craft sticks (can be used as knives), cookie cutters, stamps, beads, pipe cleaners, plastic flowers, and a wide variety of "stuff" for children to explore.

Additional Activities

Outside: Take art outside by coloring with chalk on the playground. Also add water with or without food coloring in spray bottles for the children to use to paint.

Happy Birthday, Johnny Appleseed!

STORY TIME

Apple, Apple Alligator by William Accorsi

Apples Add Up by Megan E. Bryant and Monique Z. Stephens

Apples, Apples by Kathleen Weidner Zoehfield and Christopher Santoro

Apples Away by Megan E. Bryant and Monique Z. Stephens

Dumpy's Apple Shop by Julie Andrews Edwards, Emma Walton Hamilton and Tony Walton

Story of Johnny Appleseed by Aliki

TRANSITION

Play "hot potato" with an apple. Sit in a circle. As the music plays, pass one or two apples around the circle. When the music stops the child or children holding the apples will move on to the next activity.

SNACK

Make Taffy Apple Dip (see appendix page 300 for recipe) to go with apples.

Group Time

Tell the story of how Johnny Appleseed traveled around and gave people apple seeds to plant. He loved apple trees and apples. Read *Johnny Appleseed: A Tall Tale* by Steven Kellogg. Talk about apples. Show red, yellow, and green apples. Make patterns using different colors of apples.

Learning Center Ideas

Art: Make a wormy apple. Paint a small paper plate with a water/glue mixture (add enough water to the glue so it becomes the texture of paint). Add small pieces of red tissue paper to the apple shape. Add a cinnamon stick stem. Make a worm for the apple. Give each child a pipe cleaner about six to seven inches long. String beads on the pipe cleaner (bend the bottom up and twist it so the beads do not come off). Bend and twist the ends of the pipe cleaner worm to keep the beads on. Glue the worm to the apple.

Art: Cut apples in half. Dip them in paint and show the children how to make prints on construction paper.

Dramatic Play: Set up a stand with play apples, a cash register, scale, bags, play apples, and so on.

Science/Math: Look at red, yellow, and green apples. Cut a red, green, and a yellow apple open and invite the children to look at them with a magnifying glass. Look at how the apples are the same on the inside. Ask, "Will they taste the same?" Invite each child to try a piece of each of the three kinds of apples. Help children write their names on a color cutout of the type of apple they like the best. Graph the results.

Additional Activities

Game: Hide an apple in the classroom. Invite the children to quietly look for the apple. When they find the apple, ask the children not to tell anyone, just go back and sit down. See how long it takes for everyone to find the apple.

Project: Plant apple seeds in a pot. Help the children keep track of how much the seedlings grow, how much water they need, hours of sunlight they receive, and so on. When they are big enough, plant them outside and continue to monitor their growth and progress.

Rhythm and Rhyme: Sing "Happy Birthday" to Johnny Appleseed.

DAILY PLAN CONCEPT

A Bear-y Big Welcome

GENERAL DAILY PLAN

STORY TIME

The Brand New Kid by Katie Couric
Froggy Goes to School by Jonathan London
Max and Ruby Play School by Rosemary Wells
My First Day at Nursery School by Becky Edwards
Spot Goes to School by Eric Hill

TRANSITION

Use the "Five-Minute Warning," found on appendix page 299, to let children know when a change is coming. This is especially important on the first days of a new school year.

SNACK

Enjoy teddy bear snacks, such as Teddy Grahams® or fruit snacks and milk. If you have several kinds or colors, invite children to sort them then eat them.

Group Time

Before school, create a school building shape on a large piece of paper. Cut it out and laminate it. Attach pieces of Velcro to the school shape corresponding to the number of children in the class. Next, cut out a bear shape for each child. Write a child's name on each bear. Laminate the bears and put Velcro on their backs. At Group Time, sing the "Welcome Song" (see appendix page 300) to each child to help children learn the names of their new classmates. When a child's name is called, encourage that child to find the bear shape with his name and place it on to the school shape. (The children can do this when they come to school each day, as a name recognition and attendance activity.) **Variation:** Change the bear shape to a monthly or theme shape several times during the year. Take a picture of each activity you do during the day, from arriving at school to leaving. Make a photo sequence of the day to remind the children what will happen next.

Learning Center Ideas

Literacy: Cut out bear shapes from construction paper. Write a letter on each bear shape. Laminate the shapes. Set out small objects that start with each letter. Invite the children to put the objects on the bear with the correct beginning sound.
Math: Challenge the children to sort counting bears by color.

Additional Activities

Outside: Make a teddy bear train to go outside. The children wear teddy bear nametags of different colors. Take turns calling out, "The yellow teddy bears may line up." Children with yellow nametags line up single file. The children comprise the train cars (yellow "car," blue "car" and so on). This idea helps children who have never been to school understand what a single-file line is. As the children walk around, encourage them to stay in the line and the train will stay on track.
Small Group: Give children bear nametags in different colors. Encourage the children to listen and follow the directions. Read the "Bear Poem" on appendix page 297.

I Am Special

STORY TIME

I Like Me by Nancy Carlson
You Are Special, Little One by Nancy Tafuri

TRANSITION

Say the rhyme below for each child. The child whose name is called can do a movement before moving on to the next activity.

[Child's name] *is special.*
Yes, it's true.
Show us something
You can do.

Group Time

Before Group Time, cut out apple shapes from construction paper. Also cut out an apple tree shape from construction paper. Read *I Like Me* by Nancy Carlson. Invite each child to complete the following sentence: "I am special because...." Write their responses on apples and tape them to the apple tree.

Learning Center Ideas

Make special "me" centers.
Art: Invite the children to create pictures of themselves on paper plates. First, paint the plates in the appropriate skin color. Have several colors available. Then set out yarn, paper shreds for hair, buttons, pompoms, and other embellishments for children to make themselves. **Note:** You may want to do this activity over two days: Day 1—paint, Day 2—add face and decorations.
Science: Set out an inkpad to make fingerprints. Add magnifying glasses so the children can look at all the lines on their fingers. Emphasize how each fingerprint is unique and special.
Sensory: Set out a tub of sand for the children to practice writing their names.
Writing: Set out blank book journals. Invite the children to draw or write about anything that interests them.

Additional Activities

Game: Play "I Spy." Describe a child in the classroom. Invite the children to guess who it is.
Rhythm and Rhyme: Sing "I'm Special" (appendix page 299) and "All about Me and You" with the children (appendix page 297).
Small Group: Make a "This Is Special Me" book for each child (see appendix page 297 for instructions).

Names

STORY TIME

Andy: That's My Name by Tomie
    dePaola

Charlie, Who Couldn't Say His Name
    by Carol Inouye

Chrysanthemum by Kevin Henkes

A Goose Named Gilligan by Jerry M.
    Hay

My Name Is Alice by Jane Bayer

Names for Snow by Judi K. Beach

Group Time

Print each child's name on two sentence strips. On one strip, add the child's photo. Glue the strips back to back and laminate for durability. Hold up the sentence strip on the side without the photo. Invite the children to guess whose name it is. Then flip the sentence strip over and show them the photo to see if they are right.

Other ways to use the sentence strips include:
◆ Post the names when taking attendance.
◆ Place them in the writing center so children can practice writing friends' names.
◆ Dial the letters of the names on a phone.
◆ Post them at the sensory table and encourage children to write their names in the sand.

Learning Center Ideas

Art: Print each child's name on a cardboard strip. Encourage the children to decorate the letters of their names with sequins, glitter glue, and other embellishments.

Sensory: Write the children's names on little pieces of foam. Hide them in the sand at the Sensory Table.

Writing: Invite the children to write their names on a chalkboard.

Additional Activities

Movement: Print each child's name on a card or use the sentence strips from the Group Time activity. Put each name on a chair. Play musical chairs. Walk around the chairs as the music plays. When the music stops, the children find the chair with their name and sit down.

Outside: Print each child's name on a small cutout leaf. Hide the cutouts outside in various places on the playground. Encourage the children to find their names and give them stickers when they do.

Squares

STORY TIME

Are Eggs Square? by DK Publishing
Bear in a Square by Stella Blackstone
Blue and Square by Herve Tollet
Silly Squares by Sophie Fatus
What Is Square? by Rebecca Kai
   Dotlich

SNACK

Serve square waffles with fresh fruit.

Group Time

Use tape to make a large square shape in the Group Time area. Invite the children to sit on the tape in a square for Group Time. Discuss what makes a square a square (four equal sides). Show the children pictures of squares. Encourage the children to look around the classroom and point out objects that are square. Finally, organize children into groups of four and challenge them to make squares with their bodies.

Learning Center Ideas

Art: Set out squares of different sizes, colors, and textures, such as fabric, tissue paper, and cardboard. Invite children to make square collages by gluing the squares onto a square piece of construction paper.
Math: Use craft sticks to make squares. Set out four craft sticks. Challenge the children to make square shapes using the four sticks. Glue the squares onto pieces of paper for the children to take home.
Sensory: Encourage the children to draw squares in sand or shaving cream.

Additional Activities

Movement: Use the large tape square from the Group Time activity for this activity. Invite the children to follow your instructions:
- hop around the square
- jump around the square
- crawl around the square
- walk backwards
- walk like an elephant
- stop, turn around, and go the opposite way

Outside: Draw squares on the playground to play hopscotch and four-square with a ball.

DAILY PLAN CONCEPT

School Tools

GENERAL DAILY PLAN

STORY TIME

David Goes to School by David Shannon

First Day Jitters by Julie Danneberg

First Day, Hooray! by Nancy Poydar

Miss Bindergarten Gets Ready for Kindergarten by Joseph Slate

My Teacher's My Friend by P.K. Hallinan

Tiptoe into Kindergarten by Jacqueline Rogers

Tucker's Four-Carrot School Day by Susan Winget

RULES FOR USING SCHOOL TOOLS

◆ Use crayons, markers, and pencils on paper only.

◆ Only cut on paper with scissors.

◆ Walk, don't run, with school tools in your hand.

◆ Keep non-food items out of your mouth.

◆ Clean up your messes.

SCHOOL TOOLS

◆ blocks
◆ magnets
◆ pencil
◆ markers
◆ scissors
◆ backpack
◆ calendar
◆ paper
◆ crayons
◆ chalk
◆ beads
◆ counting bears

Group Time

Talk about the rules for using school tools. Provide some of the school tools listed at the bottom left. Ask the children to sort the items by color, by type, by size, and so on, and listen to their ideas.

Learning Center Ideas

Fine Motor: Using scissors is a difficult skill to learn. Show the children how to hold the scissors. Invite the children to snip a piece of paper to practice. Sing the "Scissors Song" (see appendix page 300) as they cut.

Math: Sort and count erasers.

Math: Make patterns with markers and crayons.

Sensory: Take turns hiding and finding erasers in the sand at the Sensory Table.

Additional Activities

Game: Play Teacher, Teacher Where's Your Chalk? Invite the children to sit in a circle except for the child who will be the "teacher." The "teacher" sits in the middle of the circle with the chalk behind her back. The teacher closes her eyes. A child sneaks up and takes the chalk. All the children in the circle hold their hands behind their backs. The "teacher" opens her eyes and tries to guess who has the chalk.

Outside: Take chalk outside and encourage children to create a mural. Explain to children that a mural is a big picture that many people work on together. In this mural, each child will have an area to draw and color with many colors of chalk. The rule is that nobody can draw over anyone else's work. Give each child an area to draw and some chalk. Encourage sharing the chalk colors. When everyone is finished, look at the mural. Discuss how everyone worked together to make one big, beautiful work of art.

Small Group: Put some school tools on a tray and tell the children to study the items and try to remember what they see. Then, ask the children to close their eyes. Take away one item on the tray. Ask children to open their eyes. What is missing? (If children can do this easily, add more items to the tray or take two items away each time.)

Animal Friends

Before using this daily plan, send a note home inviting the children to bring their favorite bear or stuffed animal to school for the day. (Note: Have extra stuffed animals on hand for the children who forget to bring one.)

STORY TIME

Bear Wants More by Karma Wilson
Biscuit Goes to School by Alyssa Satin Capucilli
Brown Bear, Brown Bear, What Do You See? by Bill Martin, Jr.
If You Take a Mouse to School by Laura Joffe Numeroff
My School's a Zoo by Stu Smith
Panda Bear, Panda Bear, What Do You See? by Bill Martin, Jr.
We're Going on a Bear Hunt by Michael Rosen

SNACK

Make bread dough bears. Give each child a piece of raw bread dough (buy frozen bread dough). Invite the children to make a bear face with raisin eyes and nose, and a string licorice mouth. Children can make either a happy face or a sad face. Ask them why they chose a frown or smile. Butter the dough and sprinkle with cinnamon and sugar. Bake and enjoy.

Group Time

Invite the children to decorate special nametags for their stuffed animals. (If you do this first, it will be easier to keep the children's stuffed animals organized.) After the children have attached their nametags to their animals, ask each child in the circle to tell the group something about the animal they brought. Ask leading questions to help the children feel comfortable speaking in the group environment. Next, use the children's stuffed animals for a sorting activity. Sort the animals by color, size, and type.

Learning Center Ideas

Art: Use playdough to make animal shapes.
Dramatic Play: Set up a veterinarian's office so the children can give their animals a checkup.
Math: Encourage the children to use animal counters or animal crackers to sort and count.

Additional Activities

Movement: Place all of the stuffed animals in the middle of a parachute and then say the rhyme below and follow the directions.

Put the bears up high.
Put the bears down low.
Make the bears go fast.
Make the bears go slow.

Small Group: Take a photo of the children and their stuffed animals, or invite children to draw a picture. Ask children to tell stories about their stuffed animal friends or answer the following questions: *What is your friend's name? What does your friend eat? What does your friend like to play?* Make a class book by combining the pictures or photos and the children's responses to the questions.

Yellow

Wear yellow today.

STORY TIME

Fuzzy Yellow Ducklings by Matthew Van Fleet

One Yellow Lion by Matthew Van Fleet

Red Lace, Yellow Lace by Mike Casey

Yellow and Round by Herve Tullet

Yellow Ice by Angie Sage

TRANSITION

Recite the rhyme below, using each child's name. The named child names something yellow as she moves on to the next activity.

> [Say a child's name twice],
> *say, "Hello!"*
> *Name something yellow as*
> *you go.*

SNACK

Make a yellow chick. Put yellow food coloring in cream cheese and spread it on an English muffin to create the chick's body. Make an orange cheese triangle beak, raisin eyes, and carrot stick legs.

Group Time

Show children yellow items. Help the children make a list of things that are yellow, and then play I Spy Something Yellow with the children.

Learning Center Activities

Art: Make a big yellow sun. Set out a big sun shape cut from construction paper. Encourage the children to work together to paint the sun shape with glue, then invite them to put yellow tissue paper squares on the sun until it is yellow.

Math: Cut out several pond shapes from blue construction paper. Give each pond shape a numeral from 1–10. Laminate the shapes. Invite the children to pretend yellow pompoms are little yellow ducks and encourage them to place the proper number of "ducks" on each pond.

Science: Put yellow and blue tempera paint in a zipper-closure plastic bag. Reinforce the zipper with duct tape. Encourage the children to mix the two colors gently. What happens? (Try the same thing with yellow and red paint, too.)

Sensory: Cut a banana shape for each child. Put banana extract in yellow tempera paint. Encourage the children to fingerpaint the banana shapes with the scented paint.

Additional Activities

Movement: Walk around the classroom as the music plays. When the music stops, touch something yellow. Try different movements; skip hop, crawl, jump, and other movements.

Rhythm and Rhyme: Sing "The Yellow Song" with the children (see appendix page 300).

Numeral 8

STORY TIME

Eight Little Monkeys by Steve
  Haskamp
Ten, Nine, Eight by Molly Bang

TRANSITION

Fill in the verse below with a child's
name. The child counts to eight and
then moves to the next activity.

> [Child's name], *you are great!*
> *Can you count to number eight?*

SNACK

Place raisins, nuts, fish crackers, and
pretzels in separate bowls. Encourage
the children to count eight of each
item for a snack.

Group Time

Write movements, such as *clap your hands, jump,* or *hop on one foot,* on
pieces of paper. Fill a jar with these papers, and have the children take
turns pulling activities from the jar. Do each activity eight times.

Learning Center Ideas

Gross Motor: Challenge children to throw eight beanbags into a basket.
Math: Help children make a racetrack. Children can cut out a figure 8 (with
adult help as needed). Encourage children to paint the shape gray to
resemble a race track. When the paint is dry, invite the children to choose
eight race car stickers to put on the track.
Math/Gross Motor: Set out a deck of cards. Turn over each card one at a
time. When the numeral 8 appears, encourage the children to slap it with
their hands.
Sensory: Suggest that children write the numeral 8 in the sand.

Additional Activities

Outside: Hide eight different items outside in the playground, and
challenge the children to find them.
Rhythm and Rhyme: Sing "Crayons" with the children (see appendix page
298).

Blue

Wear blue today.

STORY TIME

Blue Hat, Green Hat by Sandra Boynton

Charlie Parker Played BeBop by Chris Raschka

Little Boy Blue by Iona Opie

One Dad, Two Dads, Brown Dad, Blue Dad by Johnny Valentine

One Fish, Two Fish, Red Fish, Blue Fish by Dr. Seuss

SNACK

Make blueberry parfaits. Put graham cracker crumbs on the bottom of clear plastic cups. Layer yogurt and blueberries to make a delicious parfait.

Group Time

Talk about the color blue. Ask children to name their favorite colors. Make a graph of their responses. Then, create a class book. Talk with the children about things that are blue. Ask each child to finish this sentence, "A _____ is blue." Write down their responses. Then give each child a piece of paper to draw a picture of the item they named. Bind the pages together into a class "Blue" book.

Learning Center Ideas

Art: Children fingerpaint a blue sky on white construction paper. When dry, encourage them to cut out a yellow construction paper sun and white cotton ball clouds and glue them onto the sky. What else is in the sky? The children may want to add birds, airplanes, and other things in the sky.

Art: Invite the children to mix blue food coloring with shaving cream. Challenge the children to make a letter *b* for blue. Then invite children to print their names.

Art: Make a blue collage. Set out blue items, such as buttons, fabric, and glitter. Glue them on a blue paper plate.

Math: Cut out fish bowls from blue construction paper. Write different numerals on the fish bowls. Laminate them for durability. Ask the children to put the correct number of fish crackers on the fish bowls. Eat the crackers when finished playing the game.

Additional Activities

Math: Read *If You Give a Moose a Muffin* by Laura Numeroff. Cut a muffin shape from brown construction paper for each child. Invite children to make blue fingerprint berries and then count the number of blue "berries."

Rhythm and Rhyme: Sing "The Blue Song" with the children (see appendix page 298).

Feelings

STORY TIME

Glad Monster, Sad Monster by Ed Emberley

How Are You Peeling? by Saxton Freymann

My Many Colored Days by Dr. Seuss

No Matter What by Debi Cliori

Smile-a-Saurus by Matt Metler

Today I Feel Silly by Jamie Lee Curtis

When Sophie Gets Angry—Really, Really Angry . . . by Molly Bang

TRANSITION

Say this rhyme, inviting the children to take turns naming things they can do if they are mad or sad, as they move on to the next activity.

> *Are you mad?*
> *Are you blue?*
> *Tell me what you can do.*

SNACK

Spread cream cheese or peanut butter on an English muffin. Use raisins, peanuts, and cereal pieces to make a face that reflects how the children feel: happy, sad, and so on. **Note:** Check for allergies before serving this snack.

Group Time

Read *Today I Feel Silly* by Jamie Lee Curtis. Ask the children how they feel. Graph their answers. On chart paper or a chalk board, draw four different faces: happy, sad, mad, and sleepy. Put the faces along the top of the paper and make a grid. Help children to print their names and draw faces on Post-it notes that show how they are feeling at the time. (Ask them to tell you, because it might be hard to tell from some of the pictures.) Help children put their faces under the appropriate heading.

Learning Center Ideas

Set up centers that are relaxing.

Sensory: Provide sand with bowls, measuring cups, and spoons for the children to explore.

Sensory: Make your favorite playdough and add a relaxing scent.

Writing: Give each child a journal for writing and drawing to express their feelings.

Additional Activities

Movement: Play Simon Says with "feeling" words. For example, say "Simon Says, show how you look when you are sad."

Rhythm and Rhyme: Teach the children the song, "Feelings Are Okay" (see page 298 in the appendix).

Letter *H*

STORY TIME

The Hat by Jan Brett
Hedgie's Surprise by Jan Brett
A House for Hermit Crab by Eric Carle
A House Is a House for Me by Mary
    Ann Hoberman

TRANSITION

Play Pass the Hat. Sit in a circle. Pass a hat around the circle as the music plays. When the music stops, the child holding the hat moves on to the next activity.

SNACK

Make ham and cheese rollups. Spread cream cheese on tortillas. Add a slice of ham. Roll up and slice into ½" pieces.

Group Time

Talk about the letter *H* and the sound that it makes. Name words that begin with the letter *h*. Play a game with the children. Say many different words and challenge them to hop up and down if the word starts with the letter *h*.

Learning Center Ideas

Art: Make "Happy Hearts" (see appendix page 296) with the children.
Art: Help the children paint a big appliance box to use as a house.
Blocks: Put toy helicopters in the block areas for the children to play with.
Dramatic Play: Encourage the children to use the box "house" that they created in the art center. Provide props for the children to use in their pretend play.
Dramatic Play: Set up a hair salon with props that the children can use in their pretend play.

Additional Activities

Outside: Play hopscotch.
Rhythm and Rhyme: Sing "H Is for Hugs" with the children (see appendix page 299).
Small Group: Read *Hippos* by Sally M. Walker. Share the Hippopotamus Facts found on appendix page 301 with the children.

Helpfulness

STORY TIME

Can I Help? by Marily Janovitz
The Little Red Hen by Byron Barton

TRANSITION

Say this rhyme and ask the children to say what they will do to help clean up the room.

Help clean up our room today.
Together we will work and play.
_____, _____ we count on you.
Tell me something you can do.

SNACK

Invite children to help set the tables and prepare snack. Also ask children to help clean up by sweeping and doing other jobs.

Group Time

Read *The Little Red Hen* by Byron Barton. Discuss with the children how the characters would not help the hen. Talk with the children about ways they can be helpful to people. Cut out a big hand shape from butcher paper, and put it in a prominent place in the classroom. Ask the children to list ways to lend a "helping hand," and write their responses on the hand.

Learning Center Ideas

Blocks: Encourage the children to work together to make block buildings and structures.

Manipulatives: Set out a 25-50-piece puzzle, depending on the abilities of the children. Encourage the children to work together to complete the puzzle.

Sensory: Make helping hands. Invite each child to fill a disposable plastic glove with sand. Seal it tight with string or a rubber band. This helping hand is a reminder to be a helper.

Additional Activities

Rhythm and Rhyme: Invite the children to sing "I Can Be Helpful," found on appendix page 299.

Home/School Connection

Send home a note and a page of copied handprints. Ask parents to acknowledge when their child gives a "helping hand" by writing the helpful action on a handprint. The child can cut it out and bring it to school. Put the handprints up on a bulletin board and talk about the helpful actions written on each one. This is a good way to reinforce helping and encourage children to be more aware of times when help is needed.

Circles

STORY TIME

Circle Dogs by Kevin Henkes
Circles by Jan Kottke
So Many Circles, So Many Squares by Tana Hoban
What Is Round? by Rebecca Kai Dotlich
Witch Dot by Kelly Asbury

SNACK

Spread butter and sugar on pancake circles. Roll them up and eat them.

Group Time

Sit in a big circle. Discuss how a circle is round and has no sides or corners. Help children locate and name things that are circles in the classroom. Play Where's Your Circle? One child is "IT." This child sits in the middle of the circle with a small paper circle behind her back. The child closes her eyes and another child takes the circle. IT opens her eyes and tries to guess who has the circle.

Learning Center Ideas

Art: Make a Circle Collage. Set out buttons, pompoms, bubble wrap, bingo markers, and hole punches to make a collage on a paper plate.
Gross Motor: Practice position words using hula hoops. Give each child a hula hoop. Tell them, "Stand inside the hula hoop," "stand outside the hula hoop," "stand beside the hula hoop," and so on. Then invite the children to try to spin the hula hoops around their waists. Be prepared to demonstrate!
Manipulatives: Cut construction paper circles the same size as pie tins. Next, cut them into quarters, then halves. Set out the pieces and encourage the children to make whole circles.

Additional Activities

Movement: Play circle games such as Ring Around the Rosie, or invite the children to hold the edges of a round parachute and move around in a circle, holding the parachute up high, down low, and so on.
Rhythm and Rhyme: Teach the children, "Sing a Song of Circles" (see appendix page 300).

Letter *S*

STORY TIME

Baby Snake's Shapes by Neecy Twinem

Sheep in a Jeep by Nancy Shaw

Shoes by Elizabeth Winthrop

Tiny Seed by Eric Carle

Twinkle, Twinkle Little Star by Iza Trapani

Wemberly's Ice-Cream Star by Kevin Henkes

TRANSITION

Rhyme *s* words with this activity. Print words that begin with *s* on star shapes. Put the stars in a jar. Each child pulls a star out of the jar. Read the word and ask the child to name a word that rhymes with the word on the star. After the child says a rhyming word, he can move to the next activity.

Group Time

Talk about the sound the letter *s* makes. Tell the children that you will name some words. If the word begins with the same sound as snake, they should make an *s-s-s* sound.

Learning Center Ideas

Art: Cut out a snake-like letter *s* for each child. Let them decorate the *s* shape with designs. At the top of the letter *s*, glue a forked tongue. Add snake eyes.

Math/Sensory: Invite the children to sort seashells by size in a Sensory Table filled with water.

Writing: Provide letters cut from sandpaper for the children to trace.

Additional Activities

Game: Play a shoe game. Invite children to each take off a shoe and put it in the middle of the circle. Take turns picking out a shoe and guessing whose it is.

Outside: Help children name some *s* things they can do outside, for example:

◆ slide
◆ play in the sandbox
◆ swing
◆ skip

Small Group: Make "Feely Socks." Put an item in each of several socks. Put a knot in the end of the socks. Invite the children to feel the socks and guess what is in each sock.

Perseverance

I Knew You Could by Craig Dorfman
I Like Me by Nancy Carlson
The Little Engine That Could by Watty Piper

Put a sticker with the words, "I stuck to it!" on each child's shirt as their names are called and they move on to the next activity.

Group Time

Read *The Little Engine That Could* by Watty Piper. Retell the story. Invite the children to dictate something they would like to try do and encourage them to draw a picture to go with their words. Put the pictures on a construction paper train and call it the "I Think I Can" Express.

Learning Center Ideas

Create centers that focus on the idea of practicing to master a skill.
Art: Explain to children that a spider makes a web. Sometimes the web falls apart or gets broken and the spider must rebuild it and not give up. Add tempera paint to glue to make several colors of glue. Children make colored glue spider webs on black construction paper, decorate them with glitter, and then add a plastic spider.
Fine Motor: Add plaster of Paris to the inside of an old lace-up shoe. After it hardens, children may use it to practice tying a shoe.
Manipulatives: Set out new puzzles for the children to explore.
Writing: Children practice writing names in shaving cream.

Additional Activities

Game: One child hides his eyes while the teacher or another child hides an object. Then the child opens his eyes and looks for the object. Children help the child by telling him that he is "getting warmer" when he is somewhat near the object, "hot" when he's very close, and "hotter" when he is almost certain to find it. When the child finds the object, another child can take a turn.
Outside: Encourage children to try to go across the climber, or count the number of times they can jump in place. Help the children state a goal and try to reach it.
Rhythm and Rhyme: Teach the children to sing "I Think I Can" (see appendix page 299).
Small Group: Use photos to show children trying to and reaching goals. Invite children to try something new. Make sure children's goals are attainable. Take a photo of the child *before* he tries to reach his goal, *as* the child is making an attempt, and finally, *when* the child accomplishes his goal. Discuss how it feels scary and difficult to try something new, but why it is important to keep trying.

Letter *B*

STORY TIME

Big Red Barn by Margaret Wise Brown

Bright Eyes, Brown Skin by Bernette G. Ford

The Bugliest Bug by Carol Diggory Shields

Bunny Cakes Bye Rosemary Wells

Busy Toes by C.W. Bowie

TRANSITION

Use a bell to help children transition to the next activity. Repeat the verse below and add a child's name with the number of times the child should ring the bell. Then the child moves on to the next activity.

> *Ring it fast.*
> *Ring it slow.*
> [Child's name], *ring a bell,*
> *And off you go.*

SNACK

Make banana boats. Cut a banana lengthwise and form the two halves into a canoe shape. Fill it with berries, pieces of pineapple, and other fruit. Add whipped cream and put a cherry on the top.

Group Time

Talk about the letter *b* and the sound it makes. Ask the children to sit in a circle. Roll the ball to one child and ask him to name a *b* word. That child then rolls the ball to another child and the game continues.

Learning Center Ideas

Art: Children fingerpaint with brown paint on a bear shape. Draw the letter *b* in the brown paint on the bear's tummy.

Art: Children use the easel to paint on butterfly-shaped construction paper or newsprint.

Sensory: Put boats in the water table for children to explore.

Writing: Put blank books in the center for children to create their own stories.

Additional Activities

Game: Play Who's Hiding Under the Blanket? One child is "IT" and goes to another area of the classroom. Another child quickly hides under the blanket. The other child is called back to guess who is hiding under the blanket.

Outside: Encourage the children to bend pipe cleaners into the shape of the letter *b*. Provide bubble solution, and the children can use their *b*-shaped pipe cleaners as wands to blow bubbles.

Rhythm and Rhyme: Sing "The Letter B Song" with the children (see appendix page 299).

Elephant Appreciation Day

GENERAL DAILY PLAN

Ellison the Elephant by Eric Drachman

Elmer series by David McKee

Five Minutes Peace by Jill Murphy

How the Elephant Got Its Trunk by Jean Richards

Right Number of Elephants by Jeff Sheppard

Seven Blind Mice by Ed Young

TRANSITION

Say the rhyme below using the name of a child in the class. The named child moves like an elephant to the next activity.

> *Elephant, elephant moves*
> *so slow,*
> *_____, _____, it's time*
> *to go.*

SNACK

Cut bread into peanut shapes and toast it. Invite children to spread peanut butter on the peanut shapes.

Group Time

Put Elephant Facts (see appendix page 301) on peanut shapes. Invite the children to pretend to be elephants and find and pick up peanuts using their arms as trunks. Read the facts on the peanuts to the children.

Learning Center Ideas

Art: Help the children make an elephant with gray and wrinkly skin. Cut brown grocery bags until they lie flat. Encourage the children to crumple them so the bags are full of wrinkles and folds, and then press them flat again. Put out black and white fingerpaint. As the children paint the paper, the colors will mix to make gray. When the paint dries, cut the paper into elephant shapes.

Dramatic Play: Make a stuffed animal zoo, using stuffed animals and crates and laundry baskets. Have a ticket booth.

Math: Cut elephant shapes and write a numeral from 1-10 on each one. Laminate for durability. Encourage the children to put the correct number of packing peanuts on the elephants.

Additional Activities

Movement: Play Elephant, Elephant, Giraffe. One child is "IT." The children sit in a circle except for IT, who walks around the circle, tapping each child on the head saying, "elephant." When he taps a child on the head and says, "giraffe," that child jumps up and tries to tag him as he moves quickly around the circle to get to the giraffe's spot before the giraffe can tag him.

Outside: Teach children to do the Elephant Walk. Children line up single file. The first child in line bends down and puts his arm through his legs. The child behind him takes his hand, and puts her other hand through her legs. The children walk around connected to each other, in the same way that elephants hold each other's tails as they walk.

Rhythm and Rhyme: Teach the children to sing "Does Your Trunk Hang Low?" (see appendix page 298).

Small Group: Read a few selections from the series of *Elmer* books by David McKee. Talk to the children about the way the books are illustrated. Then encourage them to glue many colors of small felt squares onto a construction paper elephant.

Fall

STORY TIME

Fall by Maria Rius
Fall by Nuria Roca
Hooray for Fall by Sarah Wilson
Now It's Fall by Lois Lenski

TRANSITION

Fill in the blank with a child's name. The named child tells something that happens in fall before moving to the next activity.

> *[Child's name], _____,*
> *Tell us all*
> *About something that happens*
> *In the fall.*

SNACK

Serve warm apple cider. Add a cinnamon stick for a warm fall drink.

Group Time

Cut out the shape of a person from butcher paper. Also cut out the shape of a squirrel. On the cutout of the person write, "People and Plants in Fall" and on the squirrel cutout, write, "What Animals Do." With the children, make lists of things that happen in the fall.

Learning Center Ideas

Art: Help the children make an acorn hat. Cut an acorn and a hat pattern for each child. Print black squares with a berry basket on the brown acorn hat. Glue the hat to the bottom, and draw a happy "Fall" face.
Math: Children sort and make patterns with fall leaves and gourds.
Science: Put Indian corn, gourds, leaves, and pumpkins in the Science Center. Set out magnifying glasses, and a clipboard with paper for taking notes.

Additional Activities

Movement: Spread out fabric leaves on the floor. Play music and invite the children to pick up as many leaves as they can. When the music stops, the children stop. Encourage them to count how many leaves they were able to pick up. If the children are only able to count to 10, play the music a shorter time. Children can count their own leaves or the class can count together.
Outside: Take a sock walk. Ask parents for donations of old white tube socks (adult size). Help the children put on an old sock over their own sock and shoe. Go for a walk outside in the grass. When you come back inside, take off the socks and see what stuck to them. This shows how seeds travel. If desired, put the socks in zipper-closure bags with a little bit of water and set them in a sunny spot in the classroom. Watch what grows!

Letter C

STORY TIME

Caps for Sale by Esphyr Slobodkina
Career Day by Anne Rockwell
Clifford, the Big Red Dog by Norman Bridwell
Clifford's Family by Norman Bridwell
Clifford's Puppy Days by Norman Bridwell
A Color of His Own by Leo Lionni

Group Time

Talk about the letter *c*. Listen to the sound it makes, and then say different words, some that begin with the letter *c* and some that do not. Ask the children to clap their hands if the word begins with the letter *c*.

Learning Center Ideas

Art: Help children use a candle to write their name on white construction paper. Be sure to press hard. When they paint over the candle wax with watercolor paint, their names will appear.

Fine Motor: Challenge the children to hang clothes with clothespins.

Math: Encourage children to hang clothes from smallest to largest.

Math: Cut out shirts from construction paper and write a numeral from 1-5 or 1-10 on each one. Ask the children to hang the shirts on the clothesline in the correct order.

Sensory: Put a bag of cornmeal flour in the sensory table. Offer the children measuring cups, funnels, measuring spoons, and other items for exploring.

Additional Activities

Movement: Play Crocodile Catcher. One child is the crocodile. He opens and closes his arms like crocodile jaws. The other children line up on one side of the room. When the crocodile says "Go," the children run across the room as the crocodile tries to catch them. Children who are caught become crocodiles.

Outside: Do movements that begin with the letter *c*, such as crawling, creeping, and crabwalk.

Triangles

STORY TIME

Circles, Triangles, and Squares by Tana Hoban
Color Zoo by Lois Ehlert
The Greedy Triangle by Marilyn Burns

SNACK

Make a Triangle Treat using triangle-shaped crescent biscuits (see appendix page 300 for recipe).

Group Time

Make a large triangle with masking tape in the Group Time area. During Group Time, invite the children to walk around the triangle shape on the tape. Notice the three sides and three corners. Next, put the children in groups of three. Give each child a strip of paper. Encourage the children to work together to make triangles using the strips of paper.

Learning Center Ideas

Art: Set out a piece of contact paper for each child with the sticky side up. Set out several kinds of paper, gift wrap, tissue paper, and construction paper triangles in different sizes. Invite the children to stick the triangles to the paper. When the children are finished, add another piece of clear contact paper on the top. Then cut the whole contact paper collage into a large triangle shape.

Art: Cut strips of paper in several colors. Then, give each child a piece of construction paper cut into a large triangle shape (this will be the background). Invite the children to make triangles using the strips of paper. Remind the children that a triangle has three sides. Invite them to guess how many strips of paper they will need to make each triangle.

Math: Make patterns using precut foam shapes sold in craft stores. Use all triangles or use different shapes and encourage the children to sort out the triangles. Sort by size, color, or shape.

Sensory/Art: Cut out several sizes of triangles from cardboard, bubble wrap, and textured paper. Invite the children to make triangle rubbings. Tape the triangles to a table, and help the children to put pieces of paper over the shapes and color them with crayons. Triangles will appear on their papers.

Additional Activities

Movement: Invite the children to walk around the tape used for Group Time (see above) as the music plays. When the music stops, the children freeze. Call out a direction, such as *crawl, hop, walk backwards,* and so on. The music starts and the children follow the direction until the music stops again.

Outside: Children practice drawing triangles with chalk.

Rhythm and Rhyme: Sing "The Triangle Song" with the children (see appendix page 300).

Diamonds

GENERAL DAILY PLAN

Color Farm by Lois Ehlert
Color Zoo by Lois Ehlert
Three Pigs, One Wolf, and Seven Magic Shapes by Grace Maccarone

Each child picks a shape from a basket of shapes. He names the shape and moves on to the next activity.

Group Time

Before Group Time, put masking tape in a large diamond shape in your Group Time area. Also, make Bingo cards to play "Shape Bingo." Print a grid with nine spaces. Put the following nine shapes—square, diamond, crescent moon, triangle, rectangle, circle, heart, oval, and star—in separate squares on the grid in different orders for each card.

As the children come to Group Time, invite them to sit on the diamond tape. Talk about diamonds. Then play shape Bingo as a review. Give each child a Bingo card and use cereal or poker chips as markers. The children will have to cover all their shapes to win. This way all the children win at the same time and you can see who knows their shapes. Name a shape (you might want to make a large die cut of each shape to hold up). As you name each shape, the children cover it up.

Learning Center Ideas

Manipulatives: Cut diamond shapes from plastic canvas (found in craft stores). Invite the children to weave in and out of the holes in the canvas with pipe cleaners.
Math: Children make and/or finish patterns using foam diamond shapes.
Sensory: Children make diamond shapes from playdough using craft stick knives or cookie cutters.

Additional Activities

Movement: Play Musical Shapes. Tape cutout paper shapes all over the classroom on the floor. Play music and invite the children to dance or walk around the room, being careful not to step on the shapes while the music is playing. When the music stops, they quickly stand on a shape and name the shape. Play again. Encourage the children to stand on a different shape every time.
Outside: Encourage the children to run around the bases of a baseball diamond.
Small Group: Read *Color Farm* and *Color Zoo* by Lois Ehlert. Set out many sizes and colors of rectangles, squares, ovals, and triangles. Invite the children to make their own animals using the shapes.

Squirrels

STORY TIME

Squirrel Is Hungry by Satoshi Kitamura

Squirrel Says Thank You by Mary Mantz Simon

A Squirrel's Tale by Richard Fowler

Tale of Squirrel Nutkin by Beatrix Potter

Tale of Timmy Tiptoes by Beatrix Potter

SNACK

Make a snack a squirrel would love. Spread peanut butter on a pretzel rod. Roll the rod in sunflower seeds. Have a squirrel feast. **Safety Note:** Be sure that children do not have peanut allergies before serving this snack.

Group Time

Cut out acorn shapes. On each shape, print a squirrel fact from those found on appendix page 301. Hide the shapes around the room. Invite your little squirrels to find the acorns. Read the acorns one by one to find out all about squirrels.

Learning Center Ideas

Art: Help the children make trees with a squirrel. Start by painting each child's hand and forearm up to the elbow with brown paint. Invite the child to press his arm onto a piece of construction paper to make the tree. For the branches, paint the child's palm and fingers and have him press his palm at the top of the trunk. Encourage him to make fingerprints in yellow, red, and orange for leaves. Finally, glue on gray pompoms to make a squirrel.

Math: Cut five acorns (tops and bottoms separately) from brown construction paper. Label each top with a numeral. On each bottom, put a matching number of dots. Encourage the children to match the tops and bottoms correctly.

Additional Activities

Rhythm and Rhyme: Teach the children to sing "Gray Squirrel" (see appendix page 299).

Ovals

STORY TIME

Brown Rabbit's Shape Book by Alan Baker

Color Zoo by Lois Ehlert

My First Look at Shapes (a Dorling Kindersley Book)

Shapes, Shapes, Shapes by Tana Hoban

SNACK

Make your own egg salad. Put a peeled, hardboiled egg in a Ziploc bag for each child. (Older children can peel their own eggs). Add a tablespoon of mayonnaise and close the bag. Children can use their hands to chop up the egg and mix it with the mayonnaise to make individual egg salads. Serve it with crackers or bread.

Group Time

Talk with the children about ovals. Ask the children if they know anything that is shaped like an oval. If they can't think of anything, show them a picture of an egg. Discuss how an oval shape is different from a circle. Bring in a length of string tied together at the end. Invite each child to hold on to the string. Show them how to make the string into a circle. Then make it into an oval shape.

Learning Center Ideas

Art: Help the children cut out oval shapes from foam. Also cut out an oval in the center to make picture frames. Set out embellishments to decorate the frames. Help children to put a photo of themselves at school in the frame.

Literacy: Invite children to make oval books. Draw an oval outline on a page. Inside the oval outline print the words: _____ *is an oval.* Make copies of the pages and put them in the Literacy Center. Invite children to cut out the oval shape for each page they want in their book, draw a picture of something oval on each oval they cut out, and then dictate what each item is on the line.

Math: Set up an Estimation Station. Put I, 2, or 3 beans in plastic eggs. Set out baskets that with numerals 1, 2, and 3 on them. Children shake the eggs and decide whether there are 1, 2, or 3 beans in the egg and put it in the marked basket. When they have finished sorting, they check to see if they are correct.

Additional Activities

Project: Give each child a large oval shape to place in front of a sunny window. Invite children to set small items on their oval, such as a paper clip, marker, eraser, ruler, and so on. Leave the shapes in the sunny window with the items on top for several days. Remove the items. What happened? Why? (Hint: Use the least expensive construction paper for the oval shape. It will fade faster).

Project: Make a fingerprint number book over a period of five days (see instructions on appendix page 296).

October

Calendar Time

During Calendar Time, introduce the month of October to the children. Look at the letters in the word *October*. Name each letter, and say the sound and other words that start with the sound. Whose name begins with the letter *o*? Do this for each letter in the word during calendar time throughout the month.

Monthly Organizer

MONTH-LONG CELEBRATIONS

National Popcorn Month
National Dinosaur Month
National Pizza Month
National Stamp Collecting Month

SPECIAL DAYS AND HOLIDAYS

October 5: David Shannon's Birthday
The week beginning on the second Sunday of October: National
     School Lunch Week
The third Saturday in October: Sweetest Day
October 31: Halloween

GENERAL DAILY PLANS

Opposites
Letter *O*
Responsibility
Telephones
Fire Safety
Leaves
Letter *P*
Orange
Letter *G*
Monsters
Letter *E*

Black
Owls
Pumpkins
Bats
Miss Muffet and Spiders
Flashlights

Note: Please be sure to check for allergies before serving the snacks or doing any food-related activities.

National Popcorn Month

October is National Popcorn Month.

STORY TIME

12 Ways to Get to 11 by Eve Merriam
Bear Snores On by Karma Wilson
Miss Bindergarten Plans a Circus with Kindergarten by Joseph Slate

TRANSITION

Add a name to the rhyme below. Invite the named child to hop to the next activity.

Little popcorn pop, pop, pop
____, _____ hop, hop, hop.

SNACK

Make popcorn on the cob. Put unshucked corn cobs in brown paper bags (one in each bag) and microwave them for one minute, or until the popping slows down, and serve for the children to enjoy. Sing "The Popcorn Song" on appendix page 305 while you wait.

Group Time

On chart paper, create a large graph separated into two sections headers: "Regular" and "Cheese." Ask the children for their opinion on which kind of popcorn they prefer. Make popcorn from plain kernels. Add butter and salt to half of the batch. Sprinkle parmesan cheese or cheddar cheese on the other half. After they taste the two types of popcorn, ask the children put a tally mark on the side of the graph that they prefer. **Variation:** Put popcorn in four bowls. Add nothing to the first bowl, salt to one, butter to the next, and salt and butter to the last.

Learning Center Ideas

Literacy: Label brown lunch bags with different letters. Put words on popcorn shapes, cut and laminate. Challenge the children to put the words with the same beginning letter in the correct bag.

Math: Encourage children to trace popcorn bag shapes onto construction paper. Assign each child a number and help each child to write her number on a bag outline. Then, encourage the children to put the same number of packing popcorn pieces on the popcorn bag outline.

Additional Activities

Movement: Put ping-pong balls in the middle of a parachute. Have the children hold onto the ends of the parachute and wave it up and down, simulating the popping of popcorn. Encourage the children to vary the speed and height at which they bounce the ping-pong balls, from slow and low to fast and high, imitating the increased heat and pressure applied when cooking popcorn.

Outside: Explain to the children that animals love to eat popcorn, too. Give the children some leftover popcorn to set outside near a classroom window. Ask the children which animals they think will come to eat it. As a class, observe the animals that take the popcorn.

National Dinosaur Month

October is National Dinosaur Month.

STORY TIME

Dinosaurs Roar by Paul Stickland
How Do Dinosaurs Clean Their Rooms? by Jane Yolen
How Do Dinosaurs Say Good Night? by Jane Yolen
My First Dinosaur Board Book by DK Publishing
Touch and Feel: Dinosaur by Dave King

TRANSITION

Say a child's name in the rhyme below. When she hears her name, the child can walk like a dinosaur to the next activity.

> [Child's name]- *asaur*
> *Don't be slow.*
> *Walk like a dinosaur*
> *As you go.*

SNACK

Remind children to wash hands before cooking. Make a "dinosaur bones" snack by mixing together pretzel sticks, M&Ms, corn cereal squares, and miniature marshmallows.

Group Time

Cut out felt shapes of five dinosaurs (see appendix page 302 for patterns). Make each dinosaur a different color. Put the dinosaur shapes up on a flannel board one at a time, describing each dinosaur (see Dinosaur Facts on appendix page 308). Encourage the children to repeat aloud the traits of each different dinosaur. Once all five shapes are on the dinosaur flannel board, ask the children to close their eyes. Take one dinosaur shape away. Ask the children to open their eyes and say which dinosaur is missing.

Learning Center Ideas

Art: Cut a dinosaur shape for each child. Invite the children to finger paint the dinosaur with blue and yellow, so it will be green when it dries. Encourage the children to add glitter to the paint, so when the paint dries the dinosaur will sparkle.

Math: Cut out dinosaur and egg pairs from different patterns of wallpaper. Encourage the children to match the eggs and the dinosaurs by their wallpaper patterns.

Science: Bury the toy bones from a 3-D dinosaur puzzle in a tub of sand. Encourage the children to excavate the bones and reassemble the dinosaur.

Sensory: Add plastic dinosaurs to the Sand Table with which the children can imagine and explore.

Additional Activities

Movement: Put on music and invite the children to dance in ways they imagine resemble the movements of dinosaurs.

Outside: Cut lengths of yarn equal to the various heights and lengths of different dinosaurs (see Dinosaur Facts on appendix page 308). Keep the lengths of yarn in envelopes labeled with pictures of the appropriate dinosaurs. Take the children outside and invite them to unroll the lengths of yarn. Encourage the children to gauge the different dinosaurs' lengths using their own footsteps and body lengths as units of measure.

Rhythm and Rhyme: Sing "Dinosaur Roar" (see appendix page 303).

National Pizza Month

October is National Pizza Month.

STORY TIME

Grandpa and Me by Karen Katz
Little Red Hen Makes a Pizza by
    Philemon Storges
Pete's a Pizza by William Steig

TRANSITION

Pass the pizza box. Invite the children to sit in a circle. Put on some lively music. As the music plays, encourage the children to quickly pass a pizza box around the circle. Occasionally, stop the music. When the music stops, invite the child holding the box to move on to the next activity.

SNACK

Make healthy pizzas with the children, using wheat pita bread as the crust, spreading tomato sauce on it, and adding low-fat cheese. Microwave each for about a minute, let cool, and serve.

Group Time

Bring a pizza to group time. Talk about the shape of most whole pizzas and the shape of pizza slices. At this time, introduce the children to the food pyramid (see appendix page 309). Describe the ingredients to the children, and encourage them to guess which part of the food pyramid it is from: The crust is from the grain group, the tomato sauce is from the vegetable group, and the cheese is from the dairy group. Talk about other foods that some people like to put on a pizza, such as sausage, pepperoni, vegetables, and some fruits, including pineapple. Ask children to point to each area on the food pyramid. Talk about ways to make a healthy pizza (whole wheat crust and low-fat cheese). Cut the pizza into quarters, eighths, and so on, and explain to the children what fraction of the pizza each slice represents. When there are enough pieces for each child, invite the children to enjoy a slice of delicious pizza.

Learning Center Ideas

Dramatic Play: Make a pretend Pizza Parlor. Put a tablecloth on the table. Invite children to make their own pizza menus. Use playdough to make pizzas for the restaurant.

Literacy: Cut labels from pizza boxes, packages, or ads. Cut two labels from each place. Glue four different labels on a piece of paper. Laminate both the paper and the extra pizza labels. Children play Pizza Lotto by matching the labels to the label on the paper.

Math: Cut three brown felt circles 8" in diameter. Add felt toppings: 6" red felt circle (tomato sauce) and brown pompom meatballs. Cut one pizza in half, one pizza into fourths, and one pizza into eighths. Put each pizza in a real pizza box to store. Invite children to put the pizza puzzles together.

Additional Activities

Outside: Play Pizza Line Tag. Make huge chalk circles on the playground, and divide the circles into sections resembling slices of pizza. Encourage the children to play line tag, which is similar to regular tag, with one child being "IT," tagging the other children, only everyone must stay on the lines.

Rhythm and Rhyme: Sing "The Pizza Song" with the children (see appendix page 305).

National Stamp Collecting Month

MONTH-LONG CELEBRATION

October is National Stamp Collecting Month.

STORY TIME

A Child's World of Stamps: Stories, Poems, Fun, and Facts from Many Lands by Mildred Depree
Postmark Paris: A Story in Stamps by Leslie Jonah
Tales by Mail by Karen Cartier

SNACK

Cut cheese into square "stamps" and place the squares on crackers.

Group Time

Talk to the children about letters, mail, and the post office. Sequence what happens to a letter once it is taken to the post office. 1) The post office sorts the letters. 2) The letters are sent to the post office where they are to be delivered, either by plane or by truck. 3) The letters are delivered to the address on the envelopes. Show the children how to address an envelope and where to put the stamp.

Learning Center Ideas

Art: Show the children how to make stamps using the recipe listed on appendix page 303. Give the children several pieces of construction paper in different colors. Encourage them to draw designs on the paper. Make the glue according to the recipe, and then invite the children to spread the glue on the back of their papers. After the glue dries, encourage the children to use pinking shears to cut out stamps. The children can use the homemade stamps to make patterns on a strip of paper.

Dramatic Play: Bring one large box into class and encourage the children to use it as a public mailbox, and give each child an individual shoebox to use as a mailbox. Invite the children to write and deliver letters to each other.

Literacy: Set out old stamps, magnifying glasses, and blank books of stapled paper and invite the children to make their own stamp-collecting books.

Additional Activities

Movement: Play Stamp, Stamp, Who Has the Stamp? Invite the children to sit in a circle, except for the child who is "IT." IT sits in a chair in the middle of the circle and closes his eyes while the rest of the children pass a stamp around the circle. When IT says, "Stop!" the child with the stamp hides it behind her back. IT then opens his eyes and guesses who has the stamp.

Rhythm and Rhyme: Sing "The Stamp Song" on appendix page 306.

David Shannon's Birthday

October 5th is David Shannon's birthday.

STORY TIME

Choose from the following list of David Shannon books:
Alice the Fairy
A Bad Case of Stripes
David Gets in Trouble
David Goes to School
Duck on a Bike
How I Became a Pirate
No, David!
Oh, David!
Oops

TRANSITION

Use a magic wand to tap quiet children, allowing them to move to the next activity.

SNACK

Make and eat a "magic wand" snack. Use a small star-shaped cookie cutter to cut star shapes out of cheese slices. Put the stars on pretzel rods.

Group Time

Begin by showing some of David Shannon's books to the children and asking them if they think the books were written by one person or different people. After the children take their guesses, tell them a little bit about David Shannon (see David Shannon Facts on appendix page 309). Read *No, David!* to the children. As you read it, encourage them to retell some of the things David did.

Learning Center Ideas

Art: Remind the children that David Shannon is an author and an artist. Set up art stations with paint, chalk, and markers, and invite the children to draw their own characters and then name them.

Dramatic Play: Encourage the children to pretend to be pirates, like the character Jeremy Jacob in *How I Became a Pirate.* Help the children make props for their play: string and construction paper eye patches, a pipe cleaner hook made by putting the pipe cleaner through the bottom of a paper cup, and a pirate ship made by painting a large appliance box.

Writing/Literacy: Make your own *No, David!* books. Set out several stapled paper books for children. On the top each page, print "No, [child's name]!" Have the children fill in the blanks with their own names and draw pictures to go with the story.

Additional Activities

Rhythm and Rhyme: Sing "Play with Me" (see appendix page 305) with the children.

Small Group: Read *Alice the Fairy.* Ask the children what they would do with a magic wand. Invite children to finish the sentence: "If I had a magic wand, I would _____." Invite the children to draw pictures describing what they would do with their magic wands.

National School Lunch Week

SPECIAL DAYS AND HOLIDAYS

National School Lunch Week begins on the second Sunday in October.

STORY TIME

I Need a Lunch Box by Jeannette Franklin
Lunch by Denise Fleming
Monster Munch by Margery Facklam
What's for Lunch? by Ann Garrett

SNACK

Make a Fruit Snack (see recipe on appendix page 307).

Group Time

Use a flannel board to attach laminated pictures of the different lunchtime foods found in *Lunch* by Denise Fleming. Read *Lunch* to the children. After reading the story, ask the children to say aloud and in the correct order all of the different foods that the mouse ate. As the children name each food, attach the appropriate laminated piece to the flannel board. When all the food items are on the board, ask the children to close their eyes. Take one food item away, and then ask the children to open their eyes and guess which food is missing.

Next, show the children a picture of the food pyramid (see appendix page 309). Name and discuss the foods in each group. Ask the children what food groups they ate for breakfast. Ask, "What is your favorite food in the meat group?" "How are meats different from fruits and vegetables?"

Learning Center Ideas

Literacy: Using white construction paper, cut out 52 "slices" of bread. Next, cut out 26 round bologna shapes from pink construction paper. On each piece of bread, write a letter of the alphabet—go through the alphabet twice so there are two matching slices. Write one letter of the alphabet on each "slice" of bologna. Put all of the pieces into a lunch box. Encourage the children to make "letter sandwiches" by matching the letters on the bread with the letter on the bologna.

Math: Put two colors of beads in zipper-closure bags. Put in lace (cut in necklace-size pieces) and pipe cleaners. Children may choose to make necklaces by stringing the beads in an AB pattern, or they can make bracelets by stringing beads in an AB pattern on a pipe cleaner. Help the children wind the two ends of the pipe cleaner together and put the ends under the beads so they are not sharp.

Additional Activities

Outside: Take blankets and the children's lunches outside for a picnic. If the weather is too cold, have an "inside" picnic on the classroom floor.
Rhythm and Rhyme: With the children, sing "Lunch-O," holding up the letter cards for L-U-N-C-H (see appendix page 304).

Sweetest Day

Sweetest Day is the third Saturday in October, but it may be celebrated in the classroom the Friday before.

STORY TIME

The Elves and the Shoemaker by Paul Galdone

SNACK

Make a Sharing Snack Mix with another class (see appendix page 308).

Group Time

Explain to the children that being generous means giving time, energy, love, and gifts to other people. Ask the children to give examples of when they were generous, and make a list on chart paper of their examples. Ask the children how they felt after their acts of generosity. Ask the children whether being generous can make a person feel good on the inside, and whether generosity can be a surprise. Tell the children that on Sweetest Day, people give gifts or do something generous for those they appreciate.

Send the children home with copies of the list of generous behavior they made that day. Include a note asking family members to write down or circle the generous things their children do and for whom. Ask the children to bring these lists back to school after they have filled them out. Read each list aloud to the children, and afterwards invite each child to put their note in a "Generous Jar."

Learning Center Ideas

Blocks/Construction: Set up a Habitat for Humanity construction center. Explain to children that there is a group of people who come and build homes for people who need a place to live. Set out boxes, blocks, plastic plumbing pipes, play tools, hard hats. Invite children to build houses. Take photos of their constructions for display.

Literacy: Set up a card center to make cards. Write on a poster board a list of word/pictures that children might need to spell: *Happy Birthday, Have a Good Day, I Love You*, and so on.

Math: Invite children to bring in canned goods for a community food bank. Practice sorting the cans in different ways: big, small, by what is in the can, and so on. When finished sorting them, donate the cans to the food bank.

Additional Activities

Game: Instead of playing Doggie, Doggie, Where's Your Bone, play it backwards. Ask the children to sit in a circle, with the "doggie" sitting in the center. As the "doggie" covers her eyes, one child from the circle gives the dog a bone. Then the "doggie" opens her eyes and tries to guess the name of the generous child that gave her a bone.

Halloween

Halloween is celebrated on October 31st.

STORY TIME

Five Little Pumpkins by Dan Yaccarino

Froggy's Halloween by Jonathan London

Halloween Bugs by David A. Carter

Moonlight: The Halloween Cat by Cynthia Rylant

Trick or Treat? by Bill Martin, Jr.

TRANSITION

Recite this rhyme with the children, adding a child's name in the blank. Snap your fingers at the end of the rhyme and have the named child move to the next activity.

> *Halloween witch, Halloween cat,*
> *_____ moves on, just like that.*

Group Time

Invite the children to dress up for Halloween on this day. But remember, Halloween is sometimes scary for children. At this time in their lives, children are learning what is real and what is pretend. The suggestions and Halloween Safety Rules on appendix page 309 may help children who are afraid. Halloween and trick-or-treating are great fun. Write the Halloween Safety Rules on appendix page 309 on orange pumpkin shapes. During group time, children take turns pulling them out of a plastic pumpkin. Read and talk about each one.

Learning Center Ideas

Art: Set out orange, yellow, and black paint, and several paper bags. Invite the children to use Halloween cookie cutters to make prints on the bags and use them for their trick-or-treating.

Fine Motor/Math: Let the children cut orange playdough with Halloween cookie cutters, count how many cookies they made, and then make patterns with the cookies.

Math: Bring in plastic candy holders in pumpkin or ghost shapes (they often come in packages of six), and label each with a different number. Set out several Halloween and fall erasers and invite the children to put the correct number in each candy holder.

Sensory: Place plastic spider rings in orange shredded paper in your Sensory Table or a dishpan. Stuff a rubber glove with sand or cotton and tie it shut. Print a number on each finger of the glove. Invite children to find spider rings in the tub and put the correct number on each finger of the glove.

Additional Activities

Movement: Invite the children to walk in a circle, holding hands as they sing "The Witch Is in the House" (see appendix page 306). Choose one child to start as the "witch," and move that child to the center of the circle. At the end of the first verse, the witch chooses a child to be the "scarecrow," and the scarecrow moves into the center of the circle. Repeat with each verse.

Outside: Have a Halloween costume parade.

Opposites

STORY TIME

Clifford's Opposites by Norman Bridwell
My Opposites by Rebecca Emberley
Olivia's Opposites by Ian Falconer
Opposites by Sandra Boynton
Opposites by Robert Crowther
Opposites by Chuck Murphy

TRANSITION

Write "opposite" words on pieces of paper. Put the paper slips in a basket. Invite each child to pick one of the slips from the basket. Read the word and ask the class to help the child name what is the opposite of the word. After the child names the opposite, he can move on to the next activity.

SNACK

Serve warm cider and cold, crisp apple slices.

Group Time

Talk about what it means for a thing to have an opposite. Bring in a basket filled with soft and hard items, such as a block, blanket, pillow, toy car, stuffed animal, and pencil. Have the children sort items by soft and hard.

Learning Center Ideas

Art: Explain to the children that the opposite of black is white. To illustrate this, allow the children to make collages on black paper using cotton balls, white felt, lace, sequins, and other white items.

Science: Bring in ice cubes made with red food coloring. Ask the children to say what they think will happen when the cubes are put in a bowl of hot water. Write the class' predictions on the board, and then put the ice cubes in the bowl of hot water (**adult-only step:** keep the bowl of hot water away from the children). Let the children see and discuss what happens.

Sensory: Set out a variety of items and challenge the children to sort them based on whether they are rough or smooth.

Additional Activities

Movement: Play several "opposites" freeze games. 1) Dance while the music plays when the music stops freeze; 2) walk around when the lights are off; and 3) when the lights go on, the children freeze.

Outside: Ask two children to hold the ends of a jump rope. Depending on the height at which the rope is being held, encourage the other children to go over or under the jump rope without touching it.

Rhythm and Rhyme: Sing "The Opposite Song" on appendix page 305.

Letter O

STORY TIME

The Big Orange Splot by D. Manus Pinkwater

One Duck Stuck by Phyllis Root

One Hungry Monster by Susan Heyboer O'Keefe

Over in the Meadow by Olive A. Wadsworth

Owl Moon by Jane Yolen

Pearlie Oyster: A Tale of an Amazing Oyster by Suzanne Tate

TRANSITION

Say the rhyme below with a child's name. The child says a word and then moves to the next activity.

Name a word that starts with o,
_____, _____, off you go.

SNACK

Make Oatmeal Snack Bars using the recipe on appendix page 307.

Group Time

Print "O Is for Oatmeal," found on appendix page 305, on chart paper. Point to each word as you read. With the children, highlight every letter *o* that you see. Read the poem again, and invite the children to make an *o* with their fingers and thumbs when you read an *o* word. Make a list of children's names. Invite the children to highlight each *o* in their names.

Learning Center Ideas

Art: Make orange prints by dipping a magnetic letter *o* into orange paint and print them on paper.

Dramatic Play: Set up an office, with briefcase, phones, paper, pencils, and clipboard.

Math/Sensory: Put orange items from the classroom, such as orange crayons, orange teddy bear counters, orange beads, small orange blocks, and any other orange items, in the Sensory Table. Invite the children to sort the items.

Additional Activities

Movement: As you play music, children walk around a large rope shaped into a letter *o* (circle). When the music stops, they stand on the rope.

Outside: Show children what an oak leaf looks like. Ask the children if they have seen leaves like this outside. Go on a nature walk. Look at the leaves that have fallen off the trees. See if they look like the oak leaf example. Look for oak trees.

Rhythm and Rhyme: Teach the children the "Letter O Song" (see appendix page 304).

Small Group: Read *One Duck Stuck* by Phyllis Root. Read half way through the story. Invite children to predict what will happen. When the story is finished, invite children to help retell the story.

Responsibility

STORY TIME

The Best Me I Can Be by David Parker

TRANSITION

Say the following rhyme, naming a different child each time. After the child says what she will do, she moves on to the next activity. (This rhyme can be put in a pocket chart.)

> *Responsibility,*
> *People count on me.*
> *_____, what will you do?*
> *People count on you.*

SNACK

As a class, make Grandma A's Crumb Cake (see recipe on appendix page 307). Have two or three children be responsible for each part of the recipe. When each group does its part, the end result is delicious. As you eat the crumb cake, go around the room, asking each child to tell what they did to help make the cake. Remind children that everyone was responsible for helping to make the snack. Encourage the children to give themselves a round of applause.

Group Time

Encourage the children to talk about things they do every day, such as get dressed, brush their teeth, comb their hair, wash their hands, and come to school. Tell them these are called *responsibilities*. Explain the importance of responsibilities. Ask the children what would happen if people did not follow through on their responsibilities. What would happen, for instance, if their families stopped making breakfast or going to their jobs? Give each of the children a job to do, even small jobs. These will be the children's responsibilities for the day. At the end of the day, after all the children complete the tasks they were responsible for, give them "I am responsible" awards, and congratulate the children for fulfilling their responsibilities. Children can do things in the classroom like hold the door, help with snack, help with the calendar, set out circle time mats, wash the boards, ring the bell for cleanup, water the plants, feed the class pet, and so on.

Learning Center Ideas

Art: Make "I Am Responsible" crowns. Cut a piece of bulletin board border to fit each child's head. Print "I am Responsible" on the crown. Invite children to decorate their crowns with stickers.
Blocks: Set out cardboard roads. Encourage the children to work together to make a block community. Each child could be responsible for making a building (store, Post Office, Police Station), and then use toy cars to play in the community.
Sensory: Put soap suds and water in the Water Table. Wash the housekeeping dishes and doll clothes.

Additional Activities

Rhythm and Rhyme: Sing "Responsibility" with the children (see appendix page 306).

Telephones

STORY TIME

Alexander Graham Bell by Carin T. Ford
My Talking Telephone by Johnny Miglis
Telephone by Marc Tyler Nobleman
Telephones by Elaine Marie Aphin

Group Time

Show the children how to answer the telephone correctly, and let them take turns answering the telephone. Introduce the children to the 911 emergency services number. Warn the children only to call 911 if there is a real emergency.

Learning Center Ideas

Dramatic Play: Use a large appliance box as a phone booth, cutting a door out of it and attaching a toy phone to the wall. Let the children play telephone.

Literacy: Make Phone Books. The day before doing this, remind the children to ask their parents to send to school a sheet of paper with several friends' and relatives' phone numbers. Fold three sheets of paper together. Staple the pieces along the crease, making a blank book for each child. Print "_____'s Telephone Book" on the front of each book. Show the children a telephone address book. Explain how people put important numbers in their address books. Ask the children what phone numbers they want to include in their address books, and help them add those numbers. When their books are full of important numbers, invite the children to decorate their books.

Math/Literacy: Make a phone keypad (including the letters) out of construction paper and cover it with contact paper for durability. Help children practice spelling their names by pressing the numbers to which the letters of their names correspond.

Additional Activities

Movement: On pieces of construction paper, print each number from a telephone's key pad, adding the letters below each number. Use contact paper to attach the numbers to the floor, creating a giant telephone key pad. Invite the children to practice typing their phone numbers by jumping from number to number in order. (A variation for this is to use a white or clear shower curtain and draw the phone keypad with a permanent marker.)

Fire Safety

STORY TIME

Emergency by Margaret Mayo
Firefighter Frank by Monica
    Wellington
I Am a Firefighter by Cynthia
    Benjamin
Poinsettia and the Firefighters by
    Felicia Bond

TRANSITION

Ask one child at a time to stop, drop, and roll to the next activity.

FLOWS SAFETY STEPS

Freeze
Line up
Outside
Wait quietly
Stay with your class

Group Time

Bring in a working smoke detector. Press the test button so the children know how it sounds. Discuss what to do if there is a fire. Tell the children that when they hear a fire alarm at school, they should remember FLOWS, which will remind them of the safety steps (see FLOWS steps at left).

When the children have memorized FLOWS, practice responding to a fire alarm. At several times throughout the day, push the smoke detector test button. Have the children practice the first two of the FLOWS steps. Practice this several times throughout the day. Encourage children to talk to their parents about what they should do if there is a fire at home.

Learning Center Ideas

Dramatic Play: Paint a large appliance box so it resembles a fire truck. Have the children pretend to drive to fires and put them out.
Literacy: Make a fire hat. Cut off the corners of a 12" x 18" piece of red construction paper. Cut a large semi-circle in the middle of the paper, making a flap. Fold the flap up. Help the children glue a yellow badge to the flap that says "Firefighter _____" and print their names in the blank.
Math: Cut out dog shapes from construction paper. Children use an ink pad and cotton swabs to make 10 Dalmatian spots on the dog shapes.

Additional Activities

Game: Play a Freeze Game with a real smoke detector. Invite the children to dance to some music. Occasionally, press the test button on the smoke detector. When the children hear the smoke detector, they drop to the floor and freeze.
Outside: Show the children where they will stand for fire drills or when there is a real fire. Tell the children that if, during an emergency, any of them get lost or separated from the group, they are to come to this spot.
Rhythm and Rhyme: Teach the children "Stop, Drop, and Roll," a song about what to do if there is a fire (see appendix page 306).

Leaves

The Biggest Leaf Pile by Steve
  Metzger
The Falling Leaves by Steve Metzger
*The Falling Leaves and the
  Scarecrow* by Steve Metzger
Red Leaf, Yellow Leaf by Lois Ehlert
Why Do Leaves Change Color? by
  Betsy Maestro

TRANSITION

After reciting the rhyme below,
name a color. All the children
wearing the named color move to
the next activity. Continue naming
colors until all children have moved
to the next activity.

> *Leaf, leaf on the tree,
> What color will you be?*

SNACK

Make Fall Leaves. Make a piece of
whole-wheat toast for each child.
Help the children butter the toast
lightly, and then encourage them to
sprinkle cinnamon and orange or
yellow decorating sugar onto the
butter. Help them use a leaf cookie
cutter to cut a leaf shape from the
toast.

Group Time

Find leaves of various fall colors. Laminate the leaves for increased
durability, or use fake leaves from a craft store. Hide the leaves around the
classroom or place them on the floor in the Group Time area. Invite the
children to find and pick up as many leaves as possible. When the children
have picked up all the leaves, count the number of leaves each child
found. When counting the number of one child's leaves, ask if this number
is more or less than the number of leaves the last child found. Help the
children sort their leaves into baskets by color, shape, and size.

Learning Center Ideas

Art: Place leaves under a sheet of paper. Rub the paper with a crayon to
make leaf rubbings.

Art/Math: (Wear art smocks for this activity). Mix a teaspoon of
dishwashing soap with the paint before doing this activity. Paint each
child's hand and forearm up to the elbow with washable brown paint.
Show the children how to press their arms onto a piece of construction
paper, making tree trunk shapes. Use leaf stickers or cotton swabs dipped
in fall colors to paint leaves on the trees. Encourage the children to count
the leaves as they add them to each tree.

Math: Cut tree-shapes out of construction paper. Write a number on each
trunk and laminate for durability. Encourage the children to tape a specific
number of leaves to each tree.

Additional Activities

Rhythm and Rhyme: Put the words of "Leaves on the Tree" (see appendix
page 304) in a pocket chart. Make a leaf pointer by gluing a foam leaf
shape to a pencil. Use the pointer to point to the words as you sing. Put
laminated construction paper or foam leaves in the bottom pocket of the
pocket chart for children to look at and name the color. Invite the children
to name a color that they see.

Outside: Take child-sized rakes outside and rake the leaves into piles. Once
the piles are large enough, encourage the children to take turns jumping
in. The children can also pile leaves into forts, or rake them into number-
or letter-shaped piles.

Letter *P*

STORY TIME

Pancakes for Breakfast by Tomie dePaola

The Paperboy by Dav Pilkey

Pigsty by Mark Teague

The Principal's New Clothes by Stephanie Calmenson

TRANSITION

Play Hot Potato. The children sit in a circle. As music plays, the children pass a potato around the circle as fast as they can, pretending it is hot. When the music stops, the child holding the potato moves to the next activity.

SNACK

Make a letter *p* fruit salad. Cut up peaches, pears, and pineapples. Mix them together with a non-dairy whipped topping for a peachy fruit salad.

Group Time

Put "P Is for Pizza," found on appendix page 305, in a pocket chart or on chart paper. Read the poem, Show children a cutout *p* (from construction paper or bulletin board paper. It can be glued to a pencil or a stick as a pointer.) Name the letter and the sound it makes. Invite the children to take turns highlighting each *p* in the poem with a pink or a purple highlighter or marker. Invite the children to help you make the /p/ sound when you come to a highlighted word as you read the poem again.

Learning Center Ideas

Fine Motor: Show the children how to cut several postcards into 2- to 3-piece puzzles. Encourage the children to re-assemble the postcards to their original form.

Literacy: Set out pens and paper for the children to explore writing and drawing their names.

Math: Encourage the children to count with poker chips, putting them into an oatmeal container with a slot cut through its top.

Sensory: Put purple food coloring into pitchers of water. Children can practice pouring the purple water into different-sized pitchers in the Water Table.

Additional Activities

Outside: Take pails of water and paintbrushes outside for the children to paint their names in water on the playground.

Rhythm and Rhyme: Sing the "Letter P" Song with the children (see appendix page 304). Challenge the children to come up with new letter *p* lyrics.

Small Group: Bring in green, yellow, and red peppers. Observe the differences in each pepper's color, size, and shape. Cut the peppers open and give the children small pieces of each pepper to taste. Make a graph showing which peppers the children like best.

Orange

STORY TIME

Dance with the Orange Cow by Nancy Libbey Mills

Little Orange Submarine by Ken-Wilson Max

Orange by Gary Tauali

Why Is an Orange Called an Orange? by Cobi Ladner

TRANSITION

Play Musical Colors. Set a variety of colored circles out in a larger circle pattern. Be sure that only one or two of the colored circles are orange. When the music plays, invite the children to dance around the circle of colored circles. Explain to the children that when the music stops, they must freeze on the nearest circle. The children who stop on the orange circles move to the next activity.

SNACK

Make orange punch by mixing orange sherbet with a clear juice, such as white grape juice. Serve the punch with carrot sticks and orange slices.

Group Time

Give each child small balls of yellow and red playdough. Encourage the children to mash the two balls together. What color does it turn? Can they shape their playdough into a pumpkin? Ask, "What shape is it?"

Learning Center Ideas

Art: Give the children paper and pencils. Invite them to trace coffee can lids onto their paper. Provide orange paint and encourage the children to paint their circles so they resemble pumpkins. When the paint dries, the children can draw facial features on the circles, making jack-o-lanterns.

Sensory: Squirt a layer of shaving cream onto the table. Add red and yellow food coloring. Invite children to mix the two colors of shaving cream together. Talk about what happens. Practice writing letters and numbers in shaving cream.

Additional Activities

Movement: Play music in the classroom, inviting the children to dance around the room, waving orange streamers. Call out directions using positional words such as, "Wave your streamers *high* in the sky," and other directions.

Outside: Set up cones up on a path, with small blocks to jump over, weaving through the playground equipment. To help the children know where to go, draw a line with chalk, showing the children where to walk through the cones, over the blocks, down the slide, and so on.

Rhythm or Rhyme: Invite children to name orange things in their environment before introducing "The Orange Song" (see appendix page 305). As you sing, encourage the children to clap when they say words that make the /o/ sound.

Small Group: Provide the children with a number of goldfish-shaped construction paper cutouts. Encourage the children to fingerpaint the goldfish with yellow and red. When the paint dries, the children will see how the colors combine to make orange. Decorate the fish with sequins, glitter, or other embellishments. Invite the children to dictate a story about their fish.

Letter *G*

STORY TIME

Gingerbread Man by Jim Aylesworth
Goodnight Moon by Margaret Wise
    Brown
Green Eyes by A. Birnbaum
Growing Vegetable Soup by Lois
    Ehlert

TRANSITION

Add a child's name to the rhyme below. Ask that child to say a word that begins with *g*. When the child does so, she moves to the next activity.

_____, _____, *where can you be?*
Name a word that starts with g.

SNACK

Make green gelatin, following the package directions. Cut the gelatin into rectangles. Tell the children the rectangles are plots of green grass. Encourage the children to add gummy worms to make a sweet *g* garden.

Group Time

Write "G Is for Gorilla," found on appendix page 304, in a pocket chart or on chart paper. Read the poem and point to each word. Use a green marker to highlight all of the *g* words in the poem.

Learning Center Ideas

Art: Place a number of shirt boxes on a table. Give each child a piece of construction paper and a golf ball. Encourage the children to paint their paper by placing it inside the box, dipping the golf balls in green paint, and rolling the balls in the boxes. (Optional: Add a little glue to the green paint and shake glitter on the picture before the paint dries.)
Fine Motor: Show the children how to cut green paper to make grass. Encourage the children to experiment making grass of different lengths and widths.
Sensory: Set a pail of goldfish gravel in the sand and Water Table for children to feel and explore. Add pails and shovels and other sand toys.

Additional Activities

Outside: Invite the children to pretend they are galloping on horses. Put blocks around the area for the horses to jump over. Consider having a pretend horse show, as well.
Rhythm and Rhyme: Clap the syllables as you sing this fun song, "G, G, the Letter G" (see appendix page 304).
Small Group: Help each child trace his left and right hands onto construction paper. Cut out the hand shapes. Ask each child to tell you which glove (hand shape) is the left and which is the right. As they answer, help them label each glove; encourage the children to decorate the gloves with paint and markers.

Monsters

STORY TIME

Birthday Monster by Sandra
 Boynton
Five Ugly Monsters by Tedd Arnold
Go Away, Big Green Monster by Ed
 Emberley
M Is for Monster by Mike Wazowski
Monsters by Salina Yoon
One Hungry Monster by Susan
 Heyboer O'Keefe

TRANSITION

Say a child's name in the rhyme below. After the rhyme is finished, that child moves to a new activity. Put children's monster fears to rest with this transition.

 _____, is there a monster
 here?
 (Child shakes head and
 answers): There are no
 monsters anywhere.

SNACK

Make a monster head snack. Using green sherbet as the monster's head, encourage children to make a monster face, using chocolate chips, red licorice rope, peanuts, gummy worms, and cereal. (**Safety Note**: Check for allergies.)

Group Time 1

Make felt cutouts of the pieces of the face from *Go Away, Big Green Monster* by Ed Emberley. Read the story to the children and follow along as the monster face is created and then disappears. When a monster part is introduced in the story, attach that cutout to the flannel board. When each piece leaves the story, ask the children which piece to take down.

Group Time 2

Spread out a bed sheet in the Group Time area. Read *Five Ugly Monsters* by Tedd Arnold. As you reread the story, invite five children to act out the story, taking turns being ugly monsters jumping on the bed (sheet).

Learning Center Ideas

Literacy: Invite the children to create their own monster faces with a paper plate, pens, markers, sequins, goggle eyes, construction paper, foams, paper shreds, and felt. Ask the children to dictate a story to you about their monster. Attach both to a large piece of construction paper.
Literacy/Math: Attach several green construction paper footprints on the floor, each with a numeral and letter written on them. Invite the children to jump from footprint to footprint, naming the letter on the foot on which they land and then jumping that many times.

Additional Activities

Movement: Play the "Monster Mix Up" (see appendix page 305).
Outside: Play Monster Tag. Choose one child to be the monster. The monster must chase the other children. When the monster tags someone, the tagged child becomes the new monster.

Letter *E*

STORY TIME

Eensy-Weensy Spider by Mary Ann Hoberman

An Extraordinary Egg by Leo Lionni

TRANSITION

Insert a child's name into the rhyme below. Encourage her to say a word that begins with the letter *e* sound. Once she has, invite her to move to the next activity.

> _____, *tell me a thing you see*
> *That begins with the letter e.*

SNACK

Make Elephant Ears with the children (see appendix page 306).

Group Time

Before Group Time, obtain as many plastic eggs as you have children. Put items in the eggs; some that begin with the letter *e* (eraser, envelope, plastic elephant, earring, elastic, a piece of paper with the numeral 11 on it) and some items that do not begin with *e*. Hide the eggs around the room. Invite the children to find the eggs. Sit down with the children and take turns opening the eggs. Does the item start with the /e/ sound? If not, what sound does it make?

Learning Center Ideas

Blocks/Construction: Place some toy tools and an old motor from a clock or radio for the children to explore. Encourage the children to wear safety goggles while "working" on the motor. **Note**: Be sure to remove all potentially harmful/electrical parts of the motor before giving it to the children.

Dramatic Play: Set up a Fitness Center. Invite the children to exercise using fitness center equipment such as a mat, stopwatch, and small toy weights.

Literacy: Obtain small, cheap erasers. Write an uppercase letter on several, and their matching lowercase letters on others. Invite children to match uppercase and lowercase letters. (Start with a few letters; add more when appropriate.)

Math: Make a counting envelope book. Tie the ends of five envelopes together, leaving the flap side open. Write the numerals 1–5 on the envelopes. Put cardboard shapes of the numerals into the corresponding envelopes. Have the children take out all five cardboard shapes of the numbers, then put them back into the appropriate envelopes. Or, place one item in the envelope with the numeral l, two in the envelope with numeral 2, and so on.

Math: Put out a number of special holiday-shape erasers. Encourage the children to sort the erasers in the order in which the holidays fall in the year.

Additional Activities

Movement: Encourage the children to try various exercises, from jumping jacks to touching toes.

Project: Perform an egg experiment (see appendix page 303 for instructions).

Black

Wear black on this day.

STORY TIME

Baby Animals Black and White by
Phyllis L. Tildes
Black on White by Tana Hoban
*Tomie's Baa Baa Black Sheep and
Other Rhymes* by Tomie dePaola
White on Black by Tana Hoban

TRANSITION

Put a child's name in the rhyme
below. The child pretends to be a
black animal as they move to the
next activity. The other children
guess what animal the child is
pretending to be.

> _____, _____ let me see
> Which black animal will you
> be?

SNACK

Make a Black Dirt Cake (see
appendix page 306) for snack with
the children.

Group Time

Read *Shades of Black* by Sandra L. Pickney. Invite the children to help
define the word unique. Explain that each child is unique, and invite each
child in class to describe how another child is unique. On the blackboard,
write: "_____ is unique because_____" and fill in some of the
reasons the children suggest. Once each child has had a turn to explain
how another child is unique, invite each child to draw a self-portrait.
Display the portraits in a class book.

Learning Center Ideas

Art: Cut out numerous black cat outlines from construction paper. Make
these available to the children at the art table, along with various black
items such as black buttons, black tissue paper, black paper shreds, black
sequins, black fabric, black felt, and black sandpaper. Invite the children
to explore gluing the different materials to the black cat shapes.
Math: Provide two different stamps, paper, and black ink for the children to
make AB patterns with the stamps.
Sensory: Put a little anise in black paint. Suggest that the children make
licorice-scented paintings.

Additional Activities

Game: Hang a sheet through the center of the room, putting half of the
class on each side. Turn off the lights and shine a flashlight on the sheet.
Invite a child from one side to stand behind the sheet. Encourage the
children on the other side of the sheet to guess which child's outline they
are seeing.
Rhythm and Rhyme: Sing "The Black Song" with the children (see appendix
page 303).

Owls

STORY TIME

Good Night, Owl by Pat Htuchins
Little Owl by Diers Harper
Owl and the Pussycat by Edward Lear
Owl Babies by Martin Waddell

SNACK

Who-who-who would like a snack? Make "owl toast" for each child. Cut a slice of American cheese diagonally, and put the triangle upside down on the top of the piece of toast. Add raisin eyes and a triangle cheese cracker beak.

Group Time

Talk to the children about owls (see Owl Facts on appendix page 309). Show the book *Owl Babies* by Martin Waddell. Talk about and show the title of the story, the author's name, and the illustrator's name. Read the story, but stop before the ending. Invite children to predict what will happen next.

Learning Center Ideas

Art: Cut out several owl shapes from construction paper. Encourage the children to paint them brown and white, using feathers for brushes. When the paint dries, they can add eyes and a beak.

Art: Help children make owls from large, brown construction paper cutouts of the letter *o*. Help them cut an orange triangle and glue it on upside down from the top of the *o*, and then glue on two circles for eyes and a small triangle for a beak.

Math: Cut out owl shapes from construction paper, labeling each with a numeral. Invite the children to put that many feathers on the owl.

Sensory: Put artificially colored feathers in the Sensory Table for children to explore. Invite them to sort the feathers by color and count them.

Additional Activities

Game: Play Who-Who-Who's the Owl? The children sit in a circle. Select one child to move to the other side of the classroom and close his eyes. Once the child's eyes are closed, silently pick another child to be the owl. The owl hoots. The other child opens his eyes and guesses "whoooo" is the owl. If the child guesses incorrectly, he closes his eyes again, and the owl hoots again. Repeat this until the child guesses correctly. The owl then goes to the other side of the room and becomes the guesser.

Outside: Play a game of owl tag. One child is the owl. The owl flies around and tries to tag the other children. Pick a special spot such as a tree to be a safe spot. The owl cannot tag anyone touching the tree. When the owl tags someone, that child becomes the next owl.

Rhythm and Rhyme: Sing "Owl in a Tree" (see appendix page 305) with the children.

Pumpkins

STORY TIME

Apples and Pumpkins by Anne Rockwell

The Biggest Pumpkin Ever by Steven Kroll

It's Pumpkin Time by Zoe Hall

Plumply, Dumply, Pumpkin by Mary Serfozo

Pumpkins by Jacqueline Farmer

TRANSITION

Play Pass the Pumpkin. Seat the children in a circle and put on music. As the music plays, they pass a pumpkin around the circle. (The pumpkin can be large or a small pumpkin gourd.) When the music stops, the child holding the pumpkin moves to the next activity.

SNACK

Make Pumpkin Cookies (see recipe on appendix page 307) with the children.

Group Time

Find two pumpkins of almost identical size. Invite the children to guess which pumpkin they think is bigger. Record the children's guesses on the board, and then use yarn to measure each pumpkin's diameter, cutting each string at the appropriate length. Invite one child to hold up one string and another child to hold up the other. Compare the strings. After measuring the first two pumpkins, bring out a third pumpkin of varying size and repeat the process.

Learning Center Ideas

Art: Help the children cut pumpkin shapes out of white construction paper. Print each child's name on a shape. The children finger paint with yellow and red paint on the pumpkin shapes.

Math: Cut pumpkin shapes from orange construction paper. Write a numeral on each shape. Laminate the pumpkins. Invite children to put the number of pumpkin seeds on each pumpkin shape.

Science: Cut open a pumpkin for children to explore. Talk about the different parts of the pumpkin, such as the seeds, flesh, rind, and stem.

Additional Activities

Field Trip: Visit a pumpkin patch to see pumpkins growing on the vine. Pick out pumpkins to take home. After the field trip, invite the children to draw what they liked the best at the farm.

Movement: Play Pumpkin Seed, Pumpkin Seed, Who Has the Pumpkin Seed? The children sit in a circle, except for the child who is "IT." IT sits in the middle of the circle, and closes her eyes as the children pass a pumpkin seed around the circle. IT says, "Stop" and opens her eyes, then tries to guess who has the pumpkin seed.

Small Group: Make Pumpkin Playdough (see appendix page 308 or use any playdough) for this activity. Give each child a small ball of playdough. Show and name a letter and invite the children to try to make it with dough. Try this with several letters and numerals.

Bats

STORY TIME

Baby Bat Snuggles by Patti Jennings
Baby Bat's Lullaby by Jacquelyn Mitchard
Flying Bats by Fay Robinson
Stellaluna by Janell Cannon

TRANSITION

Name a child and repeat the rhyme below. The named child says a word that rhymes with *bat* and then moves to the next activity.

> *Tell me this.*
> *Tell me that.*
> *Name a word*
> *That rhymes with* bat.

SNACK

Make several pans of brownies. Use cookie cutters to cut bat shapes, and invite children to decorate their bats with frosting, marshmallows, raisins, and so on before eating the brownie bats.

Group Time

Talk to the children about bats. Ask them if they have seen a bat in the night sky. Share the facts about bats on appendix page 308. Read *There Was an Old Lady Who Swallowed a Bat* by Lucille Colandro. Stop the story before the ending and invite the children to guess what is going to happen.

Learning Center Ideas

Art: Make bats (see appendix page 302) to hang in the classroom. Have the children put small Styrofoam balls or wads of newspaper into the middle of several sheets of black tissue paper. Twist the tissue paper around the ball. Tie the tissue paper off on both ends of the ball. Spread the tissue out on each side to make wings. Use fabric paint to draw a face on the bat, and attach a string to hang the bats.
Literacy: Cut several bats from construction paper. Write a letter on each one. Set out die-cut foam alphabet letters or bulletin board letters. The children match the foam letters to the letters on the bats.
Math: Cut out cave shapes from construction paper, labeling them 1–10. Laminate for durability. Invite children to put the correct number of plastic or pompom bats on the numbered caves.

Additional Activities

Movement: Play Bat Catcher. One child is an owl. The other children are bats. The bats line up on one side of the room. The owl tries to catch the bats. When the owl says, "Who-who-who," the bats fly across the room. The owl tries to tag them. Any bat that is tagged becomes an owl. Play until all of the bats are caught.
Rhythm and Rhyme: Sing "Bats" with the children (see appendix page 303).
Small Group: Give each child a bat made out of paper or plastic. Recite "The Bat Says," found on appendix page 303, with the children, encouraging them to follow the directions in the verse. When children's listening skills improve, give two directions at once. For example, say, "Put your bat on your head and jump."

Miss Muffet and Spiders

STORY TIME

The Itsy Bitsy Spider by Iza Trapani
Little Miss Muffet by Heather Collins
Miss Spider Books by David Kirk
Spider on the Floor by Raffi
The Very Busy Spider by Eric Carle

SNACK

Make a peanut butter spider snack.
Safety Note: Ensure no children have peanut allergies before preparing this snack. Spread peanut butter on a round cracker. Put eight pretzel sticks out around the peanut butter cracker as spider legs. Add another peanut butter cracker on top and you have a busy spider.
(A melon scoop of cream cheese can be substituted for the peanut butter.)

Group Time

Read *Miss Spider's ABC* by David Kirk. As you retell the story, give each child a cardboard shape spider with an alphabet letter on it. When a letter is read, the child holding that "bat letter" stands up and hands it to you. As children hand you their letters, ask if they can they name another word that begins with the same letter. Teach the children "Miss Spider's ABC's" (see appendix page 304) to go with the story.

Learning Center Ideas

Art: Suggest that the children make playdough spiders. They can string beads on pipe cleaners to make legs and push the pipe cleaners into playdough.
Blocks/Construction: Use yarn to build an easy spider web obstacle course. Invite children to go through it. Make it harder by adding contact paper with a sticky side up to walk through. Explain to the children that spiders catch flies and other bugs with the sticky strings of their webs.
Math: Hide plastic bugs and spiders in the sand table. Challenge the children to find and sort the bugs and spiders by counting the legs.

Additional Activities

Outside: Find real cobwebs to save and investigate. Explain to the children that cobwebs are abandoned spider webs. Spray a piece of black construction paper with hairspray. Bring the paper up under the web until it touches and sticks. Bring the webs back to the classroom to explore with magnifying glasses.
Rhythm and Rhyme: Say the nursery rhyme "Little Miss Muffet" (see appendix page 304). Encourage the children to take turns acting out the rhyme.
Small Group: Read *The Very Busy Spider* by Eric Carle. Reread the story, inviting the children to make animal noises for each animal. The children will have to use picture clues to find out what animal noises to make.

Flashlights

Bring a flashlight to school today.

STORY TIME

Flashlight Dinosaurs, Terror in Time by Mark Shulman
Good Night, Animals by Lena Arro
My First Flashlight by Dawn Bently

TRANSITION

Say the following rhyme as you shine a flashlight around the room. Occasionally, hold the light on a child (do not shine the light directly in the child's eyes) and say her name in the rhyme. When the light lands on the child, she moves to the next activity.

> *Flashlight, flashlight, shine your light.*
> *____, ____, you are a sight.*

SNACK

Make Flashlight Cakes. With the children, prepare a yellow cake mix according to the package's directions. Instead of putting the batter into muffin liners, fill regular ice cream cones (cake cones) three quarters full. Cook according to the directions for cupcakes. Let the ice cream cones cool, then add food coloring to vanilla frosting to color the bulb of the Flashlight Cakes.

Group Time

Hide foam alphabet letters around the room. Invite the children to be detectives and use their flashlights to find the letters. Once the children find the letters and bring them to the Group Time area, ask the children to show everyone the letters and name them one by one. Invite the children to find the same letter on the Word Wall or the Alphabet Chart and shine their flashlights on it.

Learning Center Ideas

Dramatic Play: Add dress-up clothes and a light for children to pretend they are actors and actresses, singers, or other performers up on a stage. Invite them to put on a show.

Literacy: Show children how to make shadow puppets on the wall. Encourage the children to make up stories about the puppets they create.

Literacy: Put a flashlight in the book corner and invite the children to use it when reading.

Science: Set out several flashlights. Cut 8" circles from several colors of cellophane. Show children how to cover the light of the flashlight to make new colors. Invite them to try two colors together.

Additional Activities

Movement: Each child will need a flashlight for this activity. They stand up and follow the directions:

> *Shine your light up.*
> *Shine your light down.*
> *Shine your light round and round.*
> *Shine to the left.*
> *Shine to the right.*
> *Shine that flashlight out of sight.* (turn off flashlights)

Outside: Take flashlights outside to explore dark places such as the undersides of bushes. Look for all the little bugs that are hard to see without a light. Talk about all the things you saw.

Rhythm and Rhyme: Invite children to have flashlight dances to different kinds of music. Dance to classical, country, and rock music, along with the children's favorites.

November

Calendar Time

During Calendar Time, introduce the month of November to the children. Look at the letters in the word *November*. Name each letter, and say the sound and other words that start with the sound. Whose name begins with the letter *n*? Do this for each letter in the word during calendar time throughout the month.

Monthly Organizer

MONTH-LONG CELEBRATIONS

Native American Heritage Month
International Drum Month

WEEK-LONG CELEBRATIONS

National Book Week
National Family Week

SPECIAL DAYS AND HOLIDAYS

November 1: Family Literacy Day
November 27: Kevin Henkes' Birthday
Thanksgiving

GENERAL DAILY PLANS

Heading South or Hibernating?
Letter *N*
Moving Day
Scarecrows
Sponges
Turkeys
Brown
Shoes
Old Mother Hubbard
Babies
Same and Different

Safety Signs
Thankfulness
Cooperation
Hats
Calendars
Letter *I*

Note: Please be sure to check for allergies before serving the snacks or doing any food-related activities.

Native American Heritage Month

MONTH-LONG CELEBRATION

STORY TIME

Emma and the Trees by Lenore Keeshing-Tobias

The First Strawberries: A Cherokee Story by Joseph Bruchac

Giving Thanks: A Native American Good Morning Message by Chief Jake Swamp

Lessons from Turtle Island by Guy W. Jones

Old Enough by Peter Eyvindson

On Mother's Lap by Ann Herbert Scott

Sky Sister by Jan Bourdeau Waboose

The Story of the Milky Way by Joseph Bruchac

Group Time

Read *Giving Thanks: A Native American Good Morning Message* by Chief Jake Swamp. Invite the children to name something for which they are thankful. Print their responses on evergreen tree shapes and display them in the classroom.

Learning Center Ideas

Art: Set out feathers and containers of paint, inviting the children to paint sheets of construction paper, using the feathers as brushes.

Math: Set out two colors of beads, and for each child, a string with a bead tied to the end. Help the children start making necklaces with the two colors in AB patterns, letting them complete the necklaces. Encourage them to try to come up with their own patterns to follow.

Music: Set several drums for the children to play. Suggest that they make up and then follow specific rhythms. Invite the children to beat the syllables in their names with the drums.

Additional Activities

Project: Show the children various examples of pottery, explaining the process of how the objects are made. Then give each child a ball of clay and show them two ways to make bowls: by rolling the clay into a round ball and poking their thumbs into the clay, spreading it out into a bowl, or by rolling the clay into a long snake and winding it around into a bowl shape. After making the bowls, paint and bake them according to clay directions. **Safety Note:** Do not eat from these bowls, as they may contain lead.

Rhythm and Rhyme: Invite the children to sing "Thank You for the Moon So Bright" found on appendix page 314.

Small Group: Read *On Mother's Lap* by Ann Herbert Scott. Ask the children, "What would you bring to mother's lap?" Encourage each of them to draw a picture. On the bottom of each picture write, "On mother's lap, I'll bring _____. " Put each child's name on the picture and compile the pages into a class book.

International Drum Month

MONTH-LONG CELEBRATION

STORY TIME

D Is for Drums by Kay Chorao
The Happy Hedgehog by Martin
    Waddell
Thump Thump Rat-a-Tat-Tat by
    Gene Baer

TRANSITION

Take turns beating a rhythm on a drum. Invite each child to copy the same rhythm before moving on to the next activity.

SNACK

Make "drums" from toasted English muffins. Use pretzel rods as drumsticks, by dipping the ends in chocolate, and serve them for snack.

Group Time

Show the children how to clap the different rhythms of their names, using a drum to emphasize the syllables for each child's first and last name. As the children hear their names, have them find their first and last names in a pocket chart.

Learning Center Ideas

Art: Make shaker instruments. Help each child staple two paper plates together, except for a little opening. Show them how to pour beads in the opening, then staple the opening shut for a shaker instrument. Set out different materials, such as crepe paper and glue, and suggest that the children decorate their instruments. Consider giving the children markers and crayons to draw on the plates before stapling them and filling them with beads.

Literacy: Set out several drums beside pieces of paper with the children's names written on them in large print. Invite the children to beat the drum for each letter in their names, saying the letters and the sounds they make each time they hit the drum.

Additional Activities

Movement: Encourage the children to have a parade, marching to the beat of the drums they made in the art center.

Outside: Make a special drum beat for each activity for the day. Before going outside, instruct children to listen to a special drumbeat, telling the children to line up to go inside when they hear it.

Rhythm and Rhyme: Sing the songs "Listen to My Drum," (appendix page 313) and "Ten Little Beats" on page 314.

National Book Week (Third week in November)

Prior to using this daily plan, send a note home to parents asking for book donations.

STORY TIME

Ask the children to choose their favorite books and then take turns reading these books.

SNACK

Make a Bookworm snack. Help the children roll whole-wheat dough into balls and then into worm shapes. Place them in a big row on a cookie sheet. Bake Bookworms. When cool, the children decorate them with honey, jam, and raisins before eating the Bookworms for snack.

Group Time

Bring in the book, *Wild About Books* by Judy Sierra. Before reading the story, read the title and the names of the author and illustrator. Explain that Judy Sierra wrote the story and Marc Brown drew the pictures. After reading the story, encourage the children to retell the story, describing the story in order.

Learning Center Ideas

Art: Set out strips of paper and embellishments for children to make their own bookmarks. Laminate the bookmarks when they are finished so the children can enjoy them for years to come.

Dramatic Play: Set up a pretend library with a shelf, books, library pockets, and cards (for signing their names). Invite the children to sort books on the shelves, while other children pretend to come and pick out books.

Literacy: Fold pages of 8 ½" x 11" paper in half and staple them to make blank books. Help the children make their own books, using index cards with words written on them. Put a picture of the word on each card and laminate them. (Children who make books can "read" them in the Dramatic Play Library.)

Math: Make counting books. Set out sheets of numbered paper, staplers, stickers, markers, pencils, stamps, and numeral stencils. Invite the children to draw, stamp, or write numerals on the pages of their books.

Additional Activities

Movement: Make a "bookworm." Ask the children to line up single file, with their hands on the shoulders of the child in front of them, and encourage them to try walking around while staying connected.

Project: Make a Classroom Bookworm (see directions on appendix page 310).

Rhythm and Rhyme: Sing "Take a Look," found on appendix page 314, with the children.

National Family Week

National Family Week takes place during the week in which Thanksgiving falls. Write a letter to parents, asking them to send in anything they and their children would like to share with the rest of the class about their families, particularly family traditions, stories, and favorite family recipes.

STORY TIME

Just the Two of Us by Will Smith
Mama Do You Love Me? by Barbara Joosse
Night Shift Daddy by Eileen Spinelli
On Mother's Lap by Ann Herbert Scott
Sky Sisters by Jan Bourdeau Waboose
Two Homes by Claire Masurel
When Mama Comes Home Tonight by Eileen Spinelli

SNACK

Serve snack family style, where everyone sits together and passes the snack and drinks around the table.

Group Time

Read *Families Are Different* by Nina Pellegrini. Discuss how families can be big, small, or be any different number of people. Graph how many people the children have in their families. Invite the children to share their family traditions, stories, and so on.

Learning Center Ideas

Blocks: Invite the children to bring in photographs of their families. Photocopy those photographs, attach each photo to a block, and invite the children to make block families. Use blocks to make homes and other community buildings.

Literacy: Cut outlines of people from 8 ½" x 11" sheets of construction paper, and suggest that the children decorate a shape for each person in their family. Help the children print the names of their family members on each outline, and then staple the pages together to make their own family books.

Additional Activities

Movement: Play the Family in the House, as you would play the Farmer in the Dell. Invite everyone holds hands and walk in a circle. Select one child to be the "dad," and have that child stand in the middle of the circle. As the class sings the song, "Family in the House," found on appendix page 311, have the "dad" choose the "mom" by pulling another child into the center of the circle. Repeat through all family members until all children are inside the circle.

Outside: Make a list of things the children do with their families outside, such as take walks, fly kites, play catch, and so on. Do some of those activities with the children.

Project: Make a special family book. Use the items children brought in from home, making sure to copy the pictures and recipes for each child's page without ruining the real items. Also, have children draw a picture of their families on a house shape to add to the book. Set the book out for families to enjoy.

Rhythm and Rhyme: Sing "Family, Family," found on appendix page 311.

Small Group: Read *When Mama Comes Home Tonight* by Eileen Spinelli. Talk about parents who work. Ask the children, "What do you do with your parents at night?" Make a list of their responses.

Family Literacy Day

Before doing this lesson plan, invite families to come in to celebrate Family Literacy Day (see Home/School Connection below, right). Family Literacy Day is November 1st.

STORY TIME

Introduce a few books to the children and parents. Start with a good classic book such as:

The Very Hungry Caterpillar by Eric Carle,

If You Give a Mouse a Cookie by Laura Numeroff, or

Chicka Chicka Boom Boom by Bill Martin, Jr.

Before reading the book, show the children where the author's name is on the book and read it together. Explain to the children that the author is the person who wrote the book, and the illustrator is the person who drew the pictures. Read the story with the children, and then encourage the children to retell it together.

SNACK

Read *If You Give a Mouse a Cookie* by Laura Joffe Numeroff. Invite the children and their families to decorate cookies together.

Group Time

Invite a storyteller or community librarian to read or tell stories.

Learning Center Ideas

Art: Set out several paper lunch bags, glue, and decorative materials, inviting the children to make puppets. When dry, encourage the children to use the puppets to tell stories (or encourage the children to make puppets based on characters from specific books).

Art: Make several artists' picture books available to the children to look at. Invite the children to imitate the art they see in the books.

Dramatic Play: Place several cookbooks in the kitchen area, and invite the children to pretend to make the recipes found in the books.

Literacy: Set out many different books, pillows, beanbag chairs, and other things to make reading enjoyable for children and their families. Give children and their families time to read books together.

Additional Activities

Outside: If weather permits, invite families to take a blanket outside and read a book.

Rhythm and Rhyme: Read and sing along with several books, such as *The Wheels on the Bus* by Paul O. Zelinsky, *Five Little Ducks* by Pamela Paprone, and *The Itsy Bitsy Spider* by Iza Trapani.

Home/School Connection

Write a letter to the parents, telling them that November 1st is Family Literacy Day, and inviting them to come class to celebrate the day by reading with their children.

Happy Birthday, Kevin Henkes

SPECIAL DAYS AND HOLIDAYS

Kevin Henkes' birthday is November 27th.

STORY TIME

Books by Kevin Henkes:
Chrysanthemum
Julius, the Baby of the World
Lilly's Purple Plastic Purse
Owen
Sheila Rae, the Brave
A Weekend with Wendell

TRANSITION

After reading *Sheila Rae, the Brave*, have the children transition by using the "Time to Go" rhyme, found on appendix page 314. Add a child's name in the rhyme, and invite that child to move to the next activity.

SNACK

Read *Wemberly Worried* by Kevin Henkes. Talk about sharing a snack with a friend. Invite children to each bring in a piece of fruit to put in a "Friendship Fruit Salad." Mix the salad and serve it to the children.

Group Time

Introduce the children to the books of Kevin Henkes, particularly *Lilly's Purple Plastic Purse*. Set out a purple purse or gift bag with five to seven alphabet letters inside. Pull out the alphabet letters and name them one by one. Now play a missing game. Instruct the children to close their eyes. While their eyes are closed, take one letter away, and then invite the children to open their eyes and guess which letter is missing.

Learning Center Ideas

Art: Set out paint, markers, crayons, glitter, other decorative materials, and several sheets of purple construction paper cut into purse shapes (see the illustration of a purse outline on appendix page 310). Invite the children to decorate their own purple purses.

Dramatic Play: Make several small dolls and stuffed animals available for the children to play with and explore.

Literacy: Put each child's name and photo on a sentence strip. Set out several kinds of paper, tablets, pens, pencils, and markers, and invite the children to print their own names and friends' names, based on what they see on the sentence strips.

Math: Cut purse shapes from purple construction paper, and write a numeral on each purse. Set out stacks of pennies and invite the children to put the correct numbers of pennies on each purse.

Additional Activities

Rhythm and Rhyme: Sing "I Am Very Brave," found on appendix page 312, with the children.

Small Group: Introduce and read the story *Sheila Rae, the Brave* by Kevin Henkes. After reading the book, encourage the children to talk about times when they were brave. Give each child a paper that says "I was brave when I _____" at the top of the paper. Write down what the children say and then suggest that they draw a picture on the paper, depicting a time when they were brave.

Thanksgiving

Thanksgiving is celebrated on the fourth Thursday in November. Before this day, send home a note asking the families what their traditions are for celebrating Thanksgiving.

STORY TIME

A Plump and Perky Turkey by Teresa Bateman

Spot's Thanksgiving by Eric Hill

'Twas the Night Before Thanksgiving by Dav Pilkey

TRANSITION

Invite the children to recite "We're Thankful," found on appendix page 315, while moving from one activity to another. At the end of the rhyme, invite the children to call out things for which they are thankful.

SNACK

Help the children prepare turkey roll-ups. Set out soft tortillas, slices of turkey lunch meat, shredded lettuce, and mayo. Give each child a tortilla, a piece of turkey, a little shredded lettuce, and a plastic knife or craft stick with which to add a small amount of mayonnaise. Show the children how to roll the tortilla and its contents tightly. Eat and enjoy.

Group Time

During Group Time, talk about the traditions and the different things families do. Explain to the children that Thanksgiving is a good time to thank people for the things they do for one another. Go through the class list. Write each child's name on a separate piece of paper. Talk about each child with the rest of the children, inviting them to remember nice things that child has done, or to say why they like that child. Copy what the children say onto the paper and display below a banner that reads "We Are Thankful for Each Other."

Learning Center Ideas

Literacy: Set out magnetic letters and a cookie sheet for making words and names. Set out pictures of each child, with their names printed on them. Separately, set out a card with "thank you" written on it as a model for the children. Invite the children to write "thank you, _____" on the cookie sheets with magnetic letters, and outline the letters of the words and their friends' names. When the outlines are completed, invite the children to decorate the letters, and then present them to their friends.

Math: Set out three labels each of different cans of beans, corn, and peas, and invite the children to sort the labels based on type of food, color of label, and so on.

Sensory: Set out colored feathers and several balls of playdough, inviting the children to roll out the playdough and stick the feathers in them, making different designs and even outlines of turkeys.

Additional Activities

Project: Help the children make Thanksgiving cards for someone special. On the front of the cards, have the children make handprint turkeys. Paint the palms and the thumbs of the hands brown, and the fingers red, green, blue, and yellow. On the inside print the "My Hand Can Be a Turkey" rhyme, found on appendix page 313.

Rhythm and Rhyme: Invite the children to sing "Thank You," found on appendix page 314.

Heading South or Hibernating?

GENERAL DAILY PLAN

STORY TIME

Copy Me, Copycub by Richard Edwards
Time to Sleep by Denise Fleming
When Winter Comes by Nancy Van Laan

TRANSITION

Recite the following rhyme with the children, calling out a single child's name in the second line. Make a few movements for the child to copy, and after she does so, invite her to move to the next activity.

Imagine this, imagine that.
_____ is a copy cat.

SNACK

Make "Store It Up" snack mix with the children, using the recipe found on appendix page 315.

Group Time

Talk with the children about what different animals do in the wintertime, explaining that some birds fly south, some animals go to sleep, and some don't alter what they do. Make a Winter Animal Behavior Chart similar to the one on appendix page 316. Encourage the children to name different animals and categorize them in the proper columns.

Learning Center Ideas

Dramatic Play: Bring in a large box, inviting the children to make it into a cave by painting it gray. This will be perfect for the children to pretend to be animals sleeping through the winter months.

Fine Motor: Set out Canadian goose shapes cut from construction paper. (Older children may be able to cut their own shape.) Invite the children to glue black and brown feathers or regular bird feathers on the shape.

Literacy: Put word cards and pictures of animals that hibernate in a pocket chart. Give the children 8 ½" x 11" sheets of paper, divided into four equal sections, with "_____ hibernates" written on each section. Invite the children to draw an animal that hibernates in each part, and help them print the names of the animals on the line. Cut apart the pages and staple them into an emergent reader book.

Math: Set out red and blue pompom "berries" and nuts in a shell, such as walnuts. Suggest that the children sort them into an ice cube or relish tray, with many compartments.

Additional Activities

Game: Play a hibernation game. Invite everyone to sit in a circle. Ask one child to go to the other side of the room and close his eyes, then have another child hide under a blanket in the middle of the circle. Once the child is well-covered, the children in the circle say, "Hibernating, hibernating, who is hibernating?" Cue the child on the other side of the room to come back and guess who is "hibernating" under the blanket.

Small Group: Make a "Whooo Is Sleeping" book (see the directions on appendix page 310).

Letter *N*

STORY TIME

Amazing Letter N by Cynthia Fitterer Klingel
Nicest Newt by Scholastic Press
Night Shift Daddy by Eileen Spinelli

TRANSITION

Set out a basket full of number cards, inviting the children to pick one each. Begin naming numerals one at a time, inviting the child holding that numeral to move to the next activity.

Group Time

Print the following rhyme on chart paper:

> *N is for* no, never, *and* not.
> *N is for* noodles *whether they are cold or hot.*

The letter *n* is the first letter of the word *November.* Ask the children, "What other words begin with the /n/ sound?" Play an *n* word game. If the word starts with the letter *n*, tell the children to nod their heads. Then look at and read the poem on chart paper.

Learning Center Ideas

Art: Encourage children to make a "nighttime" picture by drawing a picture with a crayon, pressing hard. Then paint over the picture with black watercolor paint to make it look like nighttime.

Literacy: Suggest that children make an environmental print collage about the letter *n* using the newspaper. Print the letter *n* on a piece of paper. Help the children look through the newspaper for items that begin with each letter. Cut out the items and glue them to the paper to make a collage.

Math: Set out a bucket of foam letters that contains several letter *n's.* Invite the children to sort the *n's* from the rest of the alphabet.

Additional Activities

Outside: Go outside and take a nature walk. Collect nature items and then glue them to a nut shape cut from paper.

Moving Day

STORY TIME

Boomer's Big Day by Constance W. McGeorge
Ginger by Charolotte Voake
When Marcus Moore Moved In by Rebecca Bond

TRANSITION

Say the following rhyme with the children, inserting a different name each time. The named child moves to the next activity.

Moving vans day and night,
Moving _____ out of sight.

Group Time

Bring in several items and boxes of varying sizes. Ask the children which items will fit in the boxes. Ask the children to name different things about moving to a new house that they would like and dislike. Write what they say on a sheet of chart paper with two columns. Label one column "What I Would Like About Moving" and the other "What I Would Dislike About Moving." Encourage the children to talk about why they think each answer should go in certain column.

Learning Center Ideas

Art: Set out packing peanuts of several different colors and sizes, as well as some glue and several sheets of construction paper. Invite the children to make designs and pictures out of the packing peanuts.

Dramatic Play: Bring in boxes and packing peanuts for children to pack and unpack.

Math: Cut out box or truck shapes, writing different numerals on each shape. Laminate for durability. Encourage children to put the corresponding number of packing peanuts on each truck or box.

Additional Activities

Game: Invite the children to play "I'm Moving and I'm Taking My _____." Sit the children in a circle, inviting one to say, "I'm moving and I'm taking my _____," to the child to his right, filling in the blank with something he would take when moving. The child to the right then says, "I'm moving and I'm taking my _____ and my _____," repeating the answer the first child gave, and then adding an item of his own. Repeat this until it comes back to the first child, and encourage him to recite each item each child added to the list.

Outside: Bring several big boxes outside for the children to build, stack, and move.

Small Group: Put a mystery item in a box and wrap the box so the children can't peek. Pass the box around the group and invite children to guess what is in it. Encourage children to ask "yes" or "no" questions for hints. When someone guesses correctly, open the box.

Scarecrows

STORY TIME

I'm a Dingle Dangle Scarecrow by Annie Kubler

The Little Scarecrow Boy by Margaret Wise Brown

The Scarecrow Who Wanted a Hug by Guido Visconti

Scarecrow's Secret by Heather Amery

TRANSITION

Choose one child to be the first scarecrow. After choosing a scarecrow, recite (or sing) "One Scarecrow," found on appendix page 313, to the child, and invite that child to choose someone else to be the next scarecrow. The first child then moves to the next activity.

SNACK

Make a Scarecrow Face with an English muffin. Toast an English muffin half for each child. Invite the children to add shredded cheddar cheese hair, and raisin eyes, nose, and mouth. Yummy scarecrow!

Group Time

Engage the children in a discussion about scarecrows. Ask the children where they are found, why they are there, who uses them, how they are made, and so on. After this discussion, help the children make a scarecrow. Stuff an adult flannel shirt and pants with newspapers. Pin the pants to the shirt. Tie the ends of the pant legs to close them. Stuff an old yellow, white, or orange pillowcase with newspapers. Stuff the open end of the pillowcase into the neck of the shirt. Tie the neck closed. Ask one or two children to draw a face on it. Put a straw hat on top of its head and give it name. Use the naming process to show democracy in action. Ask children to suggest names, and then allow them to vote for their favorite name. Invite children to draw and dictate stories about the scarecrow.

Learning Center Ideas

Art: Help children make scarecrow faces. Stuff brown lunch bags with straw. Help children close the bags with rope or twine. Encourage them to draw a face on their scarecrow.

Math: Copy and color several scarecrow shapes. Mark each of them with a numeral and laminate for durability. Invite the children to put the correct number of pompoms, or "crows," on each scarecrow.

Additional Activities

Movement: Select five children to come to the front of the class and pretend to be crows, flying and pecking at the ground. Invite the rest of the children to recite the "Five Crows" action rhyme, found on appendix page 311, and select an additional child to join the crows. Repeat the rhyme, adding an additional "crow" each time, until all the children are crows together.

Rhythm and Rhyme: Sing "How Many Crows?" found on appendix page 312, to your classroom scarecrow. When you are finished, draw a number from a hat, for the number of scarecrows. Clap the number.

Small Group: Practice learning positional words through the "Little Scarecrow" rhyme, found on appendix page 313. Encourage the children to pretend to be scarecrows and touch the parts of their bodies where the crow lands.

Sponges

STORY TIME

Sponges by Mary Loque
Sponges by Jody Sullivan Rake
Sponges Are Skeletons by Barbara Juster Esbensen
Sponges: Filters of the Sea by Andreu Llamas

TRANSITION

Bring the children together in a circle, and give them a sponge to pass around while music plays. Occasionally stop the music and have the child holding the sponge move to the next activity. As the children become adept at this transition activity, pass two sponges.

SNACK

Have sponge cake for a snack. Invite the children to add strawberries, blueberries, and whipped cream to the cake.

Group Time

Before Group Time, cut out sponge shapes from construction paper. Keep both the cutout shape as well as the paper. Talk to the children about sponges. Use some of the books listed in Story Time to show the children pictures and explain where sponges live and what they do for the environment. Then, give each child a cutout sponge. Hold up the outside paper of each sponge shape. Ask, "Who has the sponge that fits inside this shape?"

Learning Center Ideas

Art: Trace around shaped sponges on a sheet of paper. Cut out the sponge shapes and then laminate the sponges and the outlines for durability. Invite the children to match the sponges to their outlines.
Art: Invite the children to use different-shaped sponges to paint.
Math: Set out several different sizes of sponges and invite the children to put them in order from small to large.
Sensory: Put water and several kinds of sponges in the Sensory Table for the children to explore.

Additional Activities

Movement: Give each child a sponge, and invite the children to recite "Put Your Sponge Way Up High," found on appendix page 314, making the appropriate gestures when prompted by the song.
Project: Trace around sponge shapes on a file folder. Poke the inside with scissors and cut out the shape from the inside (adult-only step). Help children put a paper in the file folder and then sponge paint the shape on the paper.
Rhythm and Rhyme: Invite the children to sing "I'm a Little Sponge," found on appendix page 312.

Turkeys

STORY TIME

10 Fat Turkeys by Tony Johnston
Five Little Turkeys by William Boniface
Setting the Turkeys Free by W. Nikola-Lisa
This Is the Turkey by Abby Levine

TRANSITION

Encourage children to walk like turkeys to the next activity, reciting "Turkey Walks," found on appendix page 315.

SNACK

Make "Turkey Feed" with the children by mixing corn cereal, oat cereal, pretzels, and sunflower seeds.

Group Time

Turkey starts with the letter *t*. Name words, some beginning with the letter *t*, others beginning with different letters. Ask the children to "gobble" if the word you say begins with the same beginning sound as "turkey." Next, find out what the children know about turkeys. Use chart paper and write down their thoughts. Use the Turkey Facts on appendix page 315 to help with the discussion.

Learning Center Ideas

Literacy: Cut out turkey-shaped bodies from red, blue, green, and yellow paper. Print the name of the color on the turkey. Set out craft feathers, and invite the children to put the matching colored feathers on each turkey.
Math: Set out construction paper turkey shapes with a numeral written on each turkey. Invite the children to put the matching number of feathers on each turkey shape.
Science: Obtain several real turkey feathers for the children to look at with magnifying glasses.

Additional Activities

Outside: Cut out several turkey shapes and hide them outside for the children to find.
Rhythm and Rhyme: Invite the children to recite "Three Little Turkeys," found on appendix page 314.
Small Group: Show the children how to practice remembering their phone numbers with turkey-shaped phones. Cut a turkey body (a peanut shape) from brown construction paper. Print each child's name and phone number on a bird's stomach, and set out several different feather cutouts with all digits from 0–9 written on them. Invite the children to glue the numbered feathers on their turkey-shaped phones.

Brown

STORY TIME

Brown Bear, Brown Bear, What Do You See? by Bill Martin, Jr.

Moo, Moo, Brown Cow by Jakki Wood

Mr. Brown Can Moo, Can You? by Dr. Seuss

TRANSITION

Recite the following rhyme with the children. Say a different child's name with each recitation, and invite that child to name something brown before moving to the next activity.

_____, _____, *don't let me down,*
Name something that is the color brown.

SNACK

Make a brown snack by mixing cereal, pretzel fish, crackers, and pretzels in a bowl.

Group Time

Before Group Time, get several paint strip samples in the colors blue, pink, and brown. Cut apart the color shades. During Group Time, encourage the children to sort the colors. Explain to the children that each color has many shades.

Learning Center Ideas

Blocks: Tape brown boxes shut and encourage the children to use them as giant blocks.

Math: Set out several brown construction paper cutouts of nuts and invite the children to sort them into muffin tins.

Writing: Suggest that children use cinnamon sticks to write their names on sandpaper.

Additional Activities

Outside: Encourage the children to search for brown items from nature, and bring inside to explore.

Projects: Set out wood pieces, old blocks, and craft sticks. Invite children to make wooden structures and glue them together.

Rhythm and Rhyme: Sing "Brown Is the Color of My Teddy Bear," found on appendix page 311, with the children.

Small Group: With the children, finger paint on leaf shapes with red, yellow, and green paint. Ask the children "When all the colors mix, what color does it make?"

Shoes

STORY TIME

Alligator Shoes by Arthur Dorros
Look! I Can Tie My Shoes by Susan Hood
Shoes by Linda O'Keefe
Shoes by Elizabeth Winthrop
Shoes, Shoes, Shoes by Ann Morris
Whose Shoes Are These? by Lisa Carr

TRANSITION

Name a color in the rhyme below, inviting children with that color on their clothes to line up or move on to the next activity. Repeat with different colors until all the children have transitioned to the next activity.

> *If you have _____ on your shoe,*
> *Time to line up for you.*

Group Time 1

Look at children's shoes as a group. Ask the children questions: "Who has to tie their shoes? Whose shoes have buckles and whose have Velcro?" Make a graph of the children. Invite children to line up if their shoes tie, and make other lines for Velcro, slip-ons, and buckles. Ask the children to count how many are in each line. (A variation would be to take a photo of each child's shoes. Print the child's name on the photo. Make a poster board graph. Instruct each child to put his shoe photo in the correct place on the graph.)

Group Time 2

Bring in several kinds of shoes and boots, such as baby booties, bowling shoes, ice skates, flip-flops, work boots, and ballet slippers. Talk about who uses the shoes and when they use them. After talking about each shoe, tell the children to close their eyes. Take one pair of shoes away and ask the children which pair is missing.

Learning Center Ideas

Art: Ask the children to bring in old discarded shoes, or obtain them from rummage sales. Give each child an old shoe to paint and add glitter, sequins, and other embellishments, to make shoe art. Display the shoes.
Variation: This can also be a family project. The children can bring in their own shoes.
Dramatic Play: Set up chairs in a row. Have old shoes in their shoeboxes, and a cash register and ruler for measuring feet, encouraging the children to pretend they are in a shoe store.
Math: Trace the children's shoe soles on construction paper, mix them up, and invite the children to match the prints to the appropriate shoes.

Additional Activities

Movement: Invite the children to recite "If You Have Blue on Your Shoe," found on appendix page 312, making the appropriate gestures when prompted.
Rhythm and Rhyme: Help the children learn to tie their shoes by teaching them "Criss Cross Your Shoelace," found on appendix page 311.

Old Mother Hubbard

STORY TIME

Mother Hubbard's Empty Cupboard
    by Lisa Ann Marsoli
Nursery Rhymes by Samuel and
    Nancy Butcher
Old Mother Hubbard by Colin and
    Jacqui Hawkins
Old Mother Hubbard by Sarah C.
    Martin

SNACK

Make toast with butter. Sprinkle on sugar and cinnamon. Use a dog-bone-shaped cookie cutter to cut the toast into dog bones.

Group Time

Recite "Old Mother Hubbard," found on appendix page 313, with the children, inviting them to clap along with the syllables.

Learning Center Ideas

Dramatic Play: Make dog puppets from brown lunch bags. Using the puppets, tell the dogs to bark five times for a bone. The children take turns saying different numbers for the other dogs to bark.

Manipulatives: Set out dog bone-shaped cookie cutters. Invite the children to cut playdough bones with them.

Math: Cut several paper cupboards from brown paper. Write a numeral on each one and laminate for durability. Children put the corresponding number of dog bones in each cupboard.

Additional Activities

Game: Play Doggie, Doggie, Where's Your Bone? The children sit in the circle. One child is the doggie and sits in the middle of the circle with a dog bone behind her back. The doggie covers her eyes while a child sneaks the bone. The children say, "Doggie, doggie, where's your bone? Somebody took it from your home." The doggie opens his eyes and guesses who has the bone.

Outside: Hide several paper dog bones outside. Explain to children that dogs are very good at using their noses to find things. See if the children can use their senses to find the bones.

Rhythm and Rhyme: Invite the children to recite "Old Mother Hubbard Went to the Cupboard," found on appendix page 313.

Babies

STORY TIME

Everywhere Babies by Susan Meyers

Julius, the Baby of the World by Kevin Henkes

Mama Zooms by Jane Cowen-Fletcher

TRANSITION

Repeat the rhyme below, having the children take turns naming things they are able to do now that they were not able to do as babies.

Name something special about you,

That, as a baby, you couldn't do

_____.

SNACK

Prepare a baby-friendly snack. Invite the children to help you make instant oatmeal. Talk about why oatmeal is a good food for babies, as well as for children.

Group Time

Send a note home inviting families to send in a photo of their child as a baby along with a story about the child. Talk about the photos and stories the children bring in. Talk about what the children can do now. Ask the children to help make a list of all the things they can do that babies cannot.

Learning Center Ideas

Art: On a paper plate, children draw their faces as they are now. On the other side of the paper plate, they draw baby faces. Ask the children questions: "Do they have as much hair? What about teeth?" Glue the plate to a craft stick to play a game. If you name something a baby would do, the children show the baby face. If you name something that a big kid can do, they show their big-girl or big-boy face.

Dramatic Play: Set out baby equipment such as dolls, bottles, and diapers for the children to explore.

Math: Set out rattles, teething rings, bottles, pacifiers, diapers, a football, toy cars, a jump rope, and so on. Invite the children to sort the items based on what whether the objects are appropriate for babies or children.

Additional Activities

Movement: Play Mother Says. This is a variation of Simon Says. Select a child to be Mother (or Father), and encourage the child to say things that a mother would tell her child to do, such as, "Mother says to drink your milk." When Mother prefaces her request with "Mother says," the children do what she says. When Mother does not preface her request with "Mother says" and only says, "Drink your milk," for example, the children should not do as Mother says.

Outside: Before going outside, talk about the things the children can do that babies cannot do. Practice galloping, skipping, and hopping on one foot.

Rhythm and Rhyme: Invite the children to recite "I Am Big," found on appendix page 312.

Small Group: Talk about babies in the children's families. Ask, "Who has a baby brother or sister? Do you get mad at them sometimes?" Read *Goldie Is Mad* by Margie Palatini. Sing "Goldie Is Mad," found on appendix page 312, with the children.

Same and Different

STORY TIME

Babies by Ros Asquith

Everything Is Different at Nonna's House by Caron Lee Cohen

Kids Do, Animals Too by Debora Pearson

Same and Different Puzzles by Anna Pomaska

Touch and Learn: Baby Animals by Jane Horne

What Mommies Do Best, What Daddies Do Best by Laura Numeroff

TRANSITION

Show two decks of cards. Invite one child to turn over a card from each deck. Ask, "Are the cards the same or different?" If the cards do not match, the child moves to the next activity. If the cards do match, the child stays and takes another turn.

Group Time

Set out several cutout pictures of different objects, such as boats, ducks, and so on. Cut out different construction paper outlines of the objects, so there is one outline and picture for each child. Hold each outline up individually and ask the children who has the actual picture. (A variation on this activity is to give half of the children the pictures and the other half the outlines, and invite them to find the person holding the matching cut out.)

Learning Center Ideas

Blocks: Use three or four Lego blocks to build a structure. Take a photo. Invite the children to make the same structure they see in the photo.

Sensory: Bury pennies and nickels in the Sand Table for the children to sift through and find. Ask the children if the coins are the same or different as they take them out of the sand.

Additional Activities

Movement: Invite the children to recite "My Trick," found on appendix page 313. While reciting the rhyme, begin repeating a particular gesture, like tapping your head or rubbing your belly, continue reciting the rhyme and repeating the movement until all the children are doing the same.

Rhythm and Rhyme: Set out three cards, two with the same sticker and one with a different sticker. Invite the children to sing "Two Are the Same," found on appendix page 315, as they search for cards that are the same and different.

Small Group: Bring in a laundry basket full of sock pairs of different colors and kinds. Separate the pairs and set up a rope clothesline between two chairs. Invite children to find matching pairs of socks and hang them on the clothesline with clothespins.

Safety Signs

STORY TIME

City Signs by Zoran Milich
I Read Signs by Tana Hoban
Street Safety by Giovanni Cauiezel

TRANSITION

Take out a hand-held stop sign, and have the children line up on one side of the room. Tell them to move toward you while the sign is down, then freeze when the put the sign up. The children who reach you move to the next activity.

Group Time

Read the children a book about safety signs, showing them bulletin board versions of the actual signs. Invite the children to talk about the shapes of the signs. Ask them what colors the sign are and what each sign means.

Learning Center Ideas

Art: Give each child a rectangular sheet of paper, as well as three squares, one red, one yellow, and one green. Help the children cut the edges off the squares to make circles, and then glue the circles to the rectangle in the order appropriate for a stoplight.

Blocks: Set out several small signs and toy cars among the blocks. Encourage the children to use the blocks to make roadways for the cars.

Literacy: Add books on driving and car/road safety to the book corner and encourage the children to flip through and look at the pictures.

Additional Activities

Movement: Play Red Light, Green Light. Choose one child to be "IT." The other children stand on one end of the classroom. IT says, "Green light" and turns around with his back to the class. During the green light, the children try to sneak up to tag IT. When IT says, "Red light" and turns around, the children freeze. Anyone that is still moving when IT turns around has to start over. The first one to tag IT is the next one to be IT.

Outside: Take a walk outside and look for different signs. Talk with the children about what the signs mean.

Rhythm and Rhyme: Invite the children to recite "Traffic Light," found on appendix page 314.

Small Group: Show a stop sign. Ask the children questions: "What color is it? What does it say? What letters are in the word STOP?" Give each child a red stop sign shape with the word *STOP* written on it.

DAILY PLAN CONCEPT

Thankfulness

STORY TIME

Biscuit Is Thankful by Alyssa Satin Capucilli

I Am Thankful for Each Day by P.K. Hallinan

The Most Thankful Thing by Lisa Lloyd-Jones

Thankful Together by Holly Davis

TRANSITION

Teach the children the sign for "thank you" in sign language. (Put your hand up over the mouth, and put your hand out and down, so the palm is out and open facing the other person.) Ask one child at a time to make the sign. After they make the sign, they move to the next activity.

SNACK

Make a snack mix by mixing one cup each of peanuts, raisins, O-shaped cereal, and pretzels. Put small amounts in bags, tie them with ribbon, and write small cards that read, "Thanks very munch!"

Group Time

Talk about nice things people do for each other. Tell the children that when people do nice things we say, "Thank you." Make a list of people for whom children are thankful.

Learning Center Ideas

Literacy: Set out card-making supplies. Print "thank you" on a card children can use as a model, and invite them to make thank-you notes to special people in their lives.

Sensory: Tell the children that "thank you" is a very special phrase. Explain, "When people do nice things they like to hear you say 'thank you.' It makes them feel good about helping you. In a way, the word is like a treasure, because it means so much."

Sensory: Write one of the letters in "thank you" on separate poker chips and hide the chips in the Sand Table. Suggest that the children find their "treasure" (the letters), and then put them in order to spell "thank you."

Additional Activities

Movement: Play Mother May I. For this game, have the children line up on one side of the room, except for one child, who will be the Mother. The goal is to tag the Mother. Each child takes turns asking "Mother, may I take three steps?" or any number of steps. The Mother says, "Yes" or "No." The child must say, "Thank you." If the child forgets to say "thank you," before moving, that child cannot advance.

Rhythm and Rhyme: Teach the children to sing "I Thank You for All You Do," found on appendix page 312.

Cooperation

STORY TIME

Black Dog Gets Dressed by Lizi Boyd
Cleo Cooperates by Peter Koblish
The Family of Earth by Schim
    Schimmel
Nicole's Boat by Allen Morgan

TRANSITION

Use greeting cards, playing cards, or other pictures for this activity. Cut each card in two parts. (Do not use the same picture cards. Make sure there is only on of each picture.) Cut enough cards so each child has ½ of a card, and so all pictures match. Encourage the children to find the people with the other halves of their cards. When they match cards, they move to the next activity.

Group Time

Talk to the children about how cooperation means people all working together to do something. Ask the children to thing of ways they can cooperate with each other in the classroom. Copy their ideas on poster board, and display them on the wall.

Learning Center Ideas

Art: Invite two children to paint together on a single piece of paper.
Blocks: Set out a photo of a block structure made using two or three colored blocks, and invite the children to use blocks to copy the picture.
Games: Set out games, such as tic-tac-toe, memory, and so on, and encourage the children to cooperate when playing the games.
Math: Divide the children into small groups, and give each group a puzzle, encouraging them to work together to put the puzzles together.

Additional Activities

Project: Set out a large appliance box, asking the children to decide together what they want to do with it: turn it into a car, a plane, a tree, and so on. Once the children decide show them how to cooperate to make their idea work.
Rhythm and Rhyme: Invite the children to sing "Cooperation," found on appendix page 311.

Hats

On the previous day, remind the children to wear special hats today. Have extras available in case children forget.

STORY TIME

Blue Hat, Green Hat by Sandra Boynton
Caps for Sale by Esphyr Slobodkina
The Cat in the Hat by Dr. Seuss
The Hat by Jan Brett
Jennie's Hat by Ezra Jack Keats

TRANSITION

Write each letter of the alphabet on separate small sheets of paper. Put the alphabet letters into a hat. Turn on some music and encourage the children to pass the hat. Occasionally, stop the music, and have the child holding the hat pull a letter out of the hat and say its name, then move to the next activity. Repeat until all children have moved to the next activity.

Group Time 1

Bring in different kinds of hats that people wear at work, such as a hard hat, chef hat, baseball cap, police officer helmet, football helmet, and so on. Show each hat, and ask the children questions: "Who wears this hat? What do people do who wear this hat?"

Group Time 2

Create a "hat" tree. Invite the children to donate a special warm hat and mittens to put on a special tree. When your unit is over, donate the hats to children who need warm hats and mittens.

Learning Center Ideas (Put hats in all the centers for children to use.)

Art: Give each child a construction paper cutout of a winter hat. Cut four vertical slits down the middle of the hat. Show the children how to weave strips of paper through the hat. They can decorate the woven hat and glue a pompom on the top.

Blocks/Dramatic Play: Add hard hats and clipboards for children to use as they pretend to be construction workers.

Dramatic Play: Put baker's hats in playdough area, along with rolling pins, measuring cups, and cookie cutters.

Additional Activities

Rhythm and Rhyme: Invite the children to recite "When It's Cold Outside," found on appendix page 315.

Small Group: Talk about the hats the children wear to school. Take a photo of children in their hats, and invite each child to dictate a sentence to you about her hat. Ask the children to wear their hats and then help them sort themselves into a living graph by hat color or style.

Home/School Connection

Write a letter to the children's parents, asking them to be sure their children wear special hats to school for this day.

Calendars

STORY TIME

All Year Long by Nancy Tafuri
Cookie's Week by Cindy Ward
Dear Daisy, Get Well Soon by Maggie Smith
IQ Goes to School by Mary Ann Fraser
Seven Blind Mice by Ed Young
Today Is Monday by Eric Carle

SNACK

With the children, eat chicken soup with rice. Read *Chicken Soup with Rice* by Maurice Sendak to the children as you eat.

Group Time

Use masking or duct tape to make a big calendar grid (with over 31 squares) from a shower curtain, attach construction paper numerals in each box, and use the grid for the following games:

Game #1: Place the grid on the floor. Write numerals 1–31 on individual flash cards, and invite a child to pick a card. The child says the numeral and then stands on that numeral on the grid.

Game #2: Play "Musical Month." Have each child stand on a calendar numeral on the curtain. As the music plays, encourage the children to walk in order 1–31 on the grid. When the music stops, the children stop and say the numerals they are standing on. After all the children finish saying their numerals, start the music and play again.

Learning Center Ideas

Manipulatives: Cut and laminate old calendar photos for the children to use as puzzles. Also, consider using a calendar grid as a puzzle for the children to put together.

Math: Set out a large sheet of construction paper marked with a grid and numbered as a calendar would be. Set out several numbered squares of paper the same size as the squares in the grid, and invite the children to match the numbered squares to the numerals on the grid.

Science: Look at calendars containing weather-related monthly photos with the children. Talk with them about what it is appropriate to wear outside during each month.

Additional Activities

Movement: Practice birthday months with this activity. Create a start and finish line in the classroom. Instruct children to line up at the starting line. Call out a month, such as "September." Children whose birthdays are in the named month either hop, run, skip (according to the instruction) to a given place and back. Call different months until all children have had a turn to move.

Rhythm and Rhyme: Practice days of the week by reciting "The Days Song," found on appendix page 311, with the children.

Letter *I*

STORY TIME

I Love Trains by Philemon Sturges

I Love You the Purplest by Barbara M. Joose

Inch by Inch by Leo Lionni

IQ Goes to School by Mary Ann Fraser

Itsy Bitsy Spider by Iza Trapani

TRANSITION

Say a child's name in the first line of the "Fly Away" rhyme, found on appendix page 312. Have that child name an insect in the second line, then move to the next activity, walking in a manner she thinks is similar to the way the insect she named might move.

SNACK

Help the children make their own ice cream sandwiches. Give each child two graham cracker squares. Set out ice cream and help the children spread ice cream on one graham cracker, and then put the other graham cracker on top to make a sandwich. **Note**: The sandwiches might have to cool in the freezer before eating.

Group Time

Talk about the letter *i* and the sound it makes. Say words that begin with the letter *i*, and some that do not. Suggest that the children pretend to "itch" if the words begin with the *i* sound.

Learning Center Ideas

Art: Show the children how to paint with ice cubes. To make colored ice cubes, fill an ice cube tray with water, and add food coloring to the different cubes to an assortment of colors. Put the trays in the freezer. When the ice cubes are beginning to harden, add craft sticks for the children to use as handles. After they are frozen, set out paper for the children to paint using the sticks.

Math: Set out several buttons and invite the children to sort them by color or size in ice cube trays.

Writing: Set out different kinds and colors of ink pens and paper with copies of the "Fly Away" rhyme, found on appendix page 312, written on sheets of paper. Suggest that children fill in the blanks with either words or drawings.

Additional Activities

Movement: Play In and Out the Window. All but two of the children stand in a circle holding hands. One of the two remaining children is the cat and the other is the mouse. Explain that the cat will try to catch the mouse. The children in the circle begin moving their arms up and down, as though opening and closing windows. They help the mouse escape by lifting their arms up and putting them down to keep the cat inside.

Outside: Make inchworm rulers by following the directions in the appendix on page 310.

December

Calendar Time

During Calendar Time, introduce the month of December to the children. Look at the letters in the word *December.* Name each letter, and say the sound of each letter, and say other words that start with the same sound as December. Whose name begins with the letter *d?* Do this for each letter in the word during calendar time throughout the month.

Monthly Organizer

WEEK-LONG CELEBRATIONS

Hanukkah

Kwanzaa

SPECIAL DAYS AND HOLIDAYS

December 13: Santa Lucia Day

December 25: Christmas

GENERAL DAILY PLANS

Town Mouse, Country Mouse by
     Jan Brett
Numeral 2
Homes
Sharing
Gingerbread People
Numeral 10
Five Senses
Jack Be Nimble
Ribbons and Bows
Letter *D*
Stickers
Mouse Mess by Linnea Riley
Bells

Reindeer
Greeting Cards
Magnets
Buttons
Letter *K*
Hickory Dickory Dock

Note: Please be sure to check for allergies before serving the snacks or doing any food-related activities.

Hanukkah

STORY TIME

Grandma's Latkes by Malka Drucker
Hanukkah Lights, Hanukkah Nights
    by Leslie Kimmelman
*Latkes and Applesauce: Hanukkah
    Story* by Fran Manushkin

SNACK

Make Adina Kayser's Dreidel
Sandwiches (see recipe on appendix
page 320).

Group Time

Discuss Hanukkah with the children. Ask them questions about the
holiday, using the Hanukkah Facts on appendix page 321 to direct the
conversation.

Select a few Hanukkah-related items, such as a menorah, dreidel, and Star
of David (6-point star), gelt (Jewish coins), and a candle, and put them on
a tray. Ask the children to close their eyes. When they have closed their
eyes, take one of the objects away, then ask the children to open their eyes
and guess which object is missing.

Learning Center Ideas

Art: Help the children make a collage of blue and white items on a yellow
Star of David.
Sensory: Bury gelt (coins) in the Sensory Table filled with packing peanuts.
Encourage the children to find the gelt.
Sensory/Fine Motor: Set out blue playdough and white birthday candles so
the children can make menorahs.

Additional Activities

Movement: Dance with blue and white streamers to Hanukkah music, such
as *A Taste of Chanukah* or *Classic Jewish Holiday and Shabbat Songs*.
Rhythm and Rhyme: Sing the "Dreidel Song" (see appendix page 318) with
the children and play the dreidel game.

Kwanzaa

STORY TIME

Imani' s Gift at Kwanzaa by Denise
    Burden Patmon
Kwanzaa by A. B. Porter
My Fist Kwanzaa Book by Deborah
    M. Newton Chocolate

TRANSITION

The children sit in a circle. As the music plays, pass a corncob around the circle. When the music stops, the child holding the corncob moves to the next activity.

SNACK

Give each child seven large marshmallows and seven pretzels. Color vanilla frosting red, green, and black. Each child frosts three pretzels sticks green, and one pretzel stick black. Frost the other three pretzel sticks red. Put each pretzel stick candle in a large marshmallow. Put the pretzel candles in the correct order.

Group Time

Discuss the holiday of Kwanzaa (see Kwanzaa Facts on appendix page 322). A big part of Kwanzaa is cooperation. Cooperate to make a large Kwanzaa candle. Make a large black candle shape from bulletin board paper. Cut slits lengthwise stopping about 1" from the edge in the candle (for weaving). Cut red and green strips of large construction paper. Children take turns weaving red and green strips through the candle. The class helps each child by saying, "over, under" as the child weaves.

Learning Center Ideas

Literacy: Make a K Is for Kwanzaa Game. This can be done on paper for each child or laminated on poster board to use with a dry-erase marker. Print a large *k* in the middle of the paper to show the children what letter they are looking for. Then print small letters all over the paper, including many *k*s. Invite the children to find the *k*s and circles them.

Math: Make special Kwanzaa headbands and practice creating patterns. Set out black paper strips to use for headbands. Cut 1" squares in green and red. Glue squares in an AB pattern. Encourage the children to follow the AB pattern or create their own pattern with the green and red squares.

Additional Activities

Movement: Dance to Kwanzaa music (two good CDs are, "Kwanzaa Music" or "Kwanzaa Party!") with streamers of red, green, and black crepe paper.

Santa Lucia Day

STORY TIME

Lucia, Child of Light: The History and Traditions of Sweden's Lucia Celebration by Florence Ekstrand

SNACK

Make special bread in honor of Santa Lucia Day. Give each child an uncooked breadstick from a can of dough. Invite the children to make either an *s* or *x* shape with the dough (this is the traditional shape of the bread). Add butter, cinnamon, and sugar and bake according to package directions.

Group Time

Introduce the children to Santa Lucia Day using the following facts:

- The holiday is celebrated in many places around the world, including Italy and France, but is especially important in Sweden.
- The legend of Santa Lucia says that she wore white robes and a crown of light and brought food to the poor in the middle of the night. (See more St. Lucia facts on appendix page 322.)

Ask the children to bring in some canned food to donate to a local food pantry in honor of St. Lucia Day. Make gingerbread cookies with the class to celebrate St. Lucia Day. Wear the St. Lucia headbands.

Learning Center Ideas

Art: Help the children make candle headbands. Cut a strip of green construction paper for each child. Have green leaf shapes for children to glue on the strips (there are usually green leaves at the bases of the candles used on St. Lucia Day). Give each child seven white birthday candles to glue on the headband. When the headband is dry, fit it to each child's head and staple the ends together.

Dramatic Play: Provide white dresses or oversized shirts and pieces of red cloth and wreaths for the children to put on and pretend they are Santa Lucia, waking up their parents.

Additional Activities

Movement: Play Follow the Leader. The child who is the leader wears a St. Lucia crown. Walk around the classroom, and then play again with a new leader.

Outside: Invite the children to put on the headbands and white shirts and dresses from the Learning Center Ideas and have a St. Lucia parade around the playground.

Rhythm and Rhyme: Teach the children "Saint Lucia" (see appendix page 319).

Small Group: Make several colors of candles out of felt. Invite the children to do count the number of candles on the flannel board or to make patterns on the flannel board with the candles.

Christmas

It is important to respect and celebrate all cultures and religions. If you choose to share this daily plan with the children, be sure to offer daily plans that focus on other religions, as well.

STORY TIME

The Christmas Alphabet by Robert Sabuda

The Jolly Christmas Postman by Janet and Allan Ahlberg

Santa's Favorite Story by Hisaka Aoki

TRANSITION

The children sit in a circle. As you play music, the children pass a candy cane around the circle. When the music stops, the child holding the candy cane moves to the next activity.

Group Time

Talk about the Christmas holiday. Use the Christmas Facts on appendix page 321 to help explain to children why some people celebrate Christmas. Also discuss other holidays, such as Hanukkah and Kwanzaa. Explain to children that they will learn about those holidays, too. Ask children to share what they know about Christmas.

Before the children arrive, put a Christmas item, such as a candy cane, jingle bell, or an ornament, in a sock. Tie a knot in the end of the sock, and pass the sock around the circle. On a piece of poster board, write down three different possibilities for what the object in the sock might be, then invite the children to vote by a show of hands which object they think is in the sock.

Learning Center Ideas

Art: Help the children make a collage of red and green items on a construction paper cutout of a Christmas tree shape.

Dramatic Play: Set up a small pretend Christmas tree with garland and unbreakable ornaments for the children to decorate.

Fine Motor: Set out green playdough with holiday cookie cutters for the children to use.

Sensory/Fine Motor: Put scissors, ribbons, bows, and pieces of wrapping paper in the Sensory Table. Encourage the children to explore the items.

Additional Activities

Movement: Dance and sing to holiday carols with red and green streamers.

Rhythm and Rhyme: Sing traditional holiday carols with the children.

Town Mouse, Country Mouse by Jan Brett

GENERAL DAILY PLAN

STORY TIME

Enjoy some of these Jan Brett Books:

Annie and the Wild Animals
Comet's Nine Lives
Fritz and the Beautiful Horses
Gingerbread Baby
The Hat
The Mitten
The Night Before Christmas
On Noah's Ark
Scary, Scary Halloween
St. Patrick's Day in the Morning
The Umbrella
Valentine Bears
Who's That Knocking on Christmas Eve?
Wild Christmas Reindeer

TRANSITION

Invite the children to say if they would like to be a city mouse or a country mouse. Put each child's name on a clothespin. As the children move to the next activity, ask them to attach their clothespin to a graph that shows a picture of the city mouse on one side and the country mouse on the other.

If you were a little mouse,
Would you live in a city or
country house?

SNACK

Have a snack of Mouse's favorite cheese cubes and crackers.

Group Time

Introduce the children to the book, *Town Mouse, Country Mouse* by Jan Brett. Ask the children what they think the title refers to, and what the story will be about. Explain to the children that Jan Brett is the author and illustrator of the book, and that she has written many books. After introducing Jan Brett and the book, read it to the children. Invite the children to compare the Town Mouse and the Country Mouse in the story. Ask in what ways they are similar and different. Show the children items such as plant seeds, high-heeled shoes, toy buses and cars, jewelry, trowels and other gardening tools, and other items that are found in the city and the country. With the children's help, sort the items based on whether you would see the items in the country or the city.

Learning Center Ideas

Art: Give each child a house-shaped piece of paper. Invite them to decorate it with plastic leaves, flowers, and garden moss like the country mouse, or with sequins and glittery items that the city mouse would use.

Dramatic Play: Set up a "country" play area and a "city" play area and encourage the children to act out the story.

Additional Activities

Movement: Play Catch the Mouse. One child is the cat, and one child is the owl. The rest of the children are mice. The mice line up on one side of the room. The mice scurry from one side of the room to the next, while the cat and owl try to tag them. Children who are tagged become owls and cats and help catch the other mice.

Rhythm and Rhyme: Sing "Country Mouse, City Mouse" with the children (see appendix page 317).

Numeral 2

STORY TIME

1, 2, 3 to the Zoo by Eric Carle
Chicka, Chicka, 1, 2, 3 by Bill Martin
My Book of Number Games 1 to 70
    edited by Shinobu Akaishi and
    Eno Sarris
One, Two, Three by Sandra Boynton

SNACK

Break apples into two pieces for the children to share with a friend.

Group Time

Before Group Time, find a deck of Memory cards to use. Talk about the word *pair*. Explain that a *pair* is made up of two items that match. Give each child a card at Group Time. Hold up a card and ask the children, "Who has the matching card to make a pair?" Or, give each child a card and encourage them to find the other child with the same card to make a matching pair.

Learning Center Ideas

Literacy: From different colors of construction paper, cut out pairs of matching sock shapes. Write a letter in uppercase on one sock and the same letter in lowercase on the second sock. Put all the socks into a laundry basket, and invite the children to look for the matching socks.
Math: Play Memory. Set out a card deck, and invite the children to place all the cards face down on a table in four rows of 13. Invite the children to take turns flipping over one card, then another. If the cards are the same numeral, the children can keep the pair. If the cards do not match, the children turn them face down again. If a child correctly turns a matching pair, that child can continue turning cards. If not, the other child gets to turn the cards.
Sensory: Hide several matching pairs of plastic animals in the Sand Table, inviting the children to dig around, hunting for matching pairs.

Additional Activities

Movement: Invite the children to follow the directions as you recite the poem, "Two Hands, Two Feet" (see appendix page 320).
Outside: Play Partner Tag. Each child holds a friend's hand at all times. One pair of friends is "IT." They try to tag another two friends who become IT.
Rhythm and Rhyme: Sing the song, "I Like Two" with the children (see appendix page 318).

Homes

Before this unit, send a disposable camera around to each house for a night, for each family to take a picture of their house and send it back to school. In a letter brought with the camera, ask that parents list their addresses, so the children can learn them in class. Develop the film before this lesson. Be sensitive to the variety of homes that children live in. If you feel that a child in the class may feel uncomfortable, consider skipping this part of the daily plan.

STORY TIME

Home for a Bunny by Margaret Wise Brown

A House Is a House for Me by Mary Ann Hoberman

A House for Hermit Crab by Eric Carle

This Is the House That Jack Built by Jeannette Winter

Two Homes by Claire Masurel

TRANSITION

Before each child moves to the next activity, recite "Animals, Animals," found on appendix page 317, and invite the named child to tell where the animal lives.

SNACK

Make a house using a square or rectangle cracker. Cut cheese to make windows and doors.

Group Time

Talk about how animals and people live in different types of homes, but all homes do the same thing—protect humans and animals from weather and keep us safe. Bring in the pictures of the children's homes (taken previously). Show the pictures of the homes and invite the children to guess who lives there. You can sort and/or graph the homes by apartment, house, and so on.

Learning Center Ideas

Art: Bring in an appliance box, such as a refrigerator box, and set out crayons, markers, paints, and other materials for the children to decorate the box as though it were their house.

Blocks: After reading, *This Is the House That Jack Built* by Jeannette Winter, set out several blocks for children to build houses with, and take photos of the children with their homes. After the photos are developed, put the photos up on the wall with the title "These Are the Houses That We Built" written over them on construction paper.

Dramatic Play: Place several blankets over the sides of chairs or a table and invite the children to pretend they are living in tents.

Additional Activities

Movement: Tape five cutouts of house shapes on the floor. Play tag. The child who is "IT" can tag anyone not standing on a house. Children can stand on a house shape and count to 10, and then they must run again.

Outside: Go for a walk and look at different kinds of homes. Choose one home and count how many windows it has. What shape is the house? Talk about what you saw when you get back to school.

Rhythm and Rhyme: Sing "Homes" with the children (see appendix page 318).

Small Group: Read the story of "The Three Little Pigs" (many version available) to the children. Talk about the story. Then give each child a paper with, "This is the house that _____ built" printed on the top. Set out yarn, craft sticks, fabric scraps, toothpicks, and other items for the children to make houses. Print the child's name in the title. Invite the child to tell you about the house she made and write her words on the bottom of the page. Make a class book.

DAILY PLAN CONCEPT

Sharing

STORY TIME

The Doorbell Rang by Pat Hutchins
It's Mine by Leo Lionni
Me Too by Mercer Mayer

TRANSITION

Invite each child to finish the statement before he moves to the next activity.

> A way to show a friend I care
> Is when I have a toy,
> I _____.

SNACK

Invite each child to bring in a snack to share.

Group Time

Read *The Doorbell Rang* by Pat Hutchins. Talk about what happens in this funny story. Ask the children how they might feel if that happened to them. Talk about sharing of all kinds—sharing toys, sharing with people who need food and shelter, sharing time, and so on. Invite children to take turns sharing something special with the class. It can be a story, a special toy or other object, something that makes their families special, or anything each child would like to share. Remind the children that it is important to listen to their friends as they share.

Learning Center Ideas

Blocks: In addition to sharing the blocks, provide toy cars that the children can share as they play with the blocks.

Sensory: Provide playdough for the children and focus on how they all share the playdough.

Sensory: Place a few sand toys in the Sand Table and encourage the children to share the toys as they play in the sand.

Additional Activities

Movement: Encourage the children to share a beanbag with a friend and play catch together.

Project: The children can share an easel, paper, and paints with a friend to make a picture together.

Rhythm and Rhyme: Sing the song, "I Like You" with the children (see appendix page 318).

Small Group: Challenge the children to work together to make a chain with sticky tape, sharing both the sticky tape and the scissors. In the end, children's cooperation and sharing make a beautiful chain.

Gingerbread Friends

STORY TIME

Gingerbread Baby by Jan Brett

Maisy Makes Gingerbread by Lucy Cousins

Snowflake Kisses and Gingerbread Smiles by Toni Trent Parker

TRANSITION

Recite the "Gingerbread Man" rhyme on appendix page 318, adding a child's name and an action such as *hop, gallop, run,* or *walk* in the two blanks in the first line, encouraging that child to perform the action, then move to the next activity.

SNACK

Give each child a piece of thawed frozen bread dough. Let the children shape their pieces into gingerbread people. Butter the tops and sprinkle with cinnamon and sugar. If desired, make faces with raisins and/or M&Ms. Let the dough rise, and then bake it according to the package directions.

Group Time

Read the following stories to the children, *The Gingerbread Boy* by Paul Galdone, and *Gingerbread Baby* by Jan Brett. Afterward reading the books, set out several large and small construction paper cutouts of gingerbread figures, and make a graph with two columns. Write one of the book titles at the top of one of the columns. Invite the children to attach a large gingerbread cutout to the *Gingerbread Boy* side of the graph if they preferred that book, or to attach one of the small cutouts to the other side of the graph if they preferred *Gingerbread Baby.*

Learning Center Ideas

Art: Add a little ginger to brown finger paint. Let the children use it to fingerpaint on white paper. When dried, they can make sweet-smelling gingerbread people.

Art: Cut a gingerbread house shape from brown foam for each child; cut a small circle and put a child's photo on each one. Glue another house shape on the back. Invite the children to decorate their gingerbread shape with white glitter, white, pink and blue sequins, and small gingerbread people shapes. Add a string to make a great ornament for the classroom or for the children to take home.

Additional Activities

Movement: Play Hide the Gingerbread Man. One child goes to another part of the room and closes his eyes. The teacher quietly hides the gingerbread man (one of the cutouts from the Group Time activity). The class calls the other child to come back to find the gingerbread man. The class helps by giving the child clues and directions, such as, "It's on the other side of the room," "You are getting closer," "You've gone too far," and so on.

Outside: Play "The Gingerbread Man Says." Give directions. If you say, "The Gingerbread Man says," with the direction, the children should follow it. If not, they should not follow the direction.

Numeral 10

STORY TIME

10 Fat Turkeys by Tony Johnston
10 Little Rubber Ducks by Eric Carle
Feast for 10 by Cathryn Falwell
Kipper's Book of Numbers by Mick Inkpen
Spot Counts from 1 to 10 by Eric Hill

TRANSITION

Invite each child to "count to 10 or act like a hen" before moving to the next activity.

SNACK

Set up bowls of crackers, raisins, and pretzels, and ask each child to count out 10 of each for a snack.

Group Time

Read *The Big Fat Hen* by Keith Baker. As you reread the story, invite the children to do the actions.

Learning Center Ideas

Math: Print the numerals 1–10 on 10 different hen-shaped cutouts. Laminate. Invite the children to put the hens in numerical order.
Math/Sensory: Encourage children to find the foam numerals from 1–10 in the sand at the Sensory Table and then put them in order.

Additional Activities

Movement: Pretend to be a rocket counting down to blast off. Encourage the children to crouch down low as they count down. When they say, "Blast off!" they can jump up high.
Outside: Make photo fact families. Go outside and use 10 children to make 1+9=10. Take a photo of one child and another photo of nine children. Then take another photo of all 10 children together. Do this with other children and other facts of 10. Use the photos to show the numerals that make 10. Display the photos.
Small Group: Read *Ten Black Dots* by Donald Crews. Talk about what the black dots can make. Make a book. Give each child 10 red dots. Talk about what the dots could be. Give each child a paper to put the dots on and draw a picture. Invite children to dictate a sentence about the dots.

Five Senses

STORY TIME

The Five Senses by Keith Faulkner
Me and My Senses by Joan Sweeney
My Five Senses by Margaret Miller
Smelly Socks by Robert Munsch

TRANSITION

Each child smells a flavored votive candle and names the flavor before moving to the next activity.

SNACK

Bring in pickles, pretzels, lemons, grapes, and other foods with strong flavors. Invite children to try a little bit of each food. Create a chart with the following headings: Sweet, Sour, Salty, Bitter, and Spicy. Ask the children to put each food under the proper heading. Next, try an experiment: Ask the children to hold their noses closed while they taste the food. Does the food taste the same?

Group Time

Introduce the children to the five senses. Ask if any of the children can name the five senses, and help them name each sense if they are having difficulty. After naming each sense, ask the children to name a part of the body associated with that sense. Explain that the senses work together, but they can also work individually. As an example, blindfold one of the children, and give him a toy. Ask the child to guess what he is holding. If the child has trouble guessing the type of toy using only the sense of touch, invite the other children to give him hints by making sounds that might be associated with the toy. Repeat with other children.

Learning Center Ideas

Art: Make a scratch-and-sniff book. Bring in four different smelling scratch-and-sniff stickers. Children smell the stickers and draw what the sticker smells like.
Art/Writing: Make a Five Senses Wintertime Book (see appendix page 317).
Science: Put a different scent on each of several sponges by wetting the sponge and putting several drops of extract on the sponge. Invite the children to name each smell.
Sensory: Make Kool-Aid™ playdough (see appendix page 320).

Additional Activities

Movement: Play Who Has the Bell? The children sit in a circle, except for the child who is "IT." He sits in the middle of the circle. IT closes his eyes. The teacher gives one child a bell but all of the children put their hands behind their backs. Everyone is very quiet while the child rings the bell. IT opens his eyes and tries to guess who has the bell by listening very carefully.
Outside: Take a five senses walk. Ask the children to point out the things they see, hear, smell, and touch. Bring a small snack for each child to consume as they walk. When you return to the classroom, ask the children to help you make a list of "What We Saw, What We Heard, What We Tasted, What We Smelled, and What We Touched."
Rhythm and Rhyme: Sing "My Senses" with the children (see appendix page 319).

Jack Be Nimble

STORY TIME

Book of Mother Goose by Arnold Lobel

First Rhymes by Jane Swift

Mother Goose's Nursery Rhymes by Robert Frederick

TRANSITION

Take turns putting each child's name in the "Jack Be Nimble" rhyme. The named child jumps over a candlestick (block) and moves to the next activity.

[Child's name] *be nimble.*
[Child's name] *be quick.*
[Child's name] *jump over the candlestick.*

Group Time

Repeat the "Jack Be Nimble" Nursery Rhyme. Then talk about candles, and the different scents they come in. Bring in several different kinds of scented candles. Invite the children to smell them and guess what scent they are.

Learning Center Ideas

Art: Take a photo of each child jumping. After developing the photos, help the children glue them to sheets of construction paper, and invite the children to draw an object below them, so they appear to be jumping over that object. At the top of the page, write "_____ jumped over _____," and help the children fill in their names and the names of the objects they are jumping over in the pictures.

Art: Use a thick white candlestick to help the children write their names or draw pictures on white paper. Be sure to press hard when drawing. Then invite the children to paint the whole paper with watercolor paint. The candle drawing will show through.

Math: Set out a box of several different colored candles, and invite the children to sort them by color.

Science: Set out a bucket of water and several candles. Invite the children to guess whether the candles will sink or float, and then have the children put them in the water one at a time. Record the results on a graph.

Additional Activities

Movement: Try different ways to jump over the candlestick. Invite the children to take turns jumping over two, three, four, and five candlesticks on the floor. Substitute skip, hop, walk, and other motions for jump over the candlestick.

Outside: Set out several different sizes of candles, making a sort of obstacle course. Invite the children to run through the course, jumping over the candles.

Rhythm and Rhyme: Recite the rhyme, "Jack Be Nimble" with the children (see Transition, above left).

Ribbons and Bows

STORY TIME

Emily's Ballet by Claire Masural
My Hair Is Beautiful by Paula Dejoie
The Secret Fairy by Claire Freeman

TRANSITION

Invite each child to choose a bow and then listen to the directions. When children hear their color of bow, they put their bows in a box and move to the next activity.

> If _____ is the color of your
>   bow,
> It's time to get up now and go.

Group Time

Use ribbon to measure each child. Cut the length of the ribbon the same height as the child. Put the child's name on the ribbon. Use the ribbons to measure things in the room. Ask the children, "Is your ribbon longer than the table?" Invite children to compare their ribbons. "Whose ribbon is longer? Why?"

Show children several pieces of gift wrap—a small piece, a medium piece, and a whole roll—and boxes or items to wrap. Show children a large item. Which wrap would you need for this: little, medium or large? Show all the items. Which wrap would you use?

Learning Center Ideas

Art: Set out different kinds of gift wrap and ribbons for children to cut and paste to make a collage.
Fine Motor: Provide boxes for the children to wrap with paper, ribbons, and tape.
Math: Set out wrapped presents. Print a numeral on each box. Encourage the children to put that number of bows on the box. (Take the sticky part off the bows for this game.)
Math: Encourage the children to sort the bows by color. Start a pattern using bows; invite children to continue that pattern.

Additional Activities

Movement: Use a long piece of ribbon to play Limbo. With another adult, hold the ribbon up high and invite the children to walk under it single-file. When the leader gets back to the front, lower the ribbon a little bit. Encourage the children to try to go under the ribbon without touching it.
Outside: Hide a bow outside. Give one or two hints to the children about where the ribbon is hidden. Invite the children to try to find it.

Letter *D*

STORY TIME

10 Little Rubber Ducks by Eric Carle

The Dump Truck by Craig Robert Carey

Dumpy to the Rescue by Julie Andrews

Good Dog Carl by Alexandra Day

One Duck Stuck by Phyllis Root

TRANSITION

Name one child at a time. Before the named child moves on to the next activity-they name a word that begins with the letter *d*.

SNACK

Make a delicious Italian or Taco Dip (see appendix page 321 for recipes).

Group Time

Talk about the word *diamond*. Show the children a diamond shape. Ask them what letter the word diamond begins with. Explain to the children that December also begins with the letter *d*. Talk about the letter *d* and the sound it makes. *D* is also for duck. Say different words and encourage the children to quack like a duck if the word begins with a *d*.

Learning Center Ideas

Dramatic Play: Set up a doctor office with several toy doctor sets, a box of bandages, and cotton balls. Invite the young doctors to work on dolls or stuffed animals.

Math: Create six columns on a sheet of paper; write one of the numerals from 1–6 at the top of each column. Set out several dice; invite the children to roll the dice, and put a tally mark by the number that comes up on each die. Continue until all digits have come up once. Which number was rolled most frequently, which was rolled the least?

Math: Set out a bowl of pennies and dimes. Invite children to sort them on a paper plate with "1¢" written on one plate and "10¢" written on the other. **Safety Note:** Do not do this activity if children still put items in their mouths.

Sensory: Put a mixture of dishwashing soap and water in the Sensory Table. Invite the children to wash the plastic dishes from the Home Living Center.

Additional Activities

Movement: Encourage the children to follow the directions in the fun rhyme, "Dance, Dance, Dance" (see appendix page 317).

Outside: Show children how to dribble a ball.

Project: Encourage the children to make dot pictures with several different color bingo markers.

Rhythm and Rhyme: Teach the children how to sing "The D Song" (see appendix page 317).

Stickers

Make stickers for this daily plan using the recipe on appendix page 321, or use pre-made stickers. As children come to school, put a sticker circle on each child to use for different activities throughout the day.

STORY TIME

Bring in a collection of sticker books for the children to explore.

SNACK

Put a sticker by each snack. Children find the sticker that matches the sticker they are wearing on their shirt to find their snack.

Group Time

Share several seasonal stickers with the children. Help the children sort the stickers by season, putting winter stickers on a mitten shape, spring stickers on a kite shape, summer stickers on a sun shape, and fall on a leaf shape.

Learning Center Ideas

Art: Invite the children to use stickers and markers to make a picture, and then dictate a story about their pictures.

Math: Use stickers to make a lotto game. Use two of each sticker. Make lotto cards, separating the cards into six boxes. Put a sticker on the box and the other of the same sticker on an index card. Laminate both. Turn index cards face down. The children turn the cards over one at a time and match them to the stickers on their game card.

Math: Play Memory. Stick two of each kind of sticker on separate index cards. Put them face down on a table. The children take turns turning over two cards at a time. If they turn over the same cards, they keep the cards and take another turn.

Additional Activities

Movement: If the children are wearing different-colored stickers, play a game using the rhyme, "The Sticker Game" (see appendix page 320).

Outside: Create an obstacle course sticker trail for the children to follow through the playground equipment.

Small Group: Make a counting book by folding and stapling several sheets of paper together. Print the numerals 1–5 in sequential order on the pages. Each numeral is on a separate page. The children put the number of stickers on the each page that matches the numeral on that page.

Mouse Mess by Linnea Riley

GENERAL DAILY PLAN

STORY TIME

If You Give a Mouse a Cookie by Laura Numeroff

If You Take a Mouse to School by Laura Numeroff

Mouse Count by Ellen Stoll Walsh

Mouse Paint by Ellen Stoll Walsh

SNACK

Make a muffin mouse. Make an English muffin for each child in the class. Give each child a muffin, a craft stick, and soft cream cheese. Invite children to frost their muffins. Add raisin eyes, mini-butter cracker ears, and a licorice tail.

Group Time

Read *Mouse Mess* by Linnea Riley. As you read the story again, pretend to act it out with the following actions:

cracker: crunch, crunch
cookie: munch, munch
cornflakes: crackle, sweep
milk and cheese: sniff, sniff
milk: splish and splash
sugar: pour and pat
water: gurgle and bubble

Learning Center Ideas

Art: Make mice by helping the children cut out heart shapes from gray or white construction paper. Fold the hearts and glue them shut. The point of the heart is the mouse's nose. Help the children glue a ribbon tail into the fold.

Math: Give the children yellow foam triangles (cheese), with a different numeral written on each piece. Invite the children to put the correct number of pompoms on each piece of cheese.

Writing: Ask the children if they can say "Mouse Mess." Ask them if they know what letter each word begins with. Then, invite the children to think of words that begin with the same letter as their name, such as "Bashful Brian." Encourage them to draw a picture of themselves. Print their alliterative name above it. Make a class book of the pictures.

Additional Activities

Movement: Play parachute games with a red plastic tablecloth. Encourage the children to hold onto the tablecloth like a parachute. Put in plastic food and make the tablecloth go high, low, fast, and slow. Then, remove the food and as the tablecloth goes up and down, name two children. They quickly and quietly sneak under the cloth like little mice and change places.

Rhythm and Rhyme: Sing "A Mouse Mess Song" (see appendix page 319) to accompany the story *Mouse Mess* by Linnea Riley.

Bells

For this day, make a bracelet for each child by stringing several bells on a pipe cleaner. Twist the pipe cleaner shut. Use this for several activities throughout the day.

STORY TIME

Jingle Bear by Stephen Cosgrove
Jingle Bells by Michael Scott
Ring the Bells by Billy Davis
Silver Bells by Jay Livingston
Stopping by Woods on a Snowy Evening, by Robert Frost, illustrated by Susan Jeffers

TRANSITION

Say the following rhyme and then ring a bell. Ask one child to say how many times she heard the bell ring. Then that child moves to the next activity.

Listen as I ring the bell,
How many times, can you tell?

SNACK

Make bell toast. Make a piece of toast for each child. Invite the children to spread jelly on the toast. Use a bell shaped cookie cutter to cut the toast into a bell.

Group Time

Bring in different kinds of bells (commonly found in craft stores). Explore each bell and the sound it makes. Arrange the bells in order from smallest to largest. Then put the bells in order from softest to loudest. Is the order the same?

Learning Center Ideas

Art: Encourage the children to make a bell and bead necklace. First they string 10 pony beads (or any kind of bead) on a ribbon, then a jingle bell, and then 10 more beads. Help them tie the ends together to make a necklace.

Math: Cut out a construction paper horse for each child. Write a numeral on each horse shape. Invite the children to glue the correct number of jingle bells on each horse.

Math: Children take turns drawing a number card. They name the numeral and then ring a bell that many times.

Sensory: Challenge the children to find jingle bells hidden in paper shreds in the sensory table.

Additional Activities

Movement: Put a red pipe cleaner with a jingle bell on each child's left wrist. Put a blue pipe cleaner with a jingle bell on each child's right wrist. Encourage the children to follow the directions:

1. Shake the red bell on your left wrist two times.
2. Shake the blue bell four times.
3. Shake both bells 1, 2, 3. Turn around and sit happily.

Outside: One child hides with a bell. The child rings the bell. The remaining children try to find the child by listening and moving to the sound of the bell.

Rhythm and Rhyme: Sing "Ring My Bell" with the children (see appendix page 319).

Reindeer

STORY TIME

Ingor's Promise by Jamie Parkison
Maya's World: Izak of Lapland by
    Maya Angelou
Reindeer by Emilie Lephien
The Wild Christmas Reindeer by Jan
Brett

SNACK

Make reindeer toast. Make toast. Cut off the crusts so there is a square. Cut each square in half to make two triangles. Give each child a triangle reindeer head. Spread peanut butter on the toast. Add two raisin eyes and a raisin nose on the tip. Add pretzel stick antlers.

Group Time

Set out one reindeer cardboard shape for every two children in the class, and write a reindeer fact on each cutout (see appendix page 322 for Reindeer Facts). Cut each reindeer in half in a jagged manner, so each piece only connects with its appropriate half, and give each half to a different child. When two children match their halves, invite them to share their reindeer facts (help them read their facts).

Learning Center Ideas

Art: Set out several construction paper cutouts of reindeer and containers of fingerpaint, inviting the children to decorate the reindeer.

Math: Tape several construction paper cutouts of reindeer to the wall, from the floor to five feet up the wall (the average height of a reindeer is 5'). Measure the height of each child and mark it on the reindeer, so the children can see how tall they are in relation to a reindeer.

Science: Set out a globe and explain to the children that reindeer thrive in cold climates. Give the children small reindeer cutouts to tape to the globe on those places they think reindeer would most likely be found. Show the children which country has the highest population of reindeer (Norway).

Additional Activities

Movement: Invite the children to gallop like reindeer as the music plays. Set out blocks for them to jump over.

Rhythm and Rhyme: Sing "Reindeer, Reindeer Go Away" (see appendix page 319) with the children.

Greeting Cards

GENERAL DAILY PLAN

STORY TIME

Show the children a card with an interesting image on the front, and encourage them to make up a story based on the image. Write down a sentence or two on a sheet of paper, and invite the children to illustrate the rest of the story.

My Very Favorite Art Book by Jennifer Lipsey Edwards
Paper by Helen Bliss
Paper Folding Fun by Ginger Johnson

Group Time

Collect old greeting cards and cut them in half. Give each child one half of a card. Children must find the child who has the other half of their card. Talk about why people give cards and talk about the pictures on the cards.

Learning Center Ideas

Fine Motor: Punch holes around the edges of the cards. Invite the children to sew around the edges with lacing or shoestrings.
Literacy: Encourage children to sort cards by holiday or special day.
Writing: Provide card-making supplies. Talk about why people send cards to each other. Invite children to make their own cards.
Writing: Invite children to choose a card and create a story about the picture. Write down what the child says. Show the cards and read the stories that go with them to the class.

Additional Activities

Movement: Encourage the children to pretend they are mail carriers delivering cards in this variation of Duck, Duck, Goose. The children sit in a circle. One child is the mail carrier. The mail carrier walks around the outside of the circle with a card. He drops the card behind someone's back, and hurries around the circle. The child with the card gets up and runs around the circle trying to tag the mail carrier before the carrier sits in his spot.
Outside: Help the children write a card to someone in their family. Help them address the envelope to each child's home and place a stamp on the letter. Walk to a mailbox to mail the cards.

Magnets

STORY TIME

Help children with storytelling. Copy, color, and cut storybook figures. Laminate them for durability. Put a magnetic strip on the back of each figure. Put them on a cookie sheet and encourage the children to move the figures as you tell stories. Then encourage them to make up their own stories.

TRANSITION

Print each child's name on a page of lined paper. Laminate the names, and glue a piece of magnetic tape to the back. Put them on a cookie sheet, and mix them up when dry. At the end of an activity, set out the cookie sheet and invite each child to find her name. After finding their names, invite the children to put the magnets in a basket and then move to the next activity.

Group Time

Set out two cookie sheets and a basket of magnetic numerals and letters. Invite the children to take turns choosing a magnet and deciding whether it is a letter or a numeral. Sort the magnets using the two cookie sheets.

Learning Center Ideas

Art: Help children try magnetic painting. Put a sheet of paper in a shirt box. Children add a teaspoon of paint and several paper clips in the box. They drag a magnet under the box to make designs by moving the paper clips with the magnet.

Literacy: Set out alphabet magnets and children's name cards with photos. Children practice spelling the names with the magnets on a cookie sheet.

Science: Is it magnetic or not? Set out several items, such as marbles, paper clips, nail, pencils, and so on. Bring in cereal fortified with iron. Ask children to predict whether the magnet will pick up the items. Write down the predictions. Try them and see who was correct.

Additional Activities

Movement: The children pretend they are magnets. As the music plays they walk around. When the music stops, they stick to something like a magnet.

Outside: Children take magnets outside and experiment with them.

Rhythm and Rhyme: Teach the children the "Magnets" song (see appendix page 319).

Buttons

Invite the children to wear clothes that have as many buttons as possible on this day.

STORY TIME

10 Button Book by William Accorsi

The Button Box by Margarette S. Reid

Buttons for General Washington by Peter Geiger Roop

Grandma's Button Box by Linda Williams Aber

SNACK

Make a fun Bacon Ranch Dip to eat with carrot buttons (slices) (see appendix page 320 for recipe).

Group Time

Children will be wearing clothing that has as many buttons as possible on this day. Count the number of buttons on each child. Make a list with the child's name and the number of buttons. Look at the list. Who wore the most? How many children had the same number of buttons?

Learning Center Ideas

Art: Set out bags of old buttons. Invite children to make bracelets or necklaces by stringing them on lacing, shoelaces, or pipe cleaners.

Fine Motor: Save old clothing items that have buttons, zippers, and snaps. Invite the children to practice buttoning, zipping, and snapping the clothing.

Math: Cut out shirt shapes from several different colors of construction paper. Write a different numeral on each shirt and laminate them. Invite the children to spread the shirts out on the table or floor and put that matching number of buttons on each shirt.

Math: Set out several buttons in different colors, make patterns with the buttons, and invite children to continue the patterns. Encourage the children to make their own patterns, too.

Additional Activities

Outside: Glue several buttons on a gingerbread person shape, but leave a space for a missing button. Hide a button outside. Invite the children to find the missing button. The child who finds the button can hide it for the next round of the game.

Rhythm and Rhyme: Sing "My Very Own Button" with the children (see appendix page 319).

Letter *K*

STORY TIME

Blue Kangaroo Books by Emma
  Chichester Clark
Color Kittens by Margaret Wise
  Brown
*Does a Kangaroo Have a Mother
  Too?* by Eric Carle
Kipper's Kite by Mick Inkpen

TRANSITION

Name a child and repeat this verse.
Each child names a word that
begins with the letter *k* before
moving to the next activity.

> *Before your snack,*
> *Before you play,*
> *Please name a word*
> *That starts with k.*

Group Time

Wear a king's crown to Group Time. Tell children that *king* begins with the
letter *k*. What other words start with the same sound as *king*? Say a few
words, and ask the children to blow a kiss if the word starts with the
sound */k/*.

Introduce the idea of kindness, which starts with the letter *k*. Talk about
being kind to other children. Make a list of ways to be kind or do kind
things for other people. Throughout the day give a chocolate "Kiss for
Kindness" to every child who does something nice for another child.
Be sure that every child receives a chocolate kiss at some point during
the day.

Learning Center Ideas

Art: Help children make a keychain. Loop a ribbon through a key chain
ring in a slipknot for each child. Invite the children to string beads on both
of the ribbon strings. Tie a double knot to keep the beads secure.
Dramatic Play: Set up a kitchen in the Home Living Center. Encourage the
children to pretend they are cooking dinner for their families.
Fine Motor: Provide keys and locks for the children to practice turning a
key to open a lock.

Additional Activities

Movement: Move like animals that have names beginning with the letter *k*,
such as koala, kangaroo, and kitten.
Outside: Show the children how to fly a kite.
Rhythm and Rhyme: Share "The K Song" with the children (see appendix
page 319).

Hickory Dickory Dock

Although children are not developmentally ready to learn to tell time, this daily plan simply exposes them to clocks and introduces the concept of telling time.

STORY TIME

Book of Mother Goose by Arnold Lobel

First Rhymes by Jane Swift

Mother Goose's Nursery Rhymes by Robert Frederick

SNACK

Make a tortilla clock to eat. Spread cream cheese on a tortilla shell. Add two carrot sticks as clock hands. Time to eat!

Group Time

Say the rhyme "Hickory Dickory Dock" (see appendix page 318) with the children. Repeat it, and after each line say, "Tick tock," as you sway to the left and right. Encourage the children to follow your example.

Bring out a box of clocks to share with the children. Encourage them to explore many different kinds of clocks, including watches, digital clocks, clock radios, and wind-up clocks. Ask them which ones they like and why.

Learning Center Ideas

Art: Cut a circle or use a paper plate to make a clock face. Use paper fasteners to add hands. Add numerals to the clock. Invite the children to glue the clock faces to grandfather clock shapes that have been cut out beforehand. Glue a small mouse shape to a gray ribbon or string that looks like a tail. Punch a hole into the bottom of the clock and tie on the string or ribbon. Now say the rhyme, and encourage the children to move the mice up and down the clocks.

Math: Provide construction paper circles for the children. Help them write the numerals around the edge of the circle to make a clock face.

Math: Use different lengths of ribbon to make mice with tails of different lengths. Challenge children to put the tail lengths in order from shortest to longest.

Additional Activities

Outside: Draw a giant clock for children to play on. Invite children to jump the correct number of times on each numeral.

Rhythm and Rhyme: As you say "Hickory Dickory Dock," encourage children to tap sticks or beat on drums to the rhythm of the rhyme.

January

Calendar Time

During Calendar Time, introduce the month of January to the children. Look at the letters in the word *January*. Name each letter, and say the sound and other words that start with the sound. Whose name begins with the letter *j*? Do this for each letter in the word during calendar time throughout the month.

Monthly Organizer

SPECIAL DAYS AND HOLIDAYS

Happy New Year
Martin Luther King, Jr. Day
National Pie Day
National Puzzle Day

GENERAL DAILY PLANS

Winter Weather
Winter Olympics
Eyes
Snowflakes
Snow Friends
Mittens
Ice
Letter *N*
Pajama Party
Penguins
Soup
Polar Bears
Spinning Yarns
Polka Dots
Bear Snores On by Karma Wilson
The Baker's Batter

There Was an Old Woman
Letter *O*
Go, Super Bowl
Learn with Cans
Nose for Newspapers
Kangaroo Capers
A Week of Days
Quirky Letter *Q*
Cozy Blankets

Note: Please be sure to check for allergies before serving the snacks or doing any food-related activities.

Happy New Year

STORY TIME

Happy New Year, Pooh by Kathleen Weidner Zoefield

A Happy New Year's Day by Roch Carrier

P. Bear's New Year's Party: A Counting Book by Paul Owen Lewis

TRANSITION

Invite the children to take turns telling something new they want to do in the New Year. As each child names something new, invite her to move to the next activity.

SNACK

Make edible party hats. Give each child a sugar ice cream cone placed upside down on a paper plate. Invite the children to use decorator frosting, raisins, cereal, and sprinkles to make Happy New Year party hats.

Group Time

Introduce the children to the concept of resolutions, explaining that people often make resolutions at the start of a new year. Encourage the children to think of resolutions they would like to make this New Year, such as "I will pick up toys at cleanup time," "I will be nice to my friends," and so on. As each child chooses a resolution, write the resolutions on a banner (long piece of butcher paper). Invite the children to decorate the banner after all the resolutions have been copied onto it, and hang it in the classroom.

Learning Center Ideas

Art/Fine Motor: Make confetti, sequins, and foam shapes available for the children to use to create New Year's pictures.

Dramatic Play: Put a set of Happy New Year party supplies (on sale at stores after New Year's) in the Home Living area. Encourage the children to pretend to have New Year's parties together.

Writing: Provide New Year's cards and envelopes, inviting the children to write Happy New Year or thank-you cards for friends, family, and each other.

Additional Activities

Movement: Invite the children to say the "New Year" rhyme on appendix page 325 and suit their actions to the words.

Small Group: Give the children journals (these can be spiral notebooks or construction paper and blank pages stapled together). Explain that many people start new journals or diaries at the beginning of the year. Encourage the children to draw or write in their journals. Provide different kinds of colored pencils, pens, markers, crayons, and other writing utensils.

Martin Luther King, Jr. Day

Martin Luther King, Jr. Day is on the third Monday in January.

STORY TIME

Happy Birthday, Martin Luther King Jr. by Jean Marzollo

I Have a Dream by Martin Luther King Jr.

A Lesson for Martin Luther King Jr. by Denise Lewis Patrick

My Brother Martin by Christine King Farris

A Picture Book of Martin Luther King Jr. by David A. Adler

SNACK

Give each child two cookies to decorate with frosting. After each child has decorated two cookies, invite them to exchange one cookie with another child.

Group Time

Martin Luther King, Jr. was a great role model for being kind to others. Invite the children to explain what acts of kindness are, and ask them how they feel when someone does something nice for them. Give the children examples of different acts of kindness to get them started. Write "I am kind when_____" on several large construction paper hearts. Ask each child to say how he would finish the sentence and write down what each child says. Then ask him to draw a picture on his heart. After all the children have finished drawing, tie the hearts together with ribbon and put them into a class book.

Learning Center Ideas

Literacy: Provide several clip clothespins painted a particular color on one side, and with one word from a sentence on the other side. With markers, put dots of color along a sheet of construction paper, and invite the children to attach the clothespins to the matching colors, making a complete sentence.

Math: Provide a number of laminated construction paper hearts cut in half for the children to match into pairs. The hearts can be numbered or lettered, so the children have more than one clue to look for when seeking a match.

Additional Activities

Movement: Invite the children to sit in a circle with you. Ask the children to reach out to each side, taking hold of two other children's hands. When all children are holding two hands, squeeze one of the hands you are holding and invite that child to pass the squeeze (hand hug) along to the other hand he holds. When he squeezes the next child's hand, that child squeezes the other hand that he holds until the squeezes go all the way around the circle.

Outside: Invite the children to set out birdseed and carrots for animals that are hungry and cold in the winter.

Rhythm and Rhyme: Sing "I Am Kind to My Friends" (see appendix page 324).

National Pie Day

January 23rd is National Pie Day.

STORY TIME

The Apple Pie Tree by Zoe Hall
Grow a Pumpkin by Janet Gerver
I Know an Old Lady Who Swallowed a Pie by Allison Jackson
A Mud Pie for Mother by Scott Beck

TRANSITION

Invite the children to sit in a circle. Ask one child to say the first word of "Peaches, Cherries, Pears, and Plums" on appendix page 326, and invite the children to go around the circle, reciting the next word of the rhyme. When the rhyme ends, ask the next child in the circle to say her birthday, then move to the next activity.

SNACK

Give each child a small pie tin filled with banana slices covered in vanilla pudding. Add a spoonful of whipped topping to the pies. Enjoy!

Group Time

Set out several types of pie (apple, pumpkin, blueberry) beside sheets of paper with the pies' names written at the top of the paper. Invite the children to sample the various types of pie. After each child has tried all the different types of pie, ask each child to clip a clothespin with her name on it to the sheet of paper beside her favorite type of pie.

Learning Center Ideas

Art/Sensory: Help the children make paper Scratch-and-Sniff Pies (see instructions on appendix page 323).
Fine Motor: Show the children how to make Playdough Pies (see appendix page 323).
Math: Set out several pie tins and construction paper pie-shaped pieces cut into fourths, thirds, and halves. Invite the children to put the appropriate portions into pie tins marked ½, ⅓, and ¼.

Additional Activities

Outside: Play Fruit Pie Upset. Give one third of the children headbands with apples on them, one third with oranges, and one third with bananas. Place enough hula hoops on the ground so three children (one from each fruit group) can stand in a single hula hoop. After each child is standing in a hoop, call out a fruit, such as bananas. All the bananas must each find a new hula hoop to stand in (switching spots with another banana). Occasionally say "Fruit Pie Upset," to which all children must switch. Tell the children that there can be only one of each fruit in each hula hoop.
Rhythm and Rhyme: Write each line of "Little Jack Horner" (see appendix page 325) on sentence strips in a pocket chart. Also, put each word on a word card and invite the children to recite the rhyme again, matching the word cards to the sentence strips.

National Puzzle Day

January 29th is National Puzzle Day.

STORY TIME

Guess Whose Shadow by Stephen R. Swinburne

Look Look Look by Tana Hoban

My First Riddles by Judith Hoffman Corwin

What Am I? An Animal Guessing Game by Iza Trapani

Who Took the Cookies from the Cookie Jar? by Bonnie Lass and Philemon Sturges

TRANSITION

On green construction paper, draw a large snake shape. Print one numeral for each child in the class, then cut out each numbered section of the snake. Hand out the pieces of puzzle to the children, encouraging them to put the snake puzzle together in correct numerical order. When the snake is in order, invite the children to move to another activity.

SNACK

Make gelatin jigglers for the children in a 13" x 9" pan. After the gelatin hardens, give the children puzzle-piece shaped cookie cutters and invite them to cut the gelatin into puzzle pieces.

Group Time

Give each child one piece of a large puzzle. (Make sure there are only as many pieces to the puzzle as there are children, or put together a portion of the puzzle, and hand all the remaining pieces to the children.) Encourage the children to add their pieces to the puzzle and then sit down. When all the children are sitting, the puzzle should be complete. Invite the children to talk about how they connected the pieces and cooperated to finish the puzzle.

Learning Center Ideas

Art: Make your own puzzles. Set out several sheets of paper, pens, markers, crayons, and other art materials so the children can draw pictures. When the picture is complete, help the children cut it into several intricate pieces, making a puzzle.

Literacy: Make alphabet puzzles. On several word cards, print the uppercase and lowercase versions of a letter, and then cut the two matching letters apart. Set the individual cards out, inviting the children to match them.

Additional Activities

Movement: Cut out several construction paper shapes, then cut them in half, creating two-piece puzzles. Distribute one half of a puzzle to each child, and invite the children to find the children with the other halves of their puzzles. When all the children find the other halves of their puzzles, turn on music and encourage the children to dance in pairs.

Rhythm and Rhyme: Talk to the children about riddles. Explain that they are like word puzzles. Tell a few rhyming riddles, inviting the children to put the pieces of the word puzzles together. For example:

You can drive this near and far.
It has four tires; it is a_____."

Encourage the children to make up their own riddles.

Winter Weather

STORY TIME

Bear Snores On by Karma Wilson
Froggy Gets Dressed by Jonathan London
Frozen Noses by Jan Carr
The Hat by Jan Brett
Huggly's Snow Day by Tedd Arnold

TRANSITION

Recite "I Like Winter," found on appendix page 325. Once you have recited the rhyme, point to a child in the room. Invite that child to name something she likes about winter. Once the child names something he likes about winter, invite him to repeat the rhyme and select another child, repeating the process. The first child then moves to the next activity.

SNACK

Make Snowman Food (see recipe on appendix page 328) for snack.

Group Time

Read *Froggy Gets Dressed* by Jonathan London. After reading, encourage the children to talk about what happened at the beginning, middle, and the end of the story. After discussing the story, re-read it to the children, inviting them to put their hands on their heads when the word "hat" is read, or to pretend zipping their coats when the word "zip" is read.

Learning Center Ideas

Math: Set out a laundry basket holding pairs of mittens and socks for the children to practice matching and sorting.
Science: Place a thermometer outside the window, making sure a red line is visible at the 32 degree mark. Encourage the children to check the temperature each day. Keep track of how many days the thermometer goes above the red line, and how many days it stays below.
Sensory: Put real snow or ice cubes in the Sensory Table for the children to explore. Encourage the children to describe how each substance melts.

Additional Activities

Movement: Invite the children to play "Simon Says" using paper or foam snowflakes.
Outside: Encourage the children to use snow blocks to build forts in the snow.
Rhythm and Rhyme: Sing "The Winter Clothes Song" (see appendix page 327) and suit their actions to the words.

Winter Olympics

STORY TIME

Figure Skating in Action by Kate Calder

Snowboarding in Action by Bobbie Kalman

TRANSITION

Play "The Star Spangled Banner" in between activities, so the children learn to recognize it. When the song is playing, invite the children to stop what they are doing, clean up, and sit down. Then they are ready for the next activity.

SNACK

Serve the children Olympic Energy Treats (see appendix page 327). Explain to the children that Olympic athletes will often eat a snack to give them energy to do their best when they compete.

Group Time

Begin by asking the children to describe what they know about the Olympics. If the children are not familiar with the Olympics, explain to them how the Olympics are a group of special games that take place every two years, either in the summer or the winter. Talk with the children about how in the Olympics, like in any game, there are rules to follow. Today the children will have an opportunity to participate in some Olympic activities (see below). With the children, come up with a set of rules for the Classroom Olympics, such as:

> *Do your best.*
> *Be a good sport.*
> *Take turns.*
> *Have fun.*

Classroom Olympics

Sock Skating: Invite the children to remove their shoes and slide around on their socks, pretending to be Olympic skaters.

Ice Hockey: Set out two cones, and have the children take turns using a broom (hockey stick) to shoot a soft ball (puck) between the two cones.

Luge: Set out little scooters for the children to wheel around on their stomachs, as though they are in a luge competition.

Ice Dancing: Explain to the children that ice dancing is ice skating to music. Turn on several different kinds of music (classical, jazz, country, and so on), encouraging the children to ice dance to the different rhythms. After dancing, ask the children how each kind of music made them feel.

Additional Activities

Art/Literacy: Invite each child to dictate a sentence to you about one thing they did at the Classroom Olympics. Copy each child's sentence onto a sheet of paper, and invite the children to draw pictures of what the sentences describes. Write each child's name on the appropriate paper, and create a class book by stapling the pages together.

Rhythm and Rhyme: Teach the children to sing "The Olympic Song" (see appendix page 326) and fill in the blank with something people do in the Olympics.

Eyes

January 4th is Louis Braille's Birthday.

STORY TIME

Brown Bear, Brown Bear, What Do You See? by Bill Martin Jr.

Eyes, Nose, Fingers, and Toes by Judy Hindley

Fish Eyes: A Book You Can Count On by Lois Ehlert

Googly Eyes: Dinosaur Sleep by Jessica Nickelson

TRANSITION

Ask the children to line up by eye color. Tell one group at a time to move to the next activity.

Group Time

Before this Group Time activity, take individual photos of the children's faces. Glue each photo to a piece of construction paper. For all the photos, cover all the features, except the eyes, with additional pieces of paper. Hold up one photo and invite the children to guess whose eyes they are. After each child guesses, lift up the additional pieces of paper to show the whole photo of the child's face. If there is time after the children have guessed all the faces, give each child a photo of his eyes and suggest that the children draw the rest of their facial features around the eyes. When done, display the pictures on the wall.

Learning Center Ideas

Dramatic Play: Provide eye charts and old glasses frames for the children to play eye doctor and pretend to give eye exams.

Math: Invite the children to sort blue and brown pompom "eyes" by color.

Science: Talk with the children about what a magnifying glass looks like and what it does. Provide the children with several colors of cellophane with which they can make magnifying glasses by gluing colored cellophane paper in between two magnifying glass-shaped patterns.

Additional Activities

Movement: To begin this activity, choose one child to stand on one side of the room, and ask everyone else to stand in a row on the opposite side of the room. The child standing by himself is "IT." When you say, "Eyes closed," IT closes his eyes. The rest of the class tries to move up to tag IT. When you say, "Eyes open," IT opens his eyes. The other children must freeze before IT opens his eyes and sees them move. If IT sees someone move, that child must go back to the beginning and start over. The first person to sneak up and tag IT is the next IT.

Outside: Go on a nature walk. After the walk, invite the children to name five things they saw. Make a list of all these things and hang it on the wall.

Small Group: Play I Spy with the children. Ask one child to pick something in the room and give one hint, such as, "I spy something green." The other children guess what it is.

Snowflakes

STORY TIME

Don't Wake Up the Bear by Marjorie Dennis Murray

Dream Snow by Eric Carle

First Snow Day by Arnold Emily McCully

The Jacket I Wear in the Snow by Shirley Neitzel

Names for Snow by Judi K. Beach

Snow by Uri Shulevitz

Snowy Day by Ezra Jack Keats

The Tiny Snowflake by Arthur Ginolfi

TRANSITION

Invite the children to recite the "Snowflakes" rhyme on appendix page 327. As they are reciting it, point to one or two children to quietly line up or move to the next activity.

SNACK

Make Snowflake Pancakes (see appendix page 328).

Group Time

Bring in a basket of clothes. Hold up the items one at a time and ask the children to sort the clothes by season.

Learning Center Ideas

Art: Invite the children to twist together silver or white pipe cleaners to make a special snowflake. Show the children how to add beads to the ends of each pipe cleaner and twist them to make each one special and different. Using string, help the children hang their snowflakes from the ceiling for fun winter decorations.

Literacy: Write uppercase and lowercase letters on two sets of cardboard cutout snowflakes. Invite the children to match the lowercase letters with the uppercase letters. (Use only 4–5 letters at a time.)

Math: Number cutout snowflakes from 1–5 (or 1–10 depending on the age and ability of the children) and encourage the children to put the snowflakes in numerical order.

Additional Activities

Movement: This is a seasonal movement game. Invite the children to pantomime the different actions for each season:

    winter—throwing snowballs;
    spring—hopping like a bunny;
    summer—pretending to swim; and
    fall—pretending to rake leaves.

Call out a season, and have the children to act out the action for that season.

Outdoors: Take black construction paper outside for the children to catch snowflakes as they fall. On the black paper, they can observe how different the flakes are from one another.

Rhythm and Rhyme: Sing "I'm a Little Snowflake" (see appendix page 325) with the children.

Snow Friends

STORY TIME

All You Need for a Snowman by Alice Schertle
Frosty the Snowman by Jack Rollins
Snowballs by Lois Ehlert
The Snow Ghosts by Leo Landry
Snowman by Raymond Briggs

TRANSITION

Invite the children to recite "I Have a Little Snow Friend" on appendix page 325. As the children recite the rhyme, point to a few of children, inviting them to line up or move to the next activity.

SNACK

Make Snow Friend Snacks (see appendix page 328).

Group Time

Invite the children to act out the "Five Little Snowmen" fingerplay (see appendix page 324).

Learning Center Ideas

Art: Set out several pre-cut circles of felt, in three different sizes, as well as smaller orange triangles, small black circles, and other shapes, and invite the children to glue them to a separate sheet of construction paper in the shape of a snow person.

Art: Provide paint, brushes, markers, crayons, and other art materials and suggest that the children make snow friend pictures.

Math: Set out several snow people shapes with one of several differently colored pairs of buttons glued to each. Provide matching buttons and encourage the children to match the buttons.

Additional Activities

Movement: Select one child to be The Sun, and another child to be Winter Freeze. Tell the rest of the children that they will be Snow Friends. The Snow Friends run around, avoiding Winter Freeze. When Winter Freeze touches a child, that child must stand frozen until The Sun can touch the child. Occasionally change which child is The Sun and Winter Freeze.

Rhythm and Rhyme: Attach small bells to the ends of pipe cleaners for the children to shake at they sing or listen to "Frosty the Snowman" on a tape or CD.

Small Group: Introduce the children to the concepts of small, medium, and large. Help the children cut out pre-traced large, medium, and small white construction paper circles. Invite them to add a face, fabric scarf, and craft stick arms to make snow people.

Mittens

STORY TIME

Andrew's Magnificent Mountain of Mittens by Deanne Lee Bingham
Froggy Gets Dressed by Jonathan London
The Hat by Jan Brett
Missing Mitten Mystery by Steven Kellogg
Missing Mittens by Stuart J. Murphy
The Mitten by Jan Brett
The Mitten by Alvin R. Tresselt
Three Little Kittens by Anna Alter
Three Little Kittens by Paul Galdone

SNACK

Make mitten sandwiches. Use cookie cutters to cut handprint shapes out of slices of cheese. Cut mitten shapes from different kinds of bread to make mitten sandwiches.

Group Time

Before Group Time, hide a number of different-colored mittens around the room. When the children gather for Group Time, ask them to find the mittens. Once the children find all the hidden mittens, help them sort the mittens by color. With the children's assistance, graph the different mittens' colors on a large poster board or chalk board.

Learning Center Ideas

Art: Provide construction paper mitten cutouts and suggest that the children decorate a matching pairs with markers, glue, felt scraps, and other art materials.

Math: Provide a number of different pairs of mittens for the children to sort and match, reinforcing the skills first practiced during Group Time.

Math: Set out a number of snowballs (cotton balls), and a number of laminated mitten shapes, each marked with a different numeral. Invite the children to place the matching number of snowballs onto the different laminated mittens.

Additional Activities

Movement: Play Drop the Mitten. Invite the children to sit around a circle. Choose one child to walk around behind the children, carrying a mitten. This child is "IT." IT drops the mitten quietly behind one of the sitting children, and then runs around the circle. The child behind whom the mitten was dropped gets up and chases IT until IT sits in the other child's place in the circle. If the child cannot catch IT before IT reaches the child's place in the circle, that child becomes the new IT. If the child catches IT, IT repeats the process again

Rhythm and Rhyme: Teach the children "The Mitten Rhyme" (see appendix page 325).

Ice

STORY TIME

Angelina Ice Skates by Katherine Holabird

Five Little Penguins Slipping on the Ice by Steve Metzger

Pearl's New Skates by Holly Keller

TRANSITION

Play music, inviting the children to dance around as it plays. Stop the music suddenly and tell the children to freeze. With a "magic snowflake wand" made of foam glued to a straw, dowel, or pencil, tap one or two children, unfreezing them to move to the next activity. Start the music again. When the music starts, everybody resumes dancing. Repeat until all the children have moved to the next activity.

SNACK

Put ice in a blender and chop it up (adult-only step). Help the children put ice into cups and add their preferred type of juice, making snow cones.

Group Time

Show the children pictures that relate to the concepts of hot or cold. Encourage the children to sort pictures based on whether they show something hot or something cold. As the class sorts the photos, attach them to separate pieces of construction paper labeled "Hot" or "Cold." Consider cutting the two pieces of paper into hot and cold shapes, such as a sun and a mitten.

Learning Center Ideas

Art: Before the children arrive, freeze paint mixed with water in ice cube trays, with a craft stick in each cube. Once the cubes are frozen, make them available for the children to paint with ice cubes.

Science: Ask the children where ice comes from. If they are not sure, explain that ice is frozen water. Help the children put different amounts of water in several cups, and take the cups to a predetermined location outside when the temperature is below freezing (32° F). Every 10 minutes, invite a few children to check on the progress of the water's freezing, taking note of the time and progress each time the cups are checked. Once all the ice is frozen, help the children tally the different lengths of time and make charts of the results on construction paper cut into igloo shapes. Talk with the children about their conclusions.

Additional Activities

Movement: Invite the children to slide along the floor in their stocking feet, pretending to ice skate.

Outdoors: Go on an ice hunt with the children. Ask them to find places outside with ice and record those locations on a clipboard. Ask the children to discuss the common and uncommon places where ice forms.

Rhythm and Rhyme: Play "Ring Around the Ice Rink" (see appendix page 326).

Small Group: Ask the children to think of words that rhyme with ice. Make a list of the words they say. Once there are a number of words on the board, invite the children to help you make up silly rhyming sentences: *The ice is nice. I eat rice, sitting on the nice ice.*

Letter *N*

STORY TIME

Good Night Moon by Margaret Wise Brown

The Napping House by Audrey Wood

Nathan and Nicholas Alexander by Lulu Delacre

The Nose Book by Al Perkins

Nuts to You by Lois Ehlert

TRANSITION

Invite the children to raise their hands if they can think of a word that ends with an *n* sound. Call on individual children. When they name a word that ends with an *n* sound, invite them to move to the next activity.

Group Time

Place a number of things throughout the classroom, the names of which start with the letter *n*. Ask the children to find these objects and bring them to the Group Time area. Put the objects into a large bag or box that is out of sight. Select one of the objects and give the children clues about the object. Ask the children to guess which object you have selected. Suggestions for clues include "I have something that starts with the letter *n*. You use it to wipe your face when you are eating." When the children correctly guess the object, take it out of the box or bag.

Learning Center Ideas

Art: Provide buttons, string, and other objects for the children to make necklaces.

Literacy: Provide newspapers for the children to look at in the Reading Corner. Suggest that they highlight all the words that start with *n*.

Literacy: Provide crayons, markers, and notebooks on which the children can practice printing the letter *n* and different *n* words, such as *nose, no, nut,* and *nap*.

Additional Activities

Movement: Place napkins on the floor around the room, making sure there are the same number of napkins and children. Play music, inviting the children to dance around the room. Occasionally stop the music. When the music stops, tell the children that they must find a napkin on which to stand.

Rhythm and Rhyme: Teach the children to sing "The Letter *N* Song" (see appendix page 325).

Small Group: Read the story *Good Night Mr. Night* by Dan Yaccarino. Afterwards, give the children black construction paper and toothbrushes dipped in white paint, so the children can flick white specks of paint on the paper shapes, making stars.

Pajama Party

Prior to Pajama Day, invite the children to wear cozy pajamas and bring blankets and pillows to school.

STORY TIME

Are You Ready for Bed? by Jane Johnson
Good Night, Gorilla by Peggy Rathmann
Good Night, Moon by Margaret Wise Brown
Good Night, Mr. Night by Dan Yaccarino
Good Night, Sleep Tight, Don't Let the Bed Bugs Bite by Diane deGroot
Good Night, Spot by Eric Hill
How Do Dinosaurs Say Good Night? by Jane Yolen
In the Night Kitchen by Maurice Sendak

TRANSITION

Cut out a number of star shapes, printing a direction on the back of each one (see appendix page 329). Put the stars in a jar, and invite the children to pick a star and follow the star's direction before moving to the next activity.

SNACK

Give the children a bedtime snack of graham crackers and milk. Decorate graham crackers with chocolate frosting. Add little frosting decorator stars.

Group Time

Invite the children to name events and activities that occur throughout the day. Explain to the children that if the named activity or event occurs during the day, the children should sit up straight. If the activity or event named happens at night, the children should pretend to sleep.

Learning Center Ideas

Art: Provide black fingerpaint with which the children can paint a nightscape. When the paint dries, invite the children to glue paper moons and sticker stars to their nightscapes.
Math: Help each child cut an 8 ½" x 11" sheet of paper into four pieces and staple them together for a book. Help them mark each page with a consecutive number of sticker stars.

Additional Activities

Game: Suggest that the children play Flashlight Tag. Turn off the classroom lights, and put on music. The children dance in the dark. From time to time, shine the flashlight beam around the room. Whomever the flashlight beam shines on must freeze until the beam touches them again.
Rhythm and Rhyme: Invite the children to sing "Good Night, Girls and Boys" (see appendix page 324).
Small Group: Read *Good Night, Moon.* After reading the book, encourage the children to make their own books: Good Night, _____. Help the children write the names of objects they can say good night to, and encourage them to draw pictures of those objects. Once all the children complete their pages, staple the pages together in a class book.

Penguins

STORY TIME

Busy Penguins by John Schindel
Five Little Penguins Slipping on the Ice by Steve Metzger
Penguin Pete by Marcus Pfister
Plenty of Penguins by Sonia W. Black
Tackylocks and the Three Bears by Helen Lester

TRANSITION

Encourage the children to waddle like penguins as they move from one activity to the next.

SNACK

Make penguin food for snack by mixing fish crackers and raisins, which will help your little "penguins" waddle fast.

Group Time

Using the Penguin Facts on appendix page 329, talk with the children about penguins. Ask the children to compare penguins and other birds, naming similarities and differences. Record their responses. Read *Penguin Pete* by Marcus Pfister.

Learning Center Ideas

Art: Provide art materials for children to make penguin pictures. Help the children display their penguins on a bulletin board covered with wax paper or aluminum foil "ice."

Math: Before this activity, make several outlines of penguins in various sizes, labeling each with a different number, making sure the size of the number is consistent with the size of the penguin (for example, put the 1 on the smallest penguin, and the 9 on the largest penguin). Glue a paper cup to each penguin cutout. Make several small fish cutouts, and laminate them for durability. Tell the children that penguins love to eat fish, and invite them to put the correct number of fish in each penguin's cup.

Sensory: If available, put snow in the Sensory Table, and invite the children to explore it.

Additional Activities

Movement: Encourage the children to chant "Penguins High, Penguins Low" (see appendix page 326) and suit their actions to the words. Male penguins and female penguins take turns caring for their eggs and penguin babies.

Rhythm and Rhyme: Sing "I'm a Little Penguin" with the children (see appendix page 325).

Soup

On the previous day, ask all the children to bring in one can of coup. Be sure to have extra cans in case children forget to bring in a can.

STORY TIME

Chicken Soup with Rice by Maurice Sendak
Growing Vegetable Soup by Lois Ehlert
Hammer Soup by Ingrid Schubert
Seaweed Soup by Stuart J. Murphy
Slop Goes the Soup by Pamela D. Edwards
Stone Soup by Jon J. Muth

TRANSITION

Invite the children to recite "Stirring Soup" on appendix page 327. After reciting the rhyme, encourage the children to name words that start with that letter. Once a child has named a word that starts with that letter, she moves to the next activity.

SNACK

Show the children how to hollow out rolls to make bread bowls. Heat up chili or soup and serve in the bowls with crackers.

Group Time

Gather all the cans of soup. Count and sort each can by holding them up before the children and separating them by type. Later, when preparing the soups, heat two at a time, encouraging the children to try each type. After the children try each soup, invite them to put their spoons in the can of the soup they prefer. Once all the children have tried each type of soup, count the spoons to see which soup your class likes the best.

Learning Center Ideas

Art: Provide soup can labels, pages of construction paper, and glue for the children to create soup label books. Help the children staple their book pages together.

Blocks: Provide a number of empty soup cans for children to use as building blocks. **Note:** Smooth out or cover any rough or sharp edges on the cans.

Math: Write numbers on a few soup bowls and suggest that the children put the corresponding number of spoons in each bowl.

Additional Activities

Project: Ask each child to bring in a can of her favorite soup. After this unit is over, donate any extra cans to a local food pantry.

Rhythm and Rhyme: Sing "The Soup Song" with the children (see appendix page 327). If you put a *b* in the song, think of words that start with the letter *b* to put in the soup, such as bacon, beans, broccoli, and so on.

Polar Bears

GENERAL DAILY PLAN

Follow the Polar Bears by Sonia W. Black

Little Polar Bear: Just Like Father by Hans de Beer

Polar Bear, Polar Bear What Do You Hear? by Bill Martin, Jr.

TRANSITION

Ask the children to walk like polar bears to the next activity.

Group Time

Introduce the children to polar bears using the Polar Bear Facts on appendix page 329, and showing them photos of polar bears. Invite the children to imagine they are polar bears, pretending to slide down a snow hill, using their backs like sled, or to pretending to swim and float on small icebergs.

Learning Center Ideas

Art: Make a mixture of ⅓ cup white glue and 2 cups white, non-menthol shaving cream. Let the children paint with this mixture on construction paper, making polar bear pictures.

Art/Sensory: Provide ping-pong balls on which the children can draw polar bear faces. Invite the children to float their new "polar bears" in the Water Table.

Fine Motor: Invite the children to make polar bears from white playdough (see appendix page 328).

Math: Make several black, white, and brown pompoms (different species of bear) available for the children to set out in different patterns. Suggest that one child make a pattern, and challenge another to match it.

Additional Activities

Movement: Play Brown Bear, Brown Bear, Polar Bear. Invite the whole class to sit in a circle, except for the child chosen to be the "Polar Bear." "Polar Bear" walks around the outside of the circle, tapping children and saying "Brown Bear." When "Polar Bear" taps a child and says "Polar Bear," the tapped child must jump up and chase "Polar Bear" around the circle, trying to tag "Polar Bear" before he sits in that child's spot. If the tagged child can't catch "Polar Bear," the tagged child becomes the new "Polar Bear," and the game starts again.

Rhythm and Rhyme: Sing "The Polar Bear Song" with the children (see appendix page 326).

Spinning Yarns

STORY TIME

Invite the children to sit in a circle. When everyone is seated, start telling a story, using a phrase such as, "Danny had a pet dinosaur named Fred," "Amber found a magic wand," "Johnny heard a loud crash," "Once there was a beautiful princess," and so on. After starting the story, roll a ball of yarn to another child, asking her to add a little to the story. As the child tells her part of the story, write it down. When the child is done with her part of the story, have her hold the end of the yarn and roll the ball to someone else. Repeat the process until everyone has contributed a part to the story.

Group Time

Invite the children to sit in a circle. Tell the children that they are special individuals, with their own stories and life experiences. Ask the children to think about what makes them special. Then, roll a ball of yarn to one of the children, inviting her to say what makes her special. After the child answers the question, invite the child to roll the ball of yarn to another child. Repeat the process until each child has had a turn. The yarn should then have crossed over itself many times. Explain to the children that even though each child has her own life story, each child is connected to the other, just like the yarn.

Learning Center Ideas

Art: Set out glue, construction paper, and several different types of yarn so the children can experiment with making yarn collages.

Fine Motor: Provide several long lengths of unrolled yarn for the children to practice rolling into balls.

Fine Motor: Set out a number of paper plates with several 2" slits cut from the edges in. Invite the children to weave yarn through the slits. If the children weave the yarn tightly and pull the slits up they can make a basket.

Math: Set out several 12" pieces of yarn and invite the children to use the pieces of yarn to measure different objects in the classroom.

Additional Activities

Movement: Play Yarn Limbo. Turn on upbeat music, and ask two children to hold a piece of yarn at waist height. Invite the other children to try to go under the yarn without touching it. Ask the children holding the yarn to lower it about 2" after everyone has gone under it. Keep going until the children lose interest.

Movement: Use yarn to tie two friends together at the knees. Invite them to try to walk and do other things. Explain that they must cooperate with each other to get things done.

Outside: Help the children to place several very small pieces of yarn on the ground outside. Explain to them that birds like to use yarn in their nests. Watch as birds pick up the yarn.

Polka Dots

On the previous day, remind the children to wear polka dots for this day.

STORY TIME

Polka Dot Moon by Carolyn Moe
Polka Dot, Polka Dot by William Joyce
Ten Black Dots by Donald Crews

Group Time

Before Group Time, cut red, blue, green, and yellow circles from construction paper for the children to sit on. Place the dots in a circle. When the children come in, invite them to look at the color of the dot they are sitting on. Read the rhyme, "Dots," on appendix page 324, and ask the children to follow the instructions.

Learning Center Ideas

Art: Provide colored plates. Give the children sequins, pompoms, bingo markers, hole punches, and dot stickers to make dot collages on the plates.

Literacy: Provide each child with large construction paper cutouts of the letters in their names. Encourage the children to decorate the letters of their names by tracing and coloring them, or attaching circle sequins or foam circles to the letters.

Math: Provide a number of poker chips for the children to sort and count.

Additional Activities

Games: Provide a number of games that involve dots (colored dot dominoes, tic-tac-toe with different colored poker chip markers) for the children to play.

Movement: Play Musical Dots. Set several dots on the floor. Play music, inviting the children to walk around the circle of dots. Occasionally, stop the music. When the music stops, the children should find a dot to stand on. There should be enough dots for each child to stand on as the music stops. When putting the music back on, encourage the children to change the way they move around the circle, such as hop around the dots, skip around the dots, and so on.

Outside: Set out several paths of dots in different colors, inviting the children to follow the different paths. Be sure to make the paths intersect at different locations.

Rhythm and Rhyme: Teach the children to recite "The Polka Dot Rhyme" (see appendix page 326) and suit their actions to the words.

Bear Snores On by Karma Wilson

STORY TIME

Bear Wants More by Karma Wilson
Bear's New Friend by Karma Wilson

TRANSITION

Invite the children to lie down and snore loudly, pretending to sleep. Move through the children and tap a sleeping child on the head. After tapping a child, invite him to wake up, sneeze like a bear, and move to the next activity.

SNACK

Make a "stew" of honey nut cereal, popcorn, and pretzels. Serve with hot chocolate for snack.

Group Time

Read *Bear Snores On*. Invite the children to talk about what happens in the story, asking them to describe the book's events in the order in which they happened. Encourage the children to act out the story's scenes as they retell them.

Learning Center Ideas

Art: Invite the children to draw their favorite scenes from *Bear Snores On*.

Art: Fold a brown sheet of construction paper in half, and cut a semicircle out of it, making sure the fold remains attached at the top of the semicircle, and acts as a flap. Give each child a semicircle, explaining how the shape resembles a cave entrance. Help the children glue the cave entrance to a piece of black construction paper. Turn the cave entrance's flap down and encourage the children to sponge paint the paper with white to make snow. Once the snow dries, invite the children to draw bear shapes inside the cave.

Additional Activities

Movement: Place a toy tea kettle at the center of the room. Put on some invigorating music, and encourage the children to dance around the kettle. Occasionally, stop the music, instructing the children to lie down, pretending to sleep and snore. When you start the music again, invite the children to jump and dance again.

Rhythm and Rhyme: Sing "The Snore Song" (see appendix page 327) with the children.

The Baker's Batter

STORY TIME

Froggy Bakes a Cake by Jonathan London

Maisy Makes Gingerbread by Lucy Cousins

Pancakes, Pancakes by Eric Carle

Spot Bakes a Cake by Eric Hill

Walter the Baker by Eric Carle

TRANSITION

Say "The Cake Rhyme" on appendix page 323, adding a different child's name in to this rhyme. Encourage that child to name a kind of cake she would like to bake, and then move to the next activity.

SNACK

Provide the children with breadstick dough to shape into the first letters of their names. Bake the letters (adult-only step), cool, decorate, and eat.

Group Time

Write the words to "Pat a Cake" on sentence strips and on the pocket chart. Leave out the missing words as indicated (see appendix page 326), and substitute a word from the list of baked goods (see appendix page 328). Include the letter the cooked item starts with in the second blank in the rhyme (*b* for bread, *p* for pie, for example). Encourage the children to think of items they would like to bake.

Learning Center Ideas

Blocks: Provide several empty cake mix boxes for the children to build with.

Book Corner: Add cookbooks to the other bakery and nursery rhyme books for the children to explore in the book corner.

Dramatic Play: Provide several baking materials (rollers, cookie sheets, oven mitts, baker's hats) for the children's play. Encourage them to bake playdough doughnuts, cakes, and other bakery items.

Sensory: Provide flour, salt, spoons, cups, and bowls in the Sensory Table for the children to explore.

Additional Activities

Field Trip: Take the children on a field trip to a bakery.

Movement: Encourage the children to pretend they are all pretzel dough, twisting into the shapes of different letters of the alphabet. Consider having the children choose partners for this activity, so one child will act as the baker, and the other as the dough.

Rhythm and Rhyme: Using the "Pat a Cake" rhyme on the pocket chart from the Group Time activity, invite the children to clap the rhythm of the rhyme, or tap the rhyme's rhythm with drums, sticks, and other rhythm instruments.

Small Group: Make an ABC book. Set out markers, crayons, and construction paper, inviting each child to draw a picture that starts with a different letter of an item that a baker might bake (see list of baked goods on page 328).

There Was an Old Woman

GENERAL DAILY PLAN

STORY TIME

Tell the children the following rhyme.

> There was an old woman who
>   lived in a shoe.
> She had so many children she
>   didn't know what to do.
> She gave them some broth,
> She gave them some bread,
> Then she gave them a kiss and
>   sent them off to bed.

SNACK

Serve apple juice (broth) and bread and butter for snack.

Group Time

Before Group Time, print the rhyme on sentence strips for the pocket chart. When the children gather for Group Time, invite them to say the rhyme together. As the children recite each word of the rhyme, point to the words on the pocket chart. Encourage the children to clap out the rhythm of the rhyme as they recite it.

Learning Center Ideas

Dramatic Play: Provide large cardboard boxes fitted together and painted to resemble a shoe. Suggest that the children use them to act out the rhyme.

Literacy: Using the pocket chart version of the rhyme, set out note cards with each word copied onto them that the children use to match the words on the pocket chart.

Math: Make several shoe-shaped construction paper cutouts and give dot stickers to the children. Encourage the children to draw faces on the stickers and attach them to the shoe patterns, counting the number of stickers as they go.

Sensory: Make a number of different types of shoes (sandals, boots, shoes with buckles, Velcro, laces) available for the children to try on and play with.

Additional Activities

Movement: Inflate a Mylar balloon for every four or five children. Have the children toss the balloons in the air, and encourage them to tap the balloons back and forth between one another, seeing how long they can keep them from hitting the ground. Held the children count the number of times in a row they can tap the balloons.

Rhythm and Rhyme: Invite the children to recite the old woman rhyme, substituting different words for shoe, such as boot, slipper, sandal, and so on.

Letter *O*

STORY TIME

Old MacDonald Had a Farm by Carol Jones

Ostrich by Patricia Whitehouse

Over in the Meadow by Ezra Jack Keats

Owl Babies by Martin Waddell

TRANSITION

When the children are sitting in a circle, put on some music, and hand one child an orange. Tell this child to pass the orange around the circle. Occasionally, stop the music, and let the child holding the orange move to the next activity.

SNACK

Invite the children to help squeeze orange juice and serve it as part of snack.

Group Time

Show the children several photos of ostriches and owls, encouraging them to describe the birds. Point out that both bird names begin with the letter *o*. Write several descriptive details about the birds (providing some if necessary). Encourage the children to use the details to explain the differences between the two birds. For example: Owls fly and ostriches do not fly. Ostriches are big and owls are small. Owls are awake at night and ostriches are awake during the day.

Learning Center Ideas

Blocks: Provide blocks for the children to create obstacle courses for miniature cars.

Dramatic Play: Set out old glasses frames, eye charts, and other materials and invite the children to play that they are in an optometrist's office.

Fine Motor: String *o*-shaped cereal on strings. Put the strings on a bush or tree outside that is near a window where the children can watch birds eat the cereal.

Sensory: Make several bottles filled with oil, water, and confetti available for the children to observe. **Note:** Close the caps tightly and then seal with duct tape.

Additional Activities

Movement: Explain the concept of obstacle courses to the children, and invite them to make an obstacle course in the classroom.

Outside: Give the children several pieces of chalk, encouraging them to draw the letter *o* on the playground. If it is snowy outside, add food coloring to spray bottles filled with water, and invite the children to spray the letter *o* in the snow.

Rhythm and Rhyme: Recite "The O Rhyme" with the children (see appendix page 325).

Small Group: Encourage the children to think of words that begin with the letter *o*. Copy down the words as the children think of them. Once the children have thought of a number of *o* words, invite them to make up silly sentences with as many of the words as possible. Write the sentences down on poster board, and invite the children to draw pictures of their silly sentences, "Oscar the owl ate olives at the ocean."

Go, Super Bowl

The day before, remind the children to dress up in numbered shirts or football jerseys. If a child does not have a number shirt, you can easily add a number to any shirt with masking tape.

STORY TIME

My Football Book by Gail Gibbons
NFL Big and Small by DK Publishing
NFL Colors by DK Publishing
T Is for Touchdown by Brad Herzog

TRANSITION

Invite the children to line up according to the numbers on their shirts. Call out numbers, letting children wearing that number move to the next activity.

SNACK

Give each child one uncooked piece of biscuit dough, encouraging the children to shape their biscuits to resemble footballs. Bake the biscuits as directed (adult-only step).

Group Time

Ask the children if they are familiar with football. If some children are, invite them to explain the basic rules and idea behind the sport, helping the children to clarify various points where they are unclear. Specifically, explain to the children that in football, the field is 100 yards long, and that the players have to throw or run the ball toward the end zone. To illustrate this, take 10 steps, saying a multiple of 10 with each step, until you reach 100. When you reach 100, jump up and down and say "touchdown." After illustrating this to the children, invite them all to repeat the process with you.

Learning Center Ideas

Math: Set out several numbered helmets and footballs, inviting the children to match the footballs with the helmets.
Sensory: Make brown playdough available for the children to make football shapes.

Additional Activities

Movement: Invite the children to recite "Go, Team, Go!" (see appendix page 324) and suit their actions to the words.
Outside: Set out several sponges cut in the shape of footballs and encourage the children to throw them into laundry baskets. Help the children count how many passes they can get into the basket.
Small Group: Provide each child with a small rectangle of cardboard with several holes punched on one of the long sides, and a length of shoelace. Show the children how to string the lace through the holes to resemble the lacing on a football.

Learn with Cans

The day before, ask each child to bring in one or two cans of food. When the day is finished, donate the cans to a local food pantry. Have several spare cans available for children who forget to bring cans with them.

STORY TIME

I Can Do It! by Jana Novotny Hunter
I Can Fly by Ruth Krauss
Look What I Can Do by Jose Aruego
Recycle! by Gail Gibbons

SNACK

Invite the children to help prepare some of the canned foods they brought into class that day.

Group Time

Before Group Time, attach several small pictures (horses, cars, flowers, and so on) to little squares of paper. Write the name of the object on the back of the square, and put the squares into a tin can. At Group Time, invite the children to pull the squares out of the can. When a child pulls a square from the can, encourage the children to say the sound the word starts with, name a word that rhymes with the image on the square, and clap the syllables of the object's name.

Learning Center Ideas

Literacy/Math: Provide several cans of food (many cans of three or four different brands or kinds of food) with their labels still on them. Write each brand or kind of food at the top of separate pieces of construction paper and place the papers on the floor in a grid. Invite the children to sort the remaining cans in each part of this grid, making an object graph. When all the cans are in the correct place, ask the children which type of food has the most cans, and the least.

Math: Set out a scale so the children can weigh the cans.

Additional Activities

Rhythm and Rhyme: Encourage the children to sing "I Can Do Whatever I Try" (see appendix page 324).

Small Group: If it is close to January 24th, tell the children that it is National Compliment Day. Explain that the children can compliment one another by using *can* in a sentence. For example, they can say to another child, "_____, you *can* color very well," and so on. Ask the children to think of several compliments that they can give other children. Write them several times on slips of paper, and keep them at your desk. Give each child a can and a piece of paper that says, "The *Can* Can," and invite the children to decorate the piece of paper. When they are finished, help the children glue the paper to the outside of their cans. Through the day, if a child compliments another child, put a copy of that compliment slip in the child's can. At the end of the day, invite the children to listen as you read the slips of paper.

Nose for Newspapers

STORY TIME

The Furry News: How to Make a Newspaper by Loreen Leedy
The Paperboy by Dav Pilkey

TRANSITION

Have the children gather in a single group to play "I Spy," using rolled sheets of newspaper. Give one child the rolled newspaper and tell him to point it towards group of children, say, "I spy," and describe one child from the group. The rest of the class guesses which child he is describing, and the child who correctly guesses who is being described moves to the next activity.

Group Time

Bring in several food ads from newspapers and magazines. Show the ads to the children and explain that the ads are trying to sell the products featured in them. Hold up each ad individually, and ask the children what they think it is selling, and whether it makes them want to eat the food advertised. Afterwards, set up a graph with two columns, one labeled "healthy" and the other "unhealthy." Ask the children to tape the ads of each food on the side they think describes it best.

Learning Center Ideas

Art: Set out several sheets of newspaper, sets of paints, and paintbrushes for the children to paint with. After the paint dries, invite the children to cut the newspaper into interesting shapes.

Art: Set out several newspapers, inviting the children to cut out and glue together different pictures and comics.

Literacy: Give each child one page of the local newspaper. Invite the children to look through the pages and highlight the first letter of their names when they see the letter. Encourage the children to look for other letters from their names as well.

Additional Activities

Rhythm and Rhyme: Roll a newspaper into a telescope for each child. The children use their telescopes to follow directions of "The Telescope Rhyme" (see appendix page 327).

Small Group: Give each child a sheet of newspaper. Show the children how to fold the paper into hat shapes. When each child has made a hat, set out feathers, buttons, and foam shapes, and encourage them to decorate their new hats.

Kangaroo Capers

Prior to this activity, review the list of Kangaroo Facts (see appendix page 329).

STORY TIME

Does a Kangaroo Have a Mother Too? by Eric Carle

Elmer and the Kangaroo by David McKee

Norma Jean, Jumping Bean by Joanna Cole

Where Are You, Blue Kangaroo? by Emma Chichester Clark

TRANSITION

Encourage the children to hop like kangaroos as they line up or move to the next activity.

SNACK

Give each child a piece of pita bread (also called pocket bread). Set out several kinds of cheeses, meats, lettuce, tomatoes for children to make their own sandwiches.

Group Time

Before Group Time, make a large construction paper kangaroo with a large pocket. Put several cutout shapes with the names of the shapes written on one side of the cutout in the kangaroo pocket. At Group Time, invite each child to pull a shape out and try to identify it. After the children name all the different shapes, use the pouch to introduce and practice numbers and letters.

Learning Center Ideas

Art: Set out brown markers, crayons, and paints and brushes for the children to create kangaroo pictures.

Blocks: Set out blocks and several different plastic animals with which the children can build zoos.

Gross Motor: Tape large lengths of bubble wrap to the floor and invite the children to jump on and pop the bubbles.

Additional Activities

Rhythm and Rhyme: Write the words to "Hopping High, Hopping Low" on sentence strips and in the pocket chart (see appendix page 324). Encourage the children to clap out the rhythm. Give the children word cards with the words from the rhyme, and invite them to match the word cards to the words in the rhyme. Suggest that the children act out "Hopping High, Hopping Low."

Small Group: Make a concentration board with four pockets across and four pockets down, using library pockets and tag board. Make two sets of eight numbered cards, putting one card face down in each pocket. Invite each child to come up to the tag board and take two cards out of the pockets as the other children look on. If the child pulls two matching cards, he gets to pull two more cards. If he does not pull matching cards, the next child gets a chance to pull two cards. Continue until all the cards are pulled from their pockets. This game can also be used to match uppercase and lowercase letters, colors, and sight words.

A Week of Days

STORY TIME

Cookie's Week by Cindy Ward

Max and Ruby's Week by Rosemary Wells

Today Is Monday by Eric Carle

Very Hungry Caterpillar by Eric Carle

Wednesday Is Spaghetti Day by Maryann Coccaby Leffler

TRANSITION

Invite the children to sit in a circle. Ask the children to name the day of the week. After the children say what day of the week it is, start walking around the circle, tapping each child on the head, and saying each day of the week in order. For instance, if it is a Monday, tap the first child and say, "Tuesday," and continue until you get to "Monday." When you get to Monday, the child you tap moves to the next activity.

SNACK

Set out a large bowl, and each day of the week fill it with a different snack: On Monday fill it with pretzel sticks, on Tuesday fish crackers, on Wednesday M&M's, on Thursday O-shaped cereal, and on Friday tiny marshmallows. At the end of the week, mix all the ingredients, serve some to each child, and eat.

Group Time

Before Group Time, make word cards for each day of the week. Encourage the children to name the days of the week. When the children name a weekday, hold up its word card, asking the children to help put them in order on a flannel board.

Learning Center Ideas

Math: Set out a calendar and several small squares with the numbers of the dates of each month on them. Invite the children to put numbers in order on the calendar. For younger children, let them match the numbers to a calendar with numbers on it. For older children, consider putting a blank calendar out, and encourage the children to put the numbers in the proper order.

Additional Activities

Outside: Invite the children to help you draw a large calendar grid with chalk on the playground. Encourage the children to walk through the days of the week physically so they can see how the days repeat through the course of the month.

Projects: Read *Today Is Monday* by Eric Carle. After finishing the book, give each child a sheet of paper that reads "On Monday, I...," and several crayons, markers, and other art materials. Invite them to make a drawing of something they did that day. Repeat this every day for a week. At the end of the week, help the children staple their pages together to make their own book of the week.

Rhythm and Rhyme: Sing "The Days of the Week" with the children (see appendix page 323).

Quirky Letter Q

STORY TIME

Cassie's Word Quilt by Faith Ringgold
Quick as a Cricket by Audrey Wood
Quiet by Paul Bright
A Quilt for Baby by Kim Lewis
The Very Quiet Cricket by Eric Carle

SNACK

Make quick bread. Explain to the children that quick bread is considered "quick" because, unlike other breads, when it is made, it does not have to rise. Use a box mix to make banana or another kind of quick bread, inviting the children to help measure the ingredients and stir. When the mix is ready, simply bake (adult-only step), let cool, and serve.

Group Time

Read *The Very Quiet Cricket* by Eric Carle. After finishing the book, ask the children some questions about the story, such as who was the story about? What happened first? Then what? What happened next? How did the story end?

Learning Center Ideas

Art: Set out several pieces of construction paper, markers, rickrack, fabric and felt pieces, and glue. Suggest that the children create quilt squares.
Art: Provide Q-tips, paint, and paper for the children to create paintings.
Literacy: Give the children newspapers and highlighters. Ask them to search for and highlight the letter *q* wherever they see it in the newspapers.

Additional Activities

Movement: Prior to activity, develop a list of words that begin with the letter *q*. Print the letters of the alphabet on individual index cards, making sure there is one letter *q* for each child, and two or three cards for every other letter of the alphabet. Mix up all the cards, then stand in front of the children, and slowly begin flipping the cards up one at a time. Before doing this, explain to the children that if a *q* card comes up, they are to remain quiet. If a card with a different letter comes up, the children say the first word they can think of that begins with that letter. After doing this, consider placing all the cards on the floor and turning on music to which the children can dance. Tell them that whenever the music stops, they have to find a *q* card to stand on. This is particularly helpful with teaching the children to differentiate between *b, d, g, p,* and *q.*
Rhythm and Rhyme: Invite the children to sing "The Loud and Quiet Song" (see appendix page 325) and suit their actions to the words.
Small Group: Open a deck of cards in front of the children, slowly turning over individual cards. Tell the children that they are looking for the queen. When a queen is turned over, invite the children to put their hands on their heads, fingers out, imitating a crown. As the activity progresses, consider adding different actions for other cards, like holding up five fingers whenever a five card is displayed.

Cozy Blankets

STORY TIME

Baby Duck and the Cozy Blanket by Amy Hest

Dinosaur's Binkit by Sandra Boynton

The Red Blanket by Eliza Thomas

The Red Woolen Blanket by Bob Graham

Tracy's Snuggly Blanket by Marc Brown

TRANSITION

Set out red, blue, yellow, and green felt pieces (blankets) for the children to sit on during Group Time. Call out a color type and invite the group of children sitting on that color to move to the next activity. Repeat this until all children have transitioned to the next activity.

Group Time

Provide each child with a small piece of flannel. Encourage the children to sing "The Blanket Song" (see appendix page 323), putting the piece of flannel on whichever body part is named.

Learning Center Ideas

Literacy: Set out a few small pieces of felt or flannel (blanket) with a different letter of the alphabet written on each and different small items that begins with the various letters. Suggest that the children put each item on the appropriate blanket.

Math: Challenge the children to match the correct number of teddy bear counters to the numeral on small pieces of felt or flannel.

Math: Set out several small pieces of red, green, yellow, and blue felt or flannel for the children to sort teddy bear counters on, separating the teddy bear counters by color.

Additional Activities

Rhythm and Rhyme: Write the words to "Roll Over" (see appendix page 326) on sentence strips and put them in the pocket chart. Point to each word as the children recite the rhyme. Put in a different number card as the number diminishes in each verse. Invite the children to lie down on a blanket to act out the song, and to clap the words' syllables as the children sing.

Small Group: Set out several fabric crayons and pieces of cloth, inviting the children to decorate a piece. When all children have decorated a piece of cloth, help the children glue them together to make a class quilt.

February

Calendar Time

During Calendar Time, introduce the month of February to the children. Look at the letters in the word *February.* Name each letter, and say the sound and other words that start with the sound. Whose name begins with the letter *f?* Do this for each letter in the word during calendar time throughout the month.

Monthly Organizer

MONTH-LONG CELEBRATIONS

National Wild Bird Feed Month
Black History Month
National Cherry Month
Healthy Heart Month

SPECIAL DAYS AND HOLIDAYS

February 2: Groundhog Day
February 5: Weather People Day
February 11: Thomas Edison's Birthday
February 12: National Lost Penny Day
February 14: Valentine's Day

GENERAL DAILY PLANS

Letter *V*
Red
Pink
Letter *R*
Hearts
Post Office
Froggy Bakes a Cake by
    Jonathan London
In My World by Lois Ehlert
Soapy Clean
Grocery Store
Letter *F*

USA
I Stay Healthy
Hospitals
Teeth
Blocks

Note: Please be sure to check for allergies before serving the snacks or doing any food-related activities.

National Wild Bird Feed Month

February is National Wild Bird Feed Month.

STORY TIME

Are You My Mother? by Philip D. Eastman
Beautiful Black Bird by Ashley Bryan
Bird Alphabet by Teresa McKemen
An Extraordinary Egg by Leo Lionni
Owl Babies by Martin Waddell

SNACK

Make Bird's Nests with the children using the recipe on appendix page 334 (**Safety Note:** Be sure to check for allergies).

Group Time

Invite the children to share what they know about birds: different types of birds, where birds go in the winter, what they eat, where they sleep, and so on. Write down their thoughts on a sheet of construction paper. Then ask the children if there is anything they want to know about birds. Copy this information onto a separate sheet of construction paper and put each sheet up on the wall.

Set out several chenille stems on which the children can string cereal and dried fruit, to make feeders for birds. Tie the ends together in the shape of a heart and hang the feeders outside near the classroom window as a special treat for the birds.

Learning Center Ideas

Art: Explain to the children that different birds prefer different kinds of seeds. Name a few examples for the children, and then invite them to help make a Birdseed Book of birds and their favorite types of seeds (see appendix page 330 for instructions).
Math: Set out a number of red and blue pompoms as though they were berries, encouraging the children to put them in patterns. Begin by making several simple patterns of your own, and inviting the children to copy them. Later, let the children make and copy their own patterns.
Sensory: Put bird seed in the sensory tub for the children to explore.

Additional Activities

Rhythm and Rhyme: Sing I'm a Little Cardinal" with the children (see appendix page 332). Then, play a counting and rhyming game with them. Choose five children from the class and give each one a number—one through five. Encourage all the children to recite "Five Little Birds" (see appendix page 331) and invite the five children with numbers to pretend they are the little birds. Give all children an opportunity to be birds.
Outside: Invite the children to make binoculars by taping two toilet paper tubes together. Take the children on a walk, encouraging them to use their binoculars to look for birds.

DAILY PLAN CONCEPT

Black History Month

February is Black History Month.

STORY TIME

Duke Ellington: The Piano Prince and His Orchestra by Andrea Davis Pinkney

Happy Birthday, Martin Luther King, Jr. by Jean Marzollo

A Kid's Guide to African American History by Nancy I. Sanders

A Picture Book of Jackie Robinson by David A. Adler

A Picture Book of Martin Luther King, Jr. by David A. Adler

A Weed Is a Flower: The Life of George Washington Carver by Aliki

Group Time

Introduce the children to Martin Luther King, giving a quick summary of his life. Possibly play a recording of or read to the children from King's "I Have a Dream Speech," and explain that it was King's dream to have everyone get along. Encourage the children to suggest what they can do to get along better, adding suggestions if the children are slow to respond. Write down a suggestion or two from each child and keep these on hand. After discussing this with the children, paint each child's hand in white paint and invite them to stamp their hands on sheets of paper, making dove shapes. Help the children cut out the dove shapes, and help them draw an eye or glue a plastic leaf to the beak. Have children dictate what they will do to help be peaceful. On each dove, help the children print a phrase or two from those they offered earlier as ways by which they can better get along. Hang the doves around the room as reminders to the children to be peaceful.

Learning Center Ideas

Benjamin Banneker Center: Introduce the children to Benjamin Banneker, explaining that he invented the first striking clock made totally in America. Set out several paper plates and construction paper cutouts of clock hands. Attach them to them the paper plates with paper fasteners. Help the children print the numbers of the different hours around the edge of the clock, or set out several numbers and help the children glue them to the plates.

George Washington Carver Center: Introduce the children to George Washington Carver, explaining that he was an agricultural chemist, which means he used plants to invent things. Set out several paper cups, soil, and seeds, and invite the children to plant and care for their seedlings.

Jackie Robinson Center: Set out a paper towel tube and a wad of paper, inviting the children to use them as a baseball and bat.

Dr. Mae Jemison Center: Explain to the children that Dr. Mae Jemison was the first black female astronaut. Invite the children to decorate pre-cut rocket shapes in honor of Dr. Jemison. Help the children glue pre-cut red and yellow rocket exhaust shapes to the bottom of the rocket. When the glue dries, give the children crayons and markers to draw on their rockets. Help the children glue photos of themselves to the windows on the rocket shapes.

National Cherry Month

February is National Cherry Month.

STORY TIME

Apple Banana Cherry by Joy Crowly
Cherries and Cherry Pits by Vera Williams

TRANSITION

Invite the children to recite the following rhyme, choosing one child (or a few children) at the end of the rhyme to move on to the next activity.

> *Cherry, cherry in the tree,*
> *Don't you dare fall down on me.*
> *Cherry, cherry, what to do,*
> *That cherry fell right down on you!*

Group Time

Before Group Time, make two flannel board cherry trees and cut out small red circles from felt. Print numbers from 1–10 on index cards. At Group Time, invite a child to draw a number card and put that many cherries on one of the cherry trees, then invite another to repeat the process. After both children have put their cherries on the trees, encourage the children to say which tree has the most cherries. Repeat this process until all the children have had a turn putting cherries on the tree.

Learning Center Ideas

Art: Add cherry extract to red easel paint and invite the children to make sweet smelling paintings with it.

Math: Set out several ½, ¼, and ⅛ slices of red construction paper circles that fit into aluminum pie tins, inviting the children to put pies together.

Sensory: Cherry Cake. Set out flour, one box cherry cake mix, one box of salt, and several measuring cups, spoons, pans, and so on, for the children to explore.

Rhythm and Rhyme: Invite the children to recite the following rhyme, naming numbers one through five through each verse.

> *Way up high*
> *At the top of the tree,*
> *____little cherry*
> *Fell down on me.*

Additional Activities

Movement: Before this activity, cut enough several large cherry shapes for each child in the class, and draw a triangle, square, or circle on each cherry. Make sure there is an equal number of each shape. To start the movement activity, set the cherries on the floor, invite the children to stand on each of them, and turn on some music. While the music is playing, let the children to walk from cherry to cherry. Occasionally shut off the music, encouraging the children to find a cherry with the same shape on it as the cherry on which they started.

Healthy Heart Month

February is Healthy Heart Month.

STORY TIME

All About You by Catherine and
Laurence Anholt
Bearobics by Vic Parker
Clap Your Hands by Lorinda Bryan
Cauley

TRANSITION

Put the numbers 1–10 on heart
shapes. Place the hearts in a bucket.
Select an exercise for the children to
do (toe touches, crunches, jumping
up and down, and so on), and tell
the children they will have to do the
activity between 1 and 10 times,
depending on the number on the
heart shapes. Call children up in
groups of five to pull numbered
hearts from the bucket. After each
group completes their exercise, invite
them to move on to the next activity,
and call up the next group.

SNACK

Talk to the children about heart-
healthy diets. Ask them what they
think are good foods for the heart,
then set out the following foods for
a good, heart healthy snack: flaked
tuna, cucumbers, plain low-fat
yogurt, and raisins.

Group Time

Introduce the children to the heart by showing drawings of hearts. Ask the
children if they know what hearts do, how large they are, where they are in
the body. Invite the children to hold up their fists, and tell them that their
hearts are approximately the size of their fists. Ask the children if they know
the rhythm of a heartbeat. Show children how they can feel their heartbeats
in their chests. Encourage them to put their ear up to a friend's chest and
listen to the heart beat. After listening, show the children where their pulse
points are and how they can feel their heartbeats in their necks and wrists.
Ask the children what they think happens to their heart beats after vigorous
activity. Invite them to feel their pulses, then run and jump around for a few
minutes, then check their pulses again and describe the difference in what
they feel. Begin clapping out a heartbeat, inviting the children to squeeze
their fists as though they were hearts beating. Tell the children their hearts
work very hard sending blood to all parts of our body. Show children how
much blood they have in their body by showing them eight pints of water.

Learning Center Ideas

Art: Set out several construction paper cutouts of a human body, some tubes
of glue, and several lengths of red and blue yarn. Invite the children to glue
the yarn to the body shape as though the yarn were veins.
Dramatic Play: Invite the children to pretend they are grocery shopping. Set
out several different plastic foods inviting the children to sort them based on
whether they are healthy or unhealthy. Set out two plastic bags, one with a
smiley face and one with a frown, into which the children can put the food.
Math: Cut out several heart shapes and copy numbers onto them. Also set
out several strands of blue and red yarn, encouraging the children to put
the appropriate number of yarn strands on each numbered heart.
Science: Set out a stethoscope for children to listen to their heartbeats.

Additional Activities

Outside: Show children how to walk briskly, moving their arms for heart
healthy walking.
Rhythm and Rhyme: Sing "My Heart Beats" (see appendix page 332).

Groundhog Day

February 2nd is Groundhog Day.

STORY TIME

Bear Shadow by Frank Asch
Fluffy Meets the Groundhog by Kate McMullan
Gregory's Shadow by Don Freeman
Groundhog at Evergreen Road by Susan Korman

TRANSITION

Shine a flashlight on one child, inviting him to line up. Repeat this with all children, encouraging them follow the flashlight beam without talking.

Group Time

Read *Gregory's Shadow* by Don Freeman. Invite the children to talk about what happened first, second, and last in the story. Print each sentence of the story on sheets of construction paper, making sure there are as many pages as children, and invite the children each to illustrate one page of the story.

Learning Center Ideas

Art: Make silhouettes of the children (see appendix page 330 for directions).
Math: Cut several matching shapes out of bright and black colored paper, gluing the black shape to a larger sheet of construction paper. Set out the colorful shapes, inviting the children to match them to the "shadow" shapes glued to the construction paper.
Science: Set out a flashlight and plastic animals, encouraging the children to experiment with making shadows.

Additional Activities

Movement: Play this game outside on a sunny day when the children can see their shadows. Give directions such as, "The groundhog says, 'Make your shadow jump," encouraging the children to follow the directions. As with Simon Says, occasionally give a direction without the preface "the groundhog says." Those children who follow the directions not prefaced with "the groundhog says" must "go back to sleep."
Rhythm and Rhyme: Sing "Where, Oh, Where Is the Little Groundhog?" (see appendix page 334).

Weather People Day

February 5th is National Weatherperson's Day.

STORY TIME

Cloudy with a Chance of Meatballs by Judith Barrett
Kippers Book of Weather by Mick Inkpen
Maisy's Seasons by Lucy Cousins
Weather by DK Publishing Staff
What Makes a Rainbow? by Betty Ann Schwartz

SNACK

Early in the day, ask the children if they know how ice is made. If not, explain the process, comparing the process to changes in weather through the course of a year. Tell them that their snack will be made from frozen juice. Invite the children to pour juice into paper cups and add a craft stick, making popsicles. Put them in the freezer, allowing enough time for all of them to freeze. When they are frozen, take them out and serve as a cold, healthy snack.

Group Time

Set out a basket of items used in all kinds of weather, such as an umbrella, boots, sunglasses, a swimming pool toy, mittens, and so on. Ask the children to identify which objects they would use in sunny weather, or take an item from the basket an item and ask what kind of weather the item is designed for.

Ask the children if they know what a meteorologist (weather forecaster) is. If so, encourage them to describe what a meteorologist does. If not, explain the job to the children. Show maps and globes to the children, explaining how weather systems move over the surface of the earth. Introduce the children to various words a weather person uses, such as temperature, sunny, cloudy, hot, cold, windy, snowy, and foggy. Cut a window out of an appliance box, and invite the children to take turns pretending to be a meteorologist giving a forecast on television.

Learning Center Ideas

Fine Motor: Set out a pair of tongs, a bowl, and several white cotton ball "snowflakes," encouraging the children to lift the cotton balls with the tongs and put them in the bowl.
Literacy: Invite each child to make a Weather Words book (see appendix page 330 for directions).
Math: Mix several pairs of mittens, encouraging the children to put them in matching pairs.
Sensory: Set several ice cubes in the water table, inviting the children to observe what happens to them as they sit alone, in cold water, or in hot water.

Additional Activities

Project: Set a thermometer just outside a classroom window. Each morning and afternoon, ask one child to check the temperature, and then add the number to a list. Repeat this for four weeks, charting the results as the weeks go by.
Rhythm and Rhyme: Sing, "I'm a Weather Person" with the children (see appendix page 332).

Happy Birthday, Thomas Edison!

Thomas Edison's birthday is February 11th. Invite each child to bring in a flashlight for this day of fun activities.

STORY TIME

Thomas Edison by Haydn Middleton
Young Thomas Edison by Michael Dooling

SNACK

Give the children a "light" snack. Peel a pear for each child, slicing it in half the long way, then bend a shoestring licorice on top of it as though it were the filament of a light bulb.

Group Time

Introduce the children to Thomas Edison and his invention, the light bulb. (You might want to introduce briefly the idea of inventions.) Tell the children that it took Edison years of trial and error research to produce the light bulb, and invite the children to name some things they had to try many times before they could do them. Write down what the children say, and invite them to show other children in the class how to do the thing that they once had trouble doing.

As a preface to this activity, explain to the children that Thomas Edison is responsible for more than 1,100 inventions. Set out lots of different objects and junk, inviting the children to create their own inventions. When the children are finished creating, ask them to name their inventions and describe what they do. Take a photo of the child with his invention and make a class book.

Learning Center Ideas

Art: As Thomas Edison was called "The Wizard of Light," invite the children to make a "Wizard of Light" hat by shaping a piece of construction paper into a cone shape, and then decorating it with any materials they wish.
Literacy: Provide flashlights for the children. Invite the children to play a flashlight rhyming game. Ask each child to turn the flashlight on if you say two words that rhyme. Say several pairs of rhyming and non-rhyming words, complimenting the children when they correctly turn on their flashlights after hearing a rhyming pair of words.

Additional Activities

Rhythm and Rhyme: Ask each child to take out his flashlight. With the lights out, sing "On Goes My Flashlight" with the children (see appendix page 332), inviting the children to turn on their flashlights when they sing the word "on." As a variation on this activity, print the song's words on sentence strips to hang up on a story chart, inviting the children to blink their flashlights to the rhythm of the rhyme, or to use the flashlights to highlight each word as it is said.

National Lost Penny Day

SPECIAL DAYS AND HOLIDAYS

February 12th is National Lost Penny Day.

STORY TIME

Abe Lincoln's Hat by Martha Brennen

Bennie's Pennies by Pat Brisson

The Hundred Penny Box by Sharon Bell Mathis

Let's Read About Abraham Lincoln by Sonja Black

The Penny Pot by Stuart J. Murphy

SNACK

Cut carrots into little slices, call them carrot pennies and serve them with a favorite vegetable dip.

Group Time

Introduce the children to President Abraham Lincoln. After giving the children a brief history, hand out a penny to each child, asking them whose face they see. Read *Let's Read About Abraham Lincoln* by Sonja Black.

Learning Center Ideas

Dramatic Play/Math: Introduce the children to the concept of pricing and value. Attach several cutout images of toys the children would likely enjoy to a flannel board. Add prices to the images, and give each child a certain amount of small change. Invite the children to go shopping, and to see whether they have the correct amount of change to purchase the toys on the flannel board. Be sure you are present to help with this activity. Remember, children are not developmentally ready to count money, so this is a pretend activity.

Math: Set several pennies, nickels, and sheets of paper pre-marked with tic-tac-toe boards, inviting the children to use the change to play the game.

Additional Activities

Game: Invite the children to play "Who Took the Penny From the Piggy Bank?" Ask the children to sit in a circle, and encourage them to clap their hands and slap their knees in time to the following rhyme. Ask the children to recite the rhyme, adding a child's name to the first blank. Encourage the named child to say the response lines, and name a new child at the end of the rhyme. Repeat until each child's name has been called.

> (Class) *Who took the penny from the piggy bank?*
> (First child's name) *took the penny from the piggy bank.*
> (Named child) *Who me?*
> (Class) *Yes you.*
> (Named child) *Couldn't be.*
> (Class) *When who?*

Rhythm and Rhyme: Sing "Saw a Penny" with the children (see appendix page 333).

Happy Valentine's Day

Valentine's Day is February 14th.

STORY TIME

Clifford's First Valentine's Day by Norman Bridwell

Froggy's First Kiss by Jonathan London

Kisses by Nanda Roep

Valentine's Day at the Zoo by Nadine Bernard Westcott

The Very Special Valentine by Maggie Kneen

SNACK

Make a heart biscuit pizza (see appendix page 334 for recipe).

Group Time

Before Group Time, cut out 52 hearts from construction paper. Copy an uppercase or lowercase letter onto each heart, and hide the hearts around the room. At Group Time, invite the children to look for the valentine hearts. Encourage the children to find two or three hearts, and to help their friends find hearts. Once the children find all the hearts, invite the children to name the letters on the hearts, match the upper and lowercase letters on the hearts, think of words that begin with the letters on the hearts, and to name children whose names begin with each letter.

Learning Center Ideas

Art: Set out several white chenille stems and pink and white pony beads. Encourage the children to make bracelets for special people in their lives by stringing the beads on the chenille stems. When the chenille stems are full of beads, help the children twist their ends together, and bend the chenille stem into a heart shape.

Dramatic Play: Set up a post office in your writing center with stamps and stamp pads, old envelopes, old junk mail, and a list of class names available for the children.

Math: Provide several small valentine cards cut in half, encouraging the children to sort through and match the halves.

Math: Give each child a paper grid and a small cup of different-colored heart stickers. Invite the children to practice sorting the hearts on a grid, dividing them by color.

Additional Activities

Outside: Add food coloring to several spray bottles full of water. Invite the children to use the spray bottles to draw hearts and write "I LOVE YOU" in the snow.

Rhythm and Rhyme: Sing "Happy Valentine's Day" with the children (see appendix page 331).

Letter *V*

STORY TIME

Let's Go Visiting by Sue Williams
The Velveteen Rabbit by Margery Williams
Vegetable Soup by Judy Freudberg
The Very Quiet Cricket by Eric Carle

SNACK

Provide the children with several kinds of raw vegetables as a healthy snack.

Group Time

Introduce the children to the letter *v*, naming words that include the letter. Show the children how to make the letter *v* with their fingers, and encourage them to make a *v* whenever someone uses a *v* word through the day.

Take a class vote. Make a T graph on poster board, one side marked "Yes" and the other marked "No". On the top of the graph ask one of the below "yes or no" questions, such as, "Do you like ice cream?" "Do you like winter?" "Do you like dogs?" and so on. Put each child's name on both sides of clip clothespins, and invite the children to take turns voting by clipping their clothespin on that side of the graph. After each child has had a chance to vote, add up the totals.

Learning Center Ideas

Art: Make vests. Set out several paper grocery bags, sponges, stamps, and paint. Invite the children to decorate bags for themselves, and then help them cut the bags into vests.

Math: Set out two paper plates, one with a sticker of a vegetable attached and the word "Vegetable" written on it, and another with a fruit sticker attached and the word "Fruit" written on it. Set out several plastic pieces of fruit and vegetables, encouraging the children to sort them on the appropriate plates.

Math: Cut several cheap valentine cards in half, inviting the children to sort through and match the separated halves.

Science: Bring several violet seeds and small pots so the children can plant violets and watch them grow.

Additional Activities

Rhythm or Rhyme: Sing "The V Song" with the children. Invite them to name a vegetable to include at the end of the song (see appendix page 333).

Movement: Invite the children to stand in a circle and bounce a volleyball to each other As each child bounces the ball, invite him to say a word that begins with or includes *v*.

Red

Remind the children to wear something red to school.

STORY TIME

Big Red Barn by Margaret Wise Brown

Clifford the Big Red Dog by Norman Bridwell

Little Red Hen by Byron Barton

Little Red Hen Makes a Pizza retold by Philemon Sturges

One Fish, Two Fish by Dr. Seuss

TRANSITION

Invite the children to recite the following rhyme, and call on a child to name something red. After that child names a red object, invite him to move on to the next activity.

Red for you and red for me
Name something red that you
can see.

Group Time

During Group Time, help the children count how many red items they are wearing. (Be sure to have some extra red items available for children who forget to wear red to school.) Graph your results, separating the results into pants, shirts, socks, and so on, encouraging the children to help identify which type of red clothing is the most popular, original, and so on. Afterwards, take a picture of the red class.

Learning Center Ideas

Art: Set out various small red items, such as paper, ribbons, stickers, fabric, felt, tissue paper, buttons and bows. Give a square of clear contact paper. Invite the children to place the contact paper with the adhesive side up, and cover the sheet with red items. When they are finished, help the children put on another sheet of contact paper, sealing the objects between the two sheets. Help the children cut each square into a heart shape, and invite the children to decorate the room with their hearts.

Art: Make tubes of red fingerpaint and several sheets of heart and apple shaped fingerpaint paper available for the children to fingerpaint.

Blocks: If possible, provide a toy red barn for the children. Invite them to use the blocks to make a farm around the red barn.

Math/Fine Motor: Set out string, chenille stems, and red pony beads, inviting the children to make bracelets for themselves.

Additional Activities

Movement: Invite the children to play the game Red Means Stop, in which one child holds a stop sign and stands before the other children. The other children walk around the room, but must freeze whenever the child with the stop sign raises it into the air. The last child to see the sign and stop must sit down. The last child up will be the next person to hold the stop sign.

Rhythm and Rhyme: Ask the children to think of words that rhyme with red, writing them down on a sheet of paper. After the children have thought of all the rhyming words they can, invite them to make up silly sentences using as many of the words as possible. Write the sentences down on construction paper, and hang them from the walls.

Pink

STORY TIME

Daddy and the Pink Flash by Ellyn Bache

What Is Pink? by Cristina Rossette

Yellow and Pink by William Steig

SNACK

At snack time, add a couple of drops of red food coloring to milk to make a "pink drink."

Group Time

Invite the children to name pink objects, and explain to them that pink is made by mixing red and white. To illustrate this, set out several plastic bags, spray shaving cream into them, and add a few dots of red food coloring. Tape the bags shut, and hand them out to the children, inviting them to shake the bags until the contents have all turned pink.

Learning Center Ideas

Art: Make a cherry blossom tree. Before starting, add a few drops of cherry extract to a pot of glue and mix thoroughly. Set out several pre-cut construction paper tree trunk shapes. Invite the children to glue a tree trunk shape to blue construction paper. When this dries, invite the children to add "cherry blossoms" by crumpling small pink tissue paper squares and gluing them to the tree trunk shape, or by shaking popped popcorn in a bag of pink powdered paint and gluing the popcorn to the tree. When the glue dries, the tree will look and smell like a cherry blossom tree.

Art: Set out several containers of white and red fingerpaint. Invite the children to mix and paint on sheets of paper, noting how the colors turn pink as the children continue to paint. (Use more of the white paint and just a little bit of red to make a good pink color).

Fine Motor: Fold several different sized sheets of pink construction paper in half. Draw half of a heart shape on the fold, and invite the children to cut along the line, making hearts. Set out several crayons and markers, inviting the children to decorate the hearts they have created.

Additional Activities

Movement: Set out several pink scarves and streamers, inviting the children to dance to different kinds of music.

Letter *R*

STORY TIME

I Know a Rhino by Charles Fuge
Red Riding Hood by James Marshall
Roar by Pamela Duncan Edwards
Rosie's Walk by Pat Hutchins
Row, Row, Row Your Boat by Pippa
    Goodhart

TRANSITION

Invite five children to act out the rhyme, "Rat Race" on appendix page 333, moving to the next activity when the rhyme is complete. Select five more children, and repeat the process until everyone has transitioned to the next activity.

SNACK

Invite the children to make Rabbit Faces (see recipe on appendix page 334).

Group Time

Invite the children to talk about the letter *r* and its sound, naming words that begin with the /r/ sound. Encourage the children to hop like rabbits whenever they hear a word that starts with the /r/ sound.

Learning Center Ideas

Art: Set out two sheets of construction paper per child, and put dollops of different colors of paint on one of the sheets of paper. Suggest that the children place their second sheets of paper on top of the first sheets, and help them use a rolling pin to roll the sheets flat. When done, separate the two sheets and see what new designs the children have made. Let dry, then hang them on the wall.

Art: Invite the children to glue ribbons to a large red construction paper rectangle.

Blocks: Set out several small rocks in the block area for the children to use.

Fine Motor: Set out a rolling pin and red playdough, inviting the children to roll and flatten the playdough.

Math: Set out several rulers, inviting the children to measure the length and height of objects found in the classroom, including one another.

Science/Discovery: Using toilet paper rolls, boxes, other recycled items, rubber cement, and tape, encourage the children to build a robot. Take a photo of the children and their robot. Invite each child to make up a story about the robot. Copy the story down on construction paper, and invite the child to illustrate the story.

Additional Activities

Outside: Set out a large jump rope, inviting the children to play Over and Under, encouraging them to see how high they can jump and how low they can go under the rope.

Rhythm and Rhyme: Make a homemade tambourine by stapling two paper plates together with their faces facing each other. Leave an opening to fill the space inside with small pebbles, and then staple the opening shut. Invite the children to decorate their tambourines with markers, tissue paper, and streamers. When the tambourines are ready, invite the children to tap out favorite rhythms on them.

Hearts

STORY TIME

Arthur's Heart Mix Up by Marc Brown

Give a Little Love by Lizzie Mack

Hugs and Hearts by Toni Trent Parker

Lilly's Chocolate Heart by Kevin Henkes

SNACK

Make breadstick hearts. From a can of breadstick dough, give each child enough dough for one breadstick. Invite each child to shape his dough into a heart, by making a point at the middle of the dough and bending the sides around. Help the children twist the two ends together so the shape will stay. Bake the dough according to can directions. When cool, frost and decorate.

Group Time

Before Group Time, cut out and hide 30 construction paper hearts of different shapes and sizes. Invite the children to hunt through the room for the hearts. When the children have found all the hearts, help the children to count them and sort by size and color.

Learning Center Ideas

Art: Sprinkle cherry gelatin powder into a mixture of glue and water, then set it out for the children to paint the mixture onto pink construction paper heart cutouts.

Math: Make giant dice by covering large, cube-shaped boxes with contact paper. On each face, glue between one and six large hearts, until each box resembles a die. Set out the dice, inviting the children to roll them, then count and write down the number of hearts on the face of the die.

Math: Play Which Heart is Missing? For this game, cut out five differently-colored felt hearts, and attach them to a flannel board. Invite the children to count the hearts and name the colors. After the children have done this, turn the flannel board around and remove one heart. Turn the flannel board back around so the children can see it, and encourage them to guess which color heart is missing.

Additional Activities

Movement: Play Musical Hearts. In a large circle on the floor, set out one heart sticker per child in the classroom. Invite each child to sit on a heart. After each child selects a heart, put on music, and invite the children to walk around the circle of hearts. Occasionally stop the music, and encourage the children to run for the closest heart sticker.

Outside: Give the children bags of birdseed, inviting them to make heart shapes with the seeds. Leave the heart-shaped bird seed on the ground for the feathered friends to enjoy.

Rhythm and Rhyme: Provide the children with several red, blue, yellow, green, orange, purple, pink, and white construction paper hearts, inviting them to follow the instructions of the rhyme "Put Your Heart..." on appendix page 332.

Post Office

STORY TIME

Dear Mrs. LaRue: Letters from Obedience School by Mark Teague

The Post Office Book: Mail and How It Moves by Gail Gibbons

TRANSITION

Invite the children to sit in a circle. Hand one child a sealed envelope, turn on music, and encourage the children to pass the envelope until the music stops. Occasionally stop the music, and invite the child holding the envelope when the music stops to move on to the next activity.

SNACK

Enjoy a Mailbox Meal (see recipe on appendix page 334).

Group Time

Invite the children to talk about the post office, helping them describe what they are, how the mail is sorted, and how the mail gets to and from the post office. If possible, arrange to take the children on a field trip to a post office. After all children are familiar with the concept, bring in large boxes, old junk mail, magazines, and packages, and invite the children to sort the mail into boxes.

Learning Center Ideas

Dramatic Play: Invite the children to play post office with their friends. Children can buy stamps, mail letters, or pick up their mail.

Literacy: Invite the children to write letters to friends. Set out paper and envelopes for the children. Also make balancing scales available so the children can see how much their letters weigh.

Math: For each letter of the alphabet, put an uppercase letter on a construction paper cutout of a house, and the matching lowercase letter on an envelope. Encourage the children to match the lowercase and uppercase letters.

Additional Activities

Field Trip: To see how the mail works, ask each child to draw a picture on a postcard. Help the children address their postcards with their home addresses and label with the appropriate postage. Consider taking the children to a nearby public mailbox and invite the children to mail the postcards. Or, collect the postcards in class and mail them from school.

Rhythm and Rhyme: Sing "I'm a Mail Carrier" with the children (see appendix page 332).

Froggy Bakes a Cake by Jonathan London

GENERAL DAILY PLAN

STORY TIME

Invite the children to bring from home empty cake, brownie, cookies and frosting mixes. Help the children make an environmental print book by gluing the box fronts to paper, putting the pages into paper protectors, and collecting the filled page protectors in a binder.

SNACK

Bake a cake for the class to share.

Group Time

Show the children the book *Froggy Bakes a Cake* by Jonathan London. Show them what and where the title is on the cover of the book. Tell the children that the author is the person who writes the story and the illustrator is the person that draws the pictures. Before reading the story, show the children the pictures in the book, encouraging them to predict what will happen in the story. After they have predicted the ending, read them the story, and see whether they were correct.

Learning Center Ideas

Art: Invite the children to create pictures of their idea of the "best birthday cake ever."

Art: From construction paper, cut a cake shape for each child; yellow for vanilla, and brown for chocolate. Combine two parts non-menthol shaving cream and one part white glue to make the frosting for the cake. Invite the children to pick a vanilla or chocolate cake shape, and frost it with the shaving cream frosting. Sprinkle glitter or sequins on the cake for further decoration.

Math: Set out playdough, several toy dishes and birthday candles, and several note cards, numbered from 1–10. Invite the children to make birthday cakes from the playdough. Next, ask them to choose a note card, and put the same number of candles on their cake as are written on the card.

Additional Activities

Outside: Take a field trip to the local grocery store or bakery, or invite a cake decorator to come in and demonstrate decorating a cake.

Rhythm and Rhyme: Sing "Monster Cake" with the children (see appendix page 332).

In My World by Lois Ehlert

STORY TIME

All the Colors of the Earth by Sheila Hamanaka
Market Day by Lois Ehlert

TRANSITION

Pick the names of two children, tell the other children in the class, and encourage the children to recite the below rhyme. Invite the children whose names you picked to act out the different actions found in the rhyme. Continue until all children have transitioned to the next activity.

_____ and _____ leap like a frog.
_____ and _____ dance like a butterfly.
_____ and _____ wiggle like a worm
To the next activity.

Group Time

Before reading *In My World* by Lois Ehlert to the children, talk with them about the parts of the book, such as the title *In My World,* and that the author, Lois Ehlert, is the person who wrote the story. She is also the illustrator, which means she drew or cut out the pictures found in the book. Invite the children to look at the pictures. Ask the children, based on the illustrations of the book, what they think it will be about. Read the book to the children and let them decide if their predictions were correct.

After reading *In My World,* encourage the children make books about the things they like. Copy the below sentences on individual pages, and invite the children to make illustrations for each page.

Learning Center Ideas

Art: Prior to this center, cut several letter shapes out of one page of a file folder. Set the folder stencils out along with paper, paint, and several sponges. Invite the children to sponge paint the letters of their names onto separate sheets of paper by putting a sheet of paper into the appropriate folder stencils and dabbing them with paint. When all letters are dry, encourage the children to put then in order to spell their names.
Science/Discovery: Invite the children to use their five senses to examine a piece of fruit. Encourage them to tell you what they see, touch, taste, smell, and hear. Write down each child's responses in the child's portfolio.
Sensory: Set out plastic fish and frogs on the water table for the children to play with and explore.

Additional Activities

Movement: Invite all the children to stand. Ask them the following questions, encouraging them to act out the action mentioned in each question. Say, "Can you...creep like a bug? Wiggle like a worm? Leap like a frog? Dance like a butterfly? Flutter like a moth?
Rhythm and Rhyme: Invite the children to sing, "Thank You, World!" (see appendix page 333) and act out the actions.

Soapy Clean

The day before, encourage children to bring in a few empty soap containers and labels. Bring several containers for children who forget. Throughout the day's activities, remind the children that soap is not edible.

STORY TIME

Clean Up with the Cat by Dr. Seuss
Daddy and Me by Karen Katz
Five Little Monkeys with Nothing to Do by Eileen Christelow
Mr. Wishy Washy by Joy Cowley
Mrs. Wishy Washy Makes a Splash by Joy Cowley

Group Time

Ask the children if they know what soap is, and encourage them to explain how soap is used, and all the different types of soap there are. As the children name different types of soap, write their examples on chart paper. After the children finish naming different types of soap, invite them to take out the soap containers and labels they brought to class and organize them by type. Are there any surprise soaps?

Learning Center Ideas

Art: Invite the children to make designs on paper with a bar of soap, making sure they understand they might not yet be able to see the image or design they are drawing. When the children are done drawing their soap designs on the paper, give them watercolors and encourage them to paint lightly over their soap designs, and watch as the soap designs magically appear.

Fine Motor/Science: Use potato peelers to shave different colors of soap into shavings. Help the children press the shavings into mold a new bar of soap. A little water might help the shaved pieces of soap mold together. Explain to the children that soap is very important because it helps you stay clean. Cut one 6"x 6" square of terry cloth for each child to use as a washcloth. Put the washcloth and soap into a zippered plastic bag to take home. Glue the poem, "Soap" on appendix page 333 to the plastic bag.

Additional Activities

Rhythm and Rhyme: When singing, "This Is the Way I Wash My Body,"(see appendix page 333) practice naming lesser-known body parts, such as *knuckles, knees, shin,* and so on.

Movement: Blow bubbles, inviting the children to try to pop all the bubbles before they hit the ground.

Grocery Store

A few weeks before doing this plan, remind the children to bring in lots of empty and clean food containers and boxes. Request that the labels be left on.

STORY TIME

Grocery Store by Angela Leeper
Signs at the Store by Mary Hill
A Visit to the Supermarket by B.A. Hoena

Group Time

Set out the food containers that the children brought in to school. Cut two matching labels from several boxes and hand them out to the children, inviting them to go around the room, looking for the child who has a matching label. Once the children find their matches, begin asking the children if they see certain letters on their labels, which children have cereal labels, and who has labels for foods they like.

Learning Center Ideas

Art: Invite the children to make collages from labels and grocery boxes. Set out glue and paper on which they can make the collages.
Fine Motor: Set several coupons from newspapers and magazines in the Sensory Table for the children to practice cutting.
Literacy: Looking at several food packages, containers, and labels, ask the children how the can you tell what is in a box, whether there is a way to know if one box can hold more of a product than another might, and what special things on the label make the food inside attractive to eat.
Math: Set out several pages of coupons from the newspaper, inviting the children to match the coupons to with the empty food boxes everyone brought to class.
Math: Set out several empty food boxes and containers, inviting the children to sort them by food group into paper grocery bags.

Additional Activities

Movement: Encourage the children to design an obstacle course out of the boxes and cans they brought to class.
Outside: Bring plastic food outside and pretend to have an open market, inviting the children to pretend to buy and sell plastic fruits and vegetables in baskets. Make a scale and bags available for the children to weigh and package the produce.

Letter *F*

STORY TIME

Families Are Different by Nina
    Pellegrini
Fish Eyes by Lois Ehlert
Franklin Books by Paulette
    Bourgeois
Freight Train by Donald Crews
I'm a Fire Fighter by Mary Packard

TRANSITION

Call children in small groups to stand around you. Hold several feathers above your head, slowly dropping them, encouraging the children to try and catch them before they hit the floor. When a child catches a feather, he moves on to the next activity, and is replaced by another child from the class.

SNACK

Make fruit faces. Spread cream cheese on a rice cake. Give the children various pieces of fruit, and encourage them to put them in the cream cheese to make a face.

Group Time

Invite the children to talk about the letter *f* and the sound it makes, naming words that contain the /f/ sound. Through the course of the day, encourage the children to pretend to smell a flower when they hear a word that begins with the sound /f/.

Learning Center Ideas

Art: Set out several plastic forks and invite the children to paint with them.
Art: Provide photos of objects that start with *f*, as well as felt, fabric, feathers, foam, and fake flowers and invite the children to make collages.
Art/Literacy: Read *Rainbow Fish* by Marcus Pfister. After reading the book, help the children glue confetti and foil to construction paper fish shapes.
Science/Sensory: Let children experiment with things that float by placing various objects in a tub of water.

Additional Activities

Movement: Before this activity, invite the children to glue several small red, blue, yellow, and green flag shapes to craft sticks. When they are dry, invite the children to hold their flags and act out the actions as you recite "Wave Your Flag," found on appendix page 333.
Outside: Trace shoe prints onto sponges and cut them out. Set out washable paint, and encourage the children to use these sponges to make footprint paths outside.

USA

STORY TIME

America the Beautiful by Katharine Lee Bates

The Flag We Love by Pam Munoz Ryan

The Pledge of Allegiance by Frances Bellamy

TRANSITION

Invite a child to chant the rhyme below, adding the name of another child in the second line. The first child moves on to the next activity, and the chosen child chants the rhyme. Repeat until all children have moved on to the next activity.

> *Hey, hey, I want to say*
> *I live with ____ in the USA.*

Group Time

Ask the children if any of them can name our country. If not, tell them that the name of our country is the United States of America. Show the children a map of the United States, then take out a world map or globe and ask the children to find the United States. After the children find the United States, ask them to find the state in which they live. Going back to the world map or globe, tell the children that every country has its own flag. Ask the children if they know what the US flag looks like (colors, number of stripes and stars), then set out red and blue strips of construction paper and cutout star shapes. Invite the children to glue the stars and stripes onto white construction paper to make their own American flags.

Learning Center Ideas

Art: Set out several construction paper cutouts of the letters *U*, *S*, and *A*, inviting the children to glue them to a sheet of construction paper. When dry, encourage the children to decorate the letters with sequins and sticker stars.

Literacy: Talk about George Washington and explain that Washington was the first president of the United States. Then invite the children to talk about what the president does. After discussing what a president does, give the children several sheets of paper with "If I were President, ____" written on them, and encourage the children to draw a picture that finishes that thought. When each child has drawn a picture, create a cover and staple the pages together, making a class book.

Math: Provide several red construction paper rectangles with different numbers written on each. Die cut several star shapes, and invite the children to place the correct number of stars on each red rectangle.

Additional Activities

Movement: Introduce the children to some basic square dance steps. Explain to them that square dancing is an old American tradition. Put on square dance music and call out basic commands, encouraging the children to follow the steps.

Rhythm and Rhyme: Sing "My Country" on appendix page 332 with the children.

I Stay Healthy

STORY TIME

Body Battles by Rita Golden Gelman
Germs Germs Germs by Bobbi Katz
How Kids Grow by Jean Marzollo
Two Eyes, a Nose and a Mouth by
    Roberta Grobel Intrater

TRANSITION

At the end of this rhyme, point to a child. When the child answers you, he or she may go to the next activity.

    I stay healthy, yes I do
    I stay healthy, how about you?

SNACK

Set out an assortment of healthy foods and invite children to make their own healthy kabob snacks.

Group Time

Talk to the children about these healthy body facts: All people grow at their own rate. Eating a healthy and balanced diet gives the body energy to play and to grow. Every body grows and repairs itself at all times, even when sleeping at night. Next, read *My First Body Book* by Melanie and Chris Pike to the children.

Introduce the children to the following list of five great health ideas—eat healthy, exercise, get plenty of sleep, keep clean, and get regular checkups.

Hand out several sheets of paper with "I stay healthy by_____" written on them, and invite the children to draw a healthy thing they do. After each child finishes his drawing, staple all the drawings into a book, with the title "We Stay Healthy."

Learning Center Ideas

Math: Set out a scale for the children to practice measuring the weight of various objects, then weigh themselves. Record the results and invite the children to compare the differences.

Sensory: Set out soapy water and several play dishes in the Sensory Table for the children to pretend to clean.

Additional Activities

Movement: Invite the children to run, hop, skip, jump, and crawl around the classroom or outside.

Rhythm and Rhyme: Sing "I Eat Healthy Foods" with the children (see appendix page 331).

Hospitals

STORY TIME

Curious George Goes to the Hospital by H. A. Rey

Froggy Goes to the Doctor by Jonathan London

How Do Dinosaurs Get Well Soon? by Jane Yolen

Madeleine by Ludwig Bemelmans

Group Time

Introduce the children to the various positions people have in a hospital. Ask the children if they know why people go to a hospital and what happens there. Make a list of the answers the children give, and hang it on the wall.

Learning Center Ideas

Art: Set out bandages, cotton balls, tongue depressors, Q-tips, and gauze and invite the children to make an emergency equipment collage.

Dramatic Play: Set out several medical instruments (bandages, stethoscope, and so on) and invite the children to pretend they are working in a hospital.

Literacy: Set out several tongue depressors, inviting the children to form letters out of them.

Math: Set out several different types and sizes of bandages. Tell the children that the different bandages are for different-sized cuts. Start setting a few bandages in a sort of pattern, large to small; large, small, large; and so on. Once the children start to understand the patterns being made, invite the children to continue making the patterns, or let them try making their own patterns.

Additional Activities

Movement: Invite the children to stand in a circle. Choose one child to stand in the center of the circle, and tell that child that he is the "doctor." Sing "Hi, Ho, the Hospital" with the children (see appendix page 331). With each verse, the child in the center chooses the next person, nurse, tech, aide, and so on, and those two people change positions.

Outside: Set out several blankets and stuffed animals, inviting the children to pretend they have someone on a stretcher. Encourage them to practice working together to move an injured stuffed animal.

Rhythm and Rhyme: Sing "The Ambulance Song" with the children (see appendix page 331). Ring a bell and invite the children, who are "paramedics," to jump up and get ready to go on an emergency call.

Teeth

STORY TIME

Dear Tooth Fairy by Alan Durant

The Lost Tooth Club by Arden Johnson

Moose's Loose Tooth by Jacqueline Clark

The Tooth Fairy by Kirsten Hall

Wibble Wobble by Miriam Moss

SNACK

Serve apples with cheese and tell the children that these foods are "tooth healthy."

Group Time

Talk about teeth with the children. Find out how much they know about their teeth. Ask them questions such as "How many teeth do we have?" or "How can we make sure our teeth stay healthy?" Listen to their answers and fill in any gaps of information. Pass toothbrushes around the room and ask the children about why they brush their teeth. Encourage them to show you how they brush and tell you how often they brush. Read one of the Story Time selections to the children.

Learning Center Ideas

Art: Cut out several large yellow construction paper teeth shapes (yellow to show that they are dirty). Set out several containers of white paint and brushes, encouraging the children to paint the teeth white.

Art: Set out several white beads and lengths of dental floss, encouraging the children to string the beads on the floss to make necklaces. **Safety note:** Supervise this activity carefully.

Art: Cut out several sets of large lips from red construction paper. Invite the children to count out and glue on 16 pre-cut construction paper teeth.

Dramatic Play: Set up a dentist's office and invite the children to take turns pretending to be the dentist, patient, receptionist, and dental hygienist.

Literacy: Read *Wibble Wobble* by Miriam Moss. Invite the children to talk about silly places a lost tooth might be. After the children make several suggestions, hand out several sheets of tooth-shaped paper and invite children to draw a picture of someone losing a tooth in a silly place.

Additional Activities

Movement: Invite one child to be the Tooth Fairy, and one child to be Tooth Decay. Explain to the other children that they are all Teeth. Encourage Tooth Decay to chase the Teeth, trying to tag them. If Tooth Decay tags a child, that child must either name three healthy foods or be tagged by the Tooth Fairy to be released.

Outside: If possible, take the children on a field trip to a dentist's office.

Rhythm and Rhyme: Sing "Brush Your Teeth" with the children (see appendix page 331).

Blocks

This plan is full of activities involving little blocks, such as Legos, that snap together. Be sure you have a sizeable number of them before beginning this Daily Plan.

STORY TIME

ABC Block Books by Susan Estelle Kwas
Alphabet by Vincent Douglas
Learning Block Books by Susan Estelle Kwas

SNACK

Make several pans of gelatin jigglers, in red, blue and yellow. Cut the gelatin into blocks. Serve several blocks to each child.

Group Time

Set out a large container holding blocks of several different colors. As the children come to Group Time, invite each of them to pick up a block. When all the children have a block, ask that children holding each particular color come up and attach their blocks together. As the different colors of block add up, they will begin to make a graph, indicating which block color is the most popular.

Learning Center Ideas

Blocks: See how many blocks all of the children can count together, adding or building as they count. See how high or how long of a structure the children can make. Come back to this later in the year to see if the children can make a longer or higher structure.

Math: Set out several numbered construction paper dump truck shapes or toy dump trucks with numbers attached to their hoods, as well as several blocks. Invite the children to put the correct number of blocks on the dump truck shapes.

Math: Invite the children to make several different creations with blocks. Start by giving the each child three blocks, and work up to larger, more involved shapes. Take photos of each creation when the children finish, and set the photos in the center. As new children come into the center, invite them to try recreating the photographed shapes, then invite them to make new shapes, and photograph those as well.

Math: Set out several blocks, inviting the children to sort them by color and size.

Science/Discovery: Have an invention convention. Invite children to build inventions or masterpieces from blocks. Take a photo of the child and her creation. Ask each child to explain their invention or masterpiece, explaining what it is and what it can do.

Additional Activities

Outside: With the children's help, paint large grocery boxes red, blue yellow and green. When dry, take them outside and invite the children to use the boxes as blocks to build giant castles and pyramids.

March

Calendar Time

During Calendar Time, introduce the month of March to the children. Look at the letters in the word *March.* Name each letter, and say the sound and words that start with the sound. Whose name begins with the letter *m*? Do this for each letter in the word during calendar time throughout the month

Monthly Organizer

SPECIAL DAYS AND HOLIDAYS

March 1: National Pig Day
March 17: Saint Patrick's Day

GENERAL DAILY PLANS

Photos
Castles, Kings and Royal Things
Planting a Rainbow by
    Lois Ehlert
Breakfast
Number 6
Letter *T*
Music
Number 9
Goofy Green
Letter *U*
Potatoes
Kites
Artists
Cowboys
Chicka Chicka Boom Boom by
    Bill Martin Jr.
Trains

Spring
Fruits
Vegetables
Bread
Food Group Fun
Windy Weather
Paper Tubes
Noses
Pockets

Note: Please be sure to check for allergies before serving the snacks or doing any food-related activities.

National Pig Day

National Pig Day is on March 1st.

STORY TIME

If You Give a Pig a Pancake by Laura Joffe Numeroff

Mrs. Wishy Washy's Farm by Joy Cowley

Olivia by Ian Falconer

Pig in the Pond by Martin Waddell

Piggies by Audrey Wood

Pigs by Gail Gibbons

SNACK

Make "piggy snacks" (see appendix page 342). Invite the children to spread strawberry cream cheese on their English muffins using craft sticks. Add marshmallow noses with raisin nostrils and two blueberry eyes. Enjoy!

Group Time

Bring three large poster board pig shapes to Group Time. Review list of Pig Facts (see appendix page 344) and talk about pigs. On one pig shape, write, "What We Know About Pigs." List what children know. On the second pig shape, write, "What We Want to Know About Pigs" and list what children want to know. Display the two pig shapes on a bulletin board covered with brown paper (mud) and a fence border. On the third pig shape, write "What We Learned About Pigs." At the end of the unit, list what the children tell you they learned about pigs.

Learning Center Ideas

Art: Provide large pink circles for the children to use as the pig's body. Show them how to glue a smaller pink circle in the middle of the larger one to make the pig's head. Glue on two square legs and two triangle ears. Glue on a pink button with two holes for the nose. Draw eyes. Show the children how to wrap a pink pipe cleaner around their finger for a tail, and glue it on. Show the children how they can make their piggy muddy by dipping their fingers or a craft stick in a little bit of brown paint and painting it on the pig.

Art/Science: Put out red and white fingerpaint. Encourage the children to mix the colors together as they fingerpaint to make pink.

Math: Cut out pig shapes from construction paper and write a number on each one. Invite the children to count the correct number of pennies for each pig.

Additional Activities

Outside: Make mud pies. Make mud by adding a little water to a tub of sand. Add measuring cups, spoons, and play dishes to make great mud pies for a pretend piggy bath.

Rhythm and Rhyme: Sing "Three Little Pigs" with the children (see appendix page 341).

Small Group: Read the story, *The Three Little Pigs* by James Marshall (or another preferred version). Discuss what happened first, next, and last. As you read the story the second time, invite the children to say "Little pig, little pig, let me come in…" along with the wolf. Take turns acting out the story.

St. Patrick's Day

During the week before St. Patrick's Day, leave little messes around your classroom. On some days, make small green footprints around the classroom by dipping your finger in green paint. One day, leave a tiny piece of green felt "caught" between the window and the sash. Could it be the leprechaun's tiny pants? On St. Patrick's Day, leave a treat of rainbow-colored candy for each child.

STORY TIME

It's St. Patrick's Day by Rebecca Gomez

St. Patrick's Day by Gail Gibbons

TRANSITION

As you say the name of a child in this little verse, that child sneaks very quietly out of the group to line up or on to the next activity.

> *Leprechaun _____, sneak away!*
> *Don't let us hear you today.*

SNACK

Eat green snacks for St. Patrick's Day, or the leprechaun can leave magic powder (pistachio pudding) with a note to put the powder and some milk in a Tupperware container with a lid. Put the lid on securely and have each child shake the mixture five times. Open and find the magic snack.

Group Time

Read the story "A Sticky Situation" (see appendix page 339). About halfway through the story, stop and ask the children what they think will happen. Finish reading the story to find out. After reading the story, talk about where a leprechaun could hide in your classroom. Give each child a leprechaun sticker and a piece of paper. Draw a place for their leprechaun to hide. Finish the sentence "My leprechaun is hiding _____."

Learning Center Ideas

Art: Give each child a piece of clear contact paper with the sticky side up. Invite children to put small squares of different colors of tissue paper on, in the half circle shape of a rainbow. Cover with another piece of contact and cut it out for a window cling.

Math: Cut out 10 "pots of gold" from black construction paper, write a number on each, and set out several gold coins cut out of construction paper. Invite the children to put the correct number of coins on each "pot of gold."

Sensory: Bury several gold-painted rocks on the Sand Table, and invite the children to "hunt for gold" by digging through the sand. Change the center by changing the number of gold rocks in the sand. Display the number above the sand table, so the children know how many rocks to look for in the sand.

Additional Activities

Game: Cut, copy, and laminate a small leprechaun shape. Have the children sit on the Circle Time rug. Pick one child to go to another part of the room and hide his eyes. With the other children watching, quietly hide the leprechaun. Call the child back to the group. This child will look for the leprechaun shape, while the other children give directions. If the child is getting close, the children say "you are getting warmer" and so on. This is a good way to see who can follow directions and also who can give them.

Outside: Spray rocks with gold paint. Hide them outside for the children to find.

Rhythm and Rhyme: Sing "The Leprechaun Song" with the children (see appendix page 337).

Photos

Before doing this daily plan, take a photo of each activity you do throughout the day and develop the photographs.

STORY TIME

I Spy by Jean Marzollo
Knuffle Bunny by Mo Willems
Stranger in the Woods by Carl R. Sams

TRANSITION

Put a photo of each child in a basket. Choose a photo and ask the child pictured to line up or move on to the next activity.

Group Time

Talk about what happens first, next, and so on throughout the school day. Give the photos to the children and help them put the activities in sequential order. Hang up the pictures in sequence of the day, and the children can always look at the pictures to remind them what happens next.

Learning Center Ideas

Art: Take photos of each child and a special friend. Print a photo for each child. Help the children cut out heart-shaped frames from foam. Invite them to decorate the frames and mount the photos in the frames.

Art: Provide an old, plain white sheet and paints. Invite the children to paint a backdrop to use in the Dramatic Play center (see below).

Dramatic Play: Obtain used cameras and offer different costumes and clothing. Encourage children to set up a photography studio and take turns posing for pictures and taking pictures.

Math: Play a Memory game. Make two copies of every photo used in the Group Time activity above. Mount each photo on an index card. Place all of the index cards face down on the table. Encourage the children to take turns turning over two cards at a time. If the photos on the cards match, the children keep them. If they do not match, the children turn the cards over and continue playing.

Math: Invite the children to lie on the floor and mold their bodies together to make shapes. Put each photo on a page with the name of the shape. Laminate the pages and put them in the book.

Additional Activities

Movement: Take photos of your class playing their favorite games, such as Simon Says; Doggie, Doggie, Where's Your Bone?; and Duck, Duck, Goose. Put the photos face down. Ask a child to choose a photo, and play the game that is pictured.

Rhythm and Rhyme: Invite the children to sing "The Photograph Song" and suit their actions to the words (see appendix page 338).

DAILY PLAN CONCEPT

Castles, Kings, and Royal Things

GENERAL DAILY PLAN

STORY TIME

Good Night Princess Pruney Toes by Lisa McCourt

I Am the King by Nathalie Dieterlé

King Bidgood's in the Bathtub by Audrey Wood

Nothing King by Elle Van Lieshout

The Princess and the Pea by Hans Christian Anderson

Group Time

As you begin this theme, there are several royal words that the children might not be familiar with. Introduce the children to some "royal" wards, such as a *scepter, tiara,* and *moat.* As you discuss them, ask children what sound they hear at the beginning of the word. Clap the syllables. Read the children Hans Christian Anderson's story, *The Princess and the Pea,* and invite the children to act it out.

Learning Center Ideas

Art: Make crowns by cutting and stapling bulletin board borders to fit each child's head. Encourage the children to decorate the crowns with sequins, foam, and stickers to give them extra sparkle. (Optional: print each child's name on the front with glitter glue).

Art: Using a castle pattern, cut a castle shape from construction paper for each child. Set out foam shapes, gems, sequins, and construction paper to decorate their castle.

Art: Cut out castle shapes for children to paint at the easel. Encourage the children to paint princes and princesses on their castles, or offer prince and princess stickers to put on their paintings when they are dry.

Math: Sort craft jewels by color and put them into ice cube trays.

Sensory: Put bags of pea gravel or small pebbles in the Sensory Table and invite to pour and measure.

Writing: Talk about how every story has a beginning, middle, and end. Invite the children to dictate a story about their castles. Set out blank books for children to create and illustrate their own fairy tales. Offer assistance with writing as needed.

Additional Activities

Movement: Bring in dress-up clothes to have a Royal Ball and invite the children to wear their crowns. Dance to classical music such as "The Danube Waltz."

Rhythm and Rhyme: Sing "Down in the Kingdom" with the children (see appendix page 335).

Planting a Rainbow by Lois Ehlert

Before doing this lesson plan, make construction paper or foam flower nametag necklaces in these colors (make the same number in each color): red, orange, yellow, green, blue, indigo, and violet. The children will wear these necklaces to do some of the activities.

STORY TIME

All the Colors of the Rainbow by Allan Fowler

The Crayola Rainbow Colors Book by Salina Yoon

Rainbow Fish by Marcus Pfister

What Makes a Rainbow? A Magic Ribbon Book by Betty Ann Schwartz

TRANSITION

Encourage the children to line up when the color of their necklace is called.

> [Name a color] *flowers,*
> [Name a color] *flowers in a bouquet,*
> *It's your turn to line up today.*

SNACK

Make and eat Rainbow Bars (see appendix page 343).

Group Time

Give the children their necklaces (see left). Introduce the story *Planting a Rainbow* by Lois Ehlert. Show the children the title and the author. Explain that this author is also the illustrator. Read the story, and show the children how books are read from front to back. Read the story again. Invite the children to stand up when the color of their necklace is mentioned.

Learning Center Ideas

Literacy: Print the children's names on index cards, and arrange the index cards on cookie sheets. Set out several magnetic letters, and invite the children to find the magnetic letters that spell their names.

Math: Set out a rainbow shape. Invite children to put plastic or foam flowers on the same color on the rainbow.

Science: Give the children 2' long poles with a string and magnet attached at one end. Put several differently-colored construction paper cutouts of fish with paperclips attached to their bodies in a bucket, and invite the children to cast their fishing poles into the bucket, pull out a fish, and name its color.

Additional Ideas

Movement: Choose one child to be the "Rainbow Catcher" for this game. The other children line up on one side of the room or playground facing the "Rainbow Catcher." The "Rainbow Catcher" calls out a color. Children with the named color run across the room or playground to the other side while the "Rainbow Catcher" tries to tag them, If the "Rainbow Catcher" tags someone, that child helps the "Rainbow Catcher" tag other children. The game continues until all the children are caught.

Outside: Fill a clear drinking glass with water. Put it in the sun and help the children see that the water bends the light, which creates a rainbow.

Rhythm and Rhyme: Sing "The Flower Song" with the children (see appendix page 336).

Breakfast

STORY TIME

Max's Breakfast by Rosemary Wells

My Square Breakfast Shapes by Mark Shulman

Pancakes for Breakfast by Tomie de Paola

Pancakes, Pancakes by Eric Carle

SNACK

Give each child a crescent dinner roll triangle. Invite the child to use a craft stick to butter the raw roll. Sprinkle the roll with brown sugar and cinnamon. Roll the dough into the crescent shape and bake according to package directions.

Group Time

Talk about and make a list of the foods that children like to eat for breakfast. Make a bar graph of the results on a piece of poster board. Cut out small cereal bowls, pancakes, and eggs. Invite the children to choose the picture of their favorite breakfast food. If the child's favorite breakfast food is not present, help the child write the name of her favorite breakfast food. When the children all have pictures of their favorite breakfast foods, help them write their names on the pictures and put them up on the graph. Talk about the graph.

Learning Center Ideas

Art: Invite the children to fingerpaint with corn syrup (add a drop or two of maple extract) on a round pancake shape.

Dramatic Play: Set up a restaurant. Add plates, napkins, silverware, and empty breakfast food boxes (clean). Encourage the children to create a menu and take turns being the server.

Literacy: Draw eggs and bacon shapes on paper. Copy them and cut out the shapes. On each egg/bacon pair, write an uppercase and lowercase letter. Laminate and invite the children to match the letters. (Be sure to only use only 6–7 letter sets at a time, and change them often.)

Additional Ideas

Outside: On a sunny and warm morning, take breakfast items outside and enjoy a picnic.

Rhythm and Rhyme: Invite the children to sing and act out "Early in the Morning" (see appendix page 335).

Small Group: Fill a brown paper bag with several breakfast food containers and/or plastic breakfast foods. Play a guessing game. Give clues about a food item from the bag, and invite children to guess what it is. Older children can take turns choosing an item, give clues and let the rest of the class guess the item.

Number 6

STORY TIME

I Spy Little Numbers by Jean
    Marzollo
My Six Book by Jane Belk Moncure
My Very First Book of Numbers by
    Eric Carle
Numberlies: Number Six by Colin
    and Jacqui Hawkins
*One Is a Drummer: A Book of
    Numbers* by Roseanne Thong

SNACK

Give each child a piece of canned
breadstick dough. Invite each child
to mold their dough into a "6"
shape. Put on six raisins. Bake the
dough according to package
directions.

Group Time

Talk about the number 6. Show children what the number looks like. Use a
deck of cards to play a game. Put the cards face down. Hold up the cards
one by one and ask the children to raise their hands when they spot the
number 6.

Learning Center Ideas

Art: Look for sixes in magazines and newspapers. Cut them out and glue
them to a large shape of a six.
Fine Motor/Math: Play a card game called Slap Six. Two players divide and
deal a deck of cards face down. Children take turns turning over a card. If
a six comes up, the players try to slap the card first. Whoever is first gets
the cards. The child with the most cards wins.
Sensory/Math: Show the children how to draw a six in a tub of sand.

Additional Activities

Movement: Play "Simon Says," repeating each action six times.
Outside: Go on a "six" hunt. Give each child a paper lunch bag. Tell them
they are going on a hunt to find six of something. Each child should find
six items and put them into the bag. After the hunt, go inside to talk about
their treasures. Ask how many children brought six of the same things.
How many brought back things that were big, or little?
Rhythm and Rhyme: Sing "Six Little Cows" with the children (see appendix
page 338).
Small Group: Make flannel board shapes to go with "Six Little Kites" (see
appendix page 339). Say the rhymes using the flannel board figures. When
Group Time is finished, leave the flannel board and the shapes out for
children to count and play with.

Letter *T*

STORY TIME

I Love Trucks by Philemon Sturges
I'm a Little Teapot by Iza Trapani
"It's Simple," Said Simon by Mary Ann Hoberman
Little Tiger's Big Surprise by Julie Sykes

SNACK

Invite children to make "Tasty Tacos" using ingredients such as tortillas, cooked hamburger or ground turkey, lettuce, tomatoes, shredded cheese, sour cream, and salsa.

Group Time

Bring in a laundry basket full of toys, including balls, trucks, cars, blocks, telephones, bears, tigers, and so on. Invite the children to take turns choosing a toy from the basket, naming the toy, and deciding whether it begins with the /t/ sound or another sound.

Learning Center Ideas

Art: Help the children cut triangles out of many different types of green paper and fabric including tissue, felt, construction paper, and green fabric. Use tongue depressors as tree trunks and glue them in several places on a piece of construction paper. Glue the triangle trees over the tongue depressors to make a collage.

Art: Invite the children to paint on large tulip shapes made from construction paper.

Dramatic Play: Invite the children to have a tea party. A child-size tea set with napkins is a wonderful prop for the children to create their own tea party.

Literacy: Encourage the children to use flat toothpicks to form the letter *t*.

Math: Glue colored toothpicks in patterns on sentence strips. Invite the children to finish the patterns.

Additional Activities

Movement: Invite the children to recite "Round and Round" and suit their actions to the words (see appendix page 338).

Outside: Can you make a giant *t* with the whole class? Brainstorm how to do this and then go outside and try it.

Rhythm and Rhyme: Make a list of *t* words together. Say the words on the list aloud and tap the word parts or syllables.

Small Group: Bring in an old telephone for each small group. Demonstrate how to use the telephone. Discuss how to answer the telephone. Practice dialing and answering the play phones. (Remind them not to call 911 unless there is an emergency.)

Making Music

STORY TIME

Down by the Bay by Raffi
Hush Little Baby by Sylvia Long
The Maestro Plays by Bill Martin, Jr.
Miss Mary Mack by Mary Ann
    Hoberman
Snow Music by Lynne Rae Perkins
Today Is Monday by Eric Carle
Twinkle, Twinkle, Little Star by Iza
    Trapani

TRANSITION

Use a drum to beat the syllables in each child's name as they line up for another activity.

SNACK

Play calm and peaceful music as the children eat their snacks and lunch.

Group Time

Play Musical Chairs with the children, but with a twist—use the same number of chairs as children so there are no losers in this game. Invite each child to bring a chair to circle time. Arrange all of the chairs in a circle. Have the children stand in a circle around the chairs. Play music. As the music plays, the children walk around the chairs. When the music stops, each child sits in a chair. Introduce the children to different kinds of music during this game by playing country, classical, Latin, and other types of music from around the world.

Learning Center Ideas

Art: Invite the children to make drums by decorating coffee or snack cans with paper cutouts.

Literacy: Invite the children to use a drum to beat out the syllables of different children's names.

Math: Set out a drum and a deck of cards. Invite each child to turn one card from the deck, and beat out on the drum the number of the card as the other children count along out loud.

Sensory/Art: Make drums by decorating coffee cans or snack cans (with lids on) with construction paper or solid-color contact paper. Glue on paper or foam shapes, or small stickers. Use the drums for rhythm games. Make shakers by stapling beans between paper plates. Decorate them with crepe paper streamers, construction paper, and foam pieces. Add decorations with markers or crayons.

Additional Activities

Rhythm and Rhyme: Play different kinds of music and ask children how this music makes them feel. Invite the children to sing "If This Music Makes You Happy" and suit their actions to the words (see appendix page 336).

Number 9

STORY TIME

Engine Engine Number Nine by
  Stephanie Calmenson
My Nine Book by Jane Belk
  Moncure
Nine Animals and the Well by
  James Rumford
Numberlies: Number Nine by Colin
  and Jacqui Hawkins
Ten, Nine, Eight by Molly Bang

TRANSITION

Invite children to sit in a circle and
count aloud. The ninth child moves
on to the next activity. Have the
children count again, having the
ninth child move on. Repeat until all
children have moved on to the next
activity.

SNACK

Invite each child to make a 9 from
canned breadstick dough. Spread
the numeral with butter and
sprinkle on a mixture of sugar and
cinnamon. Bake according to
package directions.

Group Time

Sort the children into several different groups of varying numbers smaller
than nine: three, five, and so on. Encourage the groups to figure out how
many more people they would need so their group would have nine
people. Invite the groups to pair up in order to make groups of nine. After
the groups of nine have been made, set out nine stuffed bears or
dinosaurs, split the stuffed animals into two groups, one five, one four,
then six and three, then seven and two, then eight and one, showing the
children all the different ways to get the number nine.

Learning Center Ideas

Art: Make "9" bracelets. String nine colored beads on a chenille stem.
Measure and twist together the ends to form a bracelet. Cut off the excess.
Move a bead over each end or cover with tape so the bracelet doesn't have
sharp ends.

Literacy: Set out several old newspapers and magazines. Give the children
highlighters and invite them to mark number nines anywhere they find
them in the papers and magazines.

Math: Encourage the children to find all the nines in a deck of cards. Be
sure to count nine hearts, and so on, so they do not confuse nines and
sixes. Consider removing the sixes from the deck when working with
younger children.

Writing: Show the children how to practice drawing nines in a shallow tub
of sand. Tie four or five crayons together with masking tape to make a big
crayon and use it to draw "rainbow" nines.

Additional Activities

Movement: Say "The Nine Rhyme" and encourage the children to suit their
actions to the words (see appendix page 337).

Rhythm and Rhyme: Take turns acting out "Roll Over" (see appendix page
338) while the rest of the children sing and hold up the correct number of
fingers.

Goofy Green

Wear green today.

STORY TIME

Blue Hat Green Hat by Sandra Boynton

Five Green and Speckled Frogs by Priscilla Burris

Go Away, Big Green Monster by Ed Emberley

Green Eggs and Ham by Dr. Seuss

Little Green Tow Truck by Ken Wilson-Max

SNACK

Serve green grapes, kiwi fruit, and green apples.

Group Time

Read *Little Blue and Little Yellow* by Leo Lionni. Talk about what happened first, next, and last. Attach a piece of yellow cellophane to a flashlight, and blue cellophane to another flashlight. Shine the yellow light and the blue light. Take turns having the flashlights hug (place one on top of the other) so their combined beam turns green.

Learning Center Ideas

Art: Encourage the children to fingerpaint with blue and yellow paint on tree and plant shapes.

Art: Cut leaf shapes out of coffee filters. Invite the children to color their leaves all over with blue and yellow watercolor markers. Show them how to dip the coffee filter in water carefully and take it out quickly. Allow them to dry. What color are the leaves now?

Math: Bring in paint chips from home decorating stores in various shades of green, blue, and yellow. Invite the children to sort the chips by shades of color.

Math: Give the children plastic and fabric leaves, some in fall colors and some green. Sort the leaves by color.

Small Group: Put yellow tempera paint and blue tempera pain in a zipper plastic bag. Carefully let out the air as you zip the bag shut. Reinforce the zippers with electrical tape. Make other color bags such as red/white, yellow/red, red/blue. Ask the children to predict what color the bags will become as they are mixed. Help the children take turns mixing the bags to see what happens. Invite them to practice drawing the letters in their names with their fingers.

Additional Activities

Movement: Give each child a lily pad shape cut from construction paper. Invite the children to pretend they are frogs and follow the directions in "The Lily Pad Game" (see appendix page 337).

Outside: Take the children on a scavenger hunt for green things. Divide into groups. Make a list of all the green things you see.

Rhythm and Rhyme: Sing "The Green Song" with the children (see appendix page 336).

Letter *U*

STORY TIME

The Boy and the Tigers by Helen Bannerman

Hey! Wake Up! by Sandra Boynton

Ruby's Rainy Day by Rosemary Wells

Splosh by Mick Inkpen

SNACK

Make Upside-Down Strawberry Shortcake. First, put whipping cream on the bottom. Add washed strawberries. Put a slice of pound cake on the top.

Group Time

Introduce the children to the letter *u*. Ask the children to name some objects that begin with the letter *u*, or show the children several objects whose names begin with *u* and invite the children to name them. After this, read the story *The Umbrella* by Jan Brett. Talk about the parts of the book. Show the title, author, and illustrator. What is the umbrella?

Learning Center Ideas

Art: Print the letters *U-S-A* on white construction paper. Ask the children to trace over the letters with glue. Then, invite them to put red and blue stars in the glue to outline the letters *USA*.

Blocks: Set out several different kinds of blocks and small cars. Invite the children to make bridges and roads for the cars to go under.

Dramatic Play: A few days prior to using this daily plan, send the children home with requests for old uniforms. When the uniforms arrive, invite the children to dress in the uniforms, and pretend that they are working in whatever capacity is appropriate for that uniform.

Gross Motor: Encourage the children to look through their legs and view the world upside down.

Literacy: Set out an old shower curtain and cut several *u*-shapes into it, then attach one end to the top of a desk or the wall, and the other end to the floor. Give the children bean bags, and invite them to toss the bean bags underhand at the curtain, so the bags drop through.

Math: Cut out umbrella shapes and write a number from one to five on each one. Cut out 15 raindrop shapes. Laminate the pieces for durability. Encourage the children to put the correct number of raindrops on each umbrella shape.

Additional Activities

Movement: Set up a quick obstacle course, going under and around tables and chairs. Jump over blocks, make a u-turn and go back again. Put the word card "under" on things you go under.

Rhythm and Rhyme: Point to the letters of the alphabet as you sing the ABC song. Stand "up" as you sing the letter *u*.

Potatoes

Introduce the children to the history of potatoes in Ireland, and the Irish Potato Famine. Explain to the children that the potato, a hearty root that grows underground, was one of Ireland's largest crops (see potato facts on appendix page 344 for more information to share with the children).

STORY TIME

Hot Potato: Mealtime Rhymes by Neil Philip

I Spy an Eye: Mr. Potato Head Body Book by Nancy Krulik

Is This a Sack of Potatoes? by Crescent Dragonwagon

One Potato: A Counting Book of Potato Prints by Diana Pomeroy

TRANSITION

As you say this classic nursery rhyme, point to a child as you count the numbers. On each number, the child you point to lines up. When you say "more" the next two children may line up. Repeat until all the children are lined up or have moved on to the next activity.

> *One potato, two potatoes, three potatoes, four. . .*
> *Five potatoes, six potatoes, seven potatoes, more. . .*

SNACK

Make Potato Skins for the children (see recipe on appendix page 342).

Group Time

List the different ways to prepare potatoes. Make a picture graph of favorite ways to eat potatoes. On poster board, make a large graph with a column for mashed potato, baked potato, and French fries. Cut brown construction paper potato shapes (baked), white construction paper in fluffy shapes (mashed) and yellow, rectangular French fry shapes that fit into the squares of the grid. Have a taste-test party first, or just help each child print her name onto the potato she likes the best. Help children put their shapes in the correct places on the grid. Count how many children like each kind of potato.

Learning Center Ideas

Art: Set out several pieces of foam, felt, paper, and google eyes, inviting the children to make their own potato people.

Literacy: Set several books about potatoes and Ireland into a bushel basket, as well as a globe, with star stickers attached to Ireland and the location of your school. Invite the children to look at the books and globe to learn more about potatoes and Ireland.

Math: Cut out potato shapes from brown construction paper. Write a different number on each one and laminate for durability. Invite the children to put the correct number of wiggle eyes on each potato shape.

Science: Set out several sets of magnifying glasses and several kinds of potatoes: sweet potato, Idaho, red, and so on. Invite the children to examine the potatoes and describe their differences.

Additional Activities

Game: Sit the children in a circle. Pass the "hot" potato around the circle as fast as they can, while the music plays. When the music stops, the child holding the potato is out or moves on to the next activity.

Outside: Hide several balls of masking tape that resemble potatoes outside, at least one per child. Inside each "potato," hide a prize, such as a sticker, and invite the children to go on a potato hunt. Be sure the children stop after finding one potato, so each child can find one.

Rhythm and Rhyme: Encourage the children to sing "I'm a Little Potato" and suit their actions to the words (see appendix page 337).

Kites

Have a special kite day. Invite children to bring a kite to school.

STORY TIME

Berenstain Bears: We Like Kites by Jan Berenstain
The Emperor and the Kite by Jane Yolen
Kipper's Kite by Mick Inkpen
Kite by Mary Packard
Kite Flying by Grace Lin
Let's Fly a Kite by Stuart J. Murphy

TRANSITION

Practice the alphabet as you move on to the next activity. Repeat the rhyme below, putting an alphabet letter in the blanks. If your name begins with the given letter, you may line up or move on to the next activity.

Kites, kites up in the sky.
___ kites, ____ kites you can fly.

Group Time

Cut five kite shapes from felt, and attach them to a flannel board. Use the kites with "Five Little Kites" (see appendix page 336), removing one at the end of each stanza.

Next, ask the children what they think they could see if they were as high in the air as a kite. Invite the children to draw a picture of their kite adventure, illustrating things such as the string breaking and the kite flying away. Dictate a story about the kite's adventures.

Learning Center Ideas

Art: Take several index cards, and cut them diagonally into four pieces. Hand the children four corners and invite them to decorate each section. When each portion is decorated, have the children trade away three of their sections. To do this, it is easiest to ask that the children sit in a circle with their four sections in front of them. First, ask the children to pick up one piece and pass it to the person three people to the left. Then ask the children to pick up a second piece, and pass it four, or two, people to the left, then pass the final piece one or five people to the left. This way the children have four mismatched pieces. Give the children new index cards and help them glue the four pieces onto the whole index card, making a colorful kite. Attach strings to the ends of each kite, and help the children hand them around the room.

Art: Decorate a construction paper kite shape with various objects, such as foam shapes, construction paper pieces, sequins, and so on. Add a tail made from rags.

Math: Cut several kite shapes from construction paper and put a number on each. Set out several flannel cutouts of bow ties, and invite the children to add the correct number of them to the kite string.

Additional Activities

Movement: Read "Pretend You Are a Kite" (see appendix page 338) and encourage the children to suit their actions to the words.

Outside: Invite children to bring kites to school for a kite-flying day.

Rhythm and Rhyme: Sing "I'm a Little Kite" with the children (see appendix page 337).

Artists

STORY TIME

Andy Warhol by Jan Greenberg

Art Dog by Thatcher Hurd

Georgia O'Keefe: Painter by Michael L. Berry

The Magical Garden of Claude Monet by Laurence Anholt

Picasso and the Girl with the Ponytail: A Story About Pablo Picasso by Laurence Anholt

Uncle Andy's by James Warhol

When Pigasso Met Mootisse by Nina Laden

SNACK

Invite the children to create a snack by putting pretzel sticks into cubes like Tinker Toys. Build a large snack or a small one. Offer the following ingredients: pretzel sticks, cheese cubes, ham cubes, turkey cubes.

Group Time

Talk to the children about being an artist. Explain that there are many kinds of artists. Some artists use paint, chalk, colored pencils, junk, clay, and so on. Talk about the artists listed on appendix page 343-344. As you talk, pass around an object that will help them remember the artist. Show pictures of what the artists made.

Learning Center Ideas

Art: Set out many different kinds of creative materials, including paints, chalk, playdough, junk for collages, blocks, and beads. Encourage children to explore different ways to create art.

Blocks: Frank Lloyd Wright built houses. He was an architect. First he drew a picture of what he wanted the house to look like. These drawings are called *blueprints.* Give the children blue construction paper and white crayons or chalk and encourage them to draw a house. Then, ask them to make the house with blocks. Take pictures of the buildings and display the photographs next to the blueprints.

Literacy: Encourage children to look at art books and choose their favorite artist. Offer books by Mary Cassatt, Georgia O'Keefe, Claude Monet, Pablo Picasso, and others.

Additional Activities

Outside: Encourage the children to take paper and crayons or paints outside and to draw what they see, just as Monet did.

Rhythm and Rhyme: Sing "For He's a Very Good Artist" and "I'm a Little Artist" (see appendix page 336).

Small Group: Look at some of the pictures Picasso drew. Tell children Picasso went through times where he only drew blue pictures. He then he went through a period where he only drew rose-colored pictures. Pour green paint into four clear glass jars until each is half full. Add a little bit of white paint to one jar and stir. What happens? Then, add more white paint to the next jar and stir. Explain to the children that they are making shades of green. Do the same with black paint, making darker shades of green. Set out the paints and invite the children to use them to make their own green pictures in the same way Picasso did.

Cowboys

STORY TIME

Cowboy Bunnies by Christine Loomis
Cowboy Kid by Max Eilenberg
Cowboys Can Do Amazing Things Too by Kelly Stuart
Little Old Big Beard and Big Young Little Beard: A Short and Tall Tale by Remy Charlip
A Wild Cowboy by Dana Kessimakis Smith

TRANSITION

Explain that "cowpoke" is another word for "cowboy." Sing this song. Point to one or two cowpokes, and invite them to trot away to the next activity.

(Tune: I'm a Little Teapot)
I'm a little cowpoke in the sun,
And I have a lot of fun.
I get on my pony and ride away.
Yippi-ky-aye-o, yippi-ky-aye-ay!

Group Time

Invite the children to sit in a circle around a make-believe campfire. To make a campfire, lean three long blocks against each other. Add yellow and red tissue paper to create "flames." Talk to the children about cowboys. Explain that cowboys used to sit around a campfire and tell stories at night. Put several "old West" items in a paper bag, such as plastic horses, cowboy hats, ropes, and sheriff badges. Take them out one by one and use them to make up a cowpoke story. Use chart paper to write the story down.

Learning Center Ideas

Dramatic Play: Pretend to be cowboys on the range. Provide hats, vests, and the articles from Group Time and encourage the children to ride the range, cook by campfire, and sleep outside under the stars.

Literacy: Sing "Oh, Where Have You Been, Little Cowpoke?" in small groups (see appendix page 337). After singing the song, give children paper and writing utensils. Invite them to draw a picture about what they would do if they were a cowboy or cowgirl. Make a class book out of their pictures by stapling the pages together.

Math: Staple pieces of bulletin board paper that look like fence into circles. Write a number on each "fence." Encourage the children to put the correct number of plastic animals or laminated cow or horse shapes inside the fence.

Additional Activities

Movement: Explain that people liked to get together and square dance. Even now, people dress up in cowboy hats and special dresses to go square dancing. Teach the children how to do several simple square dance moves. Turn on square dance music and grab a partner for some fun, all while learning to follow directions.

Outside: Invite children to pretend they are horses. Show the horses how to gallop. When the horses are very good at galloping, set out blocks for the horses to jump over.

Rhythm and Rhyme: Sing "The Cowboy Song" with the children (see appendix page 335).

Chicka Chicka Boom Boom by Bill Martin, Jr. and John Archambault

GENERAL DAILY PLAN

STORY TIME

Barn Dance by Bill Martin, Jr.

A Beasty Story by Bill Martin Jr.

Brown Bear, Brown Bear, What Do You See? by Bill Martin, Jr.

Fire! Fire! Said Mrs. McGuire by Bill Martin, Jr.

Knots on a Counting Rope by Bill Martin, Jr.

The Maestro Plays by Bill Martin, Jr.

Panda Bear, Panda Bear, What Do You See? by Bill Martin, Jr.

Polar Bear, Polar Bear, What Do You Hear? by Bill Martin, Jr.

TRANSITION

Say the sentence below, and name different letters. The children whose names begin with that letter move to the next activity. Or, invite children to name another word that begins with the same letter before moving to the next activity.

If your name begins with _____, You may line up or move to the next activity.

SNACK

Invite the children to make Coconut Trees (see recipe on page 342).

Group Time

Read the story *Chicka Chicka Boom Boom* in small groups. During the second reading, encourage the children to repeat, "chicka chicka boom boom" along with the story.

Play a quiet game of I Spy with letters. Put up an alphabet poster with all the letters of the alphabet. Use a set of alphabet flash cards or print the letters of the alphabet on index cards. Show a flash card with a letter. Name this letter together. Next, look at the poster. Ask the children to raise their hands if they can find this letter on the poster. Invite one of the children to come up and point out the letter on the poster.

Learning Center Ideas

Art: Trace a large letter of the first letter of each child's name. Invite children to find their letter and decorate it with embellishments such as glitter, tissue paper, stickers, yarn, and feathers. Show the finished posters at group time. Make a class book, adding each child's picture to the poster.

Literacy: Set out a name card for each child in the class. Set out magnet letters and a cookie sheet. Invite the children to try writing their names and friends' names with magnetic letters.

Science: Put a real coconut on the Science Table for children to examine with magnifying glasses.

Writing: Put alphabet letter stamps and a stamp pad in the writing center for the children to print their names.

Additional Activities

Outside: Use chalk to draw alphabet letters on the sidewalk.

Rhythm and Rhyme: Sing "The Chicka Alphabet" (see appendix page 335).

Trains

STORY TIME

All Aboard Trains by Mary Harding

Chugga-Chugga Choo Choo by
    Kevin Lewis

Freight Train by Donald Crews

The Little Engine That Could by
    Watty Piper

Long Train by Sam Williams

Trains by Byron Barton

TRANSITION

Encourage children to act out this rhyme. One child is the "engine." That child chooses another child, who lines up behind the engine and puts his hands on the engine's shoulders. They walk around the classroom and pick up the other children until all of the children are in the train. The train moves on to the next activity. Say the rhyme each time a new child is added to the train.

SNACK

Make a train using several rectangle or square crackers. Fill up the "cars" with fruit or cheese.

Group Time

Talk about the different kinds of cars on a freight train such as box cars, oil cars, refrigerator cars, and so on. Cut out a train engine with several different kinds of cars. On each car, list the things the train car might hold. For example, a refrigerator car might hold ice, frozen food, and so on. Make a large class train for your classroom from boxes. Obtain large boxes (preferably one for each child) from your local grocery store. Cereal boxes also work well. Set out markers, paints, foam pieces, construction paper, and chenille stems, and invite children to decorate the train cars. When they finish, line up the cars to make a large class train.

Learning Center Ideas

Blocks: Put a small train in the Block Center. Invite children to play cars. Remind them that the cars have to stop for railroad trains coming through.

Gross Motor: Practice balancing. Bring in an old railroad tie. Invite children to walk across the train tie without falling off.

Literacy: Cut out a train engine shape and a train car in each of the following colors: red, blue, green, yellow, orange, brown, black, and purple. Print the color word on the train car. Set out several small items of each color. Invite the children to put the named color items on the car.

Math: Cut out a train engine shape and 10 train car shapes. Label the car shapes 1–10. Invite children to put the train car shapes in order from 1–10.

Additional Activities

Movement: Play Color Train. Choose one child to be the "engine." Explain to the child that he can pick up a train car that is wearing one of the colors he is wearing. For example, if the child is wearing a brown shirt and blue jeans, he must find another child who is wearing either brown or blue. Then, that child picks someone who is wearing one of the colors she has on, and so on, until everyone is on the train.

Outside: Play "Follow the Leader" train around the schoolyard.

Rhythm and Rhyme: Sing "The Train Song" with the children (see appendix page 341).

Spring

STORY TIME

Are You Spring? by Caroline Pitcher
Countdown to Spring by Janet
　　Schulman
Spring's Sprung by Greg Couch
*That's What Happens When It's
　　Spring* by Elaine W. Good
When Will It Be Spring? by Catherine
　　Walters

TRANSITION

Ask the children to name a word
that rhymes with *spring* as they
move on to the next activity.

SNACK

Put peanut butter on the top half of
a pretzel rod. Add pieces of white
puff cereal as pussy willows.

Group Time

Bring in a pussy willow or a flower bulb. Talk about spring and how this
item is a sign of spring. Pass around the pussy willow or flower bulb. As
the children hold the pussy willow, invite them to name a sign of spring.
Make a list on chart paper with a quick drawing. Put the list in the Writing
Center.

Learning Center Ideas

Art: Make spring flowers. Cut out large flower shapes in each of the eight
basic colors. Set out embellishments such as buttons, paper ribbon,
sequins, pompoms, felt and foam shapes, and other items. Set out the
flowers and invite children to work together to put the same color of
decorations on the flowers. When they are finished, display them with
stems as a spring color collage.

Literacy: Copy and cut out several baseball glove and baseball patterns.
Write an uppercase alphabet letter on each glove and a lowercase letter on
each baseball. Laminate the game for durability. Invite children to match
the uppercase glove to the lowercase baseball.

Science: Set out several kinds of flower seeds and flower bulbs for children
to examine.

Additional Activities

Movement: Invite the children to sing "The Springtime Song" (see appendix
page 339) and suit their actions to the words.

Outside: Go for a walk and look for items that are signs of spring. If
possible, bring some back to study at the science center.

Rhythm and Rhyme: Sing "The Colors of Spring" with the children (see
appendix page 335).

Fruits

STORY TIME

Apples and Pumpkins by Anne
    Rockwell
Big Hungry Bear by Audrey Wood
Eating the Alphabet by Lois Ehlert
*Pepo and Lolo and the Big Red
    Apple* by Martin Larranage

SNACK

Have a fruit-tasting party. Try the
fruit dip on appendix page 342 with
several fruits. Afterward, talk about
which fruit the children like best.

Group Time

Talk about different fruits, and the difference between a fruit and a
vegetable. Bring in a fruit bowl with four or five fruits in it. Show the fruits
and talk about each one. Then play a game. Put the fruits back in the
bowl. Cover the bowl (or children close their eyes) and take one fruit away.
Show the bowl again. Which fruit is missing?

Learning Center Ideas

Dramatic Play: Set up a play Fruit and Vegetable Stand and stock it with
plastic fruits and vegetables. Sort the veggies and fruits in baskets for
selling and set them on cardboard boxes or crates. Add price signs, cash
register, toy money and grocery bags for a fun fruit and vegetable stand.
Math: Invite children to sort small plastic fruits and vegetables into pots for
cooking.
Science: Set out real fruits and fruits cut in half and include magnifying
glasses for children to explore. Also set out paper and crayons for the
children to draw what they see.

Additional Activities

Movement: Assign each child as an apple, an orange or a banana. Give
each trio (apple, orange, and banana) a hula hoop and tell them to step
inside it as it rests on the floor. Call out a fruit, for example, "apple."
Encourage all of the children who are apples to switch spots with other
apples. Continue to call out different fruits. Then, say, "fruit basket upset!"
When the children hear this, they all change places at once. Help them
make sure that three different fruits end up in each hula hoop basket.
Project: Make a fruit bowl that smells like the real thing. For each child, cut
out a fruit bowl shape, a cherry, an orange, a strawberry, and a grape.
Give the shapes to the children and ask them to spread glue on each piece
of "fruit." Invite them to sprinkle the appropriate flavor gelatin on each
piece of fruit. Allow the fruit to dry. Show the children how to glue the
fruits onto the bowl shape to make a fruit salad. Scratch and sniff!
Rhythm and Rhyme : Sing "The Fruit Song" with the children (see appendix
page 336).

Vegetables

STORY TIME

Bean Soup by Sarah Hines-Stephens

Growing Vegetable Soup by Lois Ehlert

How Are You Peeling? by Saxton Freymann

I Eat Vegetables by Hannah Tofts

Peas and Thank You by Cindy Kenney

SNACK

Make this easy veggie dip (see the recipe on appendix page 343) with the children, and invite them to help wash the vegetables before cutting them.

Group Time

Bring in several kinds of vegetables for the children to see and touch. Then cut up several kinds of raw vegetables for children to try.

Learning Center Ideas

Art: Encourage the children to draw or paint their favorite vegetable. Put the child's name on the drawings. When dry, staple the pages into a class book.

Math: Set out two baskets. Label one "fruits" with a picture of an apple and label the other one "vegetables" with a picture of a carrot. Set out pictures of both fruits and vegetables and invite children to put the pictures in the right basket.

Science: Set up a seed observation station. Buy packets of vegetable seeds. Open the seeds and put the seeds and the packets in a zipper plastic bag. Also set out the raw vegetable. Invite children to match the real vegetable to the seed.

Additional Activities

Movement: Invite the children to sing "The Veggie Soup Song" (see appendix page 341). Have children join hands in a circle as they sing this song. Play a veggie soup version of The Farmer in the Dell. Invite one child to be the chef and wear an apron. As the children sing the verse, the chef picks a carrot. Then the carrot picks the beans, and so on. Invite children to name vegetables to add more verses. At the end, the children left in the circle shake their arms up and down pretending to stir the soup.

Outside: Plant carrot tops and potato eyes and other vegetables outside. After they grow, make your own vegetable soup, or plant the vegetable in small containers that the children can take home.

Rhythm and Rhyme: Recite "Veggies in My Lunch" with the children (see appendix page 341).

Bread

STORY TIME

If You Give a Moose a Muffin by Laura Numeroff
The Little Red Hen by Jonathan Allen
Lunch by Denise Fleming
Sun Bread by Elisa Kleven
Walter the Baker by Eric Carle

TRANSITION

Chant "The Muffin Chant" (see appendix page 337) and say one child's name. At the end of the chant, that child names a new child and moves on to a new activity.

SNACK

Make "Aunt Alvina's Banana Bread" (see appendix page 342).

Group Time

Discuss the many different kinds of breads we eat. Bring in several different kinds, for example, bagels, tortillas, French bread, white, and rye loaves. Invite children to taste the different kinds of bread. Have an election to vote for their favorite bread. Make up a ballot with pictures of the five types of breads they tried. Invite children to draw a circle around their favorite bread. Help the children fold their ballot and put them in a ballot box. As a class, count the votes to see which bread won.

Learning Center Ideas

Art: Set out brown construction paper with a muffin shape drawn on it. Invite children to cut out the muffin shape. They can add blueberries to their muffins by dipping their fingers into blue paint or ink to make fingerprint blueberries.

Math: Set out several paper cups with different numbers written on each. Invite the children to put the correct number of pretzel sticks in each cup.

Science: Before Centers begin, add yeast to warm water according to package directions. Put it in the Science Center. Invite children to come and look at (but not touch) the yeast to see what happens. Explain to the children that this is what makes bread rise.

Additional Activities

Outside: Set out stale pieces of bread for the birds to eat. Watch as the birds come and take it.

Small Group: Read *The Little Red Hen* by Jonathan Allen. Talk to the children about the setting and characters. Bring story props such as cooking supplies, an apron, or chef's hat for the children to act out the story.

Food Group Fun

STORY TIME

From Grass to Milk by Stacy Taus-Bolstad

It Looked Like Spilt Milk by Charles Green G. Shaw

Milk by Claire Llewellyn

Milk by Jillian Powell

The Milk Makers by Gail Gibbons

TRANSITION

Recite the following:

Milk, yogurt, ice cream cheese, who is ready to line up please?

Call on somebody who is sitting ready to line up to answer a food question and then line up or move to the next activity. Examples: "Name a food that begins with the /b/ sound," or "name a food that is yellow."

SNACK

Cut cheese and meat into small cubes. Invite the children to make kabobs by putting cheese and meat cubes onto sticks. Or, children can make their own Pudding in a Bag (see appendix page 343).

Group Time

Bring in plastic food meats and plastic dairy products. Talk about and name foods in the meat group. Also talk about and name foods in dairy group. Then play a game. Hold up two plastic foods and ask the children whether they are from the same food group. If they are the same, have the children put their hands on their heads. Then together name the food group or groups.

Learning Center Ideas

Dramatic Play: Make a Restaurant. Include a tablecloth, menus, and dishes for the children to pretend they are running or visiting a restaurant.

Fine Motor: Add rolling pins and cookie cutters to playdough. Also add aluminum pans for making pretend cookies and pies.

Sensory: Provide measuring cups, spoons, pots, and other dishes for the children to explore.

Additional Activities

Movement: Play The Cat and Mouse Game, where the mouse tries to get the cheese. Everyone stands in a circle holding hands except the cat and the mouse. Put a plastic food cheese in the center of the circle. The cat will try to protect the cheese and start the game in the center of the circle. The mouse tries to sneak under the children's arms to get the cheese without being tagged by the cat. The cat and mouse can only get under the arms of the children when their arms are in the air, but still holding hands.

Outside: Take a field trip to a grocery store. Go up and down the aisles looking for the different food groups.

Project: On construction paper, show the children how to paint with several colors of food coloring mixed with sweetened condensed milk. The paintings will take a long time to dry, but when dry will have an interesting effect on the paper.

Rhythm and Rhyme: Sing "Cartons of Milk" with the children (see appendix page 335).

Windy Weather

STORY TIME

Elmer Takes Off by David McKee
I Face the Wind by Vicki Cobb
It's Too Windy by Hans Wilhelm
One Windy Wednesday by Phyllis
  Root
The Wind Blew by Pat Hutchins
Wind Says Good Night by Katy
  Rydell

TRANSITION

Recite the below rhyme with the children, filling in the blank with a child's name, then having the child named pretend to blow away, moving on to the next activity.

Windy weather came to stay,
And then _____ blew away.

SNACK

Make Pinwheel Bread using canned crescent roll dough (see recipe on page 342).

Group Time

Talk about what happens on a windy day. Invite the children to sing "The Wind Song" and suit their actions to the words (see appendix page 341). Do windy experiments with the children. Set out a feather, rock, tissue paper, ball, and other interesting items. Ask the children what will happen when they blow on each item. Let the children try blowing on the objects through straws. Ask the children if their predictions are correct.

Learning Center Ideas

Art: Make wind paintings. Place a piece of paper flat inside a shirt box lid. Put small blobs of several colors of paint on the paper. Encourage the children to blow on the paint with a straw. Watch the paint move around and spread out.

Art/Science: Staple a piece of construction paper into a cylinder-shaped wind sock for each child. Invite each child to decorate his windsock with crayons, markers, die cut shapes, and foam pieces. Glue 3–4 crepe paper streamers about 12" long to the bottom of the wind sock. Hang the wind socks from the ceiling. Open the windows and watch them blow.

Math: Write different numbers on construction paper kites. Encourage the children to put the correct number of bow ties on the kite's tail.

Additional Activities

Movement: Dance to music with streamers. If possible, take the dancing outside so the streamers blow in the wind.

Outside: Hang two flags outside so the children can see them from a window. Check the flags on a calm day, and then again on a windy day and talk about the differences the children see in the flags each day.

Rhythm and Rhyme: Encourage the children to sing "Swoosh Goes the Wind" (see appendix page 341).

Paper Tubes

Before this unit, ask the children to donate paper tubes from paper towels and toilet paper. This could just be an ongoing request because there are so many things to make and do with them in the classroom

STORY TIME

Cardboard Tube Mania by Christine M. Irvin

Creative Crafts: Cardboard Tube by Nikki Connor

TRANSITION

Invite the children to sit in a circle around the tube. Spin the tube around and repeat the verse below. Whoever the ends point to may line up or move to the next activity.

Spin the tube round and round.
Sit very still, don't make a sound.
Where it stops, we don't know,
But then that friend will have
to go.

SNACK

Turn pancakes into tubes. Make pancakes using a mix, toaster, or microwave pancakes. Invite the children to put a teaspoon of apple or cherry pie filling in the middle of the pancake and roll the pancake up into a roll.

Group Time

Give each child a paper tube when they come to Group Time. Tell them to pretend they have a telescope. Invite children to pretend they are looking up to the sky. Ask them what they see, and make a list of their responses. Then, invite the children to pretend the tubes are microphones, and have them conduct interviews with the tubes. Use the microphones again while your class sings their favorite songs.

Learning Center Ideas

Construction: Add cardboard tubes, wood, and glue to your Construction Center. Invite children to construct a work of art.

Literacy: Using a toilet paper tube, glue a piece of colored construction paper on the tube. Glue another piece of flesh colored paper on the top 1/3 of the edge. Set out yarn and paper shreds, markers, glue, construction paper, and foam pieces to make a tube paper person. Invite the children to give people names, then make up stories about them.

Math: Glue paper around several tubes so they resemble flower vases. Write different numbers on each "vase." Set out several foam flowers glued to the tops of craft sticks, and challenge the children to put the correct number of flowers in the vases.

Small Motor: Glue foam pieces, yarn and other objects on cardboard tubes. When they are dry, put them in the playdough area, and invite the children to roll them in playdough.

Additional Activities

Movement: Say the "Jack Be Nimble" nursery rhyme, substituting children's names for "Jack." Invite the children to jump over a paper tube candlestick. (They can be short toilet tubes or tall paper towel candlesticks. Add red and yellow tissue pieces sticking out of the top as fire.)

Outside: Help the children staple or tape two paper tubes together to use as binoculars, then bring the children outside to go bird watching with their binoculars.

Noses

Eyes, Nose, Fingers and Toes: A First Book About You by Judy Hindley

Little Bunny Follow His Nose by Katherine Howard

The Long Nosed Pig by Keith Faulkner

Nose Book by Al Perkins

Toes, Ears, and Nose by Marion Dane Bauer

TRANSITION

Recite the following rhyme with the children, adding with each repetition a different child's name in the second line, and invite that child to move on to the following activity.

> *Touch your eyes, touch your nose.*
> *Out of the circle _____ goes.*

SNACK

Make yummy smelling Cinnamon Rolls (see appendix page 342).

Group Time

Play a nose guessing game. Before Group Time, take a close-up picture of each child's face. Make two prints of each child, then cut out two construction paper oval-shaped head patterns for each child. Staple them together along their tops. On the first head shape, cut only the nose and glue it on. On the second head shape, glue a picture of the whole head. Invite each child to add eyes, hair and a mouth to the first picture. During Group Time, play a guessing game. Show the nose picture first. Invite the children to guess whose nose it is. Lift up the head to see whose nose it is. Display for every one to guess, with the caption "Who Knows Whose Nose?"

Learning Center Ideas

Science: Set out several different scented candles and pictures of the items their smells are supposed to resemble, inviting the children to match the scents to the pictures.

Sensory: Add scented Kool-Aid Playdough to the Sensory Center (see appendix page 342).

Additional Activities

Rhythm and Rhyme: Invite the children to sing "The Smell Song" (see appendix page 339).

Small Group: Bring in several different strong smelling foods, such as cinnamon rolls, popcorn, and so on. Give each child two small pieces of the same food. Invite the children to taste the foods, then hold their noses and try tasting them a second time. Ask the children if they noticed any differences in the flavors, and if so, ask that they describe the differences.

Pockets

Before doing this lesson plan, send a note home telling families to help the children wear something with a pocket and to put something special in the pocket for show and tell. Wear clothes with as many pockets as you can on this day.

STORY TIME

Katy No Pocket by Emmy Payne
A Pocket for Corduroy by Don Freeman
Pocket Poems by Bobbi Katz
There's a Wocket in My Pocket by Dr. Seuss
What Did You Put in Your Pocket? by Beatrice Schenk De Regniers

SNACK

Serve vegetables, hummus, and cheese in pita pocket bread.

Group Time

Before Group Time, put in your pocket a letter made of paper, foam, magnetic, wood, or some other material. Sing the song below, asking the children to guess which letter is in your pocket. Each time you repeat the verse, give the children a clue about the letter. As the children begin to understand the game, have children pick objects to hide in their pockets while others recite the verse and guess what the objects might be. (This game will also work with shapes.)

> Tune: Did You Ever See a Lassie?
> *What letter's in my pocket, my pocket, my pocket?*
> *What letter's in my pocket?*
> *I'll give you a clue, _____.*

Learning Center Ideas

Art: Glue two large pocket shapes together for each child. Invite the children to use paper, sequins, markers, and other embellishments to decorate their pockets, then hang them in the room within each child's reach. At night, put a little note, piece of candy, or other surprise in the pocket for each child.

Literacy: Make a pocket book. Glue paper pockets onto pages. Invite children to staple several pages together into a book. Put something in each pocket, such as a button, crayon, and so on. At the bottom of each page print "a _____ in my pocket," and help the children write the name of what is in the pocket, or encourage them to make a drawing of the object in the pocket.

Math: Glue numbered pockets on posterboard, and challenge the children to put the correct number of craft sticks in each pocket.

Additional Activities

Outside: Invite the children to look for three things to put in their pockets and later add to the Science Table.

Rhythm and Rhyme: Recite "A Penny in My Pocket" with the children (see appendix page 337).

April

Calendar Time

During Calendar Time, introduce the month of April to the children. Look at the letters in the word *April.* Name each letter, and say the sound and other words that start with the sound. Whose name begins with the letter *a*? Do this for each letter in the word during calendar time throughout the month.

Monthly Organizer

SPECIAL DAYS AND HOLIDAYS

Arbor Day
April 22: Earth Day

GENERAL DAILY PLANS

Purple
Number 3
Letter *W*
Numbers
April Showers
Ducks
Chicks
Bunnies
Umbrellas
Letter *X*
Humpty Dumpty
Chameleons
Paper Clips
Planting Seeds

Stringy Stuff
Letter *Y*
Flowers
Worms
Mud
Letter *Z*
Bags
Letter *L*

Note: Please be sure to check for allergies before serving the snacks or doing any food-related activities.

Arbor Day

Arbor Day is the last Friday in April.

STORY TIME

Acorn and the Oak Tree by Lori Froeb
Around the Apple Tree by Karen Viola
Chicka Chicka 1,2,3 by Bill Martin Jr.
Five Little Monkeys Sitting in a Tree by Eileen Christelow
Tree Is Just a Tree? by Brenda Silsbe

TRANSITION

Give the children construction paper cutouts of leaves with numbers written on each. Invite the children to recite "The Number Rhyme," found on appendix page 348, saying a different number each time they recite the rhyme. The child holding the leaf with the recited number on it lines up to move on to the next activity. Repeat until all the children are in line.

SNACK

Set out foods that come from trees, such as apples, bananas, pears, and peaches, for the children to snack on.

Group Time

Set out several items, both objects related to trees and objects not related to trees. Invite the children to sort the items.

Learning Center Ideas

Art: Set out several different leaves and lengths of bark, inviting the children to make crayon rubbings of them on sheets of construction paper.
Science: Set out a section of a log, inviting the children to count its rings to determine the age of the tree from which it came.

Additional Activities

Outside: Invite the children to examine several different trees. Encourage the children to identify the roots, branches, trunk, and leaves of the trees, and to make comparisons between each tree. Consider using a tree guide to help the children identify the types of trees.
Projects: Stand a tree branch in a coffee can full of sand. Keep the branch in the classroom and decorate it for each season, using the list below as examples of how to decorate the tree:

> **Spring:** Attach flowers (Invite children to make tissue paper flowers).
> **Summer:** Make bugs glued to green leaves. Hang from the tree.
> **Fall:** Marble paint green leaf shapes, with yellow, orange, and brown.
> **Winter:** Cut snowflakes and hang them from the tree.

Rhythm and Rhyme: Invite the children to recite "I'm a Little Tree Changing All the Time," found on appendix page 347.
Small Group: Set out several different types of seeds, such as apple, peach, pear, and plum. Explain to the children how all trees start as seeds, and grow over several years. Take the children outside and help them to plant some of the seeds, or show the children how to plant the seeds in cups. Over time, encourage the children to check on the progress of their trees, and to water them if necessary.

Earth Day (April 22nd)

Wear green to celebrate Earth Day.

STORY TIME

The Earth and I by Frank Ashe
The Family of Earth by Schim
   Schimmel
Life on Earth by Stephen Holmes
Our Earth by Anne Rockwell
Water Hole by Graeme Base

TRANSITION

Invite the children to recite the "For What It's Worth" rhyme, found on appendix page 346. Pick a child, and ask him to suggest something he can do to help the earth, and then move on to the next activity. Repeat until all children have had a chance to say how they would help the earth.

SNACK

Invite the children to use a craft stick to spread blue cream cheese on half of an English muffin, so it resembles the earth. Add slices of bologna or carrot for land. Enjoy.

Group Time

Bring three small wastebaskets and an array of (clean) empty bottles, papers, and cans. Explain to the children that some of the things that we throw away in the garbage can be used again to make new materials. Explain that this is called recycling, and invite the children to help sort items based on whether they are glass, aluminum, or paper.

Learning Center Ideas

Art: Set out paints, markers, and other materials with which the children can decorate lunch bags, and invite them to use the bags to collect litter.
Craft: Set out several small rubber balls and sheets of blue tissue paper. Help the children glue the tissue paper to the ball to make a globe. When the glue dries, help the children glue green construction paper shapes to the globe, making continents.

Additional Activities

Movement: Encourage the children to act out the "Earth Day Helper" poem, found on appendix page 345, to help save the earth.
Outside: Bring the children outside and help them plant a flower or a tree.
Rhythm and Rhyme: Invite the children to sing "I Live on Earth, as You Can See," found on appendix page 347. After singing, ask the children to name ways they might take care of the earth, such as: turning off lights, planting seeds, planting trees, cleaning up litter, and recycling newspapers.
Small Group: Show the children a globe, asking if they can identify where they are on the globe, giving clues if necessary. Explain the equator, and how temperatures differ in different parts of the world.

Purple

STORY TIME

Harold and the Purple Crayon by Crockett Johnson

I Love You the Purplest by Barbara M. Joosse

Lilly's Purple Plastic Purse by Kevin Henkes

SNACK

Provide grape juice and halved purple grapes. (Be sure to cut the grapes, as they can be a choking hazard.)

Group Time

Read Crockett Johnson's *Harold and the Purple Crayon* to the children. After finishing the book, give each child a sheet of paper with the phrase "_____ and the _____ Crayon" written on it, and a different colored crayon, and invite them to draw their own pictures. When the children finish drawing, help them write their names and the colors of the crayons they used to draw their pictures in the spaces provided.

Learning Center Activities

Art: Set out blue and red fingerpaint and encourage the children to paint on grape-shaped sheets of paper.

Sensory: Give each child a small ball of red playdough and a small ball of blue playdough. Invite the children to roll the two balls together to make purple grapes. Encourage the children to count how many grapes they make.

Additional Activities

Movement: Before this activity, be sure there are several purple objects in the classroom. Turn on some lively music and dance with the children around the room. Occasionally, stop the music, telling the children to find and touch the closest purple object in the room.

Rhythm and Rhyme: Invite the children to recite "If You Take a Little Red," found on appendix page 346.

Small Group: Give each child a sheet of paper with his name written on it in red marker. Invite the children to trace over the letters in their names with blue marker to see what colors their names turn.

Number 3

STORY TIME

1,2,3 to the Zoo by Eric Carle
Chicka, Chicka, 1,2,3, by Bill Martin
Goldilocks and the Three Bears by Jim Aylesworth
One, Two, Three by Sandra Boynton
Three Billy Goats Gruff by Stephen Carpenter
The Three Little Pigs by Annabelle James

TRANSITION

Play hot potato, using three beanbags instead of one. Sit in a circle. As the music plays, encourage the children pass three beanbags around the circle. When the music stops, ask the three children holding the beanbags to move to the next activity.

SNACK

Help the children shape breadstick or pretzel dough into the shape of the number "3". Cook and serve.

Group Time

Hold up a cutout of a number 3, asking the children to identify the number, which numbers come before and after it, and to think of things that commonly come in threes. Encourage the children to clap three times every time someone says the number three. Read the children *Goldilocks and the Three Bears*, asking the children what there were three of in the book. After reading the book, set out three cups of varying sizes, and ask the children which bear each cup would belong to, and which one Goldilocks would want to use. (Consider repeating this part of the Group Time activity with other items, such as socks, blocks, and shoes.)

Learning Center Ideas

Art: Set out several cutouts of the number 3, as well as several pieces of felt, lace, and other decorative materials. Invite the children to choose three materials to glue to the cutouts.

Fine Motor: Set out several chenille stems for the children to shape into number threes.

Math: Set out a calendar and several square cutouts with the numbers 1–31 written on them, and challenge the children to put the numbers in order on the calendar.

Additional Activities

Movement: Play Dog Catcher. Choose three children to be dogcatchers, instead of one. Invite all the other children to line up and run from one side of the room to the other. As they run, the dogcatchers try to tag them. Children who are tagged become dogcatchers. The play continues until all the children are caught.

Outside: Take the children on a threes scavenger hunt, encouraging them to look for threes of things, such as houses, clouds, children, dogs, birds, and trees.

Rhythm and Rhyme: Invite the children to recite "Number Three," found on appendix page 348.

Letter *W*

STORY TIME

Warthogs Paint by Pamela Duncan Edwards
The Way I Feel by Janan Cain
Webster J. Duck by Martin Waddell
Wemberly Worried by Kevin Henkes
Wild About Books by Judy Sierra

SNACK

Bring in a large watermelon for the children to snack on.

Group Time

Introduce the children to words that include the letter *w*. Invite the children to name words that include *w*, and have them wave their hands as they say the words. Afterwards, go on a *w* walk. Bring the children outside, and encourage them to say the names of objects they see whose names include a *w*. Write down what they say put their ideas on posterboard in the classroom. Invite the children to recite them and say where they saw the objects outside.

Learning Center Ideas

Dramatic Play: Restaurant: Invite the children to pretend they are waiters and waitresses, setting out menus and inviting the children to take orders from one another. Set out several small notepads so the children can pretend to take down customers' orders.

Literacy: Help the children dip several different matchbox cars' tires in paint and drive them on construction paper cutouts of the letter *w*.

Math: Watermelon Counting: Number several differently-colored construction paper watermelon cutouts. Laminate for durability. Challenge the children to put the appropriate number of black pompom "seeds" on each watermelon.

Additional Activities

Movement: Play a game of "W Catcher." Separate the children into three groups: worms, woodpeckers, and whales. The children then separate into two groups who stand against either wall. Choose one child to be the "w catcher." The w catcher stands in the middle of the room, and calls out one of the three group names. Children in that group run from one side of the room to the other, and the w catcher tries to tag them. Those children tagged become w catchers, too. The game repeats until all children are caught.

Rhythm and Rhyme: Ask the children to name some of their favorite songs, and make a list of the names on posterboard. When several titles are on the list, encourage the children to whisper-sing their favorite songs. Also, encourage the children to try to whistle the songs.

Small Group: Read the children Martin Waddell's *Webster J. Duck*. After reading the story, invite the children to talk about the five Ws: who, what, when, where, why, and apply them to the story.

Numbers

STORY TIME

Chicka Chicka 1, 2, 3 by Bill Martin Jr.
I Spy Little Numbers by Jean Marzollo
My First Number Book by DK Publishing
Olivia Counts by Ian Falconer
The Right Number of Elephants by Jeff Sheppard

TRANSITION

Hand each child a note card with a number written on it. Encourage the children to put themselves in numerical order without speaking. Once the children are in the correct order, move on to the next activity.

SNACK

Make a rebus chart of the ingredients (found on appendix page 350) for a Zipper Bag Snack Mix. Invite the children to read the recipe and count the number of items included in each snack.

Group Time

Invite the children to talk about numbers, how we use them for counting, and where we might commonly see numbers. With the children, make a list of all the places and things on which numbers are commonly found. After making the list, write it on a sheet of posterboard, and invite the children to "Ten Little Numbers," found on appendix page 349, filling the blanks with words from the posterboard.

Learning Center Ideas

Literacy: Set out a calendar and several cut out squares with numbers 1–31 written on them, and invite the children to put them on the calendar in the correct order.

Math: Set out several large construction paper cutouts of numbers, and several clothespins. Invite the children to clip the correct number of clothespins to the large cardboard numbers.

Additional Activities

Movement: In a bucket, put note cards with the numbers 1–10 written on them. Invite the children to take turns pulling a card out of the bucket. Ask each child to say the number aloud, then do that many jumps, hops, claps or some other movement, and to count out the number of actions. Make sure each child has a turn, then repeat the activity, challenging all of them to count backwards as they jump, hope, clap, and so on.

Project: Read the children the story *Chicka Chicka, 1, 2, 3* by Bill Martin Jr. After the story, hand out a large posterboard cutout of a number. Invite the children to bring this number home with them at the end of the day, and with their families, decorate the number any way they wish. Remind the children to bring the number back to school the next day. When the children bring their numbers back, make a large Chicka Boom tree, and attach the children's numbers to the tree. Above the tree, write the following: "Chicka, Chicka, 1, 2, 3, See What I Made with My Family."

Rhythm and Rhyme: Invite the children to name their favorite number songs. Write the names on a posterboard, and encourage the children to teach each other the words and sing the songs together. (Examples: "Five Little Ducks", "Five Little Monkeys Jumping on the Bed".)

April Showers

STORY TIME

The Aunts Go Marching by Maurie J. Manning

In the Rain with Baby Duck by Amy Hest

Rain Feet by Angela Johnson

Rain Romp: Stomping Away a Grouchy Day by Jane Kurtz

Ruby's Rainy Day by Rosemary Wells

TRANSITION

Set out four or five construction paper raindrops on the floor, and invite the children to walk around them while you play music. Occasionally stop the music, telling the children to find a raindrop to stand on. Those children able to step on a raindrop can proceed to the next activity. Repeat this activity, removing one raindrop each time, until all children move on to the next activity.

Group Time

Set up a chart on the wall and for the next week, and as the children come gather for Group Time, ask them about the weather, then draw rain, sun, snow, or clouds on that day's section of the chart. At the end of the week, invite the children to look at the chart and say what kind of weather was most prominent.

Learning Center Ideas

Art: Set out several construction paper umbrella cutouts, and invite the children to decorate them with watercolor markers. When the children are done decorating them, use a spray bottle to spray water on the finished design, mimicking rain. Let it dry, and show the children how the colors have swirled together.

Science: Set out a bucket of water, a sheet of construction paper separated in a T- graph, with "sink" written on one side, and "float" written on the other. Set out several different objects and take photos of them. Invite the children to place the real objects in the bucket to see if they sink or float, and then have them rubber cement the photos to the correct side of the T-graph.

Additional Activities

Movement: Cut blue and brown puddle shapes, and challenge the children to jump over the imaginary rain and mud puddles.

Outside: Put a rain gauge with a container outside. After it rains, select a child to go outside to check to see how much rain fell.

Rhythm and Rhyme: Invite the children to recite "April Showers" (see appendix page 345) and "I'm a Little Duck," found on appendix page 347.

Small Group: Ask the children if they know why it rains. If the children are not able to say, help explain the process. Also, encourage the children to discuss the rain's importance and benefit to nature. After discussing, hand out construction paper raindrops to each child, help them put their names on the raindrops, and set out glue, glitter, confetti, and other materials for the children to decorate their raindrops.

Ducks

STORY TIME

Duck on a Bike by David Shannon

Ducks Don't Get Wet by Augusta Golden

Farmer Duck by Martin Waddell

Five Little Ducks by Raffi

Giggle, Giggle Quack by Doreen Cranin

One Duck Stuck by Phyllis Root

Starting Life Duck by Claire Llewellyn

SNACK

Little classroom ducks can make and enjoy a snack of "duck" food. Make a snack mix by counting 10 fish crackers, nine bread croutons, eight pretzel sticks, seven raisin bugs, and so on. Hand each child a zippered bag, and invite all of them to count out the pieces of food before eating them.

Group Time

Introduce the children to ducks, using the Duck Facts found on appendix page 351. Mention, especially, that ducks can swim in water all day long without staying wet because their bodies produce a special oil that repels water. The ducks produce the oil in a gland, and use their beaks to spread oil over their feathers. After explaining this fact to the children, invite them to experiment with feathers and oil to see if they can reproduce the effect. Hand two feathers out to each child, making sure each child gets one covered with baby oil, and another with nothing on it. Invite the children to dip both feathers in a bucket of water, and encourage them to discuss the effect the water has on their two feathers.

Learning Center Ideas

Art: Set out containers of paint and several feathers and feather dusters, and have the children feather-paint on construction paper duck shapes.

Math: Set out several construction paper duck shapes with numbers written on them, as well as a pile of feathers. Invite the children to put the correct number of feathers on each numbered duck shape.

Additional Activities

Outside: Invite the children to play Follow the Leader, and lead the children around as though they were little ducklings following the mother duck.

Rhythm and Rhyme: Invite the children to recite "Sing a Song of Baby Ducks," found on appendix page 348.

Small Group: Provide a tub of water for each small group. Set out several things that will and will not float. Before putting each object in the tub, ask the children whether they think it will float or sink. Write the predictions down on construction paper, as well as the results.

Chicks

STORY TIME

Big Fat Hen by Keith Baker

Good Morning Chick by Mirra Ginsburg

The Little Red Hen by Byron Burton

The Little Red Hen Makes a Pizza by Philemon Sturges

Tippy Toe Chick Go by George Shannon

This Little Chick by John Lawrence

TRANSITION

Play Pass the Chick. Invite the children to sit in a circle and pass a ping-pong ball "chick" between them as music plays. When the music stops, have the child holding the chick move on to the next activity. To make the game more interesting, include multiple chicks.

SNACK

Make snack nests for the baby chicks. In a pot, heat several peanut butter chips, until they begin to melt. Add chow mein noodles and stir. When the noodles are well mixed in, put a large dollop of the mixture on a piece of wax paper, allow it to cool for a moment, and invite the children to mold the mixture into nests.

Group Time

Read the children *The Little Red Hen* by Byron Burton. Invite them to talk about the book's setting and characters, then take a vote to see whether the children think the other animals should be allowed to eat. To take the vote, give each child a clothespin with his name on it and encourage the children to attach the clothespins to a sheet of posterboard marked "yes" or a sheet of posterboard marked "no." After the children vote, tally the votes to see which opinion was more popular among the children.

Learning Center Ideas

Art: Set out yellow circles of construction paper, yellow craft feathers, and glue, inviting the children to make little chick bodies with the materials. Give them chenille stems, markers, and triangles of orange paper with which to add beaks and legs to their chicks.

Sensory: Set out corn feed or cornmeal. Add measuring cups and spoons and containers. Encourage the children to experiment with the cups and spoons, seeing how many spoonfuls it takes to fill a cup, and so on.

Additional Activities

Game: Choose a child to be the Mother Hen, and invite the other children to sit in a circle. Ask the Mother Hen to cover her eyes or step outside the classroom for a moment, and while the Mother Hen is gone, choose one child to be the "baby chick." When the Mother Hen returns, the baby chick makes small, occasional peeps, as the Mother Hen tries to guess which child is the baby chick.

Rhythm and Rhyme: Use "There Was a Little Egg," found on appendix page 349, to discuss the sequence of a chick's life.

Small Groups: Set out several colored pompom "chicks" in a few simple patterns, and invite the children to add a pompom to the pattern. As the children understand the pattern concepts, try creating more various patterns.

Bunnies

STORY TIME

Guess How Much I Love You? by
    Sam McBratney
Hopper by Marcus Pfister
My Friend Rabbit by Eric Robmann
Runaway Bunny by Margaret Wise
    Brown
White Rabbits Color Book by Alan
    Baker

TRANSITION

Invite the children to sing the "Hop, Hop, Hop" song, found on appendix page 346, with you. Warn them to all keep quiet at the start of the third line, when you say one child's name. After saying a child's name, invite him to move on to the next activity. Repeat until all the children have transitioned on to the next activity.

SNACK

Make a dip to eat with raw veggies, a bunny's favorite food. Mix one packet of ranch party dip with one pint of sour cream. Serve with raw vegetables.

Group Time

Before Group Time, print each child's name on a sentence strip. On construction paper cut outs of bunnies, print each letter of the alphabet. At Group Time, give the children their name cards, and tell them you will hold up one bunny letter at a time. When holding up a bunny letter, invite the children to see if that letter is in their names. If so, encourage them to hop like bunnies.

Discuss bunnies with the children, using the Bunny Facts found on appendix page 350.

Learning Center Ideas

Art: Invite the children to paint several bunny shapes with glue. Set out several colors of tempera paint, and while the glue is still wet, use cotton balls to dab the paint onto the glued-covered bunnies. While the bunnies are still wet, press a second piece of construction paper over them and press down, making bunny prints.

Fine Motor: Invite the children to trace and cut out a bunny. Set out paper and a cardboard bunny shape as a tracer. Invite the children to trace around the bunny shape with a pencil, cut it out and color it. Show the children how to add a cotton ball tail, if they wish.

Additional Activities

Game: Cut orange carrot shapes from construction paper, writing a large motor direction on each carrot. For example: "jump as high as you can two times," "hop three times on your left foot," "hop five times on your right foot," or "hop backwards two times." Encourage the children to take turns picking a carrot out of the basket, then, pretending they are bunnies, perform the activities named on the carrots.

Outside: Invite the children to play tag while hopping like bunnies.

Rhythm and Rhyme: With the children, sing "Little Bunnies Come and Play," found on appendix page 348.

Small Group: Give each child a construction paper cut out of a bunny. With them, recite the "Bunnies Hopping" song, found on appendix page 345, and suit their actions to the words.

Umbrellas

STORY TIME

The Aunts Go Marching by Maurie J. Manning

In the Rain with Baby Duck by Amy Hest

Ruby's Rainy Day by Rosemary Wells

Splosh by Mick Inkpen

Twinkle, Twinkle, Little Star by Iza Trapani

TRANSITION

Invite the children to recite "Umbrella, Umbrella, 1, 2, 3," found on appendix page 349. Add a child's name in the blank. After the named child shakes his head and responds, "No, not me," invite him to move on to the next activity.

SNACK

Make Umbrella Breadsticks (see appendix page 350).

Group Time

Before reading *The Umbrella* by Jan Brett aloud to the children, invite the children to look at the book's pictures, and encourage the children to predict the narrative of the story. After reading the story to the children, re-enact the story together.

Learning Center Ideas

Art: Provide watercolor paints, paper, and brushes for the children to make rainy day art. Encourage them to draw umbrellas on their pictures, if they wish.

Dramatic Play: Invite the children to bundle up in rain gear and pretend to jump in and out of puddles as they carry pretend umbrellas.

Literacy: Encourage the children to dictate rainy day stories and ask them to illustrate the stories.

Math: Set out several construction paper umbrellas, each with a different number written on each of them. Set out several cutouts of raindrops and encourage the children to put the correct number of raindrops on each numbered umbrella.

Additional Activities

Outside: On a warm rainy day, give all the children umbrellas and go outside for a walk. Encourage the children to their five senses to observe the world around them. After returning to the classroom, encourage the children to finish sentences about the senses, such as: "I see...," "I smell...," "I hear...," "I feel...," and "I taste...."

Rhythm and Rhyme: Give each child a colorful construction paper cutout of an umbrella. Invite the children to sing "Under the Umbrella," found on appendix page 349, and to stand up during the verse when the color of their umbrella appears in the song. Invite the children to continue standing until all the children are standing.

Rhythm and Rhyme: Invite the children to sing "Where, Oh, Where Has the Umbrella Gone?" found on appendix page 349.

Letter *X*

STORY TIME

The Alphabet Mystery by Audrey Wood

Xavier and the Letter X by Cynthia Fitterer Klingel

TRANSITION

Invite the children to sit in a circle. Give each child a card with one letter of the alphabet on it (be sure an *x* is included if there are fewer than twenty-six children). Start to play music, and encourage the children to pass the cards to the left. Occasionally stop the music, and invite the child with the x card to stand up and move on to the next activity. Repeat activity until all children have moved on.

SNACK

Give each child a portion of canned bread stick dough. Cut each one in half, so each child has two pieces. Invite the children to make a letter *x* with the two pieces. Add butter, cinnamon and sugar. Bake according to the package directions.

Group Time

Before Group Time, cut out several uppercase and lowercase copies of the letter *x* and hide them around the room. Also, remove the *x* from the classroom alphabet. When the children arrive, tell them that the letter *x* is missing, and encourage them to search the room for the letter *x*. When every *x* is found, invite the children to sort them by color and then by size. After sorting the letter, read the children *The Alphabet Mystery* by Audrey Wood.

Learning Center Ideas

Art: Cut out several large construction paper copies of the letters *x* and *o*, explaining to the children that *x* sometimes stands for kisses and *o* for hugs. Hand out the letters, and invite the children to decorate the letters with *x* and *o* confetti and other materials.

Literacy: Fill a clean, clear empty two-liter soda bottle ¾ full with salt and plastic alphabet letters, reinforcing its cap with electrical tape. Invite the children to shake the bottle, looking for different letters of the alphabet.

Sensory: Spray some shaving cream into a flat container and invite the children to practice making the letter *x* in the shaving cream.

Additional Activities

Movement: Invite the children to lie down so they are comfortable. Be sure that each child has his own space. Encourage the children to wiggle their toes for a while, and then tell them to stop. Next, encourage them to pretend they are going to sleep. Tell them to relax their feet, then their legs, stomachs, arms, and finally their necks and heads, until their whole bodies are relaxed and they are ready to sleep.

Outside: Make a large map of the playground. Put an *x* where you have hidden a special treat. Invite the children to use the map to try to find it.

Rhythm and Rhyme: Invite the children to sing "Where, Oh, Where Has My Little X Gone?," found on appendix page 349.

Humpty Dumpty

GENERAL DAILY PLAN

STORY TIME

Chickens Are Not the Only Ones by Ruth Heller

An Extraordinary Egg by Leo Lionni

The Golden Egg Book by Margaret Wise Brown

Ollie by Oliver Dunrea

On My Way to Buy Eggs by Chih-Yuan Chen

TRANSITION

Recite a variation of the Humpty Dumpty rhyme, adding a child's name at the beginning. Invite the named child to move on to the next activity. Repeat this until all the children have moved on to the next activity.

SNACK

Invite the children to make egg salad, showing them how to peel a hardboiled egg, cut it into pieces, put it in a paper cup, add a tablespoon of mayo and stir the concoction together. Set out crackers with which the children can scoop out and enjoy their homemade egg salad.

Group Time

Invite the children to build a wall using blocks or cardboard boxes. Set a plastic egg on top of the wall, and use it to act out the story of Humpty Dumpty as the children recite the rhyme.

Learning Center Ideas

Art: Give each child a construction paper egg shape, as well as paper shreds, yarn for hair, crayons, markers, construction paper, and pompoms to make their own Humpty Dumptys. Once the children are finished, display the Humpty Dumptys on the top of a bulletin board wall made by sponge painting with a rectangle sponge and red paint.

Manipulatives: Set out several different colored plastic eggs, mix their halves, and invite the children to match them by color.

Math: Write different numbers on several plastic eggs, and invite the children to put in each numbered plastic egg the corresponding number of buttons.

Additional Activities

Movement: Play Humpty Dumpty Hokey Pokey, inviting the children to stand and sing along. Use the prompts such as, "put your egg head in," "put your left arm in," or "put your right leg in," for each verse of the song.

Rhythm and Rhyme: Repeat the Humpty Dumpty rhyme with the children. Invite the children to clap the rhythm of the rhyme, or hand out plastic eggs partially filled with buttons, and encourage the children to shake them to the rhyme's rhythm.

Small Group: Print "Humpty Dumpty Sat on the Ground," found on appendix page 346, on several sheets of paper, inviting the children to choose what word to include at the end of the rhyme. Help the children fill in the line of their sheet of paper, and encourage them to draw pictures of a healthy Humpty Dumpty eating breakfast. Once the children have completed their drawings, staple them together into a book.

Chameleons

STORY TIME

A Color of His Own by Leo Lionni
Hide Clyde by Russell Benfanti

TRANSITION

Recite "Chameleon, Where Will You Go?" found on appendix page 345. In the blank of the rhyme's first line, name a particular color, and ask all children wearing that color to find something in the room that matches that color, touch it, then move on to the next activity.

Group Time

Before Group Time, hide several construction paper cutout shapes of chameleons. Write various facts about chameleons on each and hide them around the classroom, putting them by objects of similar colors. At Group Time, invite the children to find the chameleons. When the children have found all the different chameleons, talk with the children about what they know about chameleons, using the Chameleon Facts from appendix pages 350–351.

Learning Center Ideas

Art: Set out chameleon shapes cut from construction paper. Set out small square shapes cut from sponges and two colors of paint, and encourage the children to print AB patterns across their chameleons.

Literacy: Cut chameleon shapes from green, yellow, red and blue construction paper. Print the names of the colord on each shape. Set out small colored blocks, and invite the children to match the colored blocks to the chameleons of the same colors.

Math: Cut paper chameleon shapes. Write a number on each chameleon shape, and challenge the children to put the correct number of plastic flies on the shapes.

Sensory: Provide plastic chameleons, artificial plants and sand for the children to explore.

Additional Activities

Outside: Play a "chameleon" variation of tag, in which children are safe for five seconds when touching something that is the same color as an article of their clothing.

Rhythm and Rhyme: Sing "I'm a Little Chameleon," found on appendix page 347.

Small Group: Cut chameleon and leaf shapes from different wallpaper patterns. Give each child in the group one of the different chameleons. One at a time, hold up each leaf shape cutout, and ask the child holding the matching chameleon to hold it up to the leaf cutout.

Paper Clips

STORY TIME

Invite each child to make up a story about a paper clip. Write down the children's stories as they tell them. After writing the stories, invite the children to draw pictures of their stories and glue paper clips to the drawings. When the glue dries, staple or bind all the drawings into a class book.

Group Time

Before Group Time, hide several paper clips of different colors and sizes around the classroom. When the children gather for Group Time, invite them to go on a paper clip hunt. After the children find all the paper clips, make an object graph by sorting the paper clips on a grid based on color and size, then count the numbers of each group.

Learning Center Ideas

Art: Invite the children to use colored paper clips to make paper clip necklaces or designs.

Math: On index cards, write the numbers 1–10, and invite the children to attach the appropriate number of paper clips to each card.

Science: Set out magnets with metal paper clips and plastic paper clips for the children to explore.

Additional Activities

Movement: Show the children how to use a paper clip chain to jump rope and play limbo, or reverse limbo, where the children jump over the paper clip chain.

Outside: Hide paper clips outside on the playground. Invite the children to use magnets to find the clips.

Rhythm and Rhyme: Attach a colored paper clip to each child, and encourage them all to follow the directions in "If Your Paper Clip Is Blue," found on appendix page 346.

Small Group: Show the children how to make paper clip chains, and use them to measure their height, and the length of items in the room, noting the length by number of paper clips.

Planting Seeds

STORY TIME

Carrot Seed by Ruth Kraus

My Seed Won't Grow by Steve Metzger

One Child One Seed: A South African Counting Book by Kathryn Cave

Seeds Grow by Angela Shelf Medearis

Silver Seeds by Paul Paolilli

SNACK

Make a seed snack by mixing one tablespoon each of sunflower, pumpkin, sesame seeds, and peanuts in zip-lock bags. (Be sure no child has allergies to these ingredients before proceeding.)

Group Time

Open up several real fruits and vegetables to look at the seeds with the children. Also, put seeds and a seed package in a zip-lock bag. Be sure the seed package has on it a picture of what the seeds will grow into, so the children can understand the growth process.

Learning Center Ideas

Art: Set out several seeds, sheets of paper, and glue. Encourage the children to make seed mosaics by gluing the seeds to the paper in different patterns. The children can make predetermined shapes, like sunflowers, or they can make up their own shapes.

Math: Set birdseed and measuring cups on the Sensory Table for the children to explore.

Math: Set out several pumpkin and sunflower seeds, challenging the children to sort them by seed type.

Additional Activities

Movement: Have the children pretend they are little seeds planted in the ground, and imitate the growth of the seeds into full plants. Begin with the children lying curled on the floor, as seeds. Then encourage them to pretend they are being rained on, and beginning to open up out of the soil, eventually standing fully-grown, with their branches stretched up to the sun. In the end, invite the children to open their hands, as though they were budding flowers.

Outside: Give the children seeds to set outside, observing what animals come to eat them.

Project: Invite the children to plant several kinds of seeds in small containers and watch how the plants grow. When it is warm enough, help the children transfer the plants to the school grounds, and let them grow there until the following fall, when they can be used to explore during Halloween.

Rhythm and Rhyme: Invite the children to recite "I'm a Little Seed," found on appendix page 347.

Stringy Stuff

Examples of Stringy Stuff: jump rope, silly string, yarn spaghetti, chenille stems, shoe laces, streamers, ribbon, rope, yarn.

STORY TIME

Anna Banana: 101 Jump Rope Rhymes by Joanna Cole
Moon Rope by Lois Ehlert
Red Lace, Yellow Lace by Mike Casey

SNACK

Make spaghetti noodles. Add sauce. Serve with string cheese.

Group Time

Show the children multiple examples of different string types, such as jump rope, silly string, chenille stems, shoelaces, streamers, ribbon, rope yarn, and so on. Encourage the children to discuss the differences and similarities between the materials.

Learning Center Ideas

Art: Set out sheets of construction paper, glue, and several stringy materials. Invite the children to make collages with them.

Fine Motor: Encourage the children to make shapes using rubber bands on a pegboard.

Fine Motor: Set out several twist ties and craft sticks, inviting the children to make designs with them.

Fine Motor: Fill an old tennis shoe with plaster. After the plaster dries, set it out for the children to practice tying its laces.

Math: Set out several lengths of string, inviting the children to measure the length of objects in the room with them.

Additional Activities

Movement: Hand streamers out to the children. Play different kinds of music and invite the children to wave the streamers around while they dance.

Outside: Tell the children how birds will use string, hair, and straw to build their nests. Give the children short lengths of different colored string to put on the ground, and then watch to see if birds take the string to build their nests.

Rhythm and Rhyme: Invite the children to recite "Stringy Stuff," found on appendix page 348.

Small Group: Loosely tangle several jump ropes, and encourage the children to work together to untangle them.

Letter *Y*

STORY TIME

Fuzzy Yellow Ducklings by Matthew
Van Fleet

In My New Yellow Shirt by Eileen
Spinelli

Purple, Green, and Yellow by Robert
N. Munsch

Yellow and Pink by William Steig

Yo! Yes? by Chris Raschka

TRANSITION

Invite children to sit in a circle and
give them a yam with which to play
hot potato. The children pass the
yam around while music plays.
When the music stops, have the
child holding the yam move on to
the next activity. Repeat until all
children move to the next activity.

SNACK

Make a yogurt parfait. Layer fruits
and yogurt in a cup, then add
whipped cream and sprinkles on
top.

Group Time

Invite the children to pronounce the letter *y*, and ask them to name words
that include the letter *y*. After naming several *y* words, invite the children
to pretend to yawn whenever they hear a word that includes the letter *y*.

Glue an index card on a craft stick for each child. On one side of the card
write, "yummy." Ask the children some of the questions about different
foods, inviting the children to hold up and their "yummy" card if they like
that particular food.

Learning Center Ideas

Art: Set out yellow yarn and several construction paper cut outs of the
letter *y*, inviting the children to decorate the cutouts with the yarn.

Literacy: Set out several containers of shaving cream, inviting the children
to make the letter *y* in the cream.

Math: Set out several pictures of people of all ages, and challenge the
children to separate them by age.

Math: Invite the children to measure large objects with a yardstick.

Additional Activities

Rhythm and Rhyme: Invite the children to recite "Letter Y, Letter Y," and "Y
Is for Young," found on appendix pages 348 and 350.

Flowers

STORY TIME

Flower Garden by Eve Bunting
Fran's Flower or Grow Flower Grow
    by Lisa Bruce
Planting a Rainbow by Lois Ehlert
This Is a Sunflower by Lola M.
    Schaefer

Group Time

Read Eve Bunting's *Flower Garden* to the children. Afterwards, ask the children to retell the story, prompting them with questions about what happened in each scene of the book. Also, discuss with the children the different things they do when it is their parents' birthdays.

Learning Center Ideas

Literacy: Set out several differently-colored construction paper cutouts of flowers, inviting the children to sort them by color.
Math: Wrap several empty juice cans with numbered sheets of contact paper. Set out several plastic flowers and challenge the children to put the correct number of flowers in each juice can.

Additional Activities

Movement: Cut several flower shapes from construction paper and print a different letter on each flower, then set them on the floor. Turn on some music and invite the children to walk around from flower to flower. Occasionally stop the music, and encourage the children to stand on the nearest flower. Each child must then name a word beginning with the letter on the flower on which he stands. After each child names a word, start the music again, and repeat the game.
Project: Read the story *Grow, Flowers, Grow!* by Lisa Bruce. After reading the book, ask the children what flowers need to grow. As children name the following items, take each one out from a large container: dirt, sunflower seeds, and plastic cups. Invite the children to plant several sunflower seeds in a cup, and help the children make signs reading, "feed me sunshine and water to grow" and attach them to the cups. Encourage the children to set the cups by the window, and to observe any changes made in the cups as the weeks go by.
Rhythm and Rhyme: Invite the children to recite "Flowers Don't Eat Cheeseburgers" and "Flowers Growing One by One," found on appendix pages 345 and 346.

Worms

STORY TIME

Diary of a Worm by Doreen Cronin
Very Hungry Caterpillar by Eric Carle
Worm Family by Tony Johnston

TRANSITION

Encourage the children to wiggle like worms as they move on to new activities.

SNACK

Give each child a length of breadstick dough, having each roll their dough and add raisin eyes. When they are ready, bake the breadsticks as directed on the package.

Group Time

Read *Diary of a Worm* by Doreen Cronin. After finishing the story, tell the children they will catch their own worms. Bring them outside to a patch of dirt, and help them water the soil very well. Tell the children it will take some time for the worms to arrive, and bring everyone back inside. In a couple of hours, bring the children back outside, and invite the children to carefully sift through the soil and take out any worms they see. Set out a jar of dirt for the worms to stay in, and bring the jar to the classroom's science area. Discuss worms with the children (see Worm Facts on appendix page 351).

Learning Center Ideas

Literacy: Make lengths of playdough available for the children to shape into worms and letters.
Math: Set out several various colored 2" lengths of yarn "worms" for the children to sort by size and color.
Science: Provide several worm books, clipboards and pencils, paper and magnifying glasses, inviting the children to observe the worms' activities (see Group Time above). Regularly select two children to leave small amounts of oatmeal and decaying leaves in the jar for the worms to eat, and keep the dirt moist, but not wet.

Additional Activities

Movement: Explain to the children how worms move without any arms and legs, then have the children pretend they are worms, and wiggle their way across the floor.
Rhythm and Rhyme: Invite the children to lay down and sing "I'm a Little Earthworm," found on appendix page 347, and try to move like a worm by stretching and contracting.
Small Group: Read *Inch by Inch* by Leo Lionni. Give each child a 1" long piece of yarn. Show the children how to measure using their yarn inchworms by lining the children's lengths of yarn in a row. Invite the children to measure a pencil, a block, and a book using their inchworms.

Mud

TRANSITION

Encourage the children to recite "Little Pig," found on appendix page 348, using a child's name in the blank space. After reciting the rhyme, ask that child to move on to the next activity. Repeat until all children have transitioned to the next activity.

SNACK

Make individual Mud Puddles (see appendix page 350).

Group Time

Cut out 2–6 mud puddle shapes from brown construction paper, and write a letter from the alphabet on each. Set the mud puddles out on the classroom floor so there is one for each child. Turn on some music, and invite the children to walk around the room, avoiding stepping in the mud puddles. Occasionally, stop the music, and tell the children to quickly jump into a mud puddle. Once all the children are on mud puddles, invite them to name the letter in their mud puddle. Play again and encourage the children to choose a different puddle.

Learning Center Ideas

Science: Add brown food coloring to goop recipe: 1 part cornstarch, 1 part water. Set out for the children to explore.
Sensory: Set out a tub of real mud, inviting the children to squish it in their hands. Encourage them to trace the first letters of their names in the mud, or numbers, or their whole names, depending on their ability. Provide towels and clean water for the children to clean up with after playing at this center.

Additional Activities

Movement: Use construction paper mud puddles to make a hopscotch game.
Outside: After a rain, bring the children outside to look for mud puddles. When the children find a puddle, give them lengths of string to outline the puddles. Come back in several hours to see what happened to the mud puddle.
Rhythm and Rhyme: Invite the children to recite "Mud, Mud, Mud," found on appendix page 348, making the appropriate sounds when prompted.
Small Group: Play The Piggy Says. Set out a construction paper cutout of a mud puddle for each child to stand on. Encourage the children to follow the directions you give them, but only if the direction is preceded by the phrase, "The piggy says…." Involve the mud puddle in the instructions, as in the following: "The piggy says stand in the mud," "The piggy says jump over the mud puddle," "The piggy says stand beside the mud puddle," and so on.

Letter Z

STORY TIME

Shape Hunt by Robbie Butler
Zipper, Buttons, and Bows by Karen Fung

SNACK

Invite the children to help make z-shaped breadstick dough. Add butter, sugar and cinnamon and then bake according to package directions.

Group Time

Bring in several plastic animals. Invite the children to sort them based on whether they live on a farm or in a zoo. Talk about the sound the letter *z* makes, inviting the children to name words that begin with *z*. Encourage the children to say "zap" and clap their hands when they hear a word that has a *z* in it.

Learning Center Ideas

Art: Invite the children to use paints, markers, crayons, and chalk to make *z*-art.

Fine Motor: Set out several old articles of clothing, inviting the children to practice using buttons, snaps, and zippers.

Writing: Set out a tub of sand in which the children can practice making the letter *z* and drawing zeros.

Additional Activities

Movement: Choose five children to act like zoo animals, encouraging the rest of the children to name the animal each child is imitating. If a child correctly guesses which animal another child is pretending to be, those children change places, and the new child pretends to be a different animal.

Outside: Draw a large *z* on the playground, and encourage the children to run zig-zags around it.

Rhythm and Rhyme: Invite the children to sing the "Who Lives in the Zoo?" found on appendix page 349, naming different animals for each verse. Ask the children to make a list of animals, and decide whether they should be named in the zoo or farm verses of the song.

Bags

STORY TIME

Billy the Goat by Shaheen Bilgrami

Morris's Disappearing Bag by
    Rosemary Wells

My Doctor's Bag by Golden Books

TRANSITION

Set several lunch bags on the floor, and write *Go!* on every fifth bag. Place all the bags in a circle face down on the floor. Turn on music, and encourage the children to march from bag to bag. Occasionally, stop the music, and invite the children to flip over the bags. Have those children holding bags that say *Go!* move on to the next activity. Repeat the process until each child transitions to the next activity.

SNACK

The day before, give each child a bag and note to bring home, asking them to bring in a snack in the bag to share the next day. When the children bring the bags, collect the snacks and divide them between the children.

Group Time

Set out several types of bags (clothes, grocery, school, lunch, garbage, and so on) beside several items that would normally go in each type of bag. Invite the children to choose which items belong in each bag, and have them sort the objects that way.

Learning Center Ideas

Dramatic Play: Set up a pretend grocery store and encourage the children to practice bagging groceries. Show children how to bag so objects like bread aren't damaged.

Literacy: Set out several lunch bags, writing a letter of the alphabet on each. Provide the children with various small items, and encourage them put the objects in the bags marked with the first letter of the objects' names.

Math: Write different numbers on the outsides of several paper bags, inviting the children to put the correct numbers of blocks in each numbered bag.

Additional Activities

Movement: Use large paper grocery bags to have potato sack races.

Outside: Give the children bags and invite them to search outside for special objects to share with the class.

Rhythm and Rhyme: Encourage the children to copy the actions in "Bag, Bag," found on appendix page 345.

Letter *L*

STORY TIME

Are You a Ladybug? by Judy Allen

The Grouchy Ladybug by Eric Carle

Guess How Much I Love You? by
   Sam Bratney

Mama Do You Love Me? by Barbara
   M. Joosse

SNACK

Help the children make ladybug cakes. Give each child a rice cake and a dollop of cream cheese with red food coloring in it, and invite them to spread the red cream cheese on the rice cake. Add chocolate chip spots.

Group Time

Talk about the letter *l* and the sound it makes, inviting the children to say words that start with and include the letter. Encourage the children to laugh if they hear a word that starts with the letter *l*.

Learning Center Ideas

Art: Set out several construction paper *l* cutouts, paint, and slices of lemons and limes with which the children can press-paint the *l* cutouts.

Math: Set out several articles of laundry, encouraging the children to sort them by color.

Additional Activities

Game: Set out several milk gallon lids with matching pairs of stickers on them and invite the children to play a memory game.

Literacy: Play "Logo Lotto." Cut two logos that are the same from empty food boxes. Put one logo from each box on a lotto grid. Laminate the lotto grid and the logos. Set out both, so children can match the logos, filling up the grid with matching logos.

Movement: Turn on some lively music. Choose two children to hold a jump rope, and invite the rest of the children to do the limbo. After each round, have the two children holding the rope lower it about 1". Whenever a child touches the rope while passing beneath it, that child is put in a space in the room designated the *l-lot*, and cheer on the remaining children in the limbo contest, chanting *la, la, la,* and *lower, lower, lower,* and so on.

Outside: Bring the children outside to look at leaves. Encourage the children to describe the leaf shapes (some look more like hands, others more like feathers, and so on).

Rhythm and Rhyme: Invite the children to sing "Letter L," found on appendix page 348.

May

Calendar Time

During Calendar Time, introduce the month of May to the children. Look at the letters in the word *May.* Name each letter, and say the sound and words that start with the sound. Whose name begins with the letter *M*? Do this for each letter in the word during calendar time throughout the month.

Monthly Organizer

MONTH-LONG CELEBRATIONS

Whale Awareness Month
Asian Heritage Month
National Police Officer Month

National Strawberry Month
National Bicycle Month
National Physical Fitness Month

WEEK-LONG CELEBRATION

National Pet Week (second week of May)

SPECIAL DAYS AND HOLIDAYS

May 1: May Day
May 5: Cinco de Mayo

GENERAL DAILY PLANS

Backwards Day
Number 4
Dogs
Silly Socks Day
Hamsters
Letter *M*
Mothers
Bees
Horses
Mary Had a Little Lamb
Beads

Trucks
Alligators and Crocodiles
Cats
Cars
Measurement

Note: Please be sure to check for allergies before serving the snacks or doing any food-related activities.

Whale Awareness Month

MONTH-LONG CELEBRATION

STORY TIME

Baby Whale's Journey by Jonathan London
I'm a Little Whale by Francois Crozat
In the Ocean by Neeay Twinem
Shh! The Whale Is Smiling by Josehpine Nobisso

TRANSITION

Glue a foam whale shape on the end of a dowel to make a magic wand. Tap children who are sitting quietly with the magic "whale wand" to move on to the next activity. Children can also hold the whale wand when it is their turn to talk. Everyone else should listen.

SNACK

Make Whales in the Ocean (see recipe on appendix page 358).

Group Time

Read books about whales, and share the Whale Facts on appendix page 360 with the children. Ask the children what they know about whales. Then play "Is it true or false?" Glue whale shapes on craft sticks, and give one to each child. Say statements about whales. Tell the children that if the answer is true, they hold up the whale shape. If it is false, they keep the whales in their laps. Some whale statements include:

♦ Whales have legs.
♦ Whales live in the water.
♦ Whales are little.
♦ Whales have blowholes.
♦ Whales eat hamburgers and French fries.

Learning Center Ideas

Listening: Get a CD of whale songs from a store that sells relaxation music. Set up the music as a listening center. The children could listen and draw a picture of what they think the whales are saying.

Literacy: Invite children to make a color whale book. Divide a 8 ½" x 11" piece of paper into four separate parts. Put a whale shape in each section, and under each whale print the name of a color: blue, yellow, red, and green. The child cuts apart the pieces and staples them to make a book. Then the child colors each whale the appropriate color.

Math: Cut whale shapes from three colors to make patterns. Set up two different patterns by gluing whale shapes onto sentence strips. Glue one pattern ABAB and another AAB. Invite children to extend the patterns.

Sensory: Cut whale shapes from foam. Put them in the Water Table. Add blue food coloring to make the water blue.

Additional Activities

Outside: Use a string to measure 100 feet. Take the string outside and show the children the approximate length of a blue whale. Ask the children to line up and see how long the line is. Then ask them to lie down in a row and see if they can reach the end of the string.

Asian Heritage Month

MONTH-LONG CELEBRATION

See appendix page 358 for Asian holiday information.

STORY TIME

Hush! A Thai Lullaby by Minfong Ho

Lanterns and Firecrackers: A Chinese New Year Story by Jonny Zucker

On My Way to Buy Eggs by Chih-Yuan Chen

A Pair of Red Clogs by Masako Matsuno

Toddler Two by Anastasia Suen

SNACK

Serve an assortment of Asian foods for the children to sample. Egg rolls, rice, and fortune cookies are good choices.

Group Time

Prior to Group Time, explain how important dragons are in Chinese culture. You might also invite parents of Chinese heritage to visit the classroom and talk about their culture. Talk about Asian countries and show the children where they are on the globe. Using a large sheet of bulletin board paper, invite children to help paint a dragon. Use many bright colors. When it is dry, cut one end of the paper into the shape of a large dragon head. To make the dragon "breathe fire," glue yellow and red streamers onto the dragon's mouth. Parade the dragon around the school.

Learning Center Ideas

Art: Make Chinese paper lanterns. Before class, fold a 9" x 12" piece of construction paper in half horizontally. Draw lines from the fold to 1" from the top evenly through the 12" side of the paper. Invite children to cut along the lines. Then open the paper and glue together on the outside edges. Add a string handle from the top. Invite children to glue on foam flowers as a decoration.

Art: Explain to the children that origami is a very special kind of paper folding art that is done in Asia. Set out paper in many different colors, patterns, and sizes. Leftover gift wrap or scrapbook paper will work for this. Also set out markers, crayons, scissors, and glue. Invite children to make something special. Show and let the children talk about their creations.

Math: Turn over an index card with a number written on it. Encourage the children to beat a drum as many times as the number on the index card.

Additional Activities

Outside: Play dragon tag. Make a dragon headband. The child wearing the headband is "IT." The child tagged by the person who is "IT" becomes the next dragon.

Rhythm and Rhyme: Explain to the children that during the Dragon parades, children run in and out of the dragon to show they are brave and not afraid. Sing "Mr. Dragon Says" with the children (see appendix page 356) with some children being the dragon and some being the brave children.

National Police Officer Month

STORY TIME

Policeman Dog's Storybook by Stephanie St. Pierre
Policeman Lou and Policewoman Sue by Lisa Desimini

TRANSITION

Recite the rhyme below. When is almost time to clean up at the end of Work Time, have the children stay in the Centers they are in. Then when it is time to clean up, they clean up the area where they played.

"Stop" said the police officer in the car.
Clean up, clean up where you are.

Group Time

Talk about what police officers do. Make a list of their jobs. If possible, have a police officer come and talk to the children. Be sure to emphasize that police officers are friends and can help us. Talk about calling 911 only in emergencies.

Learning Center Ideas

Art: Make a police car. Invite the children to cut out a car shape from blue construction paper. Glue on black tires and a red police light.
Blocks: Encourage the children to build a town with the blocks. Provide small police cars and fire trucks for the children to pretend to be police officers keeping the townspeople safe.
Math: Practice dialing 911 and talking on the phone.

Additional Activities

Outside: Take a safety walk around the school yard. Look for things that are unsafe and need to be fixed.
Rhythm and Rhyme: Sing "The Police Officer Is My Friend" with the children (see appendix page 356).

National Strawberry Month

MONTH-LONG CELEBRATION

STORY TIME

Big Hungry Bear by Audrey Wood
My Lunch Box by Bob Filipowich

TRANSITION

Strawberries start with the /s/ sound. Ask each child to name a word that starts with the /s/ sound before moving to the next activity.

SNACK

Dip strawberries in low-fat vanilla yogurt.

Group Time

What is your favorite kind of food made with strawberries? Make a graph grid and a strawberry cut out for each child. During Group Time, show a strawberry and talk about the many things that can be strawberry flavored. Choose the class favorite. Is it ice cream, gelatin, or jelly? Have a tasting party. Then help children print their name on a strawberry and put it on the graph by their favorite kind of strawberry. Discuss the results.

Learning Center Ideas

Art: Add red strawberry gelatin powder to tempera paint. Paint or fingerprint large strawberry shapes. When the paint is dry, glue on black buttons as seeds. Add a green leaf cap.

Literacy: S is for Strawberry. Make an *s* book. Divide an 8 ½" x 11" paper into four equal sections to make a book. Print "*S* is for____" in each section. Children cut the paper on the lines to make a book. On each page invite children to draw a picture of something that begins with the letter s.

Math: Cut strawberry shapes from red construction paper. Write a number on each shape. Invite children to put the correct number of black pompom seeds on the strawberry shapes.

Sensory: Add strawberry-flavored powdered drink mix to your favorite playdough recipe to make strawberry smelling playdough. Add cookie cutters and rolling pins. Invite children to make cookies, pies, and other yummy things, but remind them to not really eat the playdough.

Additional Activities

Outside: Plant strawberries. Plant the seeds inside during the winter and transplant them outside when it is warmer.

Rhythm and Rhyme: Sing "The Strawberry Song" with the children (see appendix page 357).

Small Group: Read *The Little Mouse, The Red Ripe Strawberry, and the Big Hungry Bear* by Audrey and Don Wood. Then reread the story, giving each child a strawberry to eat along with the mouse in the story.

National Bicycle Month

MONTH-LONG CELEBRATION

STORY TIME

Bear on a Bike by Stella Blackstone
Duck on a Bike by David Shannon
Go Fly a Bike by Bill Haduch
A Kids Guide to Staying Safe on Bikes by Maribeth Boelts
On the Road by Claire Llewellyn
Play It Safe by Mercer Mayer
Safety on Your Bicycle by Joanee Mattern

Group Time

Read *Duck on a Bike* by David Shannon. After reading the story, ask the children if they think a duck can really ride a bike. Talk about the difference between real and pretend. Show a picture of a cartoon dog and a real dog. Which one is real? Which one is pretend? Show a picture of a real cat and a cartoon cat. Which one is real? Show other pictures and decide if they are real or pretend. Talk about words that rhyme, which means they sound almost the same. Name pairs of words. Ask the children to clap their hands if the words rhyme. Then sing "The Bike Song" (see appendix page 353) with the children and ask them to name the rhyming words when the song ends.

Learning Center Ideas

Art: Provide paints, markers, crayons, and paper and invite the children to draw pictures of bikes, bike rides with their families, or places where they enjoy riding bikes.

Literacy: Bike starts with the /b/ sound. Sort small items. If they start with the /b/ sound put them in a bowl, if they don't, put them on a paper plate.

Math: Find pictures of different types of bikes, including unicycles, bicycles, tricycles, and bikes with carriage attachments. Invite the children to count the wheels on each type of bike.

Additional Activities

Movement: Invite the children to do bicycle exercises. Show them how to lie on their backs and move their legs like they are pedaling a bike.

Outside: Invite the children to ride tricycles outside on the playground. Be sure that the children wear helmets. Set up an obstacle course with roads and stop signs.

Rhythm and Rhyme: Sing "The Wheels on the Bike" with the children and encourage them to suit their actions to the words (see appendix page 357).

National Physical Fitness Month

MONTH-LONG CELEBRATION

Before Group Time obtain several pictures of people doing things that keep them healthy such as eating healthy foods, drinking milk, doing exercises or jogging, and sleeping.

STORY TIME

The Busy Body Book by Lizzy Rockwell

The Edible Pyramid by Loreen Leedy

Encounter by Jane Yolen

The Monster Healthy Book by Edward Miller

Sleep Is for Everyone by Paul Showers

TRANSITION

Name a child. Have the child follow the directions of the line below before they move to the next activity:

Jump, hop, clap stop. GO!

SNACK

Make an energy snack. Make a fruit salad with several different fruits.

Group Time

Invite the children to bring in environmental print labels for healthy food. Make a book by putting the labels in pocket protectors and into a binder. Talk about each label and decide whether it should be added or not.

Learning Center Ideas

Dramatic Play: Set up a Fitness Center. Set out mats, jump ropes, and pretend weights. Add a stop watch.

Literacy: Set out yoga books for children to look at, such as *Yoga Kids* by Marsha Wenig. Put a mat in the center so children can try different positions.

Math: Use tape on the floor to make a hopscotch grid with numbers. Show children how to play hopscotch.

Science: Set out magazines. Invite the children to cut out healthy food pictures to make a big collage, or set out a stethoscope. Show children how the stethoscope works. Invite children to listen to their heartbeats.

Additional Activities

Movement: Bring in a stethoscope to listen to heart beats. After listening, do several exercises. Then listen again.

Outside: Go for a healthy walk. Do several stretching exercises before and after. Tell children that when you warm up, you get your muscles ready to work. This helps prevent you from getting hurt.

Rhythm and Rhyme: Sing "The Exercise Song" (see appendix page 354) with the children.

Small Group: Obtain plastic food and empty real food boxes. Sort the foods into healthy and unhealthy.

National Pet Week

The second week of May is National Pet Week.

STORY TIME

Baby Pets by Margaret Miller
Emma's Pet by David McPhail
Just Me and My Puppy by Mercer Mayer
Pet Show by Ezra Jack Keats

TRANSITION

Invite the children to move, one at a time, to the next activity as if they were a certain type of pet. Invite the other children to guess the animal.

SNACK

Invite children to help roll out sugar cookie dough. Use cookie cutters in different pet shapes to make cookies. Bake as directed.

Group Time

Before Group Time, find pictures of many kinds of pets in magazines. Glue one picture inside a file folder on the right side. Cut the left side of the file folder in eight equal horizontal strips.

List the many different animals, birds, reptiles, and fish that people have as pets, referring to the Pet List as necessary (see appendix page 360). Play a game. Bring in many different items used for pets such as a dog bone, leash, carrot, and so on. If the item is for a dog, the children bark, if it is for a cat they meow, if it relates to a bunny, they wiggle their nose, and so on.

Play a guessing game. Hold up the closed folder with the photo of a pet inside. Lift one horizontal strip at a time. The children try to guess the animal by just seeing parts. Keep lifting one strip at a time until the children guess what animal it is or until the whole picture is uncovered.

Learning Center Ideas

Dramatic Play: Use stuffed animals and blocks to set up a pet store. Add a cash register and play money.
Literacy: Put rocks and permanent markers or paints in the Literacy Center. Invite children to decorate the rocks as pets. Invite the children to make up stories about their pets.
Math: Make a fish bowl counting book. Cut five pieces of paper into a fish bowl shape. On the first page put a #1. Glue on one foam fish (or sticker, or stamp or color). Do the same for pages 2–5, adding one fish each time.

Additional Activities

Movement: Name an animal and invite the children to move to music in the same way that the animal moves. Every few minutes, name a new animal.
Rhythm and Rhyme: Sing "The Pet Song" (see appendix page 356) with the children.

May Day

May Day is celebrated on the first day in May and it celebrates the changing of winter into spring. People secretly make baskets of flowers and hang them on the door of friends and neighbors. They ring the bell and run away.

TRANSITION

Use a flowery magic wand to tap the heads of quiet children. If you are tapped, move on to the next activity.

Group Time

Cut big flowers from white bulletin board paper for the children to learn a lesson in cooperation. Set out tissue paper, embellishments, and paint for the children to use to decorate the flower. Decide as a group how to decorate the group's flower. Decide what is going to be done, and who will do it. (The teacher can help the children learn about making decisions together). Display the finished flower.

Learning Center Ideas

Art: Make headbands using strips of construction paper. Decorate the headband with plastic flowers (or foam or paper) and crepe paper streamers.

Fine Motor: Weave ribbon in and out of berry baskets or laundry baskets.

Math: Set out several cups. Program each cup with a number. Put that number of plastic flowers in a cup.

Sensory: Add plastic flower and flower pots with green tissue paper.

Additional Activities

Game: Play traditional circle games such as "Ring Around the Rosie" and "The Farmer in the Dell."

Movement: Glue streamers to the end of an empty wrapping paper tube. Hold it up as the children dance around it. (You might need several Maypoles according to the number of children.)

Outside: Leave a basket of flowers by a neighbor of the school's door, or on the door of the school secretary, cook and other people who help the children all year.

Project: Make a basket by folding two of the same size circles and gluing the bottom halves of the circles together. Add a paper strip handle. Glue small foam flower onto craft sticks and put them in the basket. Leave your basket at the door of someone you love.

Rhythm and Rhyme: Sing "The May Day Song" with the children (see appendix page 356).

Cinco de Mayo

"Cinco de Mayo" means the fifth of May in Spanish. Mexico celebrates this day with parades, music, dancing, and lots of food. On May 5, 1862, Mexico won an important battle against the French army. Winning this battle led to Mexico's independence.

STORY TIME

Burro and the Basket by Lloyd Mardis

Calavera Abecedario: A Day of the Dead Alphabet Book by Jeanette Winter

Chiles for Benito by Ana Baca

Senor Don Gato by John Manders

Uno, Dos, Tres by Pat Mora

TRANSITION

Use maracas to tap the syllables in each child's name as you call them to move on to the next activity.

SNACK

Make a festive snack. Set out nacho chips, hamburger with taco seasonings, cheese, tomatoes, and lettuce and invite the children to make their own nacho snack.

Group Time

Explain to children that Cinco de Mayo is a special holiday people in Mexico celebrate. Show children how they will make special items to help celebrate today. Show the finished sample for sombrero, serape, shakers, and the piñata. Explain what each item is for and how they are involved in the celebration. Now you are ready to start the day.

Learning Center Ideas

Art: Cut sombrero hat shapes from construction paper for each child. Glue the hat shape on a strip of construction paper stapled in a head band. Decorate the hat with markers and embellishments. Make serapes (blankets) for each child by cutting muslin fabric into rectangles. Help each child fringe the short edges. Decorate the muslin with markers and fabric paint.

Art: Put candy in a large brown paper grocery bag and staple it shut. Invite children to glue on tissue paper squares and crepe paper streamers. Use as a piñata for the class.

Music: Staple dried beans or peas between two paper plates. Decorate and use as a shaker instrument.

Sensory: Make a design with glue on a piece of white construction paper. Shake dry tempera paint in red and green (Mexico flag colors) over it. Put another sheet of white construction paper over it and press down. Lift the paper off for a festive design.

Additional Activities

Movement: Play Spanish music and encourage the children to dance around a Spanish hat called a sombrero.

Outside: Celebrate Cinco de Mayo with a parade outside. Wear the sombrero and serapes the children made, and use the shakers. Take the class' piñata outside. Take turns hitting it until the piñata breaks and the candy falls out. Let each child pick a few pieces of candy.

Rhythm and Rhyme: Sing "Hola Means Hello" with the children (see appendix page 355).

Backwards Day

GENERAL DAILY PLAN

Before doing this lesson plan, send a note home to families telling them about Backwards Day. Ask them to help their child wear clothes backwards on this special day.

STORY TIME

10 Minutes till Bedtime by Peggy Rathmann

Girl Meets Boy/Boy Meets Girl by C. Raschka, V. Radunsky

One, Two Skip a Few by Roberta Arenson

Silly Sally by Audrey Wood

Ten Silly Dogs by Lisa Flather

TRANSITION

As you call on quiet children to move on to the next activity, invite them to try to walk backwards on a taped line on the floor.

SNACK

Have a lunch. Eat backwards, starting with dessert first.

Group Time

Tell children that before rockets blast off into space, the crew counts backwards from 10. After they get to one, they say, "Blast off "and the rocket goes into space. As a class, count down from 10. When you get to zero, jump up and shout, "Blast off!"

Learning Center Ideas

Art/Math: Decorate rocket shapes and use them to practice the countdown they did in Group Time.

Dramatic Play: Have a silly dress up. Encourage the children to put on the dress up clothes backwards.

Gross Motor: Set up blocks in an obstacle course. Invite children to go through the obstacle course backwards one at a time.

Additional Activities

Movement: Walk around the circle backwards as you play "Ring Around the Rosie."

Rhythm and Rhyme: Encourage the children to sing "The Backwards Song" (see appendix page 353) and suit their actions to the words.

Number 4

STORY TIME

Four Friends in Autumn by Tomie de Paola

Four Friends in the Garden by Sue Heap

We All Went on Safari by Laurie Kreb

What Comes in 2's 3's and 4's? by Suzanne Aker

When I Was Four by Jamie Lee Curtis

Group Time

Some shapes have corners and sides. Counting sides is one way to determine a shape's name. A circle has no sides, (show a circle). A triangle has three sides (show a triangle). A rectangle has four sides, and a square has four sides that are the same length. (Show each). Give each child a shape. Invite the children to tell you how many sides it has. Then graph how many circles, triangles, squares, and rectangles you have.

Learning Center Ideas

Art: Set out a cardboard number 4 shape. Invite the children to trace around the shape on paper and dut it out. Encourage them to glue four buttons on their number 4s.

Art: Talk to the children about the four seasons. Then invite them to use art supplies to create a picture of all four seasons.

Blocks: Encourage the children to make rectangles, squares, and other four-sided shapes with blocks.

Math: Set out sticky tape in four colors. Invite the children to make a paper chain using the four colors. (Older children can make a chain using the four colors in a pattern.)

Additional Activities

Movement: Create a baseball diamond and invite the children to take turns running around the four bases.

Outside: Challenge the children to find four of each item, including rocks, leaves, flowers, birds, cars, and children.

Rhythm and Rhyme: Sing "The Four Seasons" with the children (see appendix page 354).

Small Group: Name the four seasons. Bring in items to sort by the seasons. They could include: a packet of seeds, mittens, plastic pumpkin, and so on.

Dogs

STORY TIME

Baby Einstein: Dogs by Julie Aigner-Clark
A Boy, a Dog, and a Frog by Mercer Mayer
Dogs Rule by Daniel Kirk
Good Dog, Carl by Alexandra Day
Hot Dog (a Step into Reading book) by Molly Coxe

SNACK

Make Doggie Chow (for people)
See appendix page 357.

Group Time

Cut out paw prints from construction paper and tape them to the floor in a path to the Group Time area. When it is Group Time, encourage the children to follow the paw prints to Group Time. Talk about dogs. Ask the children what they know about dogs. Ask how many of them have a dog at home. Share the Dog Facts (see appendix page 359) with the children and encourage discussion.

Learning Center Ideas

Art: Give each child a large triangle cut from construction paper. Help each child put the triangle on the table with one point down. Fold the two top corners over to make ears. Add eyes and nose using markers.

Dramatic Play: Invite the children to have a dog show. Encourage some to be dogs, others to be the owners, and two or three children to be the judges. Remind the children to take turns.

Dramatic Play/Art: Turn a large appliance box into a dog house. Invite the children to paint the "house" and make it cozy for a dog.

Math: Write a different number on several paper bowls. Cut out dog bone shapes from construction paper and write corresponding numbers on each bone. Encourage the children to put the correct number of dog bones into each bowl.

Additional Activities

Movement: Play Dog Catcher. Invite each child to pretend they are a big St. Bernard, a small Scottie, or a medium black Lab. One child is the Dog Catcher. When the Dog Catcher calls a dog's name those children run to the other side of the room. The dog catcher tries to tag those children. Any child tagged becomes a dog catcher. Play until all the dogs are caught.

Rhythm and Rhyme: Cut out dogs from different colors of construction paper. Give one to each child. Encourage the children to stand up when their color is mentioned in "The Dog Song" (see appendix page 354). Substitute a different color each time you sing the song, until every color has been mentioned and all of the children are standing.

Silly Socks Day

Before doing this lesson plan, send a note home to parents asking them to have their child wear silly or mismatched socks on this day.

STORY TIME

Good Night Moon and Baby Socks
    by Margaret Wise Brown
*Rocks in My Socks and Rainbows
    Too* by Lovelle Carlson
Shoes by Elizabeth Winthrop
Smelly Socks by Robert Munsch
Socks by Janie Spaht Gill

TRANSITION

Choose a color to insert into the rhyme below. Children with the named color on their socks move to the next activity.

    _____ socks, _____ socks
        walk away.
    It's time for you to go today.

Group Time

Bring in a laundry basket full of pairs of socks. Give one sock to each child. Take turns pulling out a sock from the laundry basket. Hold it up and ask the children who has the matching sock. The child who has the match gets to put the socks together and choose the next sock from the basket.

Next, put a small item, such as a ball or a spoon, into a sock. Tie a knot in the top of the sock. Encourage the children to pass the sock around the circle and try to guess what is in the sock. Do this as long as the children are interested.

Learning Center

Art: Make sock puppets. Give each child a tube sock. Invite children to use fabric, yarn, buttons to make eyes, hair, mouth and nose. Make up stories using the puppets.
Fine Motor: Stretch a clothesline across a portion of the room. Invite the children to use clothespins to hang socks on the clothesline.
Literacy: Cut 10 sock shapes or use five pairs of old matching socks. In permanent marker print an uppercase letter on one sock and a lowercase on the other half. Invite the children to match uppercase and lowercase letters.
Math: Cut two sock shapes from each of the following colors; red, blue, green, yellow, orange, purple, black, and brown. Invite the children to match socks by color.

Additional Activities

Movement: Chant "Silly Socks" with the children (see appendix page 356) and ask them to suit their actions to the words.
Outside: Invite the children to bring in an old sock from home. Help them put the sock on over their shoes. Take a nature walk outside in the grass. After the walk, look at the socks. Notice the seeds stuck on the socks. Talk about how seeds travel from place to place. Put the socks in water and see if the seeds grow.
Rhythm and Rhyme: Sing "The Sock Song" with the children (see appendix page 357).

Hamsters

STORY TIME

Face to Face with the Hamster by
Paul Starosta
Little Hamster and the Great Flood
by Caroline Jayne Church

TRANSITION

Invite children to crawl through a
cardboard box like a hamster as
they move to the next activity.

SNACK

Make a "hamster" mix (see
appendix page 357).

Group Time

Tell the children that today they will learn about hamsters. Show children
pictures of different types of hamsters. On chart paper, make three lists:
"What We Know About Hamsters," "What We Want to Know About
Hamsters," and "What We Learned About Hampsters" (to be filled in at the
end of the day.) Ask the children what they know about hamsters and
write down what they say. Share the Hamster Facts from appendix page
360 and encourage the children to share their ideas and questions.

Learning Center Ideas

Art: Make swirl paint by pouring brown tempera into a bowl of white
tempera. Swirl the paint, but don't actually mix it. Show the children how
to dip a dishwashing scrubber or a bath puff into the swirled paint. Print
onto paper to make a swirly fluffy hamster. When the paint dries, add
wiggle eyes and marker legs.
Math: Draw squares on paper and write a number in each square.
Laminate. Encourage the children to put the correct number of pompom
hamsters on the cage.

Additional Activities

Game: Invite the children to sit in a circle except for one child who is "IT."
IT hides his eyes, and one child hides under a big cardboard grocery box
or under a blanket. IT opens his eyes and tries to guess who the hamster
in the cage is.
Rhythm and Rhyme: Sing "Little Hamsters" with the children (see appendix
page 355).
Small Group: Bring a small hamster into the classroom for the children to
look at in small groups. Make a list of the observations the class makes.
What do hamsters need?

Letter *M*

STORY TIME

Caps for Sale by Esphyr Slobodkina
*Five Little Monkeys Sitting in the
    Tree* by Eileen Christelow
If You Give a Mouse a Cookie by
    Laura Joffe Numeroff
*The Little Mouse, The Red Ripe
    Strawberry, and the Big Hungry
    Bear* by Audrey Wood
Mouse Tales by Arnold Lobel

TRANSITION

Make an easy "magic moon" wand
by hot gluing a foam "moon" to a
dowel. Jazz it up by gluing on glitter
or confetti. Use the magic wand to
tap children who are sitting quietly
to move on to the next activity.

SNACK

Make Monkey Bread (see appendix
page 358).

Group Time

May starts with the /m/ sound. Ask the children what other words start
with the /m/ sound. Make a list of the words that the children say.

Learning Center Ideas

Art: Fingerpaint a mouse shape with black and white tempera paint,
mixing the colors to make gray. When dry, add eyes, whiskers and a tail.
Math: Sort by colors. Obtain old colored envelopes and a grocery store box
that has sections or is sectioned into parts. Label each section a color. Sort
the envelopes into the sections by color. (If you cannot find colored
envelopes, use plain white envelopes, but put a colored sticker in the
corner).

Additional Activities

Movement: Use your magic wand to change your children into mice,
monkeys, monsters, or mail carriers. Encourage the children move
accordingly. Do this movement activity to music for more fun.
Outside: Go outside and look for mud. Where do you find it? What makes
mud? What makes it go away? If you can't find any, make some.
Rhythm and Rhyme: Sing "The M Song" with the children (see appendix
page 356).

Mothers

We celebrate Mother's Day in May.

STORY TIME

Are You My Mother? by Philip D. Eastman

Just Me and My Mom by Mercer Mayer

Mama Do You Love Me? by Barbara M. Joosse

Mother for Choco by Keiko Kasza

Mother Goose's Nursery Rhymes by Robert Frederick

On Mother's Lap by Ann Herbert Scott

TRANSITION

Children take turns naming something special about their mothers before moving on to the next activity.

SNACK

Decorate a special cookie for Mom. Set out large sugar cookies, several kinds of frosting and other cookie decorations. Invite children to decorate a cookie for Mom.

Group Time

Read the story *Does a Kangaroo Have a Mother, Too?* by Eric Carle. After reading the story, go through the book again, talking about the names of the mother, father, and baby. The names for each animal are given at the back of the book. Can someone else be a mother too? Talk about other Moms; stepmothers, foster mothers, grandmas, aunts, and how they are special.

Learning Center Ideas

Art: Make a gift for Mom. Set out an empty, clean, baby food jar for each child. Help the children fill the jar with potpourri. Put a circle of netting material over the top and secure it with a rubber band. Add a ribbon and a little note that says:

> *This is made especially for you,*
> *To say, "Have a Happy Mothers Day!"*

Dramatic Play: Set up an office for working mothers. A doctor's office could be set up in the Science area. Set up other areas that relate to the working mothers in your classroom.

Math: Sort plastic animals into groups of mothers and babies.

Additional Activities

Outside: Play Mother May I. The children stand on a line on one side of the playground. Choose one child to be the "Mother," who stands on the other side of the playground. The Mother gives a command to a child. The child says "Mother, may I?" The mother says, "Yes, you may," or "No, you may not." Each child has a turn and then a new mother is named.

Bees

STORY TIME

Bee Safe by Charles Reasoner
Buzz-Buzz Busy Bees by Dawn Bentley
Buzzing Bees by Wendy Mclean
How Bees Be by Alison Boyle

SNACK

Invite the children to put honey and peanut butter on English muffins for a sweet snack. **Note:** Be sure to check for allergies. Do not give honey to children under one year of age.

Group Time

As the children come to Group Time, make a low, buzzing noise pretending you are a bee. Ask them to tell you about the sound you're making. What could you be? A bee, of course! Talk about bees, using the Bee Facts (see appendix page 359). Ask the children to tell you what they know about bees. Write down their responses.

Learning Center Ideas

Art: Make a bee. Cut a circle from yellow construction paper, or paint a small paper plate yellow. Use two pieces of sticky black tape, or regular colored black masking tape to put on the circle as stripes. Cut two sets of wings from white tissue paper to glue on top. Add a happy bee face and the bee is ready to go to work.

Math: Practice one-to-one correspondence. Make a beehive from an egg carton. Put a yellow pompom bee in each hole.

Sensory: Set out yellow playdough. Invite the children to make playdough bees. For a twist cut out construction paper flowers. Program each flower with a number and laminate the flowers. Put the flowers in the playdough area. Invite children to make the programmed number of playdough bees for each flower.

Additional Activities

Movement: Teach the children about the body parts of an insect by doing the "Honey Bee Hokey Pokey" (see appendix page 355).

Movement: Invite the children to line up on one side of the playground, except for one child who is the Queen (or King) Bee. The rest of the class are the worker bees. The workers try to run across to the other side of the playground before the Queen tags them. When the workers are tagged, they have to help the Queen tag other children. The game continues until all the children are tagged.

Rhythm and Rhyme: Sing "The Bumblebee Song" with the children (see appendix page 353).

Small Group: Read "A Bee's Life" to the children and encourage them to suit their actions to the words (see appendix page 353). Help the children act out this story as they learn about a bee's life.

Horses

May is the month of the Kentucky Derby.

STORY TIME

Giddy-up! Let's Ride by Flora McDonnell
Happy Horse: A Children's Book of Horses by E. Ashe
My Pony by Susan Jeffers
Surprise for Horse by Alex Lee

TRANSITION

Sing "Gallop Around" with the children and invite them to suit their actions to the words (see appendix page 354). The child named in the song gallops around in a circle and then moves to the next activity.

SNACK

Make Haystack Cookies (see appendix page 357).

Group Time

On a horse shape, prints facts about horses (see Horse Facts on appendix page 360). Read the facts to the children and talk about them. Ask them if they have seen or ridden a horse. Talk about their experiences. Talk about horse races, and explain that a very big race, the Kentucky Derby, happens in the month of May. Using a map, show the children where Kentucky is located.

Learning Center Ideas

Art: Make horses. Have each child bring an old sock with a heel in for this project. Stuff the sock with crumpled paper. Then tie the sock to a large empty wrapping paper roll. Using markers or fabric paint, draw a face on the sock. The heel creates the top of the horse's head, and the toe is the horse's nose. (Optional: Invite the children to make Kentucky Derby wreaths for their horses by cutting out the middle of a paper plate and gluing on fabric or foam flowers.)

Dramatic Play: Set up the blocks in an obstacle course, so children can pretend to be horses. They gallop through the course jumping over blocks.

Literacy: Cut out several construction paper horses. Cut them in half down the middle. On the back end half, print an uppercase letter. On the front print its lowercase match. Invite the children to match the letters to put the letters to put the together.

Math: Tie brown yarn or rope in small circles like a fence. Give each small fence a number. Encourage the children to put the correct number of plastic horses inside each fence.

Additional Activities

Movement: Show children how to gallop. Practice galloping to music.
Rhythm and Rhyme: Sing "Galloping Horses" with the children (see appendix page 354).

Mary Had a Little Lamb

TRANSITION

Take turns singing "Mary had a Little Lamb," singing childrens' names instead of Mary. The child whose name was used moves to the next activity.

SNACK

Make a lamb face. Spread white cream cheese on an English muffin. Add two raisin eyes, and a miniature black cookie nose. Add sliced and peeled apple slice ears.

Group Time

Talk about sheep and how they are very fuzzy animals. Explain that sheep get hot in their coats in the summer, so they get a hair cut in the spring. Sheep's hair is called wool. Show children a piece of cotton batting. This is what their wool looks like when the sheep get the haircut. Then explain that wool gets spun together to make yarn. Show children a ball of yarn. Then explain that people or machines make this ball of yarn into mittens, a sweater, or even a hat. Show children several items that are made from wool. Review and sequence the steps.

Learning Center Ideas

Art: Make Mary's little lamb. Invite the children to glue cotton batting on a black sheep shape. Add eyes and nose with chalk.

Math: Cut out several sheep shapes. Write a number on each sheep. Laminate the shapes. Challenge the children to put the correct number of cotton balls on each sheep shape.

Science: Put cotton batting, yarn, and woolen mittens on the Science Table for the children to explore. Encourage them to use magnifying glasses to examine the wool and yarn.

Additional Activities

Movement: Play Mary (or Mark), Where's Your Lamb? The children sit in a circle except for the child who is "Mary." Mary sits in the middle of the circle with a plastic animal lamb behind her. Mary covers her eyes and a child sneaks the lamb. The children chant, "Mary (or Mark), where's your lamb?" Mary opens her eyes and tries to guess who has the plastic lamb.

Rhythm and Rhyme: Sing "Mary Had a Little Lamb" with the alternate verses (see appendix page 355).

Small Group: Sing "Mary had a Little Lamb," using the version of the song in Rhythm and Rhyme (see above), then invite children to pick silly animals and sing it again. Make a class book. For every child, write on a piece of paper: "_____ had a little _____." Invite the children to fill in the animal name, and then draw the animal. Make the pages into a class book.

Beads

STORY TIME

10 Beads Tall by Pam Adams
What's for Dinner? by Joanne
   Mattern

TRANSITION

Call out letters. Children with that letter on their necklaces line up or move on to the next activity.

Group Time

Children string their own alphabet bead necklaces to wear for the day. They string five beads and then an alphabet bead of the first letter of their name and then five more beads. Invite each child to name the bead on their necklace. Sing the ABC song and invite the children to stand up and quickly sit down when the letter on their necklace is sung. Start by singing the song slowly and then faster.

Learning Center Ideas

Art: Using playdough, make your own beads. When they are dry, string them to make a necklace. Make patterns on chenille stems with beads. Start with two colors, stringing every other color. Put at least four beads on the pipe cleaner and then invite the child to put the next bead on. Make bracelets with the activity, cutting off the extra pipe cleaner. Wrap the pipe cleaner together, and put the ends under beads so they do not scratch the children.

Fine Motor: Sort beads by size, color and shape in ice cube trays. Set out colored pony beads. Invite children to sort the beads by color in an ice cube tray.

Writing: Help the children use alphabet beads to spell their names on pipe cleaners or necklaces. Set out class name cards in the Center. Add other words, such as "Mom" and "Dad" in the Literacy Center. Add alphabet beads and rex lace for stringing. Encourage the children to try making a necklace for a friend.

Additional Activities

Movement: Sitting in a circle, everyone holds a colored bead. When the music plays they pass their bead to the person on their right. Children will be giving and getting beads. When the music stops, each person should have a new bead. Then give an instruction "Children holding a red bead, stand up." Play again. Then give another direction.

Rhythm and Rhyme: Sing "The Color Song" with the children (see appendix 354).

Trucks

STORY TIME

Don't Let the Pigeon Drive the Bus!
    by Mo Willems
Little Green Tow Truck by Ken
    Wilson-Max
My Truck Is Stuck by Kevin Lewis
Truck by Donald Crews
Truck Board Book DK Publishing
Trucks by Harriet Castor

TRANSITION

Children take turns naming their
favorite truck and move on to the
next activity.

SNACK

Use new, washed, plastic trucks to
deliver the snack to children. This
works the best when the snacks are
wrapped separately.

Group Time

Make a list of all the different kinds of trucks and talk about what they do.
Try to have the children organize them under these categories:

- Construction trucks
- Service trucks (fire, garbage)
- Delivery trucks

Learning Center Ideas

Blocks: Bring in small toy trucks for the block area, and make highways.
Dramatic Play: Invite children to help paint a large refrigerator box on its
side as a truck. Talk about logos on different trucks. Invite children to put
one on their truck. Pretend to pack and unpack boxes.
Literacy: Collect enough wrappers or logos from packages so every child
can choose one. Invite the children to cut out a trailer truck shape. Show
them how to glue their logos onto the box of the truck shape. Encourage
the children to draw their picture in the driver's seat of the truck.
Math: Tape uppercase letters on small trucks. Make a parking lot from
constructions paper. Write lowercase letters on the parking spaces. Park the
trucks in the correct parking spot. (**Note:** you can do the same with
numbers, rather than letters.)

Additional Activities

Outside: Watch and count the trucks that drive by.
Rhythm and Rhyme: Sing "The Truck Song" with the children (see appendix
page 357).
Small Group: Set out four or five small trucks on a tray. Talk about each
one. While children close their eyes, take one away. Ask the children to
open their eyes and guess which one is missing.

Alligators and Crocodiles

GENERAL DAILY PLAN

Apple, Apple Alligator by William Accorsi

An Extraordinary Egg by Leo Lionni

A Frog in the Bog by Karma Wilson

The Lady with the Alligator Purse by Nadine Bernard Westcott

Tales from the Outback by Melissa Lagonegro

TRANSITION

Say the rhyme below, inserting a child's name. That child moves his arms like an alligator snapping, and then he names another child. The alligator moves to the next activity and the chosen child becomes the alligator.

> _____ alligator in the bay
> Who will you pick to eat today?

SNACK

Make green gelatin according to package directions. Put the gelatin in small clear plastic cups. Put two small spoonfuls of whipped cream on top, with a raisin in the middle of each as eyes. (Note: This can be done with pistachio pudding instead.)

Group Time

Before Group Time, print several of the Alligator and Crocodile Facts close up (see appendix page 358) on small pieces of paper and put them in plastic eggs. In several eggs put small plastic or foam alligators. Start with a riddle: What is green, gets bigger than you but hatches from a small egg? Answer: An alligator. Invite each child to choose an egg. Open the egg and read the fact.

Learning Center Ideas

Literacy: Color wooden clip clothespins green to look like alligators. Cut small fish from poster board. Write an uppercase letter on each clothespin alligator. Write a corresponding lowercase letter on each fish. Invite the children to clip the alligator to the matching fish.

Math: Write different numbers on construction paper cutouts of alligators. Laminate for durability. Invite the children to put the correct number of fish crackers on the alligator shapes.

Science: Make a large and small alligator shape in green, red, orange, purple, and brown. Put the alligator shapes on the felt board. Invite the children to match the mom and the baby alligator shapes.

Additional Activities

Movement: Choose one child to be the crocodile. Ask the rest of the class to be fish—half are blue and half are red. The fish stand on one side of the playground. The crocodile calls out, "Red fish" and they pretend to swim across the playground. The crocodile tries to tag the fish. Any fish that are tagged become crocodiles, and they help tag other fish. The crocodile continues to call out, "Red fish," "Blue fish," or "All fish" until all the fish are caught.

Rhythm and Rhyme: Sing "The Crocodile Song" with the children (see appendix page 354).

Cats

STORY TIME

Cat's Vacation by Irene Schoch
Have You Seen My Cat? by Eric Carle
Mama Cat Has Three Kittens by
     Denise Fleming
Oh Cats! by Nola Buck

TRANSITION

Encourage the children to pretend they are cats. Point to a child and that child can sneak away quietly like a cat to the next activity.

SNACK

Invite each child to count out 10 cheese-flavored fish crackers and 10 pretzel-flavored fish crackers to enjoy.

Group Time

Play Cat and Mouse. The children stand in a circle holding hands. One child is the cat and one is the mouse. The cat tries to catch the mouse. The children help by lifting their arms so the mouse can go in, but putting them down quickly so the cat can't get through. Talk about cats with the children, using the list of Cat Facts (see appendix page 359).

Learning Center Ideas

Art: Invite children to trace and cut a cat shape from black construction paper. Decorate the shape with chalk, glitter, glue, and other materials.
Fine Motor: Set out small balls of yarn. Invite children to unroll and roll up a ball of yarn. This is especially good for younger children.
Literacy: Cut mouse and cat shapes from construction paper. Write an uppercase alphabet letter on each cat shape, and matching lowercase letters on the mouse shapes. Laminate. Encourage the children to match the uppercase and lowercase letters.

Additional Activities

Movement: Play Cat Catcher: Pretend each child is either a black, yellow or striped cat. One child is the Cat Catcher. the children all stand on one edge of the gym. The cat catcher calls out one color of cat. As those children run across to the other side of the room, the cat catcher tries to tag them. If they are tagged, they become cat catchers. Play until everyone is tagged.
Outside: Pretend you are a cat as you play outside. Try to catch a butterfly, chase your tail, and pretend you are sneaking up on a mouse, ready to pounce.
Rhythm and Rhyme: Sing "The Cat Song" with the children (see appendix page 354).

Cars

STORY TIME

Cars and Trucks and Things That Go
 by Richard Scarry
Five Little Monkeys Wash the Car by
 Eileen Christelow
I Spy Little Wheels by Jean Marzollo
Miss Spider's New Car by David Kirk
Sheep in a Jeep by Margot Apple

TRANSITION

Point to a child to finish the rhyme,
and then move on to a new activity.

> Cars go fast,
> Cars go slow,
> Red means stop,
> And green means _____!

Group Time

Start by giving each child a paper race car shape in either red, blue, or yellow. Then use a large rope to make a shape on the floor, such as a circle. Say this rhyme:

> Red cars on the race track,
> Drive round the _____(shape) *then come back.*

The red cars go around the jump rope and come and sit down. Change the color and change the jump rope to other shapes.

Learning Center Ideas

Art: Paint large discarded grocery boxes and encourage the children to pretend the boxes are cars. Provide supplies for decorating their cars. Add name license plates.
Literacy: Sort small cars by color or kind of car. Set out red, blue, green, and yellow construction paper. On each paper draw lines for parking spots around the edges. In the middle of the paper print the color word of the paper. Invite the children to park small toy cars in the parking spot the same color as the car.
Math: Cut squares in shoeboxes to make garages. Write a number on each box garage. Have the children drive the correct number of small cars into the garage.

Additional Activities

Movement: Play Red Light, Green Light. One child is "IT." Ask the rest of the children to line up on the other side of the classroom. It say "go" and turns with his back to the children. the children try to sneak up and tag IT. IT yells "Red light" and turns around. The children stop, and if IT sees anybody move they have to go to the back.
Small Group: Put several items in a bag with a small car. Each small group uses the items to make up a story.
Rhythm and Rhyme: Sing "If You're Riding in the Car" (see appendix page 355) with the children.

Measurement

STORY TIME

Bug Dance by Stuart Murphy
Grapes of Math by Greg Tang
How Tall by Nicolas Harris
Measure by Ivan Bulloch
Quack and Count by Keith Baker

TRANSITION

Show children how to measure (with feet end to end as they walk) how many footsteps away their next activity is. Children count their footsteps as they move on.

SNACK

Measure 1 cup of each of the following:

◆ cereal
◆ raisins
◆ marshmallow
◆ peanuts
◆ pretzels

Mix together. Then measure ¼ cup of the mixture for each child for a snack.

Group Time

Show the many different tools used for measurement and how to use them. Some to include are measuring cups, measuring spoons, tape measure, yardstick, ruler, and scale. Measure each child's height and weight.

Learning Center Ideas

Math: Set out a balance scale and counting bears. Set out classroom items, such as a block, toy car, eraser and a small book. Invite the children to see how many bears each item weighs.

Science: Set a regular weight scale and invite children to weigh themselves. Ask them to stand on the scale again, while holding a block. Does their weight stay the same? Try this with other items.

Sensory: Put measuring cups and spoons in the Sand Table. Invite the children to explore the sizes.

Additional Activities

Project: Help children make a rain gauge. Instruct each child to bring in a baby food jar. Ask for extras just in case some children don't have them. Before class mark off 1" and 2" on each jar in permanent or glass markers. During class explain that rain gauges measure the rain. Invite children to decorate their jars with stickers. Put the jars outside. After a rain, help children check their jars.

June | July | August

The Summer Months

WEEK ONE: SUMMER FUN

National Ice Cream Month   National Hot Dog Month

At the Fair   Baseball

Independence Day

WEEK TWO: AT THE BEACH

Beach   Manatees   Fish

Seahorses   Dolphins   Pirates

WEEK THREE: SUMMER SAFARI

Camping   Zebras   Tigers

Giraffes   Lions

WEEK FOUR: SPACE ADVENTURES

Space   Moon   Airplanes

Sun   Stars

WEEK FIVE: ON THE FARM

Farms   Watermelon   Corn

Farm Animals   Berries Galore

WEEK SIX: SUMMER BUGS

Picnic   Butterflies   Caterpillars

Ladybugs   Dragonflies

WEEK SEVEN: IT'S HOT OUT THERE!

Deserts   Rocks   Camels

Aloha   Snakes

WEEK EIGHT: LAZY SUMMER DAYS

Hands   Book Lovers' Day   T-shirts

Dandelions   Frogs

National Ice Cream Month

WEEK ONE: SUMMER FUN

STORY TIME

From Cow to Ice Cream by Bertram T. Knight

Ice Cream: The Full Scoop by Gail Gibbons

Milk: From Cow to Carton by Aliki

Wemberly's Ice Cream Star by Kevin Henkes

TRANSITION

Invite the children to recite "Ice Cream, Oh So Sweet," found on appendix page 362. Add color names to the second line with each repetition of the verse, inviting children wearing the named color to move to the next activity.

SNACK

Have an Ice Cream Social. Send a note home inviting each child to bring in a healthy topping for ice cream, such as graham cracker bits or cherries. Set out the toppings and have an ice cream party.

Group Time

Play ice cream balancing games. Before starting, roll brown construction paper in cone shapes and staple in place. Give each child one construction paper cone and a tennis ball to place on top of the cone. Challenge the children to walk around while balancing the ball on the cone. As the children become more proficient, see if they are able to pass a ball from one cone to another.

Learning Center Ideas

Blocks: Invite the children to use blocks to build an ice cream shop.

Dramatic Play: Encourage the children to pretend to work in an ice cream shop. Some children can scoop and others can be customers. Don't forget to have a cashier!

Literacy: Make a class ice cream book. Give each child a paper with the following written at the top: "_____'s favorite ice cream is _____." Encourage the children to draw their favorite ice cream treats. Print the names of children's favorite flavors on top of their pages, and then bind the pages into a class book.

Sensory: Set up ice cream dishes, scoops, and playdough and encourage the children to pretend they work at an ice cream parlor.

Additional Activities

Movement: Invite children to dance as music plays. When the music stops, the children must freeze like ice cream. Start the music and play again.

Outside: Bring the children outside to do an experiment. Explain that to do an experiment, they must start with a question, such as "What will happen to ice cream in the hot sun?" Ask the children to predict what they think will happen, and then take a dish of ice cream outside. Encourage the children to describe what happens. With the children, make conclusions about what happens to ice cream in the hot sun.

Rhythm and Rhyme: Invite the children to sing "Ice Cream, Ice Cream," found on appendix page 362.

At the Fair

Send a note home to parents asking them to dress their children in red, white, and blue for a class celebration of Independence Day tomorrow.

STORY TIME

Animal Fair by Anthony Browne
Blue Ribbon Henry by Mary Calhoun
Carousel by Donald Crews
County Fair by Laura Ingalls Wilder
Minerva Louise at the Fair by Janet Morgan Stoeke
Spot and His Grandparents Go to the Fair by Eric Hill

SNACK

Make caramel apples. Unwrap a bag of caramels and put them in a saucepan. Melt the caramels in the pan (adult-only step). Insert a craft stick in each apple. Supervising closely, help the children dip the apples into the caramels and then set on wax paper to dry. For younger children, provide apple slices with caramel sauce for dipping.

Group Time

Read *Blue Ribbon Henry* by Mary Calhoun to the children. Afterwards, talk with the children about judging contests, and then invite the children to judge the "Best of the Best" Blue Ribbon Food Contest. Set out three different kinds of pies: apple, cherry, pumpkin, or some other combination. Invite children to try each one. Set a paper cup in front of each pie, and tell the children to put their spoons in the cup in front of the pie they like best. Count the spoons and award the "Blue Ribbon" to the pie with the most spoons.

Learning Center Ideas

Art: Set out glitter, sequins, yarn, and fabric paint. Give each child a construction paper cutout of a horse shape (using the outline found on appendix page 361) to decorate like a merry-go-round horse. Help the children glue a large craft stick on the back.

Fine/Gross Motor: Play carnival games with the children. Challenge them to drop clothespins into milk bottles, or set out rings and see if they can toss the rings around the necks of bottles. Also, set out ping-pong balls for the children to toss into a laundry basket.

Literacy: Set out pieces of paper with different letters written on each, and encourage the children to throw beanbags onto the letters that are in their names. If necessary, give the children sentence strips with their names printed on them.

Sensory/Literacy: Print letters on the bottom of plastic ducks. Float the ducks in water in the Sensory Table, and encourage the children to lift the ducks and name the letters written on them.

Additional Activities

Outside: Use cones and flags to set up an obstacle course for children to go through.

Rhythm and Rhyme: Invite the children to sing "Going to the Fair," found on appendix page 361.

Independence Day

Encourage the children to wear red, white, and blue to celebrate the Fourth of July.

STORY TIME

Fourth of July Sparkly Sky by Amanda Haley

Hurray for the Fourth of July by Wendy Watson

Mouse's First Summer by Lauren Thompson

Story of America's Birthday by Patricia A. Pingry

TRANSITION

Encourage the children to practice marching as they move to the next activity.

SNACK

Decorate a birthday cake or cupcakes with red, white, and blue frosting. Sing the birthday song and celebrate with a birthday party.

Group Time

Talk about the story of the Fourth of July. More than 200 years ago, the King of England ruled people in this country. They had to do whatever the King said. The people wanted to have their own country with their own leaders and to make rules for themselves. So, everybody got together and fought against England for freedom. They won the war and created the United States of America on July 4, 1776. This date is our country's birthday. We celebrate with a big birthday party every year, with parades, parties, and fireworks.

Learning Center Ideas

Art: Suggest that the children make a sparkly fireworks picture to celebrate the Fourth of July. They use a glue bottle to make a glue design on a black piece of construction paper, shake on powdered tempera paint in red and blue over the glue, and then add gold or silver glitter. Shake off the excess paint and glitter. Let the picture dry. Spray the whole picture with hair spray to keep the picture from smearing (adult-only step).

Math: Cut firecracker shapes from red and blue construction paper and write a different numeral on each one. Give the children plastic stars and encourage them to count the correct number of stars for each firecracker.

Math: Suggest that the children practice making patterns using red and blue felt stars on a flannel board. Begin by using AB patterns. For older children or children who are ready for a challenge, add white stars so they can work on more complex patterning.

Additional Activities

Movement: Give the children red, white, and blue streamers, flags, and decorations to hold as they have a special parade to celebrate the Fourth of July.

Outside: Decorate the playground for the Fourth of July. With the children, weave red, white, and blue streamers through the playground fence.

Rhythm and Rhyme: Invite the children to sing "Happy Birthday" to the United States.

National Hot Dog Month

STORY TIME

Hot Dog by Molly Coxe

Hot Dog, Cool Cat: A Crazy Criss Cross Book of Opposites by Emma Dodd

Macaroni and Cheese, Hot Dogs and Peas by Christine Hickson

The Pigeon Finds a Hot Dog! by Mo Willems

TRANSITION

Ask the children to line up according to hot dog condiment preference, with ketchup lovers lining up, then mustard, then "the works." Count the number for each condiment before letting the children in each condiment line move to the next activity.

SNACK

Make a hot dog snack. (To prevent choking, be sure to cut the hot dogs lengthwise into four pieces.) Wrap the four pieces of each hot dog in a piece of crescent dough. Cook the hotdogs according to the package instructions (adult-only step). Serve them warm with condiments.

Group Time

Have a sausage tasting party. Cook and cut into small pieces a hot dog, a bratwurst, and an Italian sausage. Put a pretzel stick into each piece to make them easier to handle. Invite the children to try each one, and make a graph to determine the class favorite.

Encourage the children to recite "Ten Little Hot Dogs," found on appendix page 362, and use felt hotdog shapes on a flannel board to count down from 10–0.

Learning Center Ideas

Art: Help the children cut out hot dog shapes from brown construction paper, and cut yellow hot dog buns from yellow construction paper. Show the children how to glue the hot dog in the bun. Put red paint in a ketchup bottle and yellow paint in a mustard bottle so the children can paint ketchup and mustard designs on the hot dog.

Math: Set out several different plastic toy foods for the children to sort according to the food pyramid.

Math: Set out brown construction paper hot dog shapes, and yellow construction paper bun shapes, writing the same numeral on one of each. Laminate for durability. Shuffle the buns and dogs and invite the children to match the numerals on the hot dog shapes to the same numerals on the bun shapes.

Additional Activities

Movement: Play musical hot dogs. Arrange in a circle enough construction paper hot dog shapes on the floor for each child. As the music plays, have the children walk around the hot dogs, stopping on a hot dog shape whenever the music stops.

Rhythm and Rhyme: Invite the children to recite "Hot Dogs on the Grill," found on appendix page 362.

Baseball

STORY TIME

Babe and Me by Dan Gutman

Fenway Park 1, 2, 3 by Red Sox Wives

Major League Baseball 1, 2, 3 by James Buckley

Mickey and Me by Dan Gutman

Shoeless Joe and Me by Dan Gutman

TRANSITION

Throw a sponge baseball to a child, inviting the child to toss it back, and then move to the next activity.

SNACK

Use a melon ball kitchen tool to make melon "baseballs." Serve them with pretzel rod "bats."

Group Time

Invite the children to talk about softball and baseball, what the basic rules are, their favorite teams and players, what teams they might be on, and so on. Bring in a glove, ball, bat, catcher's mask, cleats, a hat and a base to show the children as you talk. Ask the children to close their eyes. Take one item and cover it with a blanket. As the children open their eyes, invite them to guess which item is under the blanket.

Learning Center Ideas

Fine Motor: Cut several glove shapes out of file folders, and punch holes around their edges. Be sure there is one cutout per child, and invite them to lace string or yarn around their glove shapes. When the edge of the glove is completely sewn, help the children make white construction paper cutouts of baseballs, and glue them to their gloves.

Math: Cut several construction paper bat and ball shapes. Write uppercase letters on the baseball bats and lowercase letters on the balls. Laminate the shapes and invite the children to match the uppercase and lowercase letters together.

Math: Provide several baseball cards for the children to sort and explore.

Additional Activities

Movement: Set up bases in the classroom or outside, and invite the children to run, hop, skip, and jump around the bases.

Outside: Set up a ball tee, and give each child a turn at hitting a baseball off it, using a plastic ball and bat.

Rhythm and Rhyme: Invite the children to sing the "Baseball Outside," found on appendix page 361, and perform the actions mentioned in it, holding up one, two, and three fingers as they recite it.

Beach

Before the day you wish to do this daily plan, send a note home to parents that explaining that their child will participate in a "Beach Day" at school. Ask them to send in the child's swimsuit, a towel, and to apply plenty of sunscreen for a fun day.

STORY TIME

All You Need for a Beach by Alice Schertle

At the Beach by Mandy Stanley

Just Grandma and Me by Mercer Mayer

Spot Goes to the Beach by Eric Hill

What's on the Beach? by Jo Lodge

SNACK

Keep cool with fruit juice popsicles. Help the children pour juice into paper cups, filling each cup half way. Put the cups in the freezer. When they are starting to freeze, help the children put a craft stick in the middle of each cup. Return the cups to the freezer until completely frozen. Remove the fruit juice popsicles from the cup and enjoy.

Group Time

Before Group Time, glue two 3" x 5" index cards together with a craft stick handle. Print "Yes" on one side and "No" on the other. Make one for each child. At Group Time, ask the children what sorts of things they might find at a beach. Give each child a "yes/no" sign. Next, name several different items for the children; for instance: shells, mittens, rulers, sand, pencils, computers, fish, umbrellas, and so on. Have the children hold up either their "yes" or "no" cards, depending on whether each particular item belongs on the beach. Also, encourage the children to discuss their beach experiences, or what they might like to do if they went to the beach.

Learning Center Ideas

Art: Have the children make their own beach in a baby food jar. Provide each child with a clean, clear baby food jar with a lid. Invite the children to fill their jars about half full of sand, and add several shells. When they are finished making beach jars, help them glue the lids on tight.

Art/Sensory: Put sand in paint for the children to experience using paint with a different texture.

Sensory: Put sand in a playdough recipe (or use the Coconut Playdough recipe on appendix page 364) for a different texture. Encourage the children to use fish, seashell, and star cookie cutters to make things found on a beach.

Additional Activities

Game: Play a game under a beach blanket. Invite the children to sit in a circle around the blanket, and ask them to close their eyes. Put an item, such as a sand bucket or shovel, under the blanket and tuck the blanket under the object so the children can see the form under the blanket. Invite children to open their eyes and guess what the item is. Start with easy items, such as a beach ball.

Rhythm and Rhyme: Teach the children to sing "Did You Ever See a Seashell?" (on appendix page 363). Encourage the children to make up new verses.

Seahorses

STORY TIME

Mister Seahorse by Eric Carle
Seahorses by Sylvia James
Seahorse Treasures by Laurie Ide
Secret Seahorse by Stella Blackstone

Group Time

Write the Seahorse Facts, found on appendix page 365 on pieces of paper. Read the facts to the children. Next, play a flannel board game. Cut seahorses and coral shapes from several different colors of felt. Put the coral shapes on the flannel board. Invite children to take turns choosing a felt seahorse and matching it to the same color of coral.

Learning Center Ideas

Art: Give the children seahorse shapes cut from white construction paper (see the seahorse pattern on appendix page 363). Encourage them to tear small pieces of colored tissue paper and glue them to their seahorse shapes.

Math: Cut seahorses and coral shapes from patterned paper. Invite the children to match the seahorses and the coral.

Science: Put small seahorses, stars, and pieces of coral at the Science Table to explore.

Additional Activities

Movement: Play hide and seek. Encourage the children who hide to recite "Seahorse in the Sea," found on appendix page 364.

Rhythm and Rhyme: Invite the children to sing "Seahorse, Seahorse," found on appendix page 364.

Manatees

STORY TIME

Dancing with Manatees by Faith McNulty
I'm a Manatee by John Lithgow
Manatees by Kathy Feeney
Manatees by Marianne Johnston
Manatee Winter by Kathleen Weidner Zoehfeld

SNACK

Invite the children to help make "manatee" Jell-O® by putting purple grapes into blue Jell-O®.

Group Time

Introduce the children to the manatee by showing them pictures of manatees and reading the Manatee Facts, found on appendix pages 364–365. After looking at the pictures, show the children a picture of a manatee and one of a fish, inviting them to compare the two creatures. Write their descriptions of differences and similarities on a sheet of construction paper.

Learning Center Ideas

Art: Set out black and white finger paint and several construction paper cutouts of manatees, using the manatee outline on appendix page 362, and invite the children to paint the manatees.

Math: Cut out several construction paper manatee shapes, and write different numerals on each. Set out several small toy fish or fish cutouts, and invite the children to put the correct number of fish on each manatee.

Sensory: Set out plastic versions of manatees and other water creatures for the children to explore.

Additional Activities

Game: Play Manatee, Manatee Where's Your Seaweed? Begin by inviting the children to sit in a circle, choosing one child to be the manatee. The manatee sits in the middle of the circle with a plastic plant (seaweed) behind her back. The manatee closes her eyes and one child sneaks her lunch (plant) and puts it behind her back. The manatee opens her eyes as the children chant "Manatee, manatee, where's your seaweed?" The manatee gets three guesses to figure out who has the seaweed.

Rhythm and Rhyme: Teach the children to sing "You're a Manatee," found on appendix page 364.

Small Group: Read *I'm a Manatee* by John Lithgow. After the story, invite the children to discuss what they would do if they were manatees. Copy down the children's responses, and invite them to draw pictures of themselves as manatees. When the children are finished drawing their pictures, gather them into a class book, titled, "If I Were a Manatee...."

Dolphins

STORY TIME

Dolphins by E. Melanie Lever
Dolphins by Robert Ada Morris
Snappy Little Splasher by Derek Matthews

TRANSITION

Recite "One Little Dolphin," found on appendix page 363, with the children. Choose one child to pretend to be the dolphin, and have the dolphin choose a friend to become the next dolphin, and then move to the next activity.

SNACK

Dolphins love to eat fish. Invite the children to practice using a measuring cup to mix 2 cups each of several kinds of fish crackers—a perfect dolphin snack.

Group Time

Ask the children what they know about dolphins, whether anyone has ever seen a dolphin, and if so, where. Discuss dolphins with the children, using the Dolphin Facts on appendix page 364. Explain to the children how a dolphin is related to whales. Copy all the facts the children mention regarding dolphins and whales on a separate sheet for each animal, and compare the two lists.

Learning Center Ideas

Art: Mix 2 cups of blue tempera paint, ½ cup aquarium gravel, and 4 tablespoons of white glue. Put 2–3 tablespoons of the mixture on a piece of cardboard with a few drops of green tempera. Give the children this mixture and encourage them to fingerpaint to create an ocean. Provide gray paint so they can paint dolphins into the seascape as well.

Math: Set out felt cutouts of fish, dolphins, and whales for the children to make patterns on flannel boards. Begin by making a pattern and challenging the children to continue the pattern on the flannel board. As they become more proficient, make more difficult patterns, or have them make and match patterns made by other children.

Sensory/Math: Set out several plastic dolphins and sharks in water a bucket of water, and invite the children to sort them by species.

Additional Activities

Movement: Play Dolphin, Dolphin, Shark. The children sit in a circle, except for the child who is "IT." IT walks around the circle tapping each child on the head and saying, "dolphin." IT taps one child on the head, says, "Shark" and runs around the circle. The shark gets up and tries to tag IT before she goes around the circle and sits in the "shark's" spot. The shark then becomes IT.

Outside: Take a beach ball outside. Challenge the children to try to keep it up in the air as long as possible.

Rhythm and Rhyme: Teach the children to sing "Dolphin in the Sea," found on appendix page 363.

Fish

STORY TIME

Fish Eyes: A Book You Can Count On by Lois Ehlert

Rainbow Fish by Marcus Pfister

Ten Little Fish by Audrey Wood

TRANSITION

Make a magnetic fishing pole by attaching a small magnet to a string and tying the string to a pole. Give each child a chance to fish for a magnetic letter or numeral. When they catch and name the number or letter, invite them to move to the next activity.

Group Time

Read *Fish Eyes* by Lois Ehlert. Give each child a fish with a numeral on it. As you read the story again and mention numbers of fish, invite the children to stand up when you mention the numerals on their fish.

Learning Center Ideas

Art: Help the children make a fish aquarium. Have each child bring in a 20-ounce clear, clean soda bottle with a lid. Help each child to fill the bottle ¾ full of water, add ¼ cup vegetable oil, confetti fish, and blue food coloring. Then put the cover on it and secure it with electrical tape. The children shake or roll the bottle and watch the fish swim.

Sensory: Put some confetti fish (available at gift stores) in a large container of water. Invite the children to catch confetti fish with strainers, count the number they catch, and sort them by color.

Additional Activities

Movement: Play Fisherman, Catch a Fish. Choose one child to be the fisherman. The other children line up on one side of the room. The fisherman says, "I'm going fishing," and the children pretend to swim to the other side of the room, as the fisherman tries to tag as many children as possible. The children who are tagged become fishermen and help catch others.

Rhythm and Rhyme: Invite the children to sing "Ten Little Fish," found on appendix page 364.

Small Group: Talk about being a good friend. Read *Rainbow Fish* by Marcus Pfister. With the children, make a list of the qualities of a good friend.

Pirates

STORY TIME

Do Pirates Take Baths? by Kathy Tucker

How I Became a Pirate by Melinda Long

I Spy Pirate Treasure by Jean Marzollo

Pirate School by Cathy East Dubowski

What If You Met a Pirate? by Jan Adkins

TRANSITION

Recite "Pirate Talk," found on appendix page 364, with the children, naming a child each time you recite the verse, sending that child to the next activity.

SNACK

Make pirate ships to eat. Cut an orange in half and use one-half of an orange for each child's boat. Put a paper sail on a craft stick and stick it in the orange boat.

Group Time

Talk to the children about pirates. Show pictures, ask them what they know about pirates, and if they can name any famous pirates. Hide "treasure" pennies around the classroom. Invite the children to find the treasure and bring it back to Group Time. Use the pennies to talk about the concept of *more* and *less*. Invite two children to stand up and hold out the pennies they found. Ask the children which child has more treasures. "Which child has less?" Count and see. Do this several times. Finally, count up all the treasure pennies.

Learning Center Ideas

Art: Pirates sometimes have pet parrots. Invite the children to make their own parrots by gluing colored feathers on parrot shapes, using the parrot outline on appendix page 363. Invite them to add eyes and beaks.

Dramatic Play: Help the children make a pirate ship from an appliance box, and telescopes from paper towel tubes. Encourage them to use these props to play pirates.

Sensory: Hide several small objects (shells, plastic coins, plastic jewelry and gems) in the Sand Table and invite the children to search for buried treasure.

Additional Activities

Rhythm and Rhyme: Invite the children to sing "I Am a Pirate," found on appendix page 363.

Small Group: Show the children maps. Talk about why maps are important. Maps help people find their way. Pirates made maps to help them remember and find where they buried their treasure. Make pirate treasure maps. Cut paper grocery bags into ragged edged 9" x 12" sheets. Put them in a shirt box cover. Add a little black tempera paint. Roll a marble through the paint and all around the paper. Take the paper map out and let it dry. When it is dry, crumple the paper up into a ball and spread it out again to look old. Encourage the children to write an X on their maps to mark the spot of their "treasure."

Camping

STORY TIME

Bailey Goes Camping by Kevin Henkes

Little Critter at Scout Camp by Mercer Mayer

Maisy Goes Camping by Lucy Cousins

Oswald's Camping Trip by Dan Yaccarino

Otto Goes to Camp by Todd Parr

TRANSITION

Play telephone, starting the game with "If I went camping, I would bring…." Have the children take turns finishing the sentence. As each child takes their turn, he tries to remember what the children before him said and then adds his own item at the end. Then he moves to the next activity.

SNACK

Make S'mores. Give each child two graham cracker squares (one large graham cracker broken into two pieces.) Spread marshmallow cream on one cracker. Add 4 squares of a milk chocolate candy bar on top. Microwave the bars for 10–15 seconds (adult-only step).

Group Time

Before Group Time, set up a campfire made with blocks. Use red and yellow tissue paper to create "flames" in the middle. Have Group Time around the campfire. At Group Time, ask the children if they have ever been camping. Bring in and show camping equipment. Talk about each item and what it is used for. Play camping "I Spy" with the camping equipment. Say, "I Spy with my little eye," and describe one of the camping items. The children guess what it is by listening to the description.

Learning Center Ideas

Dramatic Play: Set up a small tent in your Dramatic Play area. Find toy camping equipment to use in the tent. (If you do not have a tent, make one from sheets, blankets, and a clothesline.)

Literacy/Fine Motor: Use a small magnetic fishing pole from a fishing game for this activity. Set out small refrigerator magnetic letters. The children take turns using the fishing pole to fish for a letter. As children catch letters, encourage them to name them and make the sounds of the letter.

Math: Glue rocks and sticks on a cardboard in a pattern. Provide additional rocks and stick and invite the children to continue the pattern. Make several different pattern cards for the different ability levels in the classroom.

Additional Activities

Movement: Play Flashlight Hide and Seek. Turn off most of the lights in the classroom. Pick one child to be "IT," and have that child count to 10 as the other children hide. IT uses a flashlight to help him look for his friends that are hiding.

Outside: Set up a tent outside for camping play. Go for a walk and collect rocks, leaves, sticks, and other nature items. Back in the classroom, suggest that the children glue the items onto a piece of paper shaped like a tent.

Giraffes

STORY TIME

Baby Giraffe by Patricia A. Pingry
Giraffes by Jenny Markert
Giraffes by Ann Purmell
Giraffes Can't Dance by Giles
    Andreae
I Am a Little Giraffe by Francis
    Crozat
Memily by Stephen Cosgrove

TRANSITION

Recite the "Giraffe and Mouse" rhyme, found on appendix page 366. Put a different child's name in each part of the verse, asking the first child to name something small, and the second to name something tall, then have them both move to the next activity. Repeat until all the children have transitioned to the next activity.

SNACK

Make a giraffe snack—a tree. Dip pretzel rods in melted chocolate and then green sprinkles to make a yummy tree for snack.

Group Time

Ask the children different questions about giraffes, while showing photos of giraffes to the children. Discuss the Giraffe Facts, found on appendix page 367. Explain that adult giraffes can be about 18' tall. Measure a piece of yarn or string to be 18'. Show children how long it is. Ask the children how many of them they think it would take to make 18'. Write down their estimations, and then have the children lie down in a line until it is over 18' long.

Learning Center Ideas

Art: Provide each child with a white construction paper giraffe cutout, based on the giraffe outline on appendix page 365, and orange and tan fingerpaints, encouraging the children to make thumbprint marks on the bodies of the giraffes.

Math: Set out several plastic animals, and invite the children to sort them based on whether they belong in the zoo or on the farm.

Math: Makes several yellow construction paper giraffe cutouts, writing a different numeral on each. Laminate for durability. Set out several black pompoms, and encourage the children to put the correct number of pompom "birds" on each giraffe's back.

Additional Activities

Outside: Use the 18' length of string from the Group Time activity to draw a line on the playground as tall as the giraffe. Challenge the children to walk the line without falling off.

Rhythm and Rhyme: Invite the children to sing "Giraffes at the Zoo," found on appendix page 366.

Small Group: Talk with the children about how "tall" and "small" are opposites, and together make two lists, one of things that are tall and the other of things that are small.

Zebras

STORY TIME

How the Zebra Got His Stripes by Golden Books
Naughty by Caroline Castle
Za Za's Baby Brother by Lucy Cousins
Zee by Michel Gay
Zigby Camps Out by Brian Paterson

TRANSITION

With the children, recite "Zebra Gallop," found on appendix page 367. Name a child in the first line each time you repeat the verse. Have that child gallop to the next activity.

Group Time

Talk about zebras with the children. Use the Zebra Facts on appendix page 367 to start the conversation. With the children, compare zebras to horses. Make a list of ways that zebras are different from horses and a separate list of the ways that zebras are the same as horses.

Learning Center Ideas

Art: Set out several white and black construction paper cutouts of zebra shapes, based on the outline on appendix page 366, as well as black and white finger paint. Give each child the opportunity to paint one black cutout with white stripes, and one white cutout with black stripes.
Dramatic Play: Encourage the children to pretend they are on a safari in Africa. Invite them to look for zebras and other wildlife. If possible, provide a tent and help them build a "campfire" for cooking.
Math: Set out several black and white items, and invite the children to sort them by color.

Additional Activities

Movement: Gather the children in a circle. Choose one child to be the "animal," and have that child stand in the center of the circle, pretending to be a certain animal from the zoo while the other children guess what animal the child is imitating. When a child guesses correctly, that child gets to become the new "animal."
Outside: Encourage the children to pretend they are zebras, and have them gallop around together.
Rhythm and Rhyme: Teach the children to sing "I'm a Zebra," found on appendix page 366.

Lions

STORY TIME

Do You Know About Lions? by Stuart Trotter

Larry Lion's Rumbly Rhymes by Giles Andreae

One Yellow Lion by Matthew Van Fleet

Tawny Scrawny Lion by Gustaf Tenggren

That's Not My Lion by Fiona Watt

TRANSITION

Choose one child to be the lion. With all the children, recite "Lion on the Savannah," found on appendix page 367. At the end of the rhyme, have the lion choose another lion, then move to the next activity. Repeat the rhyme with the new lion picking the next, and so on, until all the children have moved to the next activity.

Group Time

Before Group Time, print some or all of the Lion Facts on appendix page 367 on separate construction paper cutouts of lion shapes, based on the outline on appendix page 365. Hide the lion shapes around the room. Read *We're Going on a Lion Hunt* by David Axtell. Explain to the children they are going on a lion hunt. Invite children to look for lion shapes around the classroom. When the children find the shapes, read the lion facts and talk about lions. Reread *We're Going on a Lion Hunt*, challenging the children to make the motions described in the story.

Learning Center Ideas

Art: Provide a variety of art materials including paints, brushes, markers, and crayons. Encourage the children to draw or paint lions or lion-related pictures.

Dramatic Play: Set out several stuffed animals that are zoo animals and invite the children to pretend they are working in and visiting a zoo.

Additional Activities

Movement: Play Lion Says, a variation of Simon Says, with the children. Invite the children to do the action if you say, "Lion says." If you do not say, "Lion says," they should stay still.

Outside: Lions like to catch many animals. Pretend each child is a zebra, giraffe, or an elephant, except for one child who is the lion. The animals line up and the lion calls "zebras." All the zebras run to the other side of the playground as the lion tries to tag them. If an animal is tagged they become another lion.

Tigers

WEEK THREE: SUMMER SAFARI

STORY TIME

The Boy and the Tigers by Helen Bannerman

Leo the Late Bloomer by Robert Kraus

Story of Little Babaji by Helen Bannerman

Three Little Javelinas by Susan Lowell

Tigers by Marfe Ferguson Delano

Tigers by Deri Robins

SNACK

Make a tiger snack. Wash and cut cauliflowers and broccoli into floret "flowers." Make a dip for the flowers by mixing a one-ounce packet of ranch-flavored dressing mix and one pint of sour cream. Invite children to eat the veggie flowers and dip. Add a few animal cracker tigers for a tiger snack.

Group Time

Talk about different kinds of cats. Put Tiger Facts, found on appendix page 367, on strips of orange paper. Invite each child to choose a strip of orange paper. Read the fact and help the child tape it to a black tiger shape. Talk about cats. Ask the children what all cats have in common. Make a list of the qualities they have that make them part of the cat family. Print the list on a tiger shape.

Learning Center Ideas

Art: Set out several orange poster board cutouts of tigers, based on the tiger outline on appendix page 366, for the children (tigers are actually orange with black stripes.) along with black chenille stems. Help the children punch holes along the edge of the tiger cutouts, and then encourage the children to string the chenille through the holes to make stripes on their tigers.

Math: Set out several orange construction paper tiger shapes, each with a different numeral written on it. Challenge the children to place the correct number of black construction paper tiger stripes on each tiger.

Sensory: Put several toy tigers in sand in the Sensory Table for the children to explore.

Additional Activities

Outside: Play Catch a Tiger by the Tail. Choose one child to be the tiger, and tape a streamer on the child's back. Encourage the children to catch the tiger by the tail. Whoever catches the tiger then puts the tail on his back, and becomes the next tiger.

Rhythm and Rhyme: Teach the children to sing "Great Big Tiger," and recite "Tiger on the Prowl," found on appendix pages 366-367.

Small Group: Read *Leo the Late Bloomer* by Robert Kraus. As you reread the story, suggest that the children stand up at the end of the story and say, "I made it" along with the story. Talk about something special that made each child bloom. Print what each child dictates on a flower, and put it on display with the words "We're Blooming."

Space

STORY TIME

Astronaut: Living in Space by Kate Hayden

Space by Simon Holland

Space Craze Blast Off by Alise Robinson

Space Craze Shapes in Space by Alise Robinson

There's No Place Like Space by Tish Rabe

TRANSITION

Choose five children at a time, and ask them to bend down, as low to the ground as they can get. Have everyone in the class count down from 10 to blast-off, and at "blast-off," have the crouching children leap up and move to the next activity.

SNACK

Cut bread, lunch meats, and cheese with a star-shaped cookie cutter, and invite children to make their own "out of this world" sandwiches.

Group Time

Invite the children to talk about the different things that are or might be out in space. Make a list of what the children name. Give each child a sheet of paper with the "Out in Space" rhyme, found on appendix page 368, written on it with the first line at the top of the page and the second at the bottom. Help them write their names in the top line, the thing they think they might see in space at the bottom, and encourage them to draw what they might see in space in the center of the page. When all the children are done, make a class book of their pages, and read it to the children.

Learning Center Ideas

Art: Set out various art supplies and cardboard tubes (from paper towel rolls) and encourage the children to make a rocket sculpture.

Dramatic Play: Set out a large appliance box, along with various crayons, markers, and other art materials. Invite the children to decorate it as a rocket ship, and then use it to pretend they are flying through space.

Additional Activities

Movement: Play a rocket ship game, using the appliance box rocket from the Dramatic Play center. Invite all the children to sit in a circle. Have one child leave the area and covers her eyes, then ask another child to sneak into the rocket box. Once the hiding child is ready, have the first child open her eyes and try to guess which child is hiding in the box.

Small Group: Gather the children in a circle. Ask the children to use their imaginations and pretend they are in a rocket ship. Prompt the children with the following statement, "In a rocket, I would...," and have each child around the circle to give an answer. Write down each child's answer. After this, give each child a piece of construction paper cut out to resemble a rocket ship, and invite the children to draw what they would do in a rocket ship, or where they think the ship would go.

Sun

STORY TIME

Good Night Sun, Hello Moon by Karne Viola

I Love You, Moon by Karen Randall

Sun Bread by Elisa Kleven

The Sun Is My Favorite Star by Frank Asch

What the Sun Sees/What the Moon Sees by Nancy Tafuri

TRANSITION

Gather the children together, and ask them to raise their hands when they think of something they like to do when it is sunny. Call on the children to name the things they like to do, and after they say them, ask them to line up and move to the next activity.

SNACK

Place chocolate squares on top of graham crackers and then place them in the sun. After the sun melts the bar, spread peanut butter on another square of graham cracker. Put the two crackers together for a yummy sandwich.

Group Time

Show children illustrations depicting how the sun is the center of the universe and the planets go around it. Make a large sun shape and tie a string on it so a child can hang the sun around her neck. Do the same with cutouts of all the other planets, and give them to children to wear. Have the sun stand in the middle of the room and have and children with the planet shapes walk around the sun as they sing "Out in the Universe," found on appendix page 368, naming a different planet each time they repeat the second verse.

Learning Center Ideas

Art/Science: On a warm, sunny day, bring buckets of water and paintbrushes out to the sidewalk and invite the children to paint everything. As the water evaporates, ask the children what they think is happening. (The heat of the sun makes the water evaporate.)

Math: Set out several different items and articles of clothing that people would wear in hit and cold weather. Challenge the children to sort them according to the weather in which the articles should be worn.

Additional Activities

Movement: Play Sun Tag. Choose one child to be the sun. The sun is IT. As the sun tags the other children, they melt to the ground, but can be released when other children tag them again.

Outside: Show the children how shadows move. In the morning, bring the children out onto the playground, have them stand in rows so their shadows are not touching. Write their names on the playground where they are standing. Have each child choose a partner, and give each pair of children a piece of chalk. Tell each partner to draw a line around the outline of her partner's shadow, and then have the partners switch. Once every child has a shadow outline starting at her name, bring the class inside. Occasionally through the day, bring the pairs of children back outside to draw the outline of their shadows again, and see how their shadows move.

Rhythm and Rhyme: Invite the children to sing "When I'm High in the Sky," found on appendix page 368.

Moon

July 20th is the anniversary of the Moon landing.

STORY TIME

Goodnight Moon by Margaret Wise Brown

Goodnight Sun, Hello Moon by Karen Viola

Happy Birthday, Moon by Frank Asch

Moon Rope by Lois Ehlert

Papa Please Get the Moon for Me by Eric Carle

TRANSITION

Sing "Sleep-O," found on appendix page 368, with the children, inserting one or two children's names in the blank, and invite those children move to the next activity.

SNACK

Make a "blue moon" snack. (About every two years, a full moon will occur twice in one month. The second full moon in that month is called a "blue moon.") Add blue food coloring to cream cheese. Spread on toasted English muffins.

Group Time

Ask the children to discuss the times when they see the sun and when they see the moon. Begin naming different daily activities, and have the children say whether what you mention happens when the sun is up or the moon is up. Some examples include sleeping, eating lunch, star-gazing, and going to school.

Learning Center Ideas

Art: Provide large construction paper pieces cut into circles. Add sand to white glue and gray tempera paint and invite the children to paint the construction paper circles until they resemble the moon. When the paint is dry, add a United States flag sticker.

Art: Set out big poster boards, black for night and yellow for day. Encourage the children to find pictures in magazines and newspapers of daytime images and activities, and glue them on the yellow poster board. Do the same with nighttime images and activities on the black poster board.

Sensory: Put several plastic toy astronauts and rockets in sand for the children to explore.

Additional Activities

Movement: Talk with the children about how different animals spent their nights in different ways. Explain that animals like raccoons, possums, and owls are up at night. After discussing this with the children, tell them you will name different animals, and then turn off the lights. While the lights are off, the children should act like the named animal.

Small Group: Read *Goodnight Moon* by Margaret Wise Brown. Make a class book. On a page for each child, print "Good night, _____," and write on the line what each says. Encourage the children to draw picture of things to which they want to say good night.

Stars

STORY TIME

10 Wishing Stars by Pamela Hall

The Birth of the Moon by Coby Hol

Mommies Are for Counting Stars by Harriet Ziefert

Twinkle, Twinkle, Little Star by Iza Trapani

Wemberly's Ice Cream Star by Kevin Henkes

TRANSITION

Invite the children to recite "Twinkle, Twinkle, Quiet Star," found on appendix page 368, encouraging the children to follow the song's instruction. When a child sits quietly, invite her to move to the next activity.

SNACK

Make a nighttime sky snack by spreading chocolate frosting on a graham cracker. Add cake-decorating stars and a tiny marshmallow moon.

Group Time

Talk with the children about the stars. Show the children pictures of constellations, and talk about how groups of stars can make pictures in the sky. Afterwards, encourage the children to make their own constellations on paper by putting dots on a piece of paper, then adding sticker stars. When done, have the children name their constellations.

Learning Center Ideas

Math: Set out several sheets of paper with different numerals written on each in little dots, so the numbers resemble constellations. Also, set out several construction paper cut-outs of stars. Challenge the children to put the correct number of stars on each sheet of paper.

Additional Activities

Project: Make "Star Children." Invite the children to paint a star shape with a yellow paint/glue mixture. Sprinkle the star with glitter. When they are dry, add a photo of the child to the top point of her star.

Rhythm and Rhyme: Sing "Twinkle, Twinkle, Little Star" turning flashlights on and off to make "twinkling stars."

Small Group: Talk to the children about how people sometimes make wishes on stars. Give each child a large star-shaped piece of paper. Ask them to draw a wish on their paper. While the children make the star pictures, encourage them to recite star wishing rhymes, such as "Star Light, Star Bright." When finished with their pictures, help the children write a wish on the bottom of their star papers.

Airplanes

July 19th is National Aviation Day.

STORY TIME

A Is for Airplane by Theresa Howell
Amazing Airplanes by Tony Milton
Little Red Plane by Ken Wilson-Max
Planes at the Airport by Peter Mandel
We're Going on an Airplane by Steve Augarde

TRANSITION

Have the children pretend to be airplanes as you add their names to the "Airplane" rhyme, found on appendix page 368. After the children respond to the rhyme's question, have them move to the next activity.

SNACK

Make airplanes good enough to eat. Show the children how to peel bananas to use as the bodies of their airplanes, and how to use peanut butter to attach graham cracker wings. When the planes are finished, eat and enjoy.

Group Time

Bring in three toy airplanes: one Styrofoam, one wooden, and one paper. Bring the children outside to test flying all three planes. Ask the children to predict how well the different airplanes will fly, then choose different children to take turns throwing the planes into the air. Record the distances they travel, and how long they stay in the air each time the children throw them. After each plane has been thrown several times, bring the children inside and discuss the three sets of numbers, making a graph of the information so the children can see which plane went the furthest and shortest distances individually, which stayed up for the longest and shortest periods of time, and what the averages for each plane's flights are.

Learning Center Ideas

Blocks: Put plastic airplanes in the block area, and encourage the children to make a hanger and airport into and out of which the planes can fly.
Dramatic Play: Ask the children to describe the inside of a commercial airplane, and encourage them to set up the room in a similar manner, using chairs to make rows, the cockpit, and so on. Help the children set up an area to get airplane tickets, and pretend to go on flights around the world.

Additional Activities

Rhythm and Rhyme: Invite the children to recite "How Airplanes Fly," found on appendix page 368, while holding their arms out, following the directions of the rhyme.
Small Group: Help the children fold paper into airplanes and then decorate the airplanes with markers. Fly the airplanes inside in the classroom. Then take the group outside and fly the airplanes there.

Farms

STORY TIME

Apples Here! by Will Hubbell

Going to a Horse Farm by Shirley Kerby James

If It Weren't for Farmers by Allan Fowler

Milk: From Cow to Carton by Aliki

Mrs. Wishy Washy's Farm by Joy Cowley

Once Upon Old MacDonald's Farm by Stephen Gammell

Rosie's Walk by Pat Hutchins

The Wheat We Eat by Allan Fowler

SNACK

Invite children to enjoy a snack from the farm. Talk about each item as you serve it. For example, give the children wheat crackers and explain they are made from wheat that grows in the fields, or cheese cubes that are made from milk, which comes from a cow. Drink apple juice, which comes from an apple tree.

Group Time

Talk to the children about farms. Ask questions to find out what they know about life on a farm, and what they want to learn. Show the children pictures of different types of farms, such as a dairy farm and horse farm, as well as farms for growing crops such as corn, wheat, and vegetables. Play a Farmer's Food Game. Hold up different pictures or containers of different foods. If the food is a dairy product, encourage the children to "moo" like cows. If it is poultry, invite them to "cluck" like chickens. If the food is a vegetable, they can stomp their feet because vegetables grow in the ground, and if it is a grain, the children can clap their hands like they are putting two pieces of bread together.

Learning Center Ideas

Blocks: Set out several toy animals and craft sticks with the blocks and invite the children to make farm houses, barns, and corrals (with the craft sticks) for the animals.

Dramatic Play: Give the children farm props and encourage them to pretend to be farmers.

Literacy: Encourage the children to draw pictures of a farm that they would like to have. On each drawing, write, "If I had a farm, I would grow _____." Help the children write their responses on their pictures.

Math: Give each child a red construction paper cutout of a barn, based on the barn outline on appendix page 369, along with several farm animal stickers. Invite the children to count each farm animal sticker they add to their barns.

Science: Invite the children to plant carrot seeds in paper cups. Set them in a sunny windowsill and remind the children to water them. Watch them grow!

Additional Activities

Movement: Play The Farmer in the Dell with the children.

Rhythm and Rhyme: Invite the children to recite "The Cow Says 'Moo'" (see appendix page 370) with you.

Farm Animals

STORY TIME

Click Clack Moo: Cows That Type by Doreen Cronin

Color Farm by Lois Ehlert

Down on the Farm by Merrily Kutner

The Flea's Sneeze by Lynn Downey

How Now, Cow? by Angela Chambers

Open the Barn Door (A Chunky Flap Book) by Christopher Santoro

The Three Billy Goats Gruff by Stephen Carpenter

TRANSITION

Recite the following rhyme, adding a child's (or a few children's) name each time.

Moo, moo, brown cow,
It's time for _____ to line up now.

SNACK

Make a yogurt parfait. Invite the children to alternate layers of yogurt and fruit in a paper cup for a fun, healthy snack.

Group Time

Make a list of all the different farm animals that children can think of, including horses, cows, pigs, chickens, ducks, geese, goats, mice, turkeys, sheep, and so on. Ask the children why these animals live on farms and not in houses with people. Talk about what farm animals need to live—food, shelter, warmth, and so on. Read *Click, Clack, Moo: Cows That Type* by Doreen Cronin. Can cows really type? Make other statements about farm animals, some true and some false, and ask the children to say "True" or "False."

Learning Center Ideas

Art: Make a troll to use in the dramatic play activity below. Give each child a construction paper troll shape, based on the troll outline on appendix page 369. Set out paint, chalk, markers, and other art materials for children to make their own trolls.

Blocks: Set out blocks and plastic farm animals and encourage the children to build a farm.

Dramatic Play: After reading *The Three Billy Goats Gruff* by Stephen Carpenter to the children, give the children an appliance box that has been cut to form a bridge. Invite them to act out the story with this prop.

Dramatic Play: Set up an imaginary ice cream shop and invite the children to scoop imaginary orders of ice cream for one another. Have some children pretend to be cows and try to order only by mooing.

Literacy: Set out word cards with animals' names on one side and pictures of the animals on the other side, along with barn-shaped books and animal stickers for the children to explore.

Additional Activities

Outside: Take a field trip to a farm, if possible.

Rhythm and Rhyme: Invite the children to recite "Three Billy Goats," found on appendix page 370, and to sing, "I Am a Cow," found on appendix page 370.

Watermelon

STORY TIME

The Enormous Watermelon retold by
    Brenda Parkes and Judith Smith
Grandma Baba's Magic Watermelon
    by Wakiko Sato
Icy Watermelon by Mary Sue
    Galindo
Watermelon Day by Kathi Appelt
Watermelon Wishes by Lisa Moser

TRANSITION

Use black pompoms as watermelon seeds for this game. Hold several "seeds" while repeating "Watermelon Seeds," found on appendix page 370, naming a child at the end of the rhyme. When the child counts the seeds in your hand and says the number aloud, that child moves to the next activity.

SNACK

Make a fruit salad in a watermelon boat (see recipe on appendix page 371).

Group Time

Explore watermelons with the children. Invite each child to dictate a word to describe the watermelon and print their words on a piece of paper that has been cut into a watermelon shape. Describe how watermelons are grown and how they ripen. Talk about the seeds inside the watermelon. Then show the children a cantaloupe. Ask the children, "How are the watermelon and cantaloupe the same?" "How are they different?"

Learning Center Ideas

Art: Help the children cut out watermelon slice shapes from red construction paper. The children can drop dots of glue on the watermelon shapes and put black pompoms (watermelon seeds) on each drop of glue, or use a black marker to make watermelon seeds.

Math: Write different numerals on several construction paper cutouts of watermelons. Set out several black pompom "seeds," and challenge the children to put the correct number of seeds on each watermelon.

Writing: Set out watermelon-shaped blank books for children to use for writing. Make the books by placing one watermelon-shaped paper on top of several sheet of white paper. Staple together, and then cut the white paper to match the watermelon-shaped paper on top. The children draw watermelon pictures and/or write or dictate things about watermelons in their watermelon books.

Additional Activities

Outside: Give the children watermelon to eat. Suggest that the children count the number of seeds in their slice of watermelon.

Rhythm and Rhyme: Invite the children to sing "Watermelon, Watermelon," found on appendix page 370.

Small Group: Cut a small slice of watermelon for each group. Invite children to estimate how many black seeds are in the piece of watermelon. Find and count the seeds together.

Berries Galore

STORY TIME

Blueberries for Sal by Robert McCloskey

Blueberries for the Queen by John Paterson

Blueberry Mouse by Alice Low

Madame Blueberry Learns to Be Thankful by Cindy Kenney

White Is for Blueberry by George Shannon

TRANSITION

Make a Berry "Wand-erful" Wand by gluing a blue felt blueberry, a pink felt strawberry, and a red felt raspberry onto a dowel. Tap children on the head with the Berry Wand-erful Wand when it is time to go to the next activity.

SNACK

Make individual Blueberry Treats (see recipe on appendix page 371).

Group Time

Bring in blueberries, strawberries, and raspberries and invite the children to try each type of berry. Talk with the children about how the berries are similar and different. Attach three pieces of paper to the wall. On one paper write "blueberries," on another "strawberries," and on the third "raspberries." On each paper, list the words the children use to describe each berry. **Note**: Before serving berries or any food to children, check for allergies or food sensitivities.

Learning Center Ideas

Art: Suggest that the children make Berry Collages. They cut out pictures of different kinds of berries from magazines. Provide paper, glue, markers, crayons, fabric scraps, and other art materials for the children to create their own berries and then place them in a collage.

Art: Invite the children to finger paint on a large circle (blueberry shape) with blue paint, with blue gelatin added for a great sensory experience.

Dramatic Play: Read *Blueberries for Sal* by Robert McCloskey with the children, and then invite them to act out the story.

Math: Provide red, pink, and blue pompoms (red for raspberries, pink for strawberries, and blue for blueberries) and three containers. Encourage the children to sort the "berries" by color. If appropriate, ask the children to estimate whether there are more blue or red berries (or more red or pink berries). Count them with the children.

Sensory/Art: Provide several different berry-flavored scratch-and-sniff markers for the children. Encourage them to guess the different scents.

Additional Activities

Rhythm and Rhyme: Invite the children to sing, "Berries, Berries," found on appendix page 370.

Corn

STORY TIME

Corn Is Maize: A Gift of the Indians by Aliki

From Kernel to Corn by Robin Nelson

I Like Corn by Robin Pickering

Raccoons and Ripe Corn by Jim Arnosky

SNACK

Use a mix to make cornbread, making individual corn muffins instead of the cornbread. Serve with warm butter and honey.

Group Time

Ask the children to name items made from corn. Make a list of the things the children name. Guide them to include corn meal, cornstarch, corn cereal, corn chips, corn tortillas, and cornbread. Talk to the children about the history of corn. Corn was cultivated by people in Mexico thousands of years ago. They called it *maize*. Tell the children about all the ways that corn is used—besides eating it. For example, corn is used—as animal feed, in different cooking oils, shoe polish, glue, aspirin, ink, and corn syrup in sodas and other sweet items, and even in gasoline (gasohol). Corn is everywhere! Bring in an ear of corn, and invite the children to peel the outer covering off of it. Then allow them to pull off the corn silk to get to the kernels underneath. Cook the corn and serve it to the children.

Learning Center Ideas

Art: If possible, show the children a piece of Indian corn. Encourage the children to make a picture of Indian corn, or to use the colors of Indian corn to make a drawing/picture of their own choosing.

Literacy: Bring in boxes, ads, and other materials with *corn* written on them. (Also ask families to bring in materials with *corn* written on them.) Gather all the materials in a photo album and put the book in the reading corner. Ask the children if they know what any of the other words on the different pages mean.

Math/Sensory: Mix a batch of equal parts cornstarch and water, and set out for the children to explore and enjoy.

Sensory: Put several stalks of corn in the Sensory Table for the children to explore.

Additional Activities

Outside: If possible, go to a farm with a cornfield. Explore the cornstalks with the children. Depending on the season, see if the children are taller than the cornstalks.

Rhythm and Rhyme: Invite the children to sing, "I Eat Corn for Breakfast," found on appendix page 370. Or, sing "Oh, What a Beautiful Morning!" by Rogers and Hammerstein with the children.

Picnic

STORY TIME

The Best Picnic Ever by Clare Jarrett
It's the Bear by Jez Alborough
Let's Go Froggy by Jonathan London
Picnic: Little Kippers by Mick Inkpen

TRANSITION

Invite the children to recite "Having a Picnic," found on appendix page 372. In the final line, say a child's name, and have the child name something she will bring on the picnic to eat. After naming a snack, the child may move to the next activity

SNACK

Have a picnic. On the previous day, remind everyone to bring snacks they can share with the other children.

Group Time

Talk about going on a picnic, asking the children to name things they might need to bring with them on a picnic. Invite the children to sing "I'm Going on a Picnic," found on appendix page 372, taking turns finishing the last sentence.

Learning Center Ideas

Dramatic Play: Set out a basket, paper plates, cups, forks, and a blanket, for the children to use to pretend they are on a picnic.

Math: Set out several paper plates with different number written on each. Give the children piles of plastic ants, and challenge them to put the correct number of ants on each plate.

Additional Activities

Movement: Invite the children to come outside and have wheelbarrow races and sack races.

Rhythm and Rhyme: Invite the children to sing "The Picnic Song," found on appendix page 373.

Small Group: Set out a napkin, fork, spoon, knife, tablecloth, cup, several plastic ants, and so on, for the children to look at. After the children have had a chance to look over everything, ask them to close their eyes. When the children all have their eyes closed, take away one object, and invite the children to guess which item is missing.

Ladybugs

STORY TIME

Are You a Ladybug? by Judy Allen
Fly Away, Ladybug by Suzy McPartland
The Grouchy Ladybug by Eric Carle
Little LuLu Ladybug by Catherine Solyoem
Very Lazy Ladybug by Isobel Finn

TRANSITION

Invite the children to recite "Ladybug, Fly Away," found on appendix page 373. Name a child in the first line each time the verse repeats, and have that child "fly" to the next activity.

Group Time

Before Group Time, make ladybugs from red and black felt. Make pairs of matching ladybugs, with the same colors and numbers of spots. This can also be done on paper, laminated with a piece of felt glued on the back.

Use the Ladybug Facts on appendix page 373 as you talk about ladybugs with the children. Invite the children to share their experiences with ladybugs. When have they seen them? Have they ever held one? Next, give each child one of each two matching ladybugs. Put one ladybug on the flannel board. Look at the color and count the spots. Who has the matching ladybug?

Learning Center Ideas

Math: Cut out several red construction paper circle "ladybugs," and put a different number on each of them. Add black construction paper cutout legs. Laminate for durability. Challenge the children to put the correct number of pompom spots on each numbered ladybug.

Sensory: Make red playdough by adding red food coloring to a playdough recipe. Set out the red playdough and encourage the children to make ladybugs. Set out black foam circles for the children to press into their ladybugs, making spots.

Additional Activities

Rhythm and Rhyme: Invite the children to sing "I'm a Ladybug," found on appendix page 372.

Small Group: Read *The Grouchy Ladybug* by Eric Carle to the children. After finishing the book, talk with the children about what happened, and then reread the book to them. As you reread the story, pause occasionally, cueing the children to say certain repeating lines aloud.

Butterflies

STORY TIME

Are You a Butterfly? by Judy Allen
Butterfly Kisses by Bob Carlisle
Fly, Little Butterfly by Elizabeth
    Lawrence
Good Night, Sweet Butterflies by
    Dawn Bentley
*How to Hide a Butterfly and Other
    Insects* by Ruth Heller

TRANSITION

Invite the children to recite "Butterfly, Fly Away," found on appendix page 372. Each time the verse repeats, add a new child's name. When a child hears her name, invite her to "fly" to the next activity.

SNACK

Make "butterflies" for a snack. Cut a slice of cheese into a butterfly shape, or use a cookie cutter. Lay a pretzel rod down its center to serve as the body.

Group Time

Give each child a colored foam or construction paper butterfly cutout butterfly (based on the butterfly outline on appendix page 371) glued to a craft stick. Invite the children to recite "Butterfly, Butterfly," found on appendix page 372, encouraging them to stand up and wave their butterfly through the air when its color is mentioned.

Learning Center Ideas

Art: Help the children fold sheets of paper in half and cut half butterfly shapes out of them, so when the papers are unfolded, the full butterfly shapes appear. Provide paint for the children to put on one wing of their butterflies, and then fold the two wings together, so the patterns on the first wings will match those on the second wings.

Math: Help the children make butterfly fingerprint counting books. Set out sheets of paper and finger paint. Write different numerals on each sheet of paper, and invite the children to make the matching number of fingerprints on those pages. When the finger paints are dry, help the children draw butterfly wing shapes around the fingerprints.

Additional Activities

Movement: Provide the children with scarves and pieces of fabric to use as butterfly wings, and invite the children to fly around to classical music pieces.

Rhythm and Rhyme: Gather the children in a circle to sing and act out "Butterfly, Fly Around," found on appendix page 372. With every repetition of the song, name a different child to perform the actions of the song, along with those previously named. Repeat until all children perform the actions of the song together.

Small Group: Use the butterflies on sticks from the Group Time activity in number and counting sentences. For example: "There were three butterflies, and two more came. How many are there in total?"

Dragonflies

STORY TIME

Are You a Dragonfly? by Judy Allen
Dragonflies by Cheryl Coughlan
Dragon in the Sky by Laurence P. Pringle
Eliza and the Dragonfly by Susie Caldwell Rinehart
Sir Small and the Dragonfly by Jane O'Conner

TRANSITION

Invite the children to recite "Dragonfly, Way Up High," found on appendix page 372. Name a child in the first line each time the children repeat the verse, and have that child move to the next activity.

SNACK

Make a dragonfly snack by placing a large marshmallow (the dragonfly's head) on a plate and then arranging dry cereal to form the dragonfly's body and wings.

Group Time

Copy the Dragonfly Facts, found on appendix page 373, onto construction paper cutouts of dragonfly shapes, based on the dragonfly outline on appendix page 371, and hang them with string around the room. Invite the children to "catch" a dragonfly with a net, and then talk with all the children about the fact on that dragonfly.

Learning Center Ideas

Math: Make several construction paper cutouts of lily pads and dragonflies, based on the outline on appendix page 371. Put a matching number on each one and laminate for durability. Mix up each group and challenge the children to match the lily pads and dragonflies by number.
Sensory: Set out playdough and invite the children to make dragonfly shapes with the playdough.

Additional Activities

Movement: In this game, the frog catches the dragonflies. One child is the frog, the rest of the class are dragonflies. The dragonflies stand on one side of the playground. The frog stands in the middle of the playground. As the dragonflies fly to the other side, the frog tires to tag them. Whoever the frog tags becomes a frog too.
Outside: Bring the children on a field trip to a lake, pond, or some other body of water, and have them look for dragonflies.
Small Group: From construction paper, cut large several blue puddle and green leaf shapes. Write different numerals on the circles, and different letters on the leaves. Set the leaves and puddles out on the floor, and have the children fly around the room as though they were dragonflies, reciting "Dragonfly in the Air," found on appendix page 372. When the rhyme ends, have the children fly to the nearest puddle or leaf. Have the children say their numerals and letters out loud. As the children become more proficient at this, challenge them to recite the numerals in correct order, and then the letters in order.

Caterpillars

STORY TIME

Caterpillar Dance by Will Grace
Caterpillar Spring Butterfly Summer
   by Susan Hood
The Crunching, Munching Caterpillar
   by Sheridan Cain
Gotta Go! Gotta Go! by Sam Swope
The Hungry Caterpillar by Eric Carle
I'm a Caterpillar by Jean Marzollo

TRANSITION

Invite the children to recite the "Caterpillar Went to Play," found on appendix page 372, naming a different child at the start of the first line each time. After reciting the rhyme, invite the named child to move to the next activity.

SNACK

Use peanut butter to affix a row of dry cereal shaped like balls to a lettuce leaf, so the cereal balls resemble a caterpillar. Be sure to tell the children it is not safe to eat regular caterpillars, only those made in the classroom for snack.

Group Time

Read *The Hungry Caterpillar* by Eric Carle to the children. When finished, ask the children to retell the story by drawing one picture of each scene. As the children draw, ask them to dictate to you a summary of the scenes they are drawing, and attach the summaries to the children's drawings. When the children are finished drawing, collect the pictures together and staple them to make a new version of the book. Discuss caterpillars with the children, using the Caterpillar Facts found on appendix page 373 as prompts.

Learning Center Ideas

Art: Help the children trace and cut out leaf shapes on green construction paper. Give each child four pompoms to glue in a row on the leaf as a caterpillar.

Art: Invite the children to sponge paint circles in a row onto construction paper, making caterpillars.

Math: Write numerals onto construction paper cutouts of leaves. Set them out, along with several pipe cleaner "caterpillars," and invite the children to put the correct number of caterpillars on each numbered leaf.

Additional Activities

Movement: Invite the children to line up with their hands on the shoulders of the child in front of them, and then walk together, as one long caterpillar.

Outside: Bring the children outside, and invite them to look for caterpillars. Tell the children to be very careful if they find a caterpillar, though, because they are very delicate.

Rhythm and Rhyme: Invite the children to sing "I'm a Little Caterpillar," found on appendix page 372.

Small Group: Put a few pompoms in a patterned row, resembling a caterpillar. Invite the children to add to the caterpillar, repeating the pattern, and then encourage the children to make their own caterpillar patterns.

Deserts

STORY TIME

The Camel's Lament by Charles E. Carryl

Desert Babies by John Shaw

Desert Explorer by Greg Pyres

Look Who Lives in the Desert! by Brooke Bessesen

Way Out in the Desert by Jennifer Ward

TRANSITION

Recite the "Desert Land" rhyme, found on appendix page 374, with the children, including a child's name each time you repeat the verse, and having the child named pretend to move like a desert creature, such as a camel, lizard, ostrich, roadrunner, snake, and so on, as he transitions to the next activity. Repeat until all children have moved to the next activity.

SNACK

Make vanilla instant pudding, and put it into paper cups. Add a celery stalk (palm tree) graham cracker "sand," and animal cracker desert animals for a desert oasis snack.

Group Time

Talk about the desert with the children, using the Desert Facts on appendix page 375 to start the conversation. Encourage the children to compare the desert to where they live. Show the children a real cactus. Carefully, let them touch it. Invite children to paint giant cactus plants on bulletin board paper. Add toothpicks to make them prickly and pink tissue paper bunched into a flower shape.

Learning Center Ideas

Art: Cut out sandpaper letters for children to trace or make rubbings on paper.

Dramatic Play: Set up a tent to encourage desert-related play.

Math: Set out flowerpots (or plastic cups) with numerals written on each flowerpot. Invite children to put the correct number of scoops of sand in the flowerpots.

Additional Activities

Movement: Play music and suggest that children pretend they are out in the hot desert as the music plays. When the music stops, they find and touch something green (an oasis).

Outside: Fill two small tubs with the same amount of sand. Explain to the children that you are putting one tub in the sun and the other in the shade. Ask the children what they think will happen. Take the sand outside on a sunny day, at the beginning of class time. Check on the sand at the end of class time. "What is different about the two tubs of sand?"

Rhythm and Rhyme: Invite the children to sing "In the Desert Sun," found on appendix page 374.

Small Group: Talk about the creatures that live in the desert. Place toy animals, such as snake, lizard, rabbit, fox, and ant, on a tray. Instruct children to close their eyes and take one away. Ask them, "Which desert creature is missing?"

Aloha

STORY TIME

The Best Hawaiian Style Mother Goose Ever by Kevin Sullivan
Hina and the Sea of Stars by Michael Nordenstrom
Pele and the Rivers of Fire by Michael Nordenstrom

TRANSITION

Invite the children to recite "Aloha, Goodbye," found on appendix page 374. Include each child's name in the rhyme, and invite each child to move to the next activity after his name is called.

SNACK

Invite the children to make fruit sticks by putting pineapple pieces and grape pieces on pretzel sticks.

Group Time

Set out a map of Hawaii, and introduce the children to the state by explaining that it is a group of islands surrounded by water. Describe the topography of the islands—they are made up of volcanoes and there are beaches, sand, and palm trees on the islands. Many people like to go to Hawaii on vacation because it is almost always warm and sunny. Introduce the children to the word "luau," telling them that luaus are big parties with lots of food, drums, and dancing. After talking with the children about Hawaii, invite them to help make a volcano in a baking pan, sculpting it out of clay. After the children have made the conical clay volcano shape, scoop a little cup shape about 2" deep from the top of the cone. Place a half cup of baking soda in the cup shape. In a separate cup, add yellow and red food coloring to vinegar, and a little dishwashing liquid (for the bubbling effect). Have the children stand back, and pour the vinegar/soap mixture into the volcano cup. Watch as it bubbles and erupts.

Learning Center Ideas

Language: Set out a drum and invite the children take turns speaking and beating out the syllables in their names.
Sensory: Put sand, seashells, and starfish in the sensory table for the children to explore.

Additional Activities

Movement: Invite the children to play drums and practice hula dancing.
Project: Cut the top of a pineapple off (adult only-step) and invite the children to plant it into the ground or a flowerpot. Water it over time and observe its growth.
Rhythm and Rhyme: Invite the children to sing "Aloha Means Hello," found on appendix page 374.
Small Group: Invite the children to make leis by alternating paper or tissue flowers and 1" pieces of cut colored straw. (Optional: make hula skirts by cutting brown plastic garbage bags in several small, three quarter length strips. Cut a slit in the top for the children to put the garbage bags on, and tie them with string to keep on.)

Rocks

STORY TIME

How We Use Rock by Chris Oxlade
Rocks in My Socks and Rainbows Too by Lavelle Carlson

TRANSITION

Play Hot Potato with rocks. The children sit in a circle. As the music plays, pass one or two rocks around the circle. When the music stops, have the child or children holding the rocks move to the next activity.

SNACK

Make candy rocks with the children. Heat 1 cup of sugar and 1 cup of light corn syrup until boiling (adult-only step). Add this mixture to 1 ½ cups of peanut butter and let the children help stir. Gradually add 6 cups of crispy cereal to make a dough mixture. Invite children to roll the dough into balls (rocks). Dip them in melted chocolate to give them a muddy look, and then invite the children to eat their rocks.

Group Time

Bring in many different rocks. Print one uppercase letter on half of the rocks, and then print one lowercase letter on another rock. Give each child a rock (if you have 20 children, hand out 10 uppercase letter rocks and 10 matching lowercase letter rocks). Challenge the children to name the letters on their rocks, and then find the children with the same letters.

Learning Center Ideas

Art: Set out different paint containers and brushes, as well as several rocks. Invite the children to paint the rocks, making paperweights.

Blocks: Add several large rocks to the block area for the children to build around. Tell the children how several old castles were build around natural formations, such as large rock outcroppings, because of the protection they provided.

Sensory: Put several different types and colors of rocks out for the children to explore. Ask them to describe the different rocks, whether they are shiny, dull, colorful, hard, crumbly, and so on.

Additional Activities

Movement: Set several flat rocks around the room. Children use the rocks like stepping stones to walk around the room. (Optional: If you do not want to bring in the big heavy rocks, cut gray pieces of construction paper rocks to use instead.)

Rhythm and Rhyme: Explain to the children that different rocks come from different areas, and invite them to sing, "I Am a Rock," found on appendix page 374.

Small Group: Give each group a pile of rocks, encouraging them to sort the rocks in as many ways as they can. Set out a balance scale for the children to compare the different weights of the rocks, and to see how many small rocks it takes to equal the weight of one larger rock.

Snakes

STORY TIME

The Day Jimmy's Boa Ate the Wash
   by Trinka Hakes Noble
Verdi by Janell Cannon

TRANSITION

Recite "Snake, Snake," found on appendix page 375, with the children. Name a color in the blank space, and have all children wearing something that color line up and move to the next activity.

SNACK

Use your favorite sugar cookie dough recipe to give each child a ball of dough. Invite the children to roll the dough into snake shapes, and then bake them according to recipe directions. Serve when cool.

Group Time

Discuss snakes, using the Snake Facts found on appendix page 375. Ask the children to name the first letter in the word "snake." Explain how the letter *s* makes an *s-s-s* sound similar to the sounds snakes make. Ask the children to name other words that start with the /s/ sound and to make a snake hiss sound as they say them.

Learning Center Ideas

Literacy: Cut out several *s* shapes from construction paper. Set out paints, crayons, markers, glue, and stickers, and then give the *s* shapes to the children and encourage them to decorate them so they resemble snakes.
Sensory: Set out several containers of playdough, and invite the children to roll it into snakes. Challenge the children to make small, medium, and large snakes, as well as thin and thick snakes.

Additional Activities

Movement: Put a jump rope on the floor and shake it in a slithery motion, encouraging the children to jump over the rope without touching it.
Project: Give each child a construction paper cutout of a circle with a spiraling black line drawn from the outside edge around into the middle. Give the children materials with which they can decorate their circles, and then help them cut along the lines on their circles until they have curly snake shapes.
Rhythm and Rhyme: Invite the children to sing "Slithery and Slinky," found on appendix page 375.

Camels

STORY TIME

The Camel's Lament by Charles E. Carryl

Elvis the Camel by Barbara Devine

How the Camel Got Its Hump by Justine Fontes

Little Humpty by Margaret Wild

What's the Matter, Habibi? by Betsy Lewin

TRANSITION

Challenge the children to walk like camels as they transition to the next activity, going on all fours without bending their knees.

SNACK

Set out dates and oat bars for the children to eat.

Group Time

Talk with the children about camels. Use the Camel Facts on appendix page 375 to start the conversation.

Learning Center Ideas

Art: Cut a camel shape (based on the camel outline on appendix page 374) from the middle of a file folder, to make a stencil. Show the children how to put a sheet of paper in the file folder, close it, and sponge paint the camel shape, or add some sand to brown or tan paint for the children to use to paint a camel. When dry, help the children glue sand on the bottom of the page to make a desert scene. Display the camels on the wall together in a "caravan."

Sensory: Put sand in the Sensory Table for children to explore. Add toy camels if available.

Additional Activities

Outside: Challenge the children to pretend they are a caravan of camels. Play "Follow the Caravan Leader." Choose a leader, and have the leader walk in different ways, saying, "Follow the caravan leader" before altering his walking style, and occasionally simply changing the style without saying the "Follow the caravan leader" command. Those who change walking style at the wrong time go to the end of the caravan line.

Rhythm and Rhyme: Invite the children to recite "I'm a Camel in the Sand," found on appendix page 374.

Small Group: Talk to the children about how camels carry people and things across the desert. Set out several different plastic toy animals, and invite the children to sort the animals into two categories: animals you can ride, and animals you cannot ride. As they categorize the animals, ask the children why they can and cannot ride the different animals.

Hands

STORY TIME

Clap Hands by Helen Oxenbury
Clap Your Hands by Lorinda Bryan Cauley
Hand Rhymes by Marc Brown
Hands Can by Cheryl Willis
Here Are My Hands by Bill Martin
If You're Happy and You Know It by David A. Carter

TRANSITION

Invite the children to recite "Hands Up High," found on appendix page 376. Before reciting it, pick one or two children to perform the motions mentioned, who then move to the next activity.

SNACK

Set out several different finger foods for the children to try. Ask them what they like the most, and what they like the least. Make a graph of their responses.

Group Time

Explain to the children how some people with hearing disabilities use their hands to communicate, and show the children *Signs for Me* by Joe Bahan, encouraging the children to learn a few various simple signs, such as "I Love You."

Learning Center Ideas

Fine Motor: Set out sets of child-safe scissors, and invite the children to practice cutting out old coupons, trying to cut evenly along the lines.
Gross Motor: Clap patterns for the children, and then encourage them to mimic the patterns. Vary the difficulty according to the children's abilities.
Science: Set out finger paints and paper for the children to use to make handprints. When dry, encourage the children to compare the differences between their handprints and another child's handprints.

Additional Activities

Project: Make handprint number books. For younger children, make books with numerals 1–5. (For older children, make one with numerals 1–10.) Help all the children make five outlines of their hands on construction paper (make an additional five outlines of both hands on construction paper for the children who will make number books that go to 10). When the children are finished, give them paints and brushes, and invite the children to paint one finger on the first page, two fingers on the second page, and so on. When finished, help the children write "one finger," "two fingers," and so on at the bottom of the pages, and help them staple the pages into books.
Rhythm and Rhyme: Invite the children to recite "My Hands Can Clap," found on appendix page 377.
Small Group: Ask the children to name different things they can do with their hands. Make a list of all the ideas they name. When finished with the list, hand out several sheets of paper with "_____'s hand can ____!" on along the top, have each child pick a hand activity, help them write their names and the activities in the blanks, then encourage them to outline their hands on the rest of the paper.

Dandelions

STORY TIME

Happy Thoughts with Sandy D. Dandelion and Friends by Holly Scarabosio

The Mole Sisters and a Cool Breeze by Roslyn Schwartz

TRANSITION

Play "Pass the Flower." Gather everyone in a circle and turn on some music. As the music plays, invite the children to pass a plastic flower around the circle. Stop the music occasionally, and have the child holding the flower move to the next activity.

Group Time

Introduce dandelions to the children, using the Dandelion Facts on appendix page 377. Show the children a dandelion flower. Explain that yellow petal is a flower. In a few days, the yellow flower will be gone and there will be white seeds. (Show one.) The seeds blow away and land to make new flowers. When the dandelion becomes a head of white seeds, sometimes people make a wish and blow the white seeds away. Invite the children to blow on their dandelions and recite "Dandelions in the Grass," found on appendix page 376, making a wish at the end of the song.

Learning Center Ideas

Math: Number several green construction paper cutouts of grass, and invite the children to match the number of yellow pompom dandelions to the numerals on each cutout of grass.

Sensory: Put plastic and fabric flowers with green Styrofoam and plastic pots in the Sensory Table.

Additional Activities

Outside: Go outside and count how many dandelions you see that are yellow and how many that are white.

Small Group: Show the children real dandelions (if you can) or photos of dandelions: one that is just leaves; another that is leaves and a yellow flower, and the last one that is just the white seeds. Invite the children to recite "Dandelion, Dandelion," found on appendix page 376, and challenge the children to put the photos of the dandelions in the correct order, according to nature and the song.

Book Lovers' Day

August 9th is National Book Lover's Day.

STORY TIME

Books by Eric Carle, Laura Numeroff, Lois Ehlert, and Jamie Lee Curtis

TRANSITION

When preparing the children to move to a new activity, ask them to raise their hands if they have a favorite book. Call on each child one by one, asking them to name their favorite books. After they do so, invite them to move to the next activity.

Group Time

The day before, invite the children to bring their favorite books to school. When all children arrive with their books, take turns asking children to talk about their favorite books. Prompt the children by asking them questions, such as, "How does the story start?" "What happens in the story?" "What happens next?" "How does the story end?" "Why do you like the story?" Invite the children to draw pictures of things they like from their favorite books, and hang the children's pictures on the bulletin board.

Learning Center Ideas

Art: Set out strips of paper, along with markers, crayons, paint, brushes, and other art materials. Invite the children to make bookmarks for their favorite books.

Literacy: Ask the children to make up a story together. Bring the children together in a circle, and ask one child to say the first word or sentence of a story. Copy the child's word on chart paper, and then ask the next child to continue the story, and so on until all the children have contributed to the story. When finished, write each child's contribution on a separate sheet of paper, and invite the children to make drawings of their parts of the story.

Additional Activities

Field Trip: Take the children on a field trip to the library, or bring them into the school's library. Show the children how the library is organized, and invite the librarian to talk with the children about how to use the library and how to take care of books.

Outside: Bring blankets and good books outside and invite the children to have a book picnic.

Rhythm and Rhyme: Invite the children to recite "Ten Little Books," found on appendix page 377.

Frogs

STORY TIME

Five Green and Speckled Frogs by Priscilla Burris
A Frog in the Bog by Karma Wilson
Froggy Books by Jonathan London
Icky Sticky Frog by Dawn Bentley
Jump Frog Jump by Robert Kalan
The Wide Mouthed Frog by Keith Faulkner

TRANSITION

Use construction paper lily pad shapes, to play musical lily pads. Play music, and as it plays, the children hop along as frogs. When the music stops, encourage the children to hop to the closest lily pad. Invite the children who are not on lily pads to hop to the next activity.

SNACK

Invite the children to make frogs on a green cucumber lily pad. Slice cucumbers and spread a little ranch dip on the cucumber slice, then add bits of celery as "frogs" and raisins as "bugs."

Group Time

Set out several plastic frogs in a blue sheet or parachute. Invite the children to hold the ends of the sheet and shake it to make the frogs hop fast, slow, and then out of the parachute. As the children shake the parachute up and down, call the names of two children, and tell them to hop under the parachute and change positions.

Learning Center Ideas

Art: Invite the children to decorate construction paper frog shapes (based on the frog outlines on appendix page 376) with glue, then sprinkle on green, yellow, orange, and blue powdered tempera paint. Show the children how to place another piece of paper over the first sheet and pat it down, then pull the second sheet off the first, revealing a gluey rainforest frog on the second sheet.

Math: Set out several construction paper cutouts of frogs (using the frog outlines on appendix page 376) with various numerals written on them. Give the children little plastic bugs and encourage them to place the correct number of bugs on each frog. (Alternative: Use numbered lily pads and place the correct number of cutout frogs on the pads.)

Additional Activities

Games: Lily Pad Hopscotch: Cut lily pad shapes from green construction paper. Tape them to the floor, and number them. Cover them all with a long piece of contact paper, and invite the children to play lily pad hopscotch.

Outside: Bring the children outside to play leapfrog.

Small Group: Bring in several books with frog facts in them. Also set out three pond shapes, and write one of the following sentences on each. "What We Know About Frogs," "What We Want to Know," and "What We Learned." Ask the children to offer examples for the first list, and then ask for information to put on the second list. When the children have provided information they want to know about frogs, help them go through the books looking for answers to their questions. When someone finds an explanation, enter it onto the third sheet. Encourage the children to add to the list throughout the day.

T-Shirts

On the prior day, remind all the children to wear a special T-shirt to school. Be sure to bring several extras to school for those who might forget.

STORY TIME

Calliou's Favorite T-Shirt by Jeanne Verhoye-Millet

Hildegarde and the Great Green T-Shirt Factory by Ravay L. Snow

In My New Yellow Shirt by Eileen Spinelli

TRANSITION

When preparing to move to a new activity, challenge the children to line up based on the colors of their shirts. Organize them in the approximate order of the color wheel: red, orange, yellow, green, blue, and violet.

SNACK

Toast a piece of bread for each child, and cut each slice into a T shape. Set out small containers of peanut butter and jelly, along with plastic knives, and invite the children to decorate their T-shirt toast.

Group Time

Make a living graph, using children. Sort children by the T-shirts they are wearing, having the children stand in one line if their T-shirts are plain, another if they have writing on their shirts, another if they have pictures on their shirts, and a fourth line if they have both pictures and writing on their shirts. Count how many children are in each line.

Learning Center Ideas

Math: Set out three laundry baskets full of piles of clothes. Challenge the children to sort and fold the clothes in three categories: shirts, pants, and T-shirts, putting each in a separate laundry basket.

Math: Make several construction paper cutouts of T-shirts, using the T-shirt outline on appendix page 376. Write a different numeral on each outline. Laminate for durability. Hang a clothesline through the room, and challenge the children to use clothespins to hang the T-shirts in numerical order. Consider numbering the clothespins first, and putting them in order on the line, so the children only have to match the number on the clothespin to the number on the shirt.

Additional Activities

Movement: Invite the children to act out the directions mentioned in the "If, Then" rhyme found on appendix page 377.

Project: Tie-dye T-shirts. To make a safe dye, put a package of unsweetened Koo-Aid in a little water. Mix different packages into different containers to make different colors. Help the children take a T-shirt, bunch up some of the fabric and tie it with rubber bands, and then help the children take turns soaking parts of their T-shirts in the containers of water. (If you are using T-shirts that the children have brought from home, be sure to obtain permission from families to dye the T-shirts.) After soaking in several colors, show the children where to wring out the shirts, and set them out on a rack or clothesline to dry. At the end of the day, check to be sure the shirts are dry. If so, encourage the children to wear them for their parents when they arrive to bring them home.

Appendix

Note: All items in the appendix are original works by Sue Fleischmann unless otherwise noted.

September Appendix

Class Book

Ask each child to complete the following sentences. Write down their responses. Collect all of the pages and staple them together to make a class book.

- *I like to play _____*
  When I was little, I liked to play_____.
- *I like to eat _____.*
  When I was little, I liked to eat _____.
- *My favorite color is _____.*
  When I was little, my favorite color was _____

Fingerprint Number Book Directions

On each page, make the given number of colored fingerprints. When the fingerprints are dry, add marker lines to make pictures.

Page 1: Help each child make one yellow fingerprint. Count aloud as each child makes a print. When the print dries, add fins and an eye. Write "1 yellow goldfish" at the bottom of the page.

Page 2: Write "2 brown eggs" at the bottom of the page. Help each child put two brown fingerprints on the page. When it is dry, add ears, eyes, and a nose with black marker.

Page 3: Write "3 red apples" at the bottom of the page. Help each child put three red fingerprints on this page. When the paint dries, add a green stem and a leaf.

Page 4: Write "4 yellow cats" at the bottom of the page. Add eyes, ears, whiskers, and nose to the fingerprints to make cats.

Page 5: Write "5 pink bunnies" at the bottom of the page. Help each child print five pink fingerprints on the page. When the paint dries, add bunny ears, eyes, nose, and whiskers to the fingerprints.

Happy Hearts

Use your hands to make a handprint heart. Cover the child's hands with paint. Help the child turn his hand upside down so that the heel of his hand creates the top of one half of the heart shape and his fingers make the point at the bottom of the heart. Next, make another handprint in the same fashion, using the heel of the other hand to create the top of the other half of the heart. When the paint dries, ask the child to dictate something that makes his heart happy and write it on the paper.

Happy/Sad Stick Puppets

Glue a craft stick between two yellow circles. On one side, draw a happy face; on the other side, a sad face.

Manners Statements

Katie thanks her friend for sharing her pink marker.

John pushes his friend while standing in line.

Betsy interrupts her teacher while she is talking.

Amya makes her friend a special picture.

Daniel helps a friend clean up a spill.

Mary takes a toy away from another child.

Jose helps a friend who fell down.

Liliana asks, "May I please have a cookie?"

Bobby burps loudly at lunch.

Jacinda bumps into a friend and says, "Excuse me."

Placemats

For this activity, fold a 9" x 12" piece of construction paper in half, so the 12" side of the paper is divided in half. Starting at the fold, cut horizontally until about 1" from the outside edges. Cut 1"-wide strips of paper to weave. Show the children how the pieces of paper go in and out of the slits. When finished, glue the edges down. Laminate the weavings.

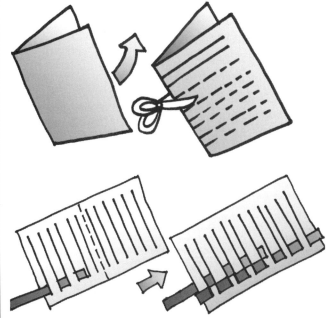

"This Is Special Me" Book

Each page is an 8 ½" x 11" sheet. Print the sentence at the bottom. Invite children to dictate answers and draw pictures for each page.

Page 1: This is me. (Ask the child to draw a picture or take a photo of the child.)

Page 2: My first name is _____.

My last name is _____.

(Invite children to print their own names.)

My birthday is _____.

I am ____ years old.

(Invite the child to draw a birthday cake with the correct number of candles.)

Page 4: My handprint (Help the child make a handprint on the page.)

Page 5: I am a special friend.

(Make a heart-shaped pocket by gluing around the bottom edges of a heart shape and glue to the page. Invite at least three friends to say how the child has been a special friend to them. Write their statements on strips of paper and place them in the heart shape on the page.)

SONGS AND POEMS

All About Me and You

Tune: I'm a Little Teapot

I have black hair, you have brown.

I wear a smile, not a frown.

I am very short, and you are tall.

But it doesn't matter at all.

Bear Poem

If you have a bear that's red

Put your bear on your head.

If you have a bear that's blue

Put your bear behind you.

If your bear is colored green
Jump three times like a jumping bean.

If your bear is the color yellow
Smile, you are a happy fellow!

All bears, all bears, go up high
All bears, all bears, pretend to fly

All bears jump fast, jump slow
All bears jump high, and jump low.

Good listening, bears, my oh my!
Sit back down and wave goodbye.

The Blue Song

Tune: Farmer in the Dell
I like the color blue.
It's on me and you.
Blue eyes, blue pants
And shirts of blue,
Blue hats and mittens, too.

The Color Song

Tune: Mary Had a Little Lamb
Rojo is the color red,
Color red, color red.
Rojo is the color red
In Espanol.

Other verses:
Azul is the color blue…
Verde is the color green…
Blanco is the color white…

Crayons

Tune: Three Blind Mice
Eight colored crayons, eight colored crayons
In a box, in a box.
Red and yellow, green and blue,
Black, brown, purple, and orange, too.
Eight colored crayons
In a box.

Does Your Trunk Hang Low?

Tune: Do Your Ears Hang Low?
Does your trunk hang low
From your head down to your toe?
Are you big and gray?
Do you like to eat hay?
Do you take a bath with
Water from your nose,
Just exactly like
A water hose?

Feelings Are Okay

Tune: Sing a Song of Sixpence
Sometimes I feel happy.
Sometimes I feel sad.
Sometimes I am lonely.
Sometimes I am glad.
But no matter how I feel,
I am still me,
And my feelings are okay,
Don't you see?

Five-Minute Warning

Tune: Mary Had a Little Lamb
We have five minutes to go.
Finish up, be fast, not slow.
Then with this we will be done,
And ready for more fun!

Gray Squirrel

Tune: Do Your Ears Hang Low?
If you have a bushy tail
And you are the color gray
And you are very busy
Both night and day.
You bury all your nuts
And jump from tree to tree
You're a squirrel, I see.

H Is for Hugs

Tune: I'm a Little Teapot
I like "h" words, yes I do.
Horn, hoop, and happy to name a few,
Hotdog, horse, hair, and hall,
But "hug" is my favorite word of all.

I Can Be Helpful

Tune: Up on the Housetop
I can be helpful every day
When I work and when I play.
If someone asks for help, I will be there.
I will show you that I care.
Help, help, help, you need me.
Help, help, help, you need me.
So if you need something I will go,
Because I love you very much, you know.

I'm Special

Tune: Mary Had a Little Lamb
I'm as special as I can be,
I can be, I can be.
I'm as special as I can be.
There's no one just like me.

I Think I Can

Tune: Sing a Song of Sixpence
I will try something new, each and every day.
It might be something hard, but I'll always say,
"I think I can do it.
Yes, I know I could!"
I'll try until I do it.
And say, "I knew I would."

The Letter B Song

Tune: Three Blind Mice
Letter B,
Letter B.
It is for me.
It is for me.
Bed, bear, bell, basket, and beat,
They all begin with the letter B.
Letter B,
Letter B.

The Manners Song

Tune: Sing a Song of Sixpence
I will use my manners each and every day.
I will use them at school, at home, and at play.
I will say, "Excuse me," "please," and
    "thank you," too.
I will listen and take turns when I talk to you.

Scissors Song

Tune: Farmer in the Dell
Open and shut,
Open and shut,
I open and shut my scissors
To cut, cut, cut.

Sing a Song of Circles

Tune: Sing a Song of Sixpence
Sing a song of circles
I see them every day.
When I eat my supper,
Or go outside and play.
I see them in a cookie jar,
A circle is my head,
I even dream of circles
Lying in my bed.

The Triangle Song

Tune: A Farmer in the Dell
Triangles have three corners.
Triangles have three corners.
Sides and corners 1, 2, 3,
A triangle is for me.

Welcome Song

Tune: Mary Had a Little Lamb
(Child's name) is at school today,
School today, school today.
(Child's name) is at school today.
Welcome to our school.

The Yellow Song

Tune: Up on the Housetop
I like bananas, yes I do.
Golden apples and yellow lemons, too.
I like pineapple all cut up,
And apple juice in a yellow cup.

RECIPES

Taffy Apple Dip

1 8-ounce container cream cheese
½ cup brown sugar
1 teaspoon vanilla
½ teaspoon caramel flavor

Blend all ingredients until smooth. Serve with sliced apples.

Triangle Treats

Triangle-shaped crescent biscuits
Vegetables, cut in bite-size pieces
Grated mozzarella cheese

Bake the crescent rolls as directed, but do not roll up the biscuits. Cover the triangle-shaped biscuits with the cheese. Add cut up vegetables, as desired.

USEFUL FACTS AND OTHER INFORMATION

Elephant Facts

- Elephants live in families, led by the oldest female elephant.
- Elephants' skin is sensitive. They take dust baths to protect their skin from sun and insects.
- When enemies come, big elephants stand in a circle around the little ones.
- Adult males wander alone.
- Elephants eat grass, seeds, fruit leaves, branches, and bark all day long.
- Elephants can eat up to 300 pounds of food a day.
- There are two kinds of elephants: Asian and African.

Hippopotamus Facts

- The hippopotamus is the third largest land mammal in the world.
- Hippopotamus means "river horse." Compare a horse to a hippo.
- Hippos are only found in Africa.
- Hippos can gallop at speeds up to 30 miles an hour.
- Hippos rest in water because they do not have sweat glands so the water keeps them cool and moist.
- A hippo's ears, eyes, and nostrils are level with each other so it only has to rise a few inches out of water to see, hear, or breathe.

Squirrel Facts

- Squirrels eat nuts, seeds, acorns, plants, insects, and grasses.
- Squirrels are found everywhere but Australia and Antarctica.
- The most common squirrels are gray squirrels. They live in trees.
- There are two kinds of squirrels; tree squirrels and ground squirrels.
- Tree squirrels spend most of their lives in trees. They build nests and do not hibernate.
- Ground squirrels live in burrows under the ground, and they hibernate.
- Squirrels that live in the ground are chipmunks, prairie dogs, and woodchucks.
- Enemies of squirrels are owls, hawks, badgers, coyote, raccoons and skunks.
- Squirrels greet each other by touching noses.
- Squirrels get into trouble by eating farmer's crops, stealing seeds from bird feeders, and chewing on electrical wires.

October Appendix

Bats

Have the children put small Styrofoam balls or wads of newspaper into the middle of several sheets of black tissue paper. Twist the tissue paper around the ball. Tie the tissue paper off on both ends of the ball. Spread the tissue out on each side to make wings. Use fabric paint to draw a face on the bat, and attach a string to hang the bats.

Dinosaur Patterns

Egg Experiment

Put two hardboiled eggs in jars of vinegar. If appropriate, tell the children that the vinegar will leech the calcium from the shells, and that over time the eggs will become "rubberized." Explain to the children that the eggs have to soak for 24–48 hours. Encourage the children to check on the eggs periodically throughout the days, noting whether they have risen or fallen in the jars, and whether they are covered with bubbles. After two days, move the eggs to jars of water. Explain to the children that the eggs will have to soak overnight. The following day, invite two children to remove the eggs from the water. Ask the children to describe any changes they see in the eggs, especially in size and softness.

Stamp Glue

2 packets of unflavored gelatin
12 tablespoons warm water
1 teaspoon mint flavoring
Paper
Pinking shears

Mix 2 packets of unflavored gelatin with 12 tablespoons of warm water and 1 teaspoon of mint flavoring to make glue. Use a paintbrush to apply the glue to the back of the paper. Allow the glue to dry. Use pinking shears to cut paper into stamps.

SONGS AND POEMS

Bats

Tune: I'm a Little Teapot
I'm a little bat outside at night.
I go to sleep when the sun is bright.
I fly high and I fly low.
Sounds help me know which way to go.

The Bat Says

Put your bat up high.
Put your bat beside you.
Put your bat under your feet.
Put your bat behind your back.

The Black Song

Tune: Three Blind Mice
Black, black, black,
The color black.
Big black cats.
Little black bats.
Black is the color of spiders and hair,
Jelly beans, sheep, and a big black bear.
Black, black, black.

Dinosaur Roar

Tune: London Bridge
I'm a great big dinosaur,   *I'm a little dinosaur,*
Dinosaur, dinosaur.   *Dinosaur, dinosaur.*
I'm a great big dinosaur.   *I'm a little dinosaur.*
Hear me roar (loudly).   *Hear me roar (softly).*

G Is for Gorilla

G is for gorilla,
Gallop, and go.
G is for watching
Green grass to grow.
(Use g words with the hard-g sound.)

G, G, the Letter G

Tune: Row, Row, Row Your Boat
G, g, the letter g,
Oh where, oh where, have you been?
In glue, and green and grapes and glove
And in my giggly grin.

Leaves on the Tree

Tune: Farmer in the Dell
Leaves on the tree,
Leaves on the tree,
What color do I see?
Leaves on the tree.

Letter O Song

Tune: Mary Had a Little Lamb
Listen for the letter o,
Letter o, letter o.
Listen for the letter o,
It makes a sound like this: (make the sound
    of an o).

Listen for the letter o,
Letter o, letter o
Listen for the letter o
It can say its name.

Letter P Song

Tune: Twinkle Little Star
I like to eat the letter p,
It tastes very good to me.
Pancakes, popcorn, peanuts, too,
Peaches and pears for me and you.
I like to eat the letter p,
It tastes very good to me.

Little Miss Muffet (Traditional)

Little Miss Muffet sat on a tuffet,
Eating her curds and whey.
Along came a spider
And sat down beside her,
And frightened Miss Muffet away.

Lunch-O

Tune: BINGO
There was a mouse who was so hungry,
And so she ate some lunch-O.
L-U-N-C-H,
L-U-N-C-H, L-U-N-C-H
And then she ate some lunch-O.

Miss Spider's ABC's

Tune: ABC Song
A, B, C, D, E, F, G,
H, I, J, K, L, M, N, O, P,
Q, R, S, T, U, V,
W, X, Y, and Z.
Miss Spider knows her ABC's,
Now have a happy birthday please.

Monster Mix Up

Tune: Hokey Pokey
Verses:
Put your monster foot in...
Put your hairy arm in...
Put your green head in...
Put your big teeth in...
Put your monster body in...

O Is for Oatmeal

O is for oatmeal,
Onion and oil.
O is for oysters
Ready to boil.

The Opposite Song

Tune: Mary Had a Little Lamb
The opposite of hot is cold
Hot is cold, hot is cold.
The opposite of hot is cold
Opposites.

(Make up other verses using opposites: on/off, fast/slow, stop/go, night/day.)

The Orange Song

Tune: Up on the Housetop
Orange is the color of a carrot stick,
Or the piece of cheese I pick.
Orange is the color of pumpkin pie,
Or of the marigold that smells, oh my!
Orange, orange, orange
Is my juice.
Orange is the beautiful sun I see
As it goes down quietly.

Owl in a Tree

Tune: I'm a Little Teapot
I am an owl up in the tree.
From this branch I can see
Bugs, animals, and birds, too.
I can even look at you.

P Is for Pizza

P is for pizza or
Pancakes on a plate.
P is for all the yummy
Popcorn that I ate.

The Pizza Song

Tune: Pop Goes the Weasel
Roll the dough so it's nice and flat,
That will be the crust.
Add sauce, meat, cheese, and onion, please.
Cook up your pizza!

Play with Me

Tune: I'm a Little Teapot
Won't you come and play with me?
I have a magic wand, you see.
We can be pirates or fairies, too,
Or animals living in the zoo.

The Popcorn Song

Tune: Pop Goes the Weasel
The popcorn seeds are in the bag
Waiting to be popped
Hotter, hotter, and hotter they get
Pop, goes the popcorn.
(The children crouch down and go up a little each time they sing "hotter," and pop up when they sing "pop.")

Responsibility

Tune: Farmer in the Dell
Responsibility,
It is a job for me.
It is something I should do,
And I will follow through.

The Stamp Song

Tune: Up on the Housetop
Wrap up myself if I am able.
I'll put on an address label.
Put on stamps with lots of glue,
Then I'll mail myself to you.

Stop, Drop, and Roll

Tune: Three Blind Mice
Remember this rule.
Remember this rule.
Stop, drop, and roll.
Stop, drop, and roll.
When you see fire on your clothes,
Don't run and look for the water hose.
Stop, drop, and roll.

The Witch Is in the House

Tune: Farmer in the Dell
The witch is in the house,
The witch is in the house,
Ha ha on Halloween,
The witch is in the house.

Additional verses:
The witch takes the scarecrow…
The scarecrow takes the cat…
The cat takes the mouse…
The mouse takes the spider…
The spider takes the ghost…
The ghost says "boo"…

Black Dirt Cake

½ stick butter
8 ounces cream cheese
1 cup powdered sugar
3 ½ cup milk
2 packages of vanilla instant pudding
12 ounces non-dairy whipped topping
1 large package of chocolate sandwich cookies
resealable zipper-closure bags
Mixing bowls and spoons
Measuring cups
Clear plastic cups, one for each child

Divide the children into three groups. One group mixes butter, cream cheese, and sugar; the second group mixes milk, pudding mix, and whipped topping; and the third group crushes the sandwich cookies in a zippered bag. Mix the first two groups' ingredients. place a bit of this mixture into clear plastic cups and then sprinkle the crushed cookie bits on top. Refrigerate before serving.

Elephant Ears

½ cup butter (melted)
2 cups flour
6 tablespoon sugar
1 teaspoon baking powder
1 teaspoon salt
⅔ cup of milk
6 tablespoon brown sugar, packed
2 teaspoon cinnamon
Mixing bowl and spoon
Measuring cups and spoons
Baking sheet or pan
Oven (adult only)

Preheat the oven to 400 degrees. Mix flour, sugar, baking soda, and salt. Add 6 tablespoons of milk and butter until you have dough. Pat the dough flat. Invite the children to brush a piece of dough with melted butter, and then add brown sugar and cinnamon to their piece of dough. Show the children how to roll the dough into an elephant ear shape and place it on a baking sheet or pan. Bake for 10–12 minutes. Take the rolls from the baking pan (adult-only step). Let cool, then serve to the children.

Fruit Snack

1 cup watermelon balls
1 cup cantaloupe balls
1 cup honeydew melon balls
1 cup pineapple chunks
½ cup blueberries
Plastic spoons and knives
Mixing cups
Large mixing bowl and spoon

Invite the children to use spoons to scoop melon balls and plastic knives to cut the pineapple into chunks. Mix the fruits together in a large bowl, pour a splash of orange juice over the fruit; chill and serve.

Grandma A's Crumb Cake

2 cups brown sugar
¾ cup butter
2 ½ cups flour
Mixing bowl and spoon
Mixing cups and spoons
1 egg
1 cup milk
1 teaspoon baking soda
1 teaspoon vanilla
pinch of salt
Mixing bowl and spoon
loaf pan
oven (adult only)

Mix the first three ingredients together like a pie crust; save 1 cup to spread on the top of the cake. Add the egg to the mixture; mix the baking soda with milk and add to the mixture. Add vanilla and salt, beating enough to make it smooth. Put it in a loaf pan and spread the extra cup of crust mix on top. Bake at 350 degrees for 30–40 minutes (adult-only step).

Oatmeal Snack Bars

½ cup butter
¼ cup white sugar
¼ cup brown sugar
1 egg
1 teaspoon vanilla
½ cup flour
¼ teaspoon salt
½ cup quick cooking oatmeal
Mixing bowl and spoon
Hand mixer (adult only)
Oven (adult only)

Cream butter and sugars; blend in vanilla and egg. Stir in remaining ingredients. Bake in a 9" x 9" pan for 20–25 minutes at 350 degrees. (This recipe can be doubled and put in a 9" x 13" pan.)

Pumpkin Cookies

½ cup butter softened
¾ cup brown sugar, firmly packed
1 large egg
1 teaspoon vanilla
½ teaspoon baking powder
¼ teaspoon salt
2 cups all purpose flour
½ cup solid-pack canned pumpkin
1 teaspoon pumpkin pie spice
Mixing bowl and spoon or hand mixer
Mixing cups and spoons
Oven (adult only)
Baking sheet or spoon

Beat butter, sugar, egg, and vanilla until fluffy. Add baking powder, salt, and flour. Then add canned pumpkin and pumpkin pie spice. Heat oven to 350 degrees. Spoon onto baking sheets or pans. Bake 10-12 minutes until lightly browned (adult-only step). Makes 4–7 dozen cookies.

Pumpkin Playdough

2 ¾ cups flour
1 cup salt
4 teaspoon cream of tartar
⅜ cup of oil
½ container of pumpkin pie spice
orange food coloring
2 cups water
Mixing bowl and spoon
Mixing cups and spoons
Stove or hot plate (adults only)

Mix all the ingredients together. Stir over medium heat until the lumps are gone. Knead dough until it is smooth (adult-only step). Store in an airtight container.

Sharing Snack Mix

3 cups pretzel sticks
5 cups round circle cereal
1 cup fish crackers
1 cup pretzel fish crackers
⅔ cup cooking oil
4 teaspoons Worcestershire sauce
cookie sheet or pan
oven (adult only)

Combine pretzels, circle cereal, and fish crackers. Stir together the Worcestershire sauce and cooking oil. Pour over the cracker mixture and stir so it is spread evenly. Spread onto a large cookie sheet or pan and bake for 30 minutes at 300 degrees (adult-only step). Serve when cool.

USEFUL FACTS AND OTHER INFORMATION

Bat Facts

- Bats are mammals because they have fur and give birth to live young.
- Bats are the only mammals that can fly.
- Bats are extremely clean and use their tongues to clean themselves.
- Bats sleep upside down during the day, hanging by their toe claws.
- A single bat can eat 600 mosquitoes an hour.
- Bats can live for 25–30 years if not eaten by natural enemies, such as owls, snakes, raccoons, and hawks.
- Most bats are very intelligent.
- Some cultures (Chinese, for example) believe bats bring good luck.
- Bats are social animals and live in large colonies.
- There are about 1,000 different kinds of bats in the world.

Dinosaur Facts

- Tyrannosaurus Rex was the king of dinosaurs. These dinosaurs were meat eaters with strong jaws and sharp teeth. They stood about 45 feet tall and walked on their hind legs.
- Apatosaurus was the largest of the land dinosaurs. Because the ground shook as these dinosaurs walked, they are nicknamed the Thunder Lizard. At over 75 feet tall, these herbivores grew so awkwardly large that they usually stayed in the water, for both protection and balance.
- Stegosaurus was about 18 feet long. These dinosaurs had protective bony plates and spines along the tail.
- Triceratops is called the three-horned dinosaur, for the two horns on the top of their heads, and third on the middle of their noses. The triceratops laid eggs and ate plants.

◆ Pterodactyl: This large, flying dinosaur had scales instead of feathers, and a wingspan of as much as 20 feet.

Facts About David Shannon

◆ David Shannon was born on October 5, 1959 in Washington, DC. He grew up in Spokane, Washington.

◆ From the time he was five, David Shannon loved drawing pictures and writing books.

◆ After he finished college, David moved to New York City and drew illustrations for famous magazines, such as Time Magazine and Rolling Stone. David Shannon created many book jackets. Then he started writing books.

◆ He writes the story and rereads it many times to figure out the best pictures.

◆ David Shannon lives in Los Angeles California with his actress wife Heidi. They have a daughter Emma and a dog named Fergus. Fergus is hiding somewhere in every one of David Shannon's books.

◆ David Shannon wrote *No, David!* when he was only five years old. It is about his life.

Food Pyramid

Halloween Suggestions and Safety Rules

Suggestions to help children who may be afraid:

◆ Acknowledge their feelings. Tell the children it is okay to be afraid, and that even grownups are scared sometimes.

◆ Ask the children what they are afraid of, and discuss their fears.

◆ Read books about characters who overcome their fears.

◆ Make scary masks, and have the children look in the mirror with them on, and then take them off to better explain the concept of pretend.

Halloween rules:

◆ Trick-or-treat in a well-lit and safe area.

◆ Go with an adult.

◆ Wear a costume that allows you to see where you are going.

◆ Take a flashlight and wear reflective clothes so cars can see you.

◆ Watch out for cars.

◆ Let an adult check your candy before you eat it.

Owl Facts

◆ Owls live everywhere on earth except Antarctica.

◆ Owls are nocturnal.

◆ Owls eat rabbits, mice, birds, and snakes. Because they cannot digest bones, feathers, teeth, and fur, they cough up these items.

◆ Owls help people by eating insects and rodents that harm crops.

◆ There are about 200 different types of owls in the world.

◆ Owls live about 25–30 years.

◆ Baby owls are called owlets.

◆ Owls fight predators by hissing, snapping, and fighting with their sharp talons.

◆ Owls have soft feathers to help them fly silently.

◆ Male owls bring food to their young.

◆ In some Native American stories, owls have magical powers.

November Appendix

Classroom Bookworm

Ask the children to tell you the names of their favorite stories. Give each child a large green circle with a smaller white paper circle inside. Help the children to draw something about their favorite story on the white circles. After they draw the picture, ask them to tell you the name of the story and write down the title of the story. Put the green circles together into a worm shape. Add a head and eyes, explaining to the children what an actual worm is, as well as explaining that avid readers are also called bookworms.

Inchworm Rulers

Mark several 2' sheets of construction paper with 1" grids. Cut each sheet into several long strips of single squares, and invite the children to draw worms in each square of their "inchworm ruler." When each child's ruler is ready, take them outside and encourage them to measure the length of different items, such as balls, sticks, slides, and other items.

Purse Outline

Use this outline for the art center idea on page 73 in the Daily Plan Concept of Happy Birthday, Kevin Henkes.

"Whooo Is Sleeping?" Book

Provide pre-cut cave shapes for each child. Give each child a piece of white construction paper to glue to the cave opening, making a flap. At the top of each cave shape, help the children write "Shhh, _____ is sleeping." Set out crayons and markers, inviting the children to make drawings of animals that hibernate in winter behind the flaps on their sheets of paper. Help the children write the name of the animal they drew. After each child finishes, bind each drawing together with string, making a book. [Illustration] Consider making several small books or one big book.

Brown Is the Color of My Teddy Bear

Tune: Up on the Housetop
Brown is the color of my teddy bear,
Autumn leaves, and children's hair.
Brown is the color of my chunky shoe,
Crackers, cookies, pudding, too.

Cooperation

Tune: London Bridge
Cooperation's what we need,
What we need, what we need.
Cooperation's what we need
To succeed.

Criss Cross Your Shoelace

Tune: Farmer in the Dell
Criss cross your shoelace.
Criss cross your shoelace.
What to do to tie your shoe,
Criss cross your shoelace.

Put one lace through and pull…
Make two bunny ears…
Criss cross the bunny ears…
Put one ear through and pull…

The Days Song

Tune: Yankee Doodle
Sunday, Monday, Tuesday, Wednesday,
Thursday, Friday, Saturday.
Sunday, Monday, Tuesday, Wednesday,
Thursday, Friday, Saturday.
Days, days of the week
Every day to play.

Sunday, Monday, Tuesday, Wednesday,
Thursday, Friday, Saturday.

Family, Family

Tune: Daisy, Daisy
Family, family,
We love our family.
It doesn't matter how big or small it might be.
Even in stormy weather,
We always stick together.
It is a treat, it is so neat
To be in my family.

Family in the House

Tune: The Farmer in the Dell
The dad takes the mom.
The dad takes the mom.
We are a family.
The dad takes the mom.

Additional verses:
The mom takes the brother…
The brother takes the sister…
The sister takes the baby…

Five Crows

Five crows all playing in the corn. (five children
   stand together pretending to be crows)
One more flew in this sunny morn. (one child joins
   them)
Now six crows are there to play.
Scarecrow, scarecrow, shoo them away! (the six
   children all pretend to fly away)

Fly Away

Insect _____ fly away,
Fly off like a _____ today.

Goldie Is Mad

Tune: Three Blind Mice
Goldie is mad. Mad, mad, mad.
Her brother spits on her little doll,
Goldie is mad and sits by the wall.
Goldie is mad. Mad, mad, mad.

How Many Crows?

Tune: Mary Had a Little Lamb
How many crows did you scare,
Did you scare, did you scare?
How many crows did you scare
In the field out there?

I Am Big

Tune: Farmer in the Dell
I am big. I am big.
There's so much that I can do.
I am big.
I can ____. I can ____
There's so much that I can do.
I can ____.

Additional verses:

walk	jump	skip
hop	talk	run

I Am Very Brave

Tune: The Farmer in the Dell
I am very brave.
I am very brave.
I come to school and try new things.
I am very brave.

If You Have Blue on Your Shoe

If you have blue on your shoe,
Stand up tall is what you do.

If you have white on your shoe,
Turn round and round is what you do.

If you have black on your shoe,
Hop on one foot is what you do.

If you have brown on your shoe,
Touch your toes is what you do.

I'm a Little Sponge

Tune: I'm a Little Teapot
I'm a little sponge and you should see
Just how clean I can make things be!
With bubbles and water I can really go,
I can clean high and I can clean low.

I Thank You for All You Do

Tune: Twinkle, Twinkle, Little Star
I thank you for all you do.
You are very special, too.
You do so much for me.
You are the very best you see.
I thank you for all you do.
You are very special, too.

Listen to My Drum

Tune: The Farmer in the Dell
Listen to my drum.
Listen to my drum.
Can you do what I do?
Listen to my drum.
(Tap out a rhythm, then invite the children to tap the same rhythm.)

Little Scarecrow

Hey, little scarecrow, be aware!
There's a crow right in your hair.

Hey, little scarecrow, look at you.
There's a crow right on your shoe.

Hey, little scarecrow, I can see
A crow that's right on your knee.

Hey, little scarecrow, please don't cry.
There's a crow right on your eye.

Hey, little scarecrow, he doesn't mean any harm.
There's a crow right on your arm.

Hey, little scarecrow, I see crows.
There's one right on your nose.

Hey, little scarecrow, scare them away.
Then we can go and play.

My Hand Can Be a Turkey

My hand can be a turkey
With feathers green and blue.
This little turkey wants to say
A great big gobble thank you!

My Trick

Here's my trick, can you see.
Can you do the same as me?

Old Mother Hubbard (Traditional)

Old Mother Hubbard
Went to her cupboard
To get her poor dog a bone.
But when she got there,
The cupboard was bare,
And so the poor doggy had none.

Old Mother Hubbard Went to the Cupboard

Tune: Skip to My Lou
Old Mother Hubbard went to the cupboard,
Old Mother Hubbard went to the cupboard,
Old Mother Hubbard went to the cupboard,
To give her dog a bone.

One Scarecrow

Tune: One Elephant
One scarecrow in the field one day
Sat in the field scaring crows away.
He had such enormous fun,
He asked another scarecrow to come.

Pipe Cleaner

(Insert color) *pipe cleaners dance around,*
Reach up high, touch the ground.
Stand on one foot, now the other one, too.
Then sit down and touch your shoe.

Put Your Sponge Way Up High

Put your sponge way up high
Reach way up to the sky.

Very good, way to go!
Now put your sponge way down low.

Throw your sponge in the air.
Catch it, catch it, if you dare.

Put your sponge on your knee.
Hold very still and count to three.

Sponge on your head, walk around,
Don't let the sponge hit the ground.

Take a Look

Tune: Do Your Ears Hang Low?
Would you like to take a look
At a very good book
About horses or cars,
Or the sun and stars,
Maybe learn a new trick?
There's so many books to pick.
I love them all!

Ten Little Beats

Tune: Ten Little Indians
1 little, 2 little, 3 little beats,
4 little, 5 little, 6 little beats,
7 little, 8 little, 9 little beats,
10 beats on my drum. (beat a drum 10 times)

Thank You

Tune: Twinkle, Twinkle, Little Star
Thank you for the friends we meet.
Thank you for the food we eat.
Thank you for our clothes to wear,
And for the families who care.
Thank you for our toys to play,
We are thankful on this day.

Thank You for the Moon So Bright

Tune: Twinkle, Twinkle, Little Star
Thank you for the moon so bright,
And the twinkling stars at night.
Thank you for the sun so high,
Shining brightly in the sky.
Thank you for the birds that sing.
We thank you for everything.

Three Little Turkeys

Tune: Bumpin' Up and Down in My Little Red Wagon
One little, two little, three little turkeys,
Four little, five little, six little turkeys,
Seven little, eight little, nine little turkeys,
Hiding from the cook.

Time to Go

_____ the brave,
It's time to go.
Don't be afraid.
Don't be slow.

Traffic Light

Tune: I'm a Little Teapot
If you see a traffic light,
There are three things you should know.
Red means stop and yellow means wait,
And don't forget that green means go.

Turkey Walks

Turkey walks with a wobble, wobble, wobble.
Turkey talks with a gobble, gobble, gobble.
With a wobble and a gobble,
The turkey walks away.
With a wobble and a gobble,
The turkey goes to play.

Two Are the Same

Tune: Farmer in the Dell
Two are the same.
Two are the same.
One is very different,
And two are the same.

We're Thankful

We're thankful for food,
A house, and more.
But who is the person
You are thankful for?

When It's Cold Outside

Tune: If You're Happy and You Know It
When it's cold outside, wear a hat.
When it's cold outside, wear a hat.
When it's cold outside, please,
You don't want your ears to freeze.
When it's cold outside, wear a hat.

Store It Up Snack Mix

2 cups oyster crackers	2 tsp dill
2 cups small pretzels	¾ cup oil
2 cups fish pretzels	garlic (optional)
2 cups O-shaped cereal	
2 packages dry ranch dressing	

Mix the ingredients and bake at 200 degrees for one hour (adult-only step), let cool, and serve.

USEFUL FACTS AND OTHER INFORMATION

Turkey Facts

- Turkeys are one of the most popular and famous birds in North America.
- There are domestic turkeys that live on farms and wild turkeys that live in the woods.
- Turkey on the farm cannot fly because they are too heavy, but wild turkeys can fly.
- Male turkeys are called "Toms" or "gobblers."
- Female turkeys are called "hens."
- Turkeys can lay up to 18 eggs at a time.
- The skin on a turkey's head can turn from gray to red when distressed or mating.

Winter Animal Behavior Chart

FLY SOUTH	SLEEP	STAY THE SAME
geese	bears	cardinals
monarch butterflies	frogs	deer
robins	woodchucks	raccoons

December Appendix

ACTIVITY DIRECTIONS

Five Senses Wintertime Book

Give each child five sheets of construction paper, with the one of the sentences found below written on each sheet, and invite the children to make drawings that relate to the sentences found on each page.

Page 1: "I see a glittery star."

Page 2: "I hear ringing bells."

Page 3: "I smell evergreen trees."

Page 4: "I touch cold, wet snow."

Page 5: "I taste hot chocolate."

SONGS AND POEMS

Animals, Animals

Animals, animals, they like to roam.
But where does a _____ make his home?

Additional verses:
squirrel (in a tree)
bear (in a cave)
fish (in water)
cow (on a farm)
bird (in a nest)

Country Mouse, City Mouse

Tune: I'm a Little Teapot
I'm a little country mouse.
I live in a country house.
I like it quiet where I stay.
It's green and beautiful where I play.

I'm a little city mouse.
I live in a city house.
I like it noisy where I stay.
It's very busy where I play.

The D Song

Tune: Farmer in the Dell
I like letter d.
Many words you see
Like duck and drum
And dinosaur
All start with letter d.

Dance, Dance, Dance

Dance fast.
Dance slow.
Dance high.
Dance low.
Dance with a hop.
Dance with a pop.
Dance round and round.
Dance upside down.

The Dreidel Song (Traditional)

Chorus:
I have a little dreidel.
I made it out of clay.
And when it's dry and ready,
Then dreidel I shall play.

Verses:
It has a lovely body,
With legs so short and thin,
And when it is so tired
It drops and then I win!

Chorus

My dreidel's always playful.
It loves to dance and spin.
A happy game of dreidel,
Come play now, let's begin!

Gingerbread Man

_____, _____, as fast as you can.
You can't catch me I'm the gingerbread man!

or

_____, _____ as slowly as you can.
You can't catch me I'm the gingerbread man!

Hickory Dickory Dock (Traditional)

Hickory Dickory Dock
The mouse ran up the clock.
The clock struck one,
The mouse ran down.
Hickory Dickory Dock.

Homes

Tune: I'm a Little Teapot
A fish lives in the great big lake
A bear in a cave, for heaven's sake.
A squirrel lives in a big old tree,
But my home's just the place for me.

I Like Two

Tune: I'm a Little Teapot
Two eyes, two ears, and two big feet,
Two hands that give me food to eat.
I really like the number two.
It means friends like me and you.

I Like You

Tune: Pop Goes the Weasel
I know something you don't know.
It is a special secret.
But I know what I want to do
Is share the secret with you.
Say (I like you).

It's a Wrap

Tune: I'm a Little Teapot
I've got wrap that's blue and green,
The prettiest wrap you've ever seen.
I've got lots of wrap, you see,
To wrap you up just for me.

Jack Be Nimble

Tune: Mary Had a Little Lamb
Jack be nimble, Jack be quick.
Jack be nimble, Jack be quick.
Jack be nimble, Jack be quick.
Jack jumped over the candlestick.

The K Song

Tune: I'm a Little Teapot
I can pretend I'm a kangaroo,
Pour ketchup and blow kisses, too.
I do things all through the day
That begin with the letter k.

Magnets

Tune: I'm a Little Teapot
I can be curved and I can be straight.
I'm a magnet but just wait.
I have something I can do.
If you wear metal, I'll stick to you!

A Mouse Mess Song

Tune: Do Your Ears Hang Low?
I'm a little brown mouse
In a very big house.
On the stairs, I hear feet,
So I know it's time to eat.
I eat crackers and cornflakes,
A big mess is what I make.
Then I go to sleep.

My Senses

Tune: Head, Shoulders, Knees and Toes
Eyes, ears, nose, mouth and hands,
   mouth and hands.
Eyes, ears, nose, mouth and hands,
   mouth and hands.
I use my senses every day.
Eyes, ears, nose, mouth and hands.
   mouth and hands.

My Very Own Button

Tune: I'm a Little Teapot
I wear a button every day,
When I work and when I play.
It's not on my shirt, pants, or hat.
It's my belly button. How about that?

Reindeer, Reindeer Go Away

Tune: Skip to My Lou
Reindeer, reindeer go away.
You don't have time to play.
You have a lot of work today,
Pulling Santa's sleigh.

Ring My Bell

Tune: London Bridge
I will ring my little bell,
Little bell, little bell
I will ring my little bell,
Ring it _____ times. (Put a number in the blank.
   The class sings the song, then rings their jingle
   bells that many times.)

Saint Lucia

Tune: Are You Sleeping?
St. Lucia, St. Lucia,
Coming soon,
Coming soon.
Bringing us light,
To make winter bright,
St. Lucia,
St. Lucia.

The Sticker Game

If you have a sticker that's red,
Pretend you are sleeping in your bed.

If you have a sticker that's blue,
Look around behind you.

If you have a sticker that's green,
Hide your face so you can't be seen

If your sticker is the color yellow,
Show a smile, you friendly fellow

If you have a sticker that's round,
Turn around and touch the ground.

Two Hands, Two Feet

Touch two hands,
Touch two feet,
Touch two heads,
It can't be beat.

Touch two fingers,
Touch two knees,
Touch two noses,
If you please.

Touch two ears,
Touch two thighs,
With two hands,
Wave goodbye!

Adina Kayser's Dreidel Sandwiches

For each child:
2 slices of bread with peanut butter and jelly
Pretzel sticks (3–4)
Celery stick

Help each child make a peanut butter and jelly sandwich. Cut each sandwich into four triangles. Show the children the Hebrew symbols; Hey, Shin, Nan, and Gimmel. Invite each child to make one of the symbols on each triangle with pretzel sticks. Add a celery handle for the top of the driedel. Enjoy.

Kool-Aid Playdough Recipe

Mixing bowl
Measuring cups and spoons
5 cups flour
1 cup salt
4 packages unsweetened Kool-Aid
4 cups boiling water
6 tablespoon vegetable oil

Mix the flour, salt, and Kool-Aid in a bowl. Add the boiling water and the oil. Mix until it forms playdough. Store in an airtight container.

Bacon Ranch Dip

1-ounce package ranch dip seasoning
1 pint sour cream
¼ cup bacon bits
1 cup shredded cheese
Mixing bowl and spoon

Mix together and chill.

Italian Dip

1 cup dairy sour cream
½ cup Zesty Italian Dressing
¼ cup grated Parmesan cheese
Mixing bowl and spoon
Mixing cups

Mix ingredients and chill.

Taco Dip

8 ounces cream cheese
8 ounces sour cream
1 package taco mix
Mixing bowl and spoon
Mixing cups

Mix ingredients and chill.

Sticker Recipe

½ cup water
2 packets of unflavored gelatin
1 teaspoon corn syrup
1 teaspoon vanilla
Saucepan
Mixing spoon
Sticker paper

Boil the water. Stir in unflavored gelatin and then mix in corn syrup and vanilla. Let cool. Brush on sticker paper and let dry. Cut into individual stickers.

USEFUL FACTS AND INFORMATION

Christmas Facts

- Christians celebrate Christmas as a day to honor the birth of Jesus.
- People give gifts at Christmas as a token of goodwill and generosity.
- Legend has it that Santa Claus comes down the chimney and leaves toys and treats for good girls and boys.

Hanukkah Facts

- Jewish people celebrate Hanukkah.
- Hanukkah begins on the 25th day of the month of Kislev, the ninth of the twelve months on the Jewish calendar.
- Hanukkah lasts for 8 days.
- Hanukkah is called the Festival of Lights, a name derived from a miracle in Jewish lore, in which the Jewish people were able to burn a light for eight days necessary for the rededication of Temple Mount in Jerusalem, though they only had enough oil to burn it for one day.
- A menorah holds candles. One is lit on each day of the celebration. Families pray while the candles are being lit.
- A game called dreidel is played with a four-sided spinning top.
- People eat latkes, which are potato pancakes.
- Some families exchange gifts on each of the 8 days.
- Hanukkah celebrates freedom and light.
  For more information, go to the following website http://www.kidsdomain.com/holiday/chanukah/index.html.

Kwanzaa Facts

- This holiday is celebrated by African Americans.
- It was started by Dr. Maulana Kerenga, Ph.D in 1966 as a way to reintroduce the harvest celebrations from traditional African cultures, as well as to celebrate the history of African American.
- Kwanzaa lasts seven days—from December 26 to January 1.
- Each of the seven days celebrates one of the seven principles:
  Self-Determination
  Purpose
  Creativity
  Unity
  Cooperative Work and Responsibility
  Cooperative Economics
  Faith
- Three colors are associated with Kwanzaa:
  Black: for color of the African race
  Red: for the blood shed by African ancestors
  Green: for the land of Africa and hope
- Kwanzaa uses seven symbols, including a mkeka (mat), Kinara (candle holder), seven candles, unity cup, crops, corn, and gifts.
- A Kinara (candle holder) sits on top of the mkeka (mat). Seven candles are placed in the Kinara, three red, one black, and three green. Each day, one candle is lit, starting with the black one in the middle, which represents unity.
- On the last day of Kwanzaa, children receive a gift. For more information, go to the following website, http://www.aakulturezone.com/kidz/abc/kwanzaa.html.

St. Lucia Facts

- In Sweden on December 13, the oldest daughter in the family dresses in a white dress with a red sash and wears a wreath of seven candles on her head. She brings coffee, buns, and gingerbread cookies to her parents. Sisters and brothers follow behind.
- St. Lucia Day is the beginning of the Christmas season in Sweden.
- This is the first day that stores decorate their windows for Christmas.
- St. Lucia is said to make lighter days by coming at the darkest time of the year.
- In Sweden, each town crowns a St. Lucia bride, who brings the message of generosity to the townspeople.

Reindeer Facts

- Reindeer are sometimes called caribou.
- Reindeer are members of the deer family.
- Both male and female reindeer have antlers.
- Female reindeer are called cows, and male reindeer are called bulls.
- Reindeer live together in herds.
- Reindeer are well adapted to winder conditions and can eat less in the winter.
- Reindeer eat lichen. In the winter, reindeer stay in forested areas because lichen grows on trees.
- Some people use reindeer as sources of food, use their hides for clothes, and harness them to sleighs for transportation.
- Reindeer are strong runners and swimmers.
- Reindeer shed their antlers each year.
- The average lifespan of a reindeer is ten years.

January Appendix

Playdough Pies

2 ½ cups flour
½ cup salt
2 package unsweetened drink mix
3 tablespoons oil
2 cups of boiling water

Invite the children to mix the dry ingredients, then add the oil and water (adult-only step), and mix quickly. After the mixture is well stirred, let it cool for 15 minutes. Store the playdough in a zipper plastic bag to keep it fresh. It's possible to make different kinds of playdough by changing the kind of unsweetened drink mix put in the mixture. If, for instance, purple mix is added, the playdough will look purple and smell like grapes. Once the playdough is ready, show the children how to roll it into pie shapes.

Scratch-and-Sniff Pies

Invite the children to cut out piecrust shapes from brown construction paper, as well as several slightly smaller, different colored construction paper circles that will serve as the pie filling. Help the children glue dry flavored gelatin mix to the pie filling pieces (use the chart beneath to match color to gelatin flavor). After the glue dries, invite the children to scratch and sniff their pies.

KIND OF PIE	COLOR OF CIRCLE	GELATIN FLAVOR
Cherry	Red	Cherry
Blueberry	Blue	Blue Raspberry
Lemon	Yellow	Lemon
Chocolate	Brown	Chocolate Pudding

The Blanket Song

Tune: Farmer in the Dell
Blankets are warm.
Blankets are warm.
I put the blanket on my _____.
Blankets are warm.

Additional verses:
Toes, nose, head, knee, eyebrow, elbow, and so on

The Cake Rhyme

_____, _____ you will bake?
You are making a _____ cake.

The Days of the Week

Tune: Mary Had a Little Lamb
Sunday, Monday, Tuesday,
Wednesday, Thursday,
Friday and Saturday.
Days of the week.

Today is Monday, Monday, Monday.
Today is Monday.
Days of the week.

Yesterday was Sunday, Sunday, Sunday.
Yesterday was Sunday,
Days of the week.

Tomorrow is Tuesday, Tuesday, Tuesday.
Tomorrow is Tuesday,
Days of the week.

Dots

If you are sitting on a dot that's red,
Stand up tall and touch your head.

If you are sitting on a dot that is blue,
Say "hello" at the person sitting next to you.

If you are sitting on a dot that is green,
Give someone a smile, do not be mean.

If you are sitting on a dot that is yellow,
Make a funny face, you are a silly fellow.

Five Little Snowmen

Five little snowmen went out to play
In the winter sun one day.
The first one wore a scarf of red.
"See my orange nose?" the second one said.
The third one had a big blue hat.
The fourth one had a little black cat.
The fifth one winked his black coal eyes.
The sun got hot that winter day,
And the five little snowmen melted away.

Go, Team, Go!

Up high,
Down low,
Round and round,
And round you go.

Shake to the left,
Shake to the right,
Go, team, go,
With all your might!

Go, team, go!

Good Night, Girls and Boys

Tune: Good Night, Ladies
Good night, girls.
Good night, boys.
Good night, girls.
We're going to sleep right now.

Wake up, girls.
Wake up, boys.
Wake up, girls.
We're getting up right now.

Hopping High, Hopping Low

Hopping high, hopping low,
Hopping is the way to go.
If you are a kangaroo,
Hopping around is what you do.
Hop! Hop! Hop!

I Am Kind to My Friends

Tune: Skip to My Lou
I am kind to my friends.
I am kind to my friends.
I am kind to my friends.
When I _____. (Let a child finish with
an answer)

I Can Do Whatever I Try

Tune: Mary Had a Little Lamb
I can do whatever I try,
Whatever I try, whatever I try.
I can do whatever I try,
If I think I can.

I Have a Little Snow Friend

Tune: Did You Ever See a Lassie?
I have a little snow friend, a snow friend, a snow friend.
I have a little snow friend and that friend is you.

I Like Winter

I like winter, yes I do
I like winter, how about you?

I'm a Little Penguin

Tune: I'm a Little Teapot
I'm a little penguin in the snow,
I waddle or swim wherever I go.
Some birds think the sun is nice,
But I really like the snow and ice.

I'm a Little Snowflake

Tune: I'm a little Teapot
I'm a little snowflake in the air,
Floating down without a care.
The wind comes and I blow around
Faster, faster to the ground.

The Letter N Song

Tune: London Bridge Is Falling Down
What words start with letter n, letter n, letter n?
What word starts with letter n?
Tell me now. (Ask the children to name n words)

Little Jack Horner (Traditional)

Little Jack Horner
Sat in a corner,
Eating his Christmas pie.
He put in his thumb

And pulled out a plum,
And said, "What a good boy am I!"

The Loud and Quiet Song

Tune: London Bridge
I am singing very loud,
Very loud, very loud.
I am singing very loud
When I yell.

I am singing quietly,
Quietly, quietly.
I am singing quietly
When I whisper.

The Mitten Rhyme

Red mittens, blue mittens,
I've got two mittens.
One for my left and
One for my right.
They keep my hands
Right out of sight.

New Year

We're starting a new year today.
Stand right up and shout hurray.
Count on your fingers one and two
For the new things we will do.
Jump three times right off your feet
For all the new friends you will meet.
Clap four times, sit down, that's cool
For all the learning you'll do at school.

The O Rhyme

Tune: Oh Dear, What Can the Matter Be?
O, O, I like the letter O.
O, O, I like the letter O.
O, O, I like the letter O.
Letter O starts the word _____

The Olympic Song

Tune: The Farmer in the Dell
In the Olympics they _____.
In the Olympics they _____.
People from all over the world
In the Olympics they _____.
For each verse, include one of the following words:
Skate, Ski, and Dance

Pat a Cake (Traditional)

Pat a cake, pat a cake,
Baker's man.
Bake me a _____
As fast as you can.
Roll it, pat it,
Mark it with _____.
Put it in the oven
For my class and me.

Peaches, Cherries, Pears, and Plums

Peaches, cherries, pears, and plums,
Tell me when your birthday comes.

Penguins High, Penguins Low

Penguins high,
Penguins low,
Penguins, penguins,
On the go.

Penguins fast,
Penguins slow,
Penguins, penguins,
On the go.

Penguins small,
Penguins grow,
Penguins, penguins,
On the go.

The Polar Bear Song

Tune: I'm a Little Teapot
I'm a big polar bear in the snow,
And I know which way to go.
I go on a hunt when I want to eat,
For some seal and whale meat.

The Polka Dot Rhyme

I'd do a lot for a little dot.
I'd jump,
I'd hop,
I'd stand,
On one foot.
I'd clap,
I'd snake,
A silly face
I'd make.
I'd do a lot for a little dot.

Ring Around the Ice Rink

Tune: Ring Around the Rosie
(Act out the words fast, slow, moving like a monster, penguin, and so on.)
Ring around the ice rink.
Pockets full of snow.
Slippery, sliding.
We all fall down.

Roll Over (Traditional)

There were five (bears, cats, dogs) in the bed,
And the little one said,
"Roll over, roll over,"
They all rolled over and one fell out....

The Snore Song

Tune: Old MacDonald Had a Farm
The little bear went to sleep,
S-N-O-R-E.
Creatures came and had a party,
S-N-O-R-E,
With an achoo here and an achoo there,
Here a party, there a party,
Then the animals went to sleep,
S-N-O-R-E.

Snowflakes

Snowflakes falling down below,
Quietly, quietly as they go.

The Soup Song

Tune: The Farmer in the Dell
I am making soup.
I am making soup.
I am making alphabet soup.
I'm putting in a _____

Stirring Soup

Stirring soup, 'round and 'round,
I'm stirring up the_____ sound.

The Telescope Rhyme

Look up to the sky.
Look down to the floor.
Look out of the window,
Now out the class door.

Look at something very big.
Look at something blue.
Look at something very small.
Turn and look behind you.

Look at something small and red.
Look at your favorite place to play.
Put your telescope on the floor,
And sit down where you were before.

The Winter Clothes Song

Tune: London Bridge
We're putting on our snow pants,
Our snow pants, our snow pants.
We're putting on our snow pants,
To go out to play.

Next we put our boots on,
Our boots on, our boots on.
Next we put our boots on,
To go out to play.

Then we put our coat on…
Then we put our hat on…
Last we put our mittens on…

Uh-oh, time to come in.
(At this point in the song, encourage the children to pretend to take each item off in reverse order and then sit down.)

RECIPES

Olympic Energy Treats

Mix 1 cup oat cereal, 1 cup raisins, 1 cup pretzels, and 1 cup of marshmallows. Serve a handful to each child.

Playdough

2 ½ cups flour
½ cup salt
2 pkg unsweetened drink mix
3 Tablespoons oil
2 cups of boiling water

Snowflake Pancakes

Give each child a pancake and a doily. Invite the children to cover the pancake with the doily, and sprinkle powdered sugar onto the doily. When the children remove the doilies, the pancakes resemble snowflakes.

Snowman Food

2 cups pretzels
2 cups graham cracker cereal
2 cups tiny marshmallows
2 cups chocolate chips

Mix it all together and serve it with warm (not hot) chocolate.

Snow Friend Snacks

For each child:
3 pieces of bread dough (1 small, 1 medium, 1 large)
Vanilla frosting
Chocolate chips, orange slices and gumdrops (optional)

Cut three pieces of bread dough for each child, one small, one medium, and one large. Encourage the children to roll the dough into balls, and let it rise. Bake according to package directions (adult-only step). When the dough is ready, provide vanilla frosting, orange slices, chocolate chips, and gumdrops for the children to decorate their snow friends.

White Playdough Recipe

4 cups flour
1 cup salt
1 ⅓ cups warm water

Mix thoroughly.

List of Baked Goods

a—apple pie
b—brownies
c—cookies
d—doughnuts
e—eggnog
f—fruit cake
g—gingerbread
h—hard rolls or hot dog buns
i—ice cream pie
j—jelly doughnuts
k—key lime pie
l—lemon pie
m—muffins
n—nut bread
o—oatmeal cookies
p—peanut butter cookies
q—quiche
r—raisin bread
s—sourdough bread
t—torte
u—upside-down cake
v—vanilla cheese cake
w—wheat bread
x—hot cross buns
y—yeast bread
z—zucchini bread

Pajama Party Transition Ideas

- Act like an owl looking for its lunch.
- Act like a raccoon washing its lunch in the stream.
- Act like the moon waking up.
- Act like the sun getting sleepy.
- Act like a star trying to twinkle.
- Act like a morning glory flower that closes at night.
- Act like an opossum running across the road.
- Act like a baker making doughnuts for the morning.
- Act like a robin going to sleep in its nest.

Kangaroo Facts

- Male kangaroos are called boomers, females are called does, and babies are called joeys.
- A group of kangaroos is called a mob.
- Kangaroos have large rear feet and smaller feet in front.
- Kangaroos are marsupials, meaning that the female has a pouch for babies.
- Most kangaroos are native to Australia.
- Kangaroo's fight by boxing and kicking their legs.
- Babies stay in the pouch for 6 months, but still go in and out of the pouch for up to one year.
- Kangaroo's eat grasses and low growing plants.

Penguin Facts

- Penguins are birds.
- Penguins cannot fly, but they are very fast and good swimmers.
- Penguins live in the Southern Hemisphere in cold climates.
- Penguins like to eat krill, fish, squid, and other sea life.
- In summer, penguins like to swim.
- In fall, penguins walk across the land to a special place to lay their eggs.
- Daddies keep the eggs warm on their feet.
- Gray baby chicks grow up together in big groups called a rockery.
- Male and female penguins look the same, but they make different sounds.
- Penguins mate for life.

Polar Bear Facts

- Polar bears are one of the biggest and strongest of all animals.
- Polar bears walk on all four feet, and love to play in the snow.
- Polar bears are strong swimmers. Their heavy coats protect them from arctic waters.
- Polar bears have black noses and skin and white fur.
- Polar bears eat fish and other animals.

February Appendix

Birdseed Book

Set out several different bird shapes and several cups of different types of seeds. Encourage the children to match certain birds to certain kinds of seeds and glue them onto individual pages. When the glue dries, help the children write the bird and seed name on the page in a manner similar to that shown below:

Page 1:

Red Cardinal, Red Cardinal, what do you need?
"I need to eat a sunflower seed."

Page2:

Black Crow, Black Crow, what do you need?
"I need to eat a black oil seed."

Page 3:

Blue Jay, Blue Jay, what do you need?
"I need to eat a sunflower seed."

Page 4

Sparrow, Sparrow, what do you need?
I need to eat a thistle seed.

Page 5

Robin, Robin, what do you need?
I need to eat some berry seeds. (small blue and red pom poms)

Page 6

All birds, all birds, what do you need?
We need water and lots of bird seed.

Silhouettes

Use an overhead projector or a flashlight to outline each child's silhouette on a large sheet of black paper attached to the wall. Encourage one child to draw in chalk the outline of the child's silhouette on the black paper. When each child has his outline drawn, carefully cut each one out. Set out several sheets of white construction paper, red and blue paint, and invite the children to marble paint the sheets. To marble paint, put a sheet of paper in a shallow shirt box lid, add a few little dabs of paint to the top of the piece of paper, and invite a child to roll a marble through the paint, making designs on the paper. When dry, cut the painted construction paper into large heart shapes and glue them to the silhouettes. Display with the title "Whose Shadow?" This makes a wonderful valentine gift.

Weather Words Book

Page 1: Sunny

Cut out white construction paper suns for the children to paint with a white glue/water mixture. Help the children cover the shapes with yellow and orange tissue paper squares. When the suns are dry, glue them to the page and write "Sunny" above them.

Page 2: Rainy

Prepare several construction paper raindrop shapes. Invite the children to cover one in glitter. Help the children cut lightning shapes out of cardboard and wrap them in aluminum foil. Glue both objects to another sheet of paper and write "Rainy" above them.

Page 3: Snowy

Prepare several cutout cardboard snowflake shapes from blue construction paper. (If children are older, they may be able to cut their own snowflakes from folded paper.) Mix glue with white glitter or salt and glue to the snowflake shape to a sheet of paper, writing the word "Snowy" above it.

Page 4: Cloudy

Mix cotton balls together in a paper bag filled with black or gray powder paint. When the cotton balls are dry, invite the children to glue the cotton balls to a sheet of paper with "Cloudy" written above them.

My World Book
Title page: My World by _____
Page 1 : Wiggling _____.
Page 2: Dancing_____.
Page 3: Growing _____.
Page 4: Glittering _____.
Page 5: Thank you, world. (Blue circle world shape)

SONGS AND POEMS

The Ambulance Song

Tune: Bumpin' Up and Down in My Little Red
    Wagon
Hurry, hurry, drive the ambulance.
Hurry, hurry drive the ambulance.
Hurry, hurry drive the ambulance.
Ding, ding, ding ding, ding.

Additional verses:
    … check the patient.
    … load the patient.
    … drive to the hospital.
    … slowly, slowly go back home.

Brush Your Teeth

Tune: Are You Sleeping?
Brush your teeth, brush your teeth,
Every day, Every day,
Eat healthy foods.
Visit the dentist
For healthy teeth, for healthy teeth.

Five Little Birds

Five little birds flew out one day
Over the trees and far away
Mama Bird said, "Cheep, cheep, cheep, cheep"
Only four flew back to sleep….

Happy Valentine's Day

Tune: Bumpin' Up and Down in My Little Red
    Wagon
One little, two little, three little hearts,
Four little, five little, six little hearts,
Seven little, eight little, nine little hearts,
Happy Valentine's Day.

Hi-Ho, the Hospital

Tune: The Farmer in the Dell
The doctor at the hospital,
The doctor at the hospital,
Hi ho hospital-o,
The doctor at the hospital.

Additional verses:
The doctor takes the nurse…
The nurse takes the tech…
The tech takes the aide…
The aide takes the patient…
The patient takes the shot!

I Eat Healthy Foods

Tune: I'm Bringing Home a Baby Bumblebee:
I eat healthy foods as you can see
Because I take good care of me
I exercise to grow so big and strong
And sleep so very well all night long

I'm a Little Cardinal

Tune: I'm a Little Teapot
I'm a little cardinal,
Look at me.
I am high in the evergreen tree.
When I get hungry, I fly away.
I could eat sunflower seeds all day.

I'm a Mail Carrier

Tune: I'm a Little Teapot
I'm a mail carrier dressed in blue.
Let me tell you what I do.
I go from house to house to deliver the mail,
In wind and snow and sleet and hail.

I'm a Weather Person

Tune: I'm a Little Teapot
I'm a weather person on TV.
I'll tell you what the weather will be.
Sometimes it's rainy, sunny, or there's snow.
Listen to me and then you'll know.

Monster Cake

Tune: I'm a Little Teapot
Take some spider legs
And wings of bat.
Stir it up with a great big splat.
Add some muddy water and let it bake,
Then you have a monster cake.

My Country

Tune: Mary Had a Little Lamb
I live in the United States, United States,
*   United States.*
I live in the United States
That's my country.

My Heart Beats

Tune: The Farmer in the Dell
My heart beats every day.
When I work and play
When I rest my heart beats slow
And faster as I go.

To have a healthy heart
I have to do my part.
Eat healthy, exercise and sleep
A healthy heart I'll keep.

On Goes My Flashlight!

Tune: Pop Goes the Weasel
I'm sitting in the dark night
I'm getting a little worried
I hear a noise go bumpity, bump
ON goes my flashlight.

Put Your Heart...

Put your heart the color red,
Way up high, on top your head.

Put your heart, the color blue
On the top of your shoe.

Yellow heart look at me.
Put your heart on top your knee.

Little green hearts who are here
Put your heart upon your ear.

Put orange hearts on your toe
Purple hearts on your elbow.

Pink hearts on your lip.
White hearts on your hip.

Rat Race

Five little rats were in a race.
Each one wanted to be in first place.
The first rat ran very slow.
The second thought hopping was the way to go.
The third little rat decided to walk.
The fourth little rat decided to run.
But it was the fifth little rat that won.

Saw a Penny

Tune: Mary Had a Little Lamb
Saw a penny, picked it up,
Picked it up, picked it up.
Saw a penny, picked it up,
Now I'll have good luck.

Soap

I wash my face everyday,
Before I go to school or play.
I wash my hands before I eat,
After the bathroom, or a treat.

Thank You, World!

Tune: Do Your Ears Hang Low:
I like wiggling worms and leaping frogs
I like singing birds and swimming fish
I like falling leaves and blooming flowers
Thank you, world!

This Is the Way I Wash My Body

Tune: Here We Go 'Round the Mulberry Bush
This is the way I wash my _____
Wash my _____, wash my ___.
This is the way I wash my _____
Every day.

The V Song

Tune: Oh Dear What Can the Matter Be?
V, V, V is for vegetable,
V, V, V is for vegetable,
V, V, V is for vegetable.
I like the vegetable _____.

Wave Your Flag

If you have a flag that's red
Move it way above your head.

All flags high, all flags low,
Round and round and round you go.

If you have a flag that's blue
Put your flag behind you

All flags high, all flags low,
Round and round and round you go.

Yellow flags go to your right
Wave them fast with all your might.

All flags high, all flags low
Round and round and round you go.

On your left, the green flags go
Wave them very, very slow.

All flags high, all flags low,
Round and round and round you go.

Where, Oh, Where Is the Little Groundhog?

Tune: Where, Oh Where Has My Little Dog Gone?
Where, oh, where is the little groundhog?
Oh where, oh where, can he be?
Will he see his shadow,
Or go back to sleep?
Oh Where oh where can he be?

RECIPES

Bird's Nests

(Safety Note: Be sure to check for allergies before making this recipe.)
1 cup corn syrup
1 cup granulated sugar
1 ½ cups peanut butter
6 cups crispy cereal
Candies, optional

Stir 1 cup corn syrup and 1 cup granulated sugar in a sauce pan over high heat until it boils. Pour the mixture into a bowl with 1 ½ cups of peanut butter. Mix. Stir until mixed. Add 6 cups of a crispy cereal and stir until mixed. Mold spoonfuls into nest shapes. When dry, add circle candies as eggs.

Heart Biscuit Pizza

Ingredients for each child:
1 canned biscuit, such as Pillsbury® dough
pizza sauce
pizza toppings

Give each child a biscuit to shape into a heart. Add pizza sauce and toppings. Bake as directed. Enjoy.

Mailbox Meal

Ingredients for each child:
1 pretzel log (wooden post)
1 white bread sandwich rectangle with the crusts cut off (mailbox)
1 mailbox flag cut from a red fruit leather

Put the pieces together to make a mailbox.

Peanut Treats

1 container (8 oz) soft cream cheese
½ cup peanut butter
1 pkg (6 oz) chocolate chips melted
2 ¼ cups graham cracker crumbs
⅔ cups finely chopped peanuts

In large mixing bowl, mix the ingredients. Shape into 1-inch balls. Chill. It makes 4 dozen.

Rabbit Faces

1 piece of toast for each child
Peanut butter
Bananas
Raisins
Black licorice

Prepare a piece of toast for each child, cutting it into a circle shape. Encourage each child to spread peanut butter on his circle, then stand a banana half (or smaller if the bananas are large) up on the toast for ears. Provide the children with several raisins for eyes and noses, and use black shoestring licorice for whiskers.

March Appendix

Cartons of Milk

Tune: 99 Bottles of Pop
Ten cartons of milk in the fridge,
Ten cartons of milk.
Take one down, pass it around,
Nine cartons of milk in the fridge.

The Chicka Alphabet

Tune: Twinkle, Twinkle, Little Star
ABCDEFG,
Going up the coconut tree,
HIJKLMN,
Going right back down again,
OPQRSTU,
What now are you going to do?
VWXYZ.
Hang out by the coconut tree!

The Colors of Spring

Tune: Up on the Housetop
The sun is shining up in the blue sky.
Fluffy white clouds are floating by.
The green grass is starting to grow.
Birds are building brown nests just so.
Red, yellow, blue flowers, too.
A purple kite high in flight
I love the colors of spring each day,
As I run and climb and play.

The Cowboy Song

Tune: The Wheels on the Bus
The song of the cowboy goes yippie ky ay,
*   yippie ky ay, yippie ky ay*
The song of the cowboy goes yippie ky aye
All across the range.

Additional verses:
The chaps on the cowboy go swish, swish, swish…
The tail of the snake goes rattle, rattle, rattle…
The cow in the herd goes moo, moo, moo…
Howl of the coyote goes yowl, yowl, yowl…

Down in the Kingdom

Tune: Up on the Housetop
Down in the kingdom's where I live.
I obey rules that the king gives.
I wear a heavy armor of gray.
And fight dragons every day.
"Ride, ride, ride, on my horse
I will save the princess, of course.
Down to the castle, I will go,
To save the kingdom from its foe.

Early in the Morning

Tune: Mulberry Bush
This is the way we stir the eggs,
Stir the eggs, stir the eggs.
This is the way we stir the eggs,
So early in the morning.

Additional verses:
…flip the pancakes…
…fry the bacon…
…set the table…
…eat the food…
…clear the table…

Five Little Kites

Five little kites way up in the sky
Blowing in the wind, flying high
They swooped way up and way down low
And one little kite hit the ground below.

Four little kites way up in the sky
Blowing in the wind, flying high.
One little kite got stuck in a tree.
Now in the sky, there's only three

Three little kites up in the sky
Blowing in the wind, flying high.
One little kite lost his tail of blue
Now in the sky there's only two

Two little kites, way up in the sky
Blowing in the wind, flying high.
One little kite said "It's been fun
But I'm going down, now there's just one.

One little kite way up in the sky
Blowing in the wind, flying high.
The last little kite flew into the sun.
Now in the sky, there are none.

The Flower Song

Tune: Twinkle, Twinkle, Little Star
Red flowers, yellow flowers, orange, and blue,
Green flowers, indigo, and violet, too.
Little flowers growing tall,
Making a rainbow with them all.
Red flowers, yellow flowers, orange, and blue
Green flowers, indigo, and violet, too.

For He's a Very Good Artist

Tune: For He's a Jolly Good Fellow
For (child's name)'s a very good artist
For (child's name)'s a very good artist

For (child's name)'s a very good artist
For he/she can (name something the child can do).

The Fruit Song

Tune: London Bridge
Apples, peaches, pears, and plums,
Pears and plums, pears and plums.
Apples, peaches, pears and plums,
Tell me when your birthday comes.

The Green Song

Tune: BINGO
I mixed blue paint with some yellow,
And it turned to green-o,
G-r-e-e-n, g-r-e-e-n, g-r-e-e-n,
And it turned to green-o.

If This Music Makes You Happy

Tune: If You're Happy and You Know It
If this music makes you happy, clap your hands.
If this music makes you happy, clap your hands.
If you're happy and you know it, then your face
*   will surely show it.*
If this music makes you happy, clap your hands.
*   (Play sad music and sing)*
If this music makes you sad, clap your hands…

I'm a Little Artist

Tune: I'm a Little Teapot
I'm a little artist as you see.
I'm the best that I can be.
I can draw pictures and paint them, too,
In red, green, yellow, black, orange and blue.

I'm a Little Kite

Tune: I'm a Little Teapot
I'm a little kite and I fly high
Way up in the bright blue sky.
When the wind stops,
I fall down,
Down, down, down, down
To the ground.

I'm a Little Potato

Tune: I'm a Little Teapot
I'm a potato, brown and round
Don't have a mouth, so I don't make a sound.
But I have eyes to help me grow.
But no nose to smell you know.

The Leprechaun Song

Tune: Oscar Mayer Weiner Song
Oh, I wish I were a little green leprechaun.
That is what I really want to be
'Cause if I were a little green leprechaun
No one would be able to see me.

The Lily Pad Game

Froggies stand on the lily pad.
Froggies stand in front of the lily pad.
Froggies stand behind the lily pad.
Froggies jump over the lily pad.
Froggies stand on the lily pad.
Jump three times on the lily pad.

The Muffin Chant

Tune: Who Stole the Cookie from the Cookie Jar?
Who took the muffin from the bakery?
_____ (child's name) took the muffin from
the bakery.
"Who Me? Couldn't be."
_____ (child names new child) stole the
muffin from the bakery.

The Nine Rhyme

Hop nine times.
Clap nine times.
Jump nine times.
Snap nine times.
Now as plain as you can see,
I'm as tired as I can be.

Oh, Where Have You Been, Little Cowpoke?

Tune: Where Have You Been, Billy Boy?
Oh, where have you been, little cowpoke, little
cowpoke?
Oh, where have you been, little cowpoke?
I've been riding on my horse
In my hat and boots, of course,
Doing tricks and roping all the cattle.

A Penny in My Pocket

I had to go to school today
I cried and made a fuss.
Mom put a penny in my pocket
And put me on the bus.

On the bus, I kicked and yelled,
And tried to get away.
The driver put a penny in my pocket,
So in my seat I'd stay.

I got to school and held on tight
I wouldn't go inside.
A penny in my pocket from a teacher
So I ran into school to hide.

Inside the school and under the desk
I refused to come out.
"I'll give you something for your pocket,"
I heard my teacher shout.

I made out pretty good at school.
Not a bad day.
I have four pennies in my pocket,
So I guess, I'll go and play.

The Photograph Song

Tune: Mary Had a Little Lamb
Who is in the photograph, photograph,
*   photograph?*
Who is in the photograph?
Please stand up. (The child in the photograph
*   stands up)

Pretend You Are a Kite

Pretend you are a kite, sailing high
In the big, wide open sky.
Here comes a cloud, now dance around,
Swoop up high, now down to the ground.
The sun is getting hot, oh my!
From way up high, you'll see the town.
Uh, oh! The wind is gone, fall back down.

Roll Over (Traditional)

There were nine in the bed and the little one said,
"Roll over, roll over."
So they all rolled over and one fell out.

There were 8 in the bed and the little one said,
"Roll over, roll over."
So they all rolled over and one fell out.

Continue until there is one in the bed.

There was one in the bed and the little one said,
"Ahhhh! Alone at last."

Round and Round

Touch two ears.
Touch your toe.
Round and round and round you go.

Touch your tummy.
Touch your toe.
Round and round and round you go.

Touch two eyes.
Touch your toe.
Round and round and round you go.

Touch two elbows.
Touch your toe.
Round and round and round you go.

Six Little Cows

Tune: Six Little Ducks That I Once Knew
Six little cows that I once knew.
Fat one, skinny ones, fair ones, too.
One little cow didn't know what to do.
He led the others with a moo, moo, moo.

Six little horses that I once knew.
Fat ones, skinny ones, fair ones too.
One little horse went to play one day.
He led the others with a neigh, neigh, neigh.

Six Little Kites

Six little kites up in the sky,
Six little kites go flying by.
Four little kites fell down, oh my,
But two are flying way up high.

Six little cookies on a plate,
Hurry let's grab them, don't be late.
Six little cookies, what should we do?
Three for me and three for you.

Six little flowers in the ground,
Growing up without a sound.
Six little flowers in a flowerbed,
Five are blue and one is red.

The Smell Song

Tune: Pop Goes the Weasel
All around the neighborhood
There is a funny smell.
I cover my nose and run and hide
P U a skunk!

The Springtime Song

Tune: Farmer in the Dell
I'm planting flower seeds.
I'm planting flower seeds.
I'm planting seeds in springtime.
I'm planting flower seeds.

Additional verses
I'm flying a kite...
I'm flying a kite in springtime

I'm riding on my bike...
I'm riding my bike in springtime

I'm jumping over puddles...
I'm jumping puddles in springtime

A Sticky Situation

Shamrocks go up, valentines come down.
That means trouble for the school side of town.
A wee little elf sneaks into the school,
And looks around for someone to fool.

Smaller than my finger, bigger than my thumb,
From over the rainbow, this leprechaun did come.
Dressed all in green from his head to his toes.
He has scruffy red hair and a lumpy nose.

He stands up straight and turns to say,
"I'll stay until St. Patrick's Day.
Ha, ha, ha, you can't catch me!
I'm Leprechaun Lee and I am free!"

He tips the plants out of the pots.
He ties the string up into knots.
He puts green paint all over the door.
He leaves green footprints on the floor.

Then he writes a little note to say,
"I'll stay until St. Patrick's Day.
Ha, ha, ha, you can't catch me!
I'm Leprechaun Lee and I am free!"

The school bell rings, the children come back.
Ready to wash their hands for a snack.
Johnny was first to the messy green door.
He yelled, "Green footprints all over the floor."

The children rush in, "The leprechaun's back!
We have not time to eat our snack.
Let's get to work and make a plan.
If anyone can catch him, we sure can."

Katie said, "Use a butterfly net."
Joey had the best idea yet.
He said, "Let's make a giant trap.
With lots of doors and a secret flap."

Hiding, Lee shook his head,
Laughed and laughed, and then he said,
"Ha, ha, ha, you can't catch me!
I'm Leprechaun Lee and I am free!"

Hammers, nails, boxes, and glue,
String and tape, and markers too.
Everyone worked, but in their haste
They dropped a little glob of paste.

The bell rang just as the work was done.
Ben said, "Tomorrow will be fun.
We'll catch a leprechaun and I'm told,
He'll have to give us the pot of gold."

The children left, the lights went out.
Out came Lee and he did shout,
"Ha, ha, ha, you can't catch me.
I'm Leprechaun Lee and I am free!"

He made a mess of all the books.
He switched the nametags on the hooks.
Lee walked over to the giant trap
And played all night with the secret flap.

Morning came, it was time to hide.
Lee took a car for one last ride.
Lee heard kids coming, and in his haste
He stepped right into that glob of paste.

Lee tried to walk and said, "Just my luck.
What will I do? My foot is stuck!"
He twisted and twirled and turned about,
He could not get his little foot out.

Lee Finally said, "I know what I'll do."
He pulled his foot right out of his shoe.
He ran and hid behind a block,
In one green shoe and one little sock.

The teacher came in and turned on the light.
"What a mess! What a horrible sight."

This leprechaun has got to go!
It is St. Patrick's Day, you know."

From the doll house, in his favorite chair,
A leprechaun, laughing to himself in there.
The kids came in and ran to the trap.
As Lee closed his eye to take a nap.

Johnny said, "The room is such a mess.
The trap idea didn't work, I guess."
Then Tim screamed, "A leprechaun shoe!
It's in that little glob of glue.

"He's in here somewhere," Ryan said.
The leprechaun jumped off the bed.
"That's it, we'll find him, he won't get away.
We'll have that pot of gold today."

The leprechaun hobbled under a chair.
"Ha ha! They'll never find me in there."
But as a big shoe started walking his way,
The leprechaun thought he'd better not stay.

He hopped to the window that was open a crack.
He had to get out and never look back.
The kids were getting closer, as he bit his lip.
Squeezing out of the window, he heard a big rip.

He shook his head as he looked down.
He looked less like a leprechaun and more like a
    clown.
This little leprechaun was standing there
With one shoe off, in his underwear.

It's St. Patrick's Day, Lee had to go
Back to his home on the rainbow.
He left candy gold coins for the class here.
He will come back to school next year.

The kids found the candy and the note to say,
"I stayed until St. Patrick's Day.

Ha ha ha, you didn't catch me!
I'm Leprechaun Lee, and I am free!

Swoosh Goes the Wind

Tune: Do Your Ears Hang Low?
Swoosh goes the wind through the leaves on the
*   trees.*
And swoosh goes the wind to the clouds that I see
And swoosh goes the wind to the kite in the sky
As it dances by.

Three Little Pigs

Tune: Three Blind Mice
Three little pigs, three little pigs,
They each built a house.
They each built a house.
One used straw and one used sticks,
One made his house with very strong bricks.
Three little pigs, three little pigs.

The Train Song

Tune: Do Your Ears Hang Low?
I'm a little train,
And I sit upon the track.
I take train cars places,
And I bring them back.
I pull heavy loads everywhere I go,
Sometimes fast and slow.
Toot! Toot!

The Veggie Soup Song

Tune: The Farmer in the Dell
I'm making veggie soup,
I'm making veggie soup,
Hi Ho, I'm healthy, so
I'm making veggie soup.

The chef takes the carrot,
The chef takes the carrot,
Hi ho he's healthy, so
The chef takes the carrot.

Additional verses
The carrot takes the beans...
The beans take the peas...
The peas take the potato...

Veggies in My Lunch

Give me veggies in my lunch.
Munch, munch, munch.
Carrots, beans, corn, and peas,
Please give me more of these!
Crunch, crunch, crunch.

The Wind Song

Tune: The Wheels on the Bus
The wind makes the trees blow back and forth
back and forth, back and forth
The wind makes the trees blow back and forth
All through the day.

Additional Verses:
The wind makes the door blow open and shut...
The wind makes the balloons go up, up, up...
The wind makes the kite go up and down...

Aunt Alvina's Banana Bread

Mix together:

½ cup butter	1 cup sugar
2 beaten eggs	½ cup hot water
2 cups flour	1 ½ tsp baking powder
1 tsp salt	½ tsp baking soda
2 mashed bananas	1 cup walnuts

Put in a loaf pan and bake at 350° for 40–60 minutes. Serve warm with butter.

Cinnamon Rolls

Buy enough frozen bread dough to give each child a ball of the dough. Invite the children to roll the dough flat. With knife or craft stick, butter the top of the dough. Next, cover the top of the butter with brown sugar. Sprinkle a layer of cinnamon on top. Roll the dough into a log. Cut the log into 1" slices. Put the dough into greased pans and put them in a warm place. Let them rise until the rolls almost double in size. Cook at 350° until brown.

Coconut Trees

Ingredients per child:
1 pretzel rod "tree trunk"
2–3 spearmint leaf candy pieces
2 "coconut" grapes
Alphabet cereal to place on the tree trunk
small paper plate

Put the pretzel rod tree trunk on the plate. Put the spearmint candy leaves on the top of the pretzel tree trunk. Add the coconut grapes. Put alphabet cereal around the tree on the plate. Enjoy.

Fruit Dip

1 7–ounce jar of marshmallow creme
1 8–ounce package of cream cheese

Kool-Aid Playdough Recipe

2 ½ cups flour	½ cup of salt
2 pkg unsweetened Kool-Aid	3 Tbsp oil
2 cups boiling water	

Mix dry ingredients. Add oil and water. Stir quickly and cool.

Piggy Snacks

(makes 1 snack)
½ English muffin, toasted
strawberry cream cheese and a craft stick to spread it
½ large marshmallow (nose)
2 raisins (nostrils)
2 blueberries (eyes)

Pinwheel Bread

Take out a square of dough for each child. Do not break it into triangles. Make another crease across the dough so the two creases make an X. Take the right side of each triangle that makes up the square in to the center and pinch it tight to make a pinwheel shape. Bake according to package directions.

Potato Skins

Clean one potato for each child and bake potatoes until done. Take the potatoes out of the oven. Cut potatoes in half and scoop the insides into a bowl. Mash the potatoes. Scoop mashed potatoes back into the potato skins. Add shredded cheese and return to the oven until the cheese melts

Pudding in a Bag

Ingredients for each child
1 zipper plastic bag
¼ cup of milk
1 tbsp instant pudding powder

Directions: Invite each student to put 1/4 cup milk and 1 tbsp pudding powder in the zipper bag. Seal the bag. Squish the bag until the milk and powder mix to make pudding.

Rainbow Bars

1 package miniature marshmallows
¼ cup butter
6 cups fruit-colored circle cereal

Melt butter in a large saucepan over low heat. Add marshmallows and stir until completely melted. Add cereal and stir. Put in a greased 9" x 13" pan. Children can eat immediately, though it is less messy and easier to clean up if the children wait before eating.

Veggie Dip

1 package of ranch dressing mix
1 small carton of sour cream

Mix together and chill.

USEFUL FACTS AND OTHER INFORMATION

Artist Facts

Oscar Claude Monet

- Monet was born in France on November 14, 1840.
- Monet started "Impressionism." He tried to paint the feeling of a place, right at the moment it was painted.
- Monet went to art school with friends Auguste Renoir, Alfred Sisley and Frederic Bazille. They were also Impressionists.
- Monet was interested in the way light changed things.
- Monet painted outside, even when it was hot, cold, or snowy.
- Monet became obsessed with landscapes of water and reflections

Georgia O'Keefe

- She was born in 1887, in Sun Prairie, WI.
- In 1905, O'Keefe attended the Art Institute of Chicago.
- She worked as a commercial artist and taught art before returning to school, attending teacher's college.
- O'Keefe met and married photographer Alfred Stiglitz after he put several of her paintings up for sale in his gallery in New York City.
- O'Keefe is best known for the flower paintings she made in the 1920s. At the end of that decade, she traveled to the Southwest, and made a number of famous landscape paintings.
- O'Keefe died in March, 1986, at the age of 98.

Pablo Picasso

- When he was born on October 25, 1881, in Spain, people thought Picasso was dead, but an uncle revived him.
- Picasso's father was a painter, but he took a job as a teacher to support the family. By age 13, Picasso's father said that Pablo had surpassed him as an artist and his father never painted again.
- Picasso thought art should reflect the artist's innermost feelings and dreams.
- Picasso changed his style of painting according to the object he painted.
- Picasso had a "Blue Period"—all his paintings are done in shades of blue. He painted poor mothers, children, and old men.
- He also had a "Rose Period"—all paintings are done in red, yellows, and soft rose pink. Most paintings in this period are of circus people.

- Picasso explored cubism in which all his paintings were geometric shapes.
- Picasso died in 1975 at the age of 91.

Andy Warhol
- Andy Warhol did not like to give out information about his past, saying that he changed it every time he had to say anything about it.
- He was born between 1927 and 1930 to Czechoslovakian immigrant parents.
- A quiet and shy child, after high school, he attended the Carnegie Institute.
- He worked in advertising after college, where he specialized in illustrations of shoes.
- In the 1950s and 1960s, Warhol helped develop Pop Art, and created his best-known works in his studio, The Factory.
- He famously said that in the future, everyone would be world famous for fifteen minutes.
- Warhol died on February 22, 1987.

Frank Lloyd Wright
- Frank Lloyd Wright was born on June 8, 1867 in Richland Center, Wisconsin.
- His mother bought him blocks when he was 9 years old to help him learn about geometry, color, and mathematics.
- He became an architect—a person who designs buildings.
- Wright liked nature and used nature's colors to make houses blend in with nature.
- Wright designed "Prairie" houses. These houses had no attics or basements. He felt things should be thrown away.
- Wright is the most famous American architect.

Pig Facts

- Pigs live everywhere in the world except Antarctica.
- The Chinese people first domesticated pigs about 7,000 years ago.
- Domesticated means "tamed."
- Pigs are scavengers, which means they will eat anything.
- Pigs are very intelligent and more trainable than dogs and cats.
- Pigs are very clean and will go to the bathroom only in certain places.
- Pigs do not sweat. They are fair skinned and can become sunburned. Pigs avoid this by wallowing in the mud to cool down.
- Pigs are social animals. They communicate with each other in a language of calls, snorts, sniffs, and whistles.
- Pigs that weigh more than 180 pounds are called hogs. Hogs are raised on farms for food.
- Female pigs are called sows, some males are called boars, and babies are piglets.
- Some people own pigs as pets.
- Resources:
  www.pbs.org/wnet/nature/critters
  www.pbs.org/wnet/nature/pigs

Potato Facts

- The potato was introduced to Ireland around the turn of the seventeenth century.
- It provided a simple and plentiful source of nourishment.
- Families often survived off potatoes when they had little else to eat.
- Unfortunately, in 1845, a fungus appeared in Ireland, destroying the potato crops for the next few years. As a result there was widespread famine and starvation throughout Ireland, killing almost one million people, and forcing another million to leave Ireland for the United States in search of a new life.

April Appendix

April Showers

Tune: London Bridge
April showers falling down,
Falling down, falling down.
April showers falling down,
Bring May flowers.

Bag, Bag

Bag, bag, what can you do?
Hold your bag in front of you.

Bag, bag, hold it high,
Hold it way up to the sky.

Bag, bag, what can you do?
Hid your bag behind you

Bag, bag, what can you do?
Put your bag under you

Bag, bag, don't be shy,
Hand in your bag and wave good bye.

Bunnies Hopping

Bunnies hopping to and fro.
Bunnies, where will you go?
Bunnies hopping through and through.
Put your bunnies _____ you.
in front of you
behind you
on top
under
beside

Chameleon, Where Will You Go?

_____ chameleon, where will you go?
So you can hide and we won't know.

Earth Day Helper

I trim the grass,
I plant some seeds,
I water flowers,
I pull out weeds.
I am an Earth Day Helper,
Keeping the Earth clean.
I want to help to keep the land
Beautiful to be seen.

Flowers Don't Eat Cheeseburgers

Tune: Did You Ever See a Lassie?
Flowers don't eat cheeseburgers, pizza or
*   ice cream.*
Flowers don't eat cookies or even dog bones.
But they do need some raindrops and sunshine
*   and dirt.*
Maybe some talking and love won't hurt.

Flowers Growing One by One

Tune: The Ants Go Marching
Flowers growing one by one hurrah, hurrah
Flowers growing one by one hurrah, hurrah
Flowers growing one by one,
With water, dirt and lots of sun
Flowers growing in the sun, in the sun.

Flowers growing two by two, hurrah, hurrah
Flowers growing two by two, hurrah, hurrah
Flowers growing two by two
Red and yellow , white and blue
Flowers growing in the sun, in the sun.

Flowers growing three by three hurrah, hurrah
Flowers growing three by three hurrah, hurrah
Flowers growing three by three
Danced on by a buzzing bee
Flowers growing in the sun, in the sun

Flowers growing four by four hurrah, hurrah
Flowers growing four by four hurrah, hurrah
Flowers growing four by four
Flowers growing more and more
Flowers growing in the sun, in the sun

Flowers growing five by five, hurrah, hurrah
Flowers growing five by five hurrah, hurrah
Flowers growing five by five
Very close to a big beehive
Flowers growing in the sun, in the sun

For What It's Worth

_____, _____ for what it's worth,
How will you take care of earth?

Hop, Hop, Hop

Hop, hop, hop,
Don't be slow,
_____ bunny,
It's time to go.

Humpty Dumpty Sat on the Ground

Humpty Dumpty sat on the ground.
There you will stay, safe and sound,
You cannot fall
Any way at all
And you can have ____ for breakfast again.

If You Take a Little Red

Tune: Do Your Ears Hang Low?
If you take a little red,
And you add a little blue,
And you mix it, mix it, mix it,
And when you're through
You will look and see:
Another color it will be.
Surprise, it's purple.

If Your Paper Clip Is Blue

If your paper clip is blue,
Take off your shoe.
If your paper clip is red,
Shake, shake, shake your head.
If your paper clip is black,
Pat yourself on your back.
If your paper clip is white ,
Hide your face out of sight.
If your paper clip is yellow,
Wave to the class, a big hello.
If your paper clip is pink,
Give a friend a great big wink.
If your paper clip is green,
Smile now and don't be mean.

I Live on Earth As You Can See

Tune: I'm Bringing Home a Baby Bumblebee
I live on the earth and as you can see.
The earth takes very good cared of me.
So I should do everything I can do.
To help take care of the earth too.

I'm a Little Chameleon

Tune: Do Your Ears Hang Low?
I'm a little chameleon dressed in yellow,
I'm a very slippery and sneaky fellow.
I can turn orange with stripes or even blue.
That's the way I can hide from you.

I'm a Little Duck

Tune: I'm a Little Teapot
I'm a little duck and I love to play
Out in raindrops on a rainy day.
I swim, take a bath and then I play.
I just love a rainy day.

I'm a Little Earthworm

Tune: I'm a Little Teapot
I'm a little earthworm in the ground.
I stretch my body to get around.
I can make my body very small.
And really stretch to make me tall.

I'm a Little Seed

Tune: I'm a Little Teapot
I'm a little seed,
I'm in the ground,
In my blanket of soil, safe and sound.
Then the sun shines and rains start to fall,
I start to grow so very tall.

I'm a Little Tree Changing All the Time

Tune: She'll be Coming 'Round the Mountain
I'm a little tree changing all the time, all the time.
I'm a little tree changing all the time, all the time.
Even though I stay right here,
I am changing through the year
I'm a little tree changing all the time, all the time.

In the Spring I have little green buds, little buds.
In the Spring, I have little green buds, little buds.
That's the way you know
That I'm starting to grow.
In the Spring, I have little green buds, little buds.

In the summer, I have big green leaves, green leaves.
In the summer, I have big green leaves, green leaves.
I will come to your aid
For my leaves will give you shade.
In the summer I have big green leaves, green leaves.

My leaves will turn colors in the Fall, in the Fall.
My leaves will turn colors in the Fall, in the Fall.
They'll turn red and orange and brown,
And fall down to the ground.
My leaves will turn colors in the Fall.

In the cold and snowy winter, I will sleep, I will sleep.
In the cold and snowy winter, I will sleep, I will sleep.
In my cozy blanket of snow
I'll rest up so I can grow.
In the cold and snowy winter I will sleep, I will sleep.

Letter L

Tune: Three Blind Mice
Letter L,
It's very swell.
It has many words, that you have heard,
Ladybug, ladder and leapfrog,
Listen, letter, lullaby and log.
Letter L,
It's very swell.

Letter Y, Letter Y

Tune: Three Blind Mice
Letter y, Letter y.
Starts many words.
Starts many words.
Like yes and yarn and yogurt too,
Yellow and yard, just to name a few.
Letter y, Letter y.

Little Bunnies Come and Play

Tune: Mary Had a Little Lamb
Little bunnies come and play,
Come and play, come and play.
Little bunnies come and play
On this _____. (Monday, Tuesday, Wednesday,
Thursday, Friday, Saturday,
Sunday)

Little Pig

Little pig, little pig sitting just so.
Little pig, _____, time to go.

Mud, Mud, Mud

Tune: Three Blind Mice
Mud mud mud,
I like mud. (snort)
I like mud between my toes. (snort)
I like mud on my big pink nose. (snort)
Mud, mud, mud,
I like mud. (snort)

The Number Rhyme

Number _____ leaf on the tree,
Quietly come line up by me.

Number Three

Tune: Three Blind Mice
Number three. I like three.
Three bears, three pigs and three blind mice.
Number three is very nice.
Number three, I like three.

Sing a Song of Baby Ducks

Tune: Sing a Song of Sixpence
Sing a song of baby ducks
All in a row.
Every where that Mommy goes
Ducklings always go.
They put their heads in water
To look for things to eat
A little bug or little fish
Yum, yum what a treat.

Stringy Stuff

Tune: Jingle Bells
Stringy stuff,
Stringy stuff,
I like stringy stuff:

Spaghetti, ribbons, lace and string
I like everything.

Ten Little Numbers

Tune: Ten Little Indians
One little, two little, three little numbers,
four little, five little, six little numbers,
seven little, eight little, nine little numbers,
On the _____.

telephone   computer
television (remote)   cash register
calendar

There Was a Little Egg

Tune: The Farmer in the Dell
There was a little egg,
There was a little egg,
Heigh ho on the farm,
There was a little egg.

Additional verses:
The little egg hatched...
A little chick popped out...
The little chick ate worms...
The little chick grew up...
Now the chick's a hen...
The hen laid an egg...

Umbrella, Umbrella, 1, 2, 3

Umbrella, umbrella, 1, 2, 3
Who's under the umbrella?
Is it _____?
(Named child responds) No, not me!

Under the Umbrella

Tune: London Bridges
I'm under the umbrella,
Umbrella, umbrella.
I'm under the umbrella
My umbrella is _____.

(red, blue, yellow, green)
I'm under the rainbow,
The rainbow, the rainbow
I'm under the rainbow
A rainbow of colors.

Where, Oh Where Has My Little X Gone?

Tune: Where Oh Where Has My Little Dog Gone?
Where oh where has little x gone?
Where oh where can she be?
She's in the word fox and in the word box
And also in ax, tax and wax.

Where, Oh, Where Has the Umbrella Gone?

Tune: Where Oh Where Has My Little Dog Gone?
Where, oh where has the umbrella gone?
Where oh where can it be?
It's raining outside and I want to play
Where oh where, can it be?

Who Lives in the Zoo?

Tune: London Bridge
_____ lives in the zoo, in the zoo, in the zoo.
_____ lives in the zoo,
With his friends.

_____ lives on the farm, on the farm, on the farm.
_____ lives on the farm,
With his friends.

Y Is for Young

Y is for young, yogurt, and yell.
It is also for yams and a yellow bell.

Mud Puddles

For each child:
¼ cup milk
2 tablespoons chocolate pudding powder
Gummy worm
Resealable baggies

Add milk and chocolate pudding powder to each resealable baggie, as well as a gummy worm or two. Zip the bags shut, and hand them out for the children to squish until they turn to "mud." When done, encourage the children to unzip them and enjoy.

Umbrella Breadsticks

For each child:
1 raw breadstick from can
1 round canned biscuit
Peanut butter, jelly, butter, or cream cheese

Give each child a raw breadstick from a can of breadsticks. Invite them to shape their breadstick into the shape of a j. Add a round biscuit from a can of biscuits, to the top of the j to make an umbrella. Cook as directed. Invite the children to spread their umbrella with peanut butter, jelly, butter, or cream cheese.

Zipper Bag Snack Mix

1 zipper bag
2 mini-cookies
3 fruit snacks
4 chocolate chips
4 mini-crackers
6 raisins
7 marshmallows
8 circle cereals
9 fish crackers
10 pretzel sticks

Bunny Facts

- Wild rabbits live in large groups together in a maze of tunnels called a warren.
- There are hundreds of breeds of pet rabbits.
- Rabbits have fluffy tails called scuts.
- They have long ears that can swivel in all directions to listen.
- Rabbits can see all around but cannot see far away.
- Rabbits eat grass, hay, and a mixture of grains.
- Rabbits' front teeth continue to grow all the time so must gnaw on things.
- Pet rabbits need company, but male rabbits fight.
- Rabbits communicate by thumping on the ground with their back feet.
- Newborn rabbits are called kittens.

Chameleon Facts

- Chameleons can change colors. In bright sunlight, they can be yellow with green spots. In the shade they turn green all over. Chameleons can change from spotted to stripes.
- Chameleons use colors to "talk." Bright colors and patterns tell other chameleons to stay away. If chameleons are fighting and one turns brown it means "I give up."

- There are more than 100 different kinds of chameleons.
- Chameleons use their tails as an extra arm or leg to climb.
- Chameleons have sharp eyes that can look in two directions at once.
- Chameleons use their sticky tongues to catch insects to eat.
- Males and females use colors to send messages to mate. The male puffs out his skin and flashes bright colors. Females get smaller and are one color.
- As chameleons grow, they shed their skin. This is molting. The old skin peels off as they grow into the new skin.
- Chameleons are reptiles.

Duck Facts

- Ducks do not get wet because they have an oil gland. Ducks use their bills to spread the oil all over their feathers. Oil makes the water roll off the feathers.
- Ducks tip their heads down into the water to find food.
- Mallard Ducks eat pond grass, wild rice, seeds and insects.
- Ducks can dive 100 feet down into the water (as high as a 10 story building) and they can swim about 300 feet underwater.
- When winter comes and the lakes freeze, they cannot find food. They have to fly south where there is open water.
- Ducks can fly as fast as 70 miles per hour.
- Ducks travel the same route south every year.
- Ducks have 12,000 feathers and each feather lasts a year.
- Ducks molt: old feathers fall out and new ones grow. It takes about three weeks. During this time, the ducks cannot fly.

Worm Facts

- Worms have rings or segments.
- Earthworms feed on decaying plants found on or near the soil surface.
- The worm must keep his body moist to move through the soil.
- There are about 1,800 species of earthworms.
- Worms are invertebrates.
- Worms are important for keeping the soil well drained, aired and healthy by burrowing.
- Worms are both male and female but two worms must mate.
- Earthworms can push objects that are 10 times their own weight.
- As worms burrow, they suck in dirt and digest the food items they need.
- Worms move by stretching its body in the direction it wants to go.

Worm Farm

- To look for worms, water the soil and leave it for a few hours and worms will come to the surface.
- Keep worms in a tall jar, keeping it cool and moist but not wet.
- Place worms on top of the soil, and they will burrow down into it.
- Worms move away from light and come out to collect food when it is dark.
- Every 6 weeks add a small amount of oatmeal and a few decaying leaves as food.

EASY DAILY PLANS | APPENDIX

May Appendix

A Bee's Life

It is a hot summer day at the beehive. The queen bee is laying eggs into each cell of the beehive. Your little brother is cleaning the beehive and feeding the baby bee larvae some nectar. A few worker bees are trying to cool down the hot beehive by flapping their wings. It's almost time to go looking for pollen from flowers to make honey. You finish eating your breakfast of honey. Your friends come by to ask you if you are ready by moving their eyes. You move your eyes to tell them yes. You and your friends fly out of the beehive to look for flowers. Your antenna smells the scent of another bee. Then you see your bee friend flying in circles ahead. That means there are flowers. You and your friend fly to them as you look into the sun to help you figure out where you are going. You and your friends dance around on the flower to get pollen on your legs. You eat the yummy nectar of the flower for lunch. Now it's your turn to fly in circles above the flowers to tell other bees to come. Then you fly back to the hive. Your bee friends ask you where you found the flowers. You do another special dance to tell them. It's been a long day of work. You are tired. But of course that is why you are called the worker bee.

The Backwards Song

Tune: Did You Ever See a Lassie?
I can hop backwards,
Hop backwards, hop backwards.
I can hop backwards
All by myself.

Additional verses
I can walk backwards...
I can jump backwards...
I can crawl backwards...

The Bike Song

Tune: Sing a Song of Sixpence
I'm a little duck and
I like to ride a bike.
All of my friends said
I'd be better off to hike.
But when my ride was over,
I turned around with glee,
All of my farm friends
Were riding bikes with me.

The Bumblebee Song

Tune: Skip to My Lou
Buzz, buzz bumblebee
Buzz, buzz bumblebee
Buzz, buzz bumblebee
Looking for a flower.

Additional verses
Dancing on a flower...
Fly back to your hive...
Making me some honey...

The Cat Song

Tune: Do Your Ears Hang Low?
Do your ears point up?
Do you have a lot of fun?
And when you are happy
Do you start to purr?
Do you like to chase a mouse,
All around the great big house?
Then, you are a cat!

The Color Song

Tune: Head, Shoulders, Knees and Toes
Red, yellow, green, and blue, green and blue
Red, yellow, green and blue, green and blue.
Orange, purple and pink beads too
Red. Yellow, green and blue, green and blue.
*Invite children to stand if they are wearing that color bead.

The Crocodile Song

Tune: Pop Goes the Weasel
Hiding down in the water so deep
Pretending to be asleep.
The crocodile sees something to munch
Snap! Time for lunch!

The Dog Song

Tune: I'm a Little Teapot
I'm a ____ dog and I like to play
Outside in the yard all day.
But if I see somebody new
I'll bark very loud so I will tell you.

The Exercise Song

Tune: Mary Had a Little Lamb
____ helps me be strong.
Me be strong, me be strong
____ helps me be strong
Every day.

Exercise
Getting rest
Eating well

The Four Seasons

Tune: Mary Had a Little Lamb
Winter, Spring, Summer, and Fall
Winter and Spring
Summer and Fall
Winter, Spring, Summer, and Fall
Four seasons in a year.

Gallop Around

Tune: Mulberry Bush
____, ____ gallop around,
Gallop around, gallop around.
____, ____ gallop around
Around in a circle.

Galloping Horses

Tune: Little Red Wagon
1 little, 2 little, 3 little horses
4 little, 5 little, 6 little horses
7 little, 8 little, 9 little horses
Running in a race.

Hola Means Hello

Tune: The Farmer in the Dell
Hola means hello.
Hola means hello.
Hola, amigos.
Hola means hello.

Additional verses
Amigos means friends...
Por favor means please...
Gracias means thank you...

Honey Bee Hokey Pokey

Tune: Hokey Pokey
Put your head in
Put your head out
Put your head in and shake it all about
You do the Bee Hokey Pokey
And you turn yourself around
That's what its all about.

Additional verses
antennas
abdomen
thorax (bottom)
legs
wings
whole bee

If You're Riding in the Car

Tune: If You're Happy and You Know It
If you're riding in the car, buckle up.
If you're riding in the car, buckle up.
When you go from place to place,
And you want to stay safe,
When you're riding in the car, buckle up.

Little Hamsters

Tune: London Bridge
Little hamsters like to chew,
Like to chew, like to chew.
Little hamsters like to chew
On cardboard tubes.

Additional verse
Little hamsters like to run...on their wheels

Mary Had a Little Lamb

Mary had a little lamb,
Little lamb, little lamb.
Mary had a little lamb
Its fleece as white as snow.

Additional verses:
Mary had a little pig,
Little pig, little pig.
Mary had a little pig
Who loved to play in mud.

Mary had a little cow
Little cow, little cow
Mary had a little cow
Who loved to eat the hay.

Mary had a little duck,
Little duck, little duck.
Mary had a little duck
Who loved to quack, quack, quack.

The May Day Song

Tune: Daisy, Daisy
May Day, May Day
It starts the month of May.
It tells me that spring is here
And I can go out and play.
Flowers for a friend
So your friendship may never end.
May Day, May Day,
It starts the month of May.

The M Song

Tune: The Farmer in the Dell
I like the letter m.
It starts many words,
Like mitten, monkey, mouse, and moon,
And others you have heard.

Mr. Dragon Says

Tune: Skip to My Lou
"I'm a dragon with people feet
I like dancing in the street
I try to scare the children away
So they won't want to come and play.

Children sing:
"Mr. Dragon you can't scare me
I'm as brave as I can be.
When you come and want to play
I'm not going to run away.

The Pet Song

Tune: Did You Ever See a Lassie?
A pet needs exercise
Exercise, exercise.
A pet needs exercise
Every day.

A pet needs good food…
A pet needs some water…
A pet needs lots of love…

The Police Officer Is My Friend

Tune: The Farmer in the Dell
Police officer is my friend.
Police officer is my friend.
Wherever I need help, I can call.
Police officer is my friend.

Silly Socks Chant

If your silly socks have red,
Reach way up and touch your head.

If your silly socks have blue,
Reach down and touch your shoe.

If your silly socks have brown,
Jump, jump, jump up and down.

If your silly socks have green,
Make a face that's very mean.

If there are stripes on your sock,
Hop, hop, hop, then walk, walk, walk.

If your silly socks are white,
Pretend you're sound asleep at night.

If there are circles on your sock,
Point up to your classroom clock.
If your silly socks have pink,
Give your friend a great big wink.

The Sock Song

Tune: I'm a Little Teapot
I'm a sock and it's a treat
When I cover up clean feet.
But if the feet are dirty, I cover my nose
Peee-yew! Clean those toes.

The Strawberry Song

Tune: Three Blind Mice
Strawberries,
Yum yum, yum!
Strawberries,
Yum, yum, yum!
I like strawberries on bagels and toast.
I like them on ice cream the most.
Strawberries,
Yum, yum, yum!

The Truck Song

Tune: Did You Ever See a Lassie?
I'm driving in my mail truck
My mail truck, my mail truck.
I'm driving in my mail truck.
I'm delivering the mail.

Additional verses
I'm driving in my fire truck…
I put out the fires.

I'm driving in my cement truck…
I'm making the roads.

The Wheels on the Bike

Tune: The Wheels on the Bus
The wheels on the bike go round and round,
Round and round, round and round.
The wheels on the bike go round and round,
All through the town.

Additional verses:
The horn on the bike goes beep, beep, beep…
The child on the bike says, "Look at me"…

RECIPES

Doggie Chow (for People)!

1 cup peanut butter
12 oz milk chocolate chips
1 stick butter
1 box cereal squares, such as Chex®
3 cups powdered sugar

Melt the peanut butter, chocolate chips, and butter and stir. Add one small box of cereal squares. Mix with 3 cups of powdered sugar.

Hamster Mix

Mix the following ingredients for a healthy hamster snack.

sunflower seeds   peanuts
raisins   non-sugary cereal O's
pretzel sticks   dried fruits

Haystack Cookies

2 bags butterscotch chips
2 bags of milk chocolate chips
2 cans of chow mein noodles

Melt the chips together and mix. Add the chow mein noodles and mix. Carefully mold into haystacks and let harden

Monkey Bread

2 cans of biscuit dough
Butter, melted
Brown Sugar
Cinnamon

Open two cans of biscuit dough. Cut each biscuit in four pieces. Dip the biscuit pieces in melted butter and then in brown sugar. Put them in a prepared pan. Sprinkle cinnamon on top. Bake according to the directions on the can.

Whales in the Ocean

For each child:
½ canned pear
Blue gelatin
2 apple slices

Add a pear whale to a blue gelatin "ocean." Make blue gelatin according to the package directions with the children. Put the gelatin in clear plastic cups to harden. Before it hardens all the way add 1/2 a canned pear as a whale body and use 2 cut apple slices as fins, one going each way out of the small end of the pear. Let harden and enjoy.

USEFUL FACTS AND OTHER INFORMATION

Alligator and Crocodile Facts

◆ Differences between crocodiles and alligators:
  ◆ Alligators have rounded snouts and crocodiles' snouts are pointed.
  ◆ When their mouths are closed, alligators' teeth cannot be seen, but crocodiles' can be seen.
  ◆ Crocodiles can live to be over 100 years old; alligators live to be 30 to 40 years.
◆ Crocodiles and alligators are usually 10 to 12 feet long but can be up to 26 feet long.

◆ Alligators look like they are sleeping in the water, but are really watching and waiting for food.
◆ Alligators lay eggs.
◆ Alligators and crocodiles spend most of their time in the water.
◆ Alligators and crocodiles like to eat fish, small animals, turtles and birds.
◆ A big crocodile can even eat a lion, hippo or a tiger.
◆ People hunt alligators for their leather for belts, shoes, and handbags.
◆ They are reptiles; land dwellers, lay eggs, breathe with lungs.
◆ There are 14 kinds of crocodiles and 2 types of alligators.
◆ Both have been around since the dinosaur time and are close relatives.
◆ By 1972, different crocodiles were threatened, endangered, or declining. Now, they are protected.

Asian Holidays

Chinese New Year:
◆ For Chinese people, this is the most important holiday of the year.
◆ Everyone celebrates the old year leaving and the birth of the New Year.
◆ "Gung Hay Fat Choy" means Happy New Year.
◆ The holiday lasts for 15 days.
◆ People decorate their houses with pink and red flowers.

Japanese Children's Day:
◆ It is celebrated on May 5.
◆ The symbol for this day is a fish because he overcomes hard obstacles.
◆ This used to be just for boys but now girls celebrate it too.
◆ The Japanese name is Kodomono-hi.
◆ A decoration for this holiday is a doll with a helmet and a sword. This is the wish of the parents; for their boy (child) to be strong and successful.

Bee Facts

- The kinds of bees are queen, drone, and worker bee.
- Bees see, move around, and communicate with other bees by using their eyes.
- Antennae allow bees to recognize the scent of other bees.
- Bees figure out where a field of flowers is by comparing the distance between the sun and the hive.
- A bee signals where flowers are to other bees by flying in circles.
- Bees feed on nectar and collect pollen to make honey.
- Each honey tastes slightly different according to the kind of flower the nectar comes from.
- Youngest bees in the hive do housekeeping, stock up on food, and feed larvae.
- During winter, bees hibernate inside the hive. They cluster and keep close to the queen. Bees feed on honey they've stored from summer.
- Bees are insects.

Cat Facts

- Adult cats weigh from 6 to 15 pounds.
- Cats have excellent vision. They see in color but cannot see in total darkness.
- Cats can hear things too faint for humans to hear.

Cats communicate their feelings.
- When cats purr, it means they are happy.
- When cats gurgle, it means they are happy.
- When cats meow, it means they are hungry or unhappy.
- When cats hiss, screech, and growl, it means they are angry.

Cat use body language.
- When they rub against someone or something, it means they are happy and affectionate.
- When they point their ears forward, it means they are interested and watchful.
- When they are angry, they raise their ears and point them forward.
- When they are defensive, they arch their backs, flatten their ears, and show their teeth.

Dog Facts

- There are many different breeds of dogs.
- There are 30 kinds of wild dogs, including the gray wolf, red fox, and coyote.
- Dogs pant to stay cool.
- Dogs' sharpest sense is smell, but they hear four times better than people.
- A small to medium dog lives about 15 years, a large dog about 10 years.
- Many scientists think dogs see in shades of gray.

Dogs need certain things to stay healthy.
- They need to be fed 1–2 times each day.
- They need exercise.
- They need fresh water.
- They need regular grooming.
- They need safe toys to play with.
- They need cozy beds to sleep in.
- They need regular visits to the veterinarian.
- They need a lot of love.

Dogs help people.
- Some dogs are guide dogs for blind people or people with disabilities.
- Some dogs help farmers round up sheep.
- Some dogs pull sleds in the snow.
- Some dogs help police officers solve crimes.
- Some dogs guard the home where they live.

Dogs communicate in different ways.
- When a dog is happy, it wags its tail.
- When a dog is angry, it bares its teeth.
- When a dog is scared, it puts its tail between its legs.

- When a dog whines, it means it is restless and/or excited.
- When a dog barks like a "woof" it is a warning.
- When a dog growls or barks, it is angry.

fish   potbelly pig
turtle   hermit crab
snake   chameleon
spider   lizard
mouse

Hamster Facts

- Hamsters are good pets. They are clean, take up very little space, and are not very noisy.
- Hamsters live about two years.
- Hamsters are rodents; they have sharp teeth and gnaw on things.
- Hamsters eat grain, seeds, roots, and fruit.
- Hamsters in the wild make burrows, come out at night when it is cooler, and hibernate in winter.
- Hamsters need a well-balanced diet, enough exercise, and a clean cage.

Horse Facts

- Horses can trot 12 miles an hour for 4 hours without stopping.
- A racehorse can run up to 42 miles an hour.
- Horses have long, very light legs.
- Hoses sleep standing up.
- Horses can see the colors red and blue, but not the other colors.
- Horses see well in poor light.
- Horses' ears can turn in the direction of sound.
- Horses smell the breeze to know that predators are near, such as coyotes or wolves.
- Horses spend at least 60% of the day eating, and their main diet is grass and hay.
- Like people, horses recognize the voices of other horses.

Pet List:

dog   hamster
cat   guinea pig
bird   horse
rabbit   goat

Whale Facts

- Whales are mammals and cannot breathe underwater. They rise to the water's surface and blow air out of blowholes on the tops of their heads.
- Whales are in the Cetacean family, which includes whales, dolphins, and porpoises.
- The sounds that whales make help them find their way and locate food by using echoes.
- Whale songs during the mating season can be up to 30 minutes long.
- Baleen whale calves are born in winter near the equator. Then, in the spring, they all swim to colder water.
- Beluga whales live in the Arctic. Beluga means white in Russian.
- An Orca is called a killer whale, but it is actually a dolphin.
- They have 40 or more teeth.
- They hunt in groups.
- They are playful and gentle with people.
- Sperm whales are the biggest whales. The female is the size of a bus, and the male is double that size.
- Baleen whales have no teeth.
- The blue whale is a type of Baleen whale, and can be up to 100 feet long.
- Whales are protected by blubber, which is a thick layer of fat.
- Whale hunting ended in 1983.

June, July, August Appendix

WEEK ONE: SUMMER FUN

The publisher grants permission for this page to be photocopied for distribution for the teacher's classroom use only.
© Gryphon House, Inc. 800.638.0928.www.gryphonhouse.com.

SONGS AND POEMS

Baseball Outside

Tune: Pop Goes the Weasel
I love to play baseball outside.
It's my turn to bat.
The ball comes fast.
I swing with my bat.
One, two, three strikes you're out.

Going to the Fair

Tune: Farmer in the Dell
I'm going to the fair.
There's lots of people there,
With food and music and lots of games,
And rides, if you dare.

Hot Dogs on the Grill

Tune: My Little Red Wagon
One little, two little, three little hot dogs.
Four little, five little, six little hot dogs.
Seven little, eight little, nine little hot dogs,
Cooking on the grill.

One little, two little, three little bites.
Four little, five little, six little bites.
Seven little, eight little, nine little bites,
Of hot dog in my tummy.

Additional verses:
On their hotdog buns...
With ketchup and mustard on...

Ice Cream, Ice Cream

Tune: Bicycle Built for Two
Ice cream, ice cream,
I eat it every day.
I love ice cream.
It makes my bones strong to play.
I'll eat it in the summer.
I'll eat it in the winter.
It's oh so sweet,
A special treat,
I love to eat ice cream!

Ice Cream, Oh So Sweet

Ice cream, ice cream, oh so sweet,
_____ ice cream is such a treat.

Merry-Go-Round and Round

Round and round, up and down.
Who is going on the merry-go-round?

Ten Little Hot Dogs

10 little hot dogs in the bun
I am hungry so I eat one.
Hot dogs, hot dogs, what a treat!
There are now ___ hot dogs left to eat.

WEEK TWO: AT THE BEACH

PATTERNS

Manatee
Parrot
Seahorse

SONGS AND POEMS

Did You Ever See a Seashell?

Tune: Did You Ever See a Lassie?
Did you ever see a seashell, a seashell, a seashell?
Did you ever see a seashell,
Down at the beach?

Additional verses:
...sailboat...
...starfish...
...lion...

Dolphin in the Sea

Tune: Twinkle, Twinkle, Little Star
Dolphin, dolphin, in the sea
Play with your friend just like me.
You leap and dive in the air
Up so high without a care.
Dolphin, dolphin, in the sea
Play with your friend just like me.

I Am a Pirate

Tune: Do Your Ears Hang Low?
With a patch upon my eye,
And a parrot who won't fly,
On my boat upon the sea,
Finding treasure all for me,
I never go slow,
Just in case you do not know,
I am a pirate.

One Little Dolphin

One little dolphin swimming in the sea,
He asked a friend, "Please swim with me."

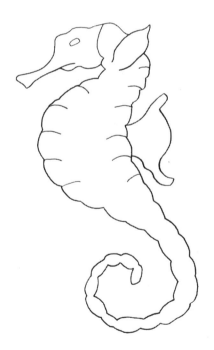

Pirate Talk

"Ahoy, Matey," is what I say,
When it is time for ____ to go and play (or away).

Seahorse in the Sea

I'm a seahorse in the sea.
Look and look but you can't find me!

Seahorse, Seahorse

Tune: Daisy, Daisy
Seahorse, seahorse,
Out in the deep blue sea.
You may change colors,
But you can't hide from me.
I know where you are.
You're by your friend, the star.
So come on out and play with me
Out in the deep blue sea.

Ten Little Fish

Tune: My Little Red Wagon
One little, two little, three little fish.
Four little, five little, six little fish.
Seven little, eight little, nine little fish,
Swimming in the sea.

You're a Manatee

Tune: Do Your Ears Hang Low?
If you're big and wide
So that you cannot hide,
And you swim in the sea,
And eat seaweed with your tea,
If you like the water warm
And you don't cause any harm,
Then you're a manatee.

Coconut Playdough Recipe

2 cups flour
1 cup salt
2 cups water
2 teaspoons coconut extract
2 tablespoons vegetable oil
4 teaspoons cream of tartar

Combine all the ingredients in a pot. Cook, over low heat, stirring until a dough forms. Let cool before using.

Dolphin Facts

◆ Dolphins are mammals, meaning they have backbones, breathe air, and their babies drink milk.
◆ Dolphins love to socialize and live in groups of thousands.
◆ The U.S. Navy uses dolphins to find explosives, find people lost at sea, and carry tools to underwater worksites.
◆ Dolphins use echolocation, or sound reverberations, like submarines, to map surroundings and find their way.
◆ Dolphins can swim up to 25 miles an hour.
◆ Dolphins group together in schools, herds, or pods.
◆ Dolphins blow bubbles to warn other dolphins of danger.
◆ Dolphins sleep by taking 5–10 minute naps that add up to 6–8 hours in a 24-hour period.

Manatee Facts

◆ Manatees are mammals, like humans, because they are warm-blooded.
◆ Manatees are gray. They have two flippers and a flat tail.

- Manatees grow to be about 10 feet and weigh about 1,200 pounds.
- Manatees live in fresh and salt water that is less than 15 feet deep and warmer than 70 degrees.
- Manatees eat mostly plants, eating up to 150 pounds of plants a day in about six to eight hours.
- Manatees are endangered because they are harmed by boat propellers.

Seahorse Facts

- A seahorse is a fish.
- Seahorses swim standing up and they move very slowly.

- Seahorses hide from enemies by changing colors to blend in.
- Male seahorses, not females, give birth to their young.
- Seahorses eat tiny shrimp. A seahorse's snout works like a vacuum cleaner to suck up food.
- Seahorses hold themselves in place by wrapping their tails around grasses.
- When a seahorse is frightened, it curls its tail around its snout and makes itself very small.
- Seahorses have cirri, which are knobs and spines on the top of their heads. The cirri protect them from being eaten by their natural enemies, such as crab, tuna, skates, and rays.
- Seahorses are in danger from fishing and water pollution that poisons their food.

WEEK THREE: SUMMER SAFARI

PATTERNS

Giraffe
Lion
Tiger
Zebra

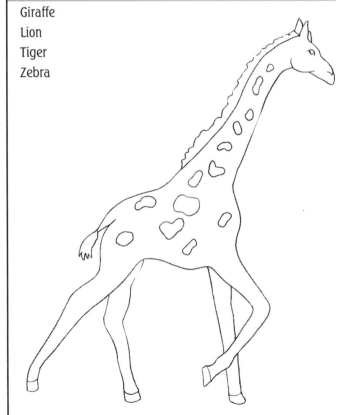

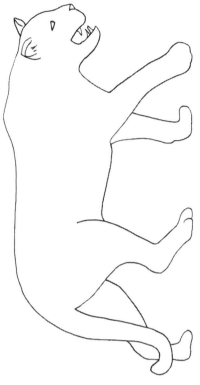
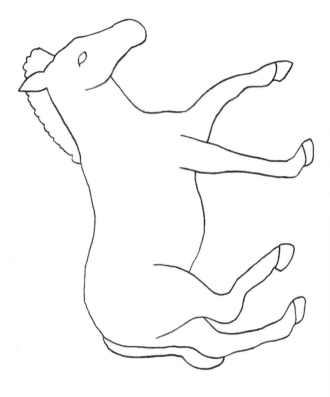

SONGS AND POEMS

Giraffe and Mouse

_____, giraffe, oh so tall,
Name something that is very small.

_____, mouse, oh so small,
Name something that is very tall.

Giraffes at the Zoo

Tune: Twinkle, Twinkle, Little Star
Giraffes, giraffes, in the zoo
I love to come and look at you.
You are so very tall.
I am so very small.
You are beautiful by the trees
In the hot summer breeze.

Great Big Tiger

Tune: I'm a Little Teapot
I'm a great big tiger.
I have stripes on my back.
I am very big
With colors orange and black.
I sleep during the day
And at night go on the prowl.
And I don't talk,
I will give a great big growl. (growl)

I'm a Zebra

Tune: I'm a Little Teapot
I'm a zebra, black and white.
I am a very handsome sight.
I run and gallop in the sun,
Eat some grass and have some fun.

Lion on the Savannah

One lion went out to play
Out on the savannah one sunny day.
He had such enormous fun,
He called another lion to come.

Tiger on the Prowl

I'm a big orange tiger.
I am going on the prowl.
If you get too close,
I will give a great big growl. (growl)

Zebra Gallop

Zebra _____ kick up high,
As you go galloping by.

USEFUL FACTS AND OTHER INFORMATION

Giraffe Facts

◆ The legs of a giraffe are taller than a person who is six feet tall.
◆ Giraffes can walk as fast as 10 miles an hour.
◆ Giraffes wrestle by swinging their heads, with the winner being the dominant mate.
◆ Babies are 6 feet tall at birth, and in 7 years they can reach 18 feet tall.
◆ Giraffes can go several days without water because there is moisture in the leaves that they eat.
◆ Giraffes consume 75 pounds of food each day.
◆ Giraffes like more than 100 different plants, but Acacia leaves are their favorites.

Lion Facts

◆ The lion is called the king of beasts.
◆ The male can grow to 10 feet long (with tail).
◆ Lions can weigh up to 500 pounds.

◆ Lions usually hunt in the evening and early morning.
◆ Lions are so good at hunting that they can stay within a five-mile radius and hunt only two or three hours a day.
◆ Lions travel in prides with up to 30 members.
◆ Lions eat everything from insects to giraffes, but prefer large animals that they share with the rest of the pride.
◆ The female usually makes the kill and the male eats it.
◆ Lions may eat up to 60 pounds of meat at one time and then not eat for another week.
◆ Lions can live for up to 25 years in captivity, but sometimes less than 10 years if they are in the wild.

Tiger Facts

◆ Tigers are the strongest and largest of all wild cats.
◆ The four great cats are lions, leopards, jaguars, and tigers.
◆ Most tigers live in different parts of Asia.
◆ There are five subspecies of tigers—Siberian, Bengal, Indochinese, South China, and Sumatran.
◆ Tigers usually live alone.
◆ Tigers sleep during the day and hunt at night.
◆ Tigers usually do not attack humans.
◆ Tigers are endangered because of poachers.

Zebra Facts

◆ Most zebras are white with black stripes.
◆ Horses and zebras are closely related.
◆ No two zebras have the same pattern of stripes.
◆ Zebras can travel up to 30 miles a day looking for food.
◆ Zebras stay together and face in opposite directions to watch for enemies.
◆ Zebras spend several hours each day grooming themselves and each other. They take dust baths.
◆ A family of zebras is usually a group of 5 to 20 members.
◆ Young male zebras are called colts; young female zebras are called fillies.

SONGS AND POEMS

Airplane

Airplane _____ in the sky,
Where are you going as you fly by?

How Airplanes Fly

Airplanes fly low.
Airplanes fly high.
Airplanes twirl round
In the big blue sky.

Airplanes fly fast.
Airplanes fly slow.
Airplanes twirl round.
Which way will they go?

Airplanes looking down,
Getting ready to land.
Put down your wheels
And land in the sand.

Out in Space

_____, _____, what do you see?
I see _____ out in space with me.

Out in the Universe

Tune: Farmer in the Dell
The sun is a star.
The sun is a star.
Out in the universe,
The sun is a star.

_____ goes 'round the sun.
_____ goes 'round the sun.
Out in the universe,
_____ goes 'round the sun

Sleep-O

Tune: BING-O
Little _____, it's time for bed.
It's time to go to sleep-o.
S-L-E-E-P, S-L-E-E-P, S-L-E-E-P,
It's time to go to sleep.

Twinkle, Twinkle, Quiet Star

Tune: Twinkle, Twinkle, Little Star
Twinkle, twinkle, quiet star,
Sit very quietly where you are.
When I see how you can do,
Then I will call on you.

When I'm High in the Sky

Tune: Do Your Ears Hang Low?
When I'm high in the sky
Then you go outside to play,
But I go down at the end of the day.
I'm a very big star, and I am very hot.
The moon I'm not!
What am I?

WEEK 5: ON THE FARM

PATTERNS

Barn
Troll

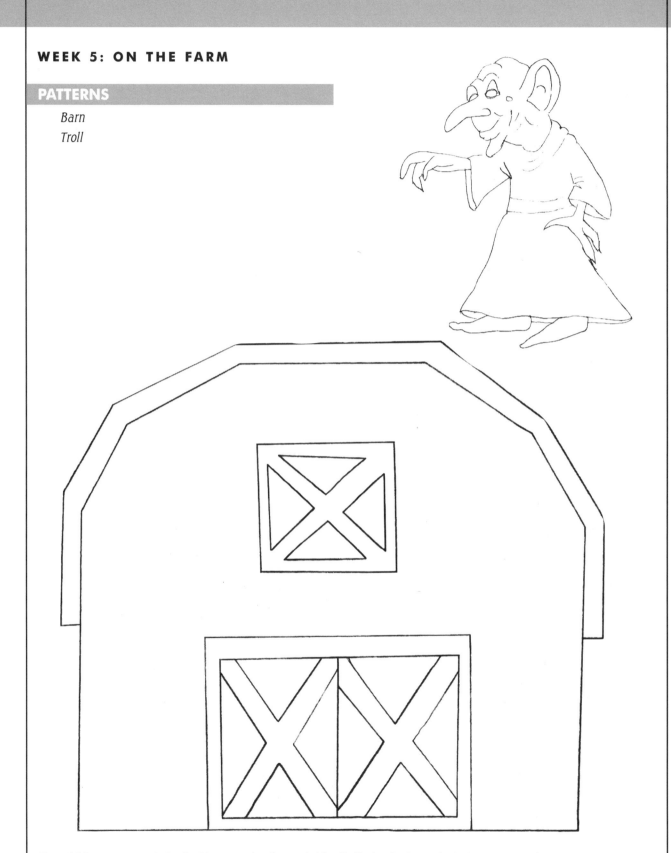

Berries, Berries

Tune: Twinkle, Twinkle, Little Star
Berries, berries,
Hiding in the woods.
Berries, berries,
You are very good.
Blueberry muffins, strawberry pie,
Raspberry ice cream, my, oh, my!
Berries, berries,
Hiding in the woods.
Berries, berries,
You are very good.

The Cow Says "Moo"

Tune: The Farmer in the Dell
The cow says, "moo,"
The cow says, "moo,"
Animal, animals on the farm,
The cow says, "moo."

Additional verses:
The horse says, "neigh"…
The pig says, "oink"…
The duck says, "quack"…
The sheep say, "baa"…

I Am a Cow

Tune: Do Your Ears Hang Low?
I go stand outside chewing cud all day.
I never run and laugh or even play.
But I have a very important job to do,
I make milk for you.

I Eat Corn for Breakfast

Tune: London Bridge
I eat corn for breakfast
For breakfast, for breakfast.
I eat corn for breakfast
In my cereal.

I eat corn for lunch,
For lunch, for lunch.
I eat corn for lunch
In my taco.

I eat corn for dinner
For dinner, for dinner.
I eat corn for dinner
In my corn on the cob.

Three Billy Goats

Tune: Three Blind Mice
Three billy goats, three billy goats,
Wanted to cross the bridge,
Wanted to cross the bridge.
Two goats said, "Wait for our brother."
Big goat pushed the troll in the water.
No more trolls!
No more trolls!

Watermelon Seeds

Watermelon seeds 1, 2, 3,
How many seeds do you see, _____?

Watermelon, Watermelon

Tune: Frere Jacques
Watermelon, watermelon,
Very sweet,
And fun to eat.
I will eat a slice,
It's so very nice.
But don't eat the seeds.
Don't eat the seeds.

RECIPES

Blueberry Treats

Give each child a foil muffin/cupcake liner. Invite them to put a vanilla cookie in the bottom of the paper, add two teaspoons of vanilla pudding on top of the cookie, and top with a teaspoon of blueberry pie filling.

Watermelon Boat Fruit Salad

Cut a watermelon in half lengthwise. Scoop out the red watermelon with a melon ball scoop or spoon until the all of the fruit has been removed. The watermelon shell becomes a boat. Mix together the watermelon scoops, cantaloupe scoops, grapes cut in half, and any other fruit you wish. Put back into the watermelon shell.

SUMMER WEEK 6: SUMMER BUGS

PATTERNS

Butterfly
Dragonfly

Butterfly, Butterfly

Butterfly, butterfly, the color blue,
Butterfly, butterfly, where are you?
Butterfly, butterfly, the color red,
Wake up from your snuggly cocoon bed
Butterfly, butterfly, dressed in green,
Hide on a leaf and you won't be seen.
Butterfly, butterfly, dressed in pink,
Are you getting a raindrop drink?
Butterfly, butterfly, dressed in yellow,
Flutter your wings for a butterfly hello.

Butterfly, Fly Around

Tune: Skip to My Lou
_____ butterfly, fly around.
Fly up high and then fly down.
Fly in a circle round and round,
Then land on the ground.

Butterfly, Fly Away

Butterfly _____, no time to play.
Butterfly _____, fly, fly, away.

Caterpillar Went to Play

_____ caterpillar went to play
Out on a big green leaf one day.
He got tired,
Went to sleep,
Woke up a butterfly and flew away.

Dragonfly in the Air

Dragonfly, dragonfly in the air,
Flying around without a care,
Looking for a place to land, I see,
Land somewhere else but not on me.

Dragonfly, Way Up High

Dragonfly _____, way up high,
Wave to your friends and you fly by.

Having a Picnic

We're going on a picnic.
We're going to bring our lunch.
We're going on a picnic.
_____ will bring _____ to munch.

I'm a Ladybug

Tune: I'm a Little Teapot
I'm a ladybug dressed in red,
Sleeping on my green leaf bed.
Don't try to catch me, I won't play.
I'll open my wings and fly away.

I'm a Little Caterpillar

Tune: Sing a Song of Sixpence
I'm a little caterpillar,
And I like to eat,
Especially on green leaves
I stand on with my feet.
I get full and tired,
Then I go to sleep. (yawn)
I wake up as a butterfly
With beautiful wings to keep.

I'm Going on a Picnic

Tune: Mary Had a Little Lamb
I'm going on a picnic,
A picnic, a picnic.
I'm going on a picnic,
And I'll bring some _____.

Ladybug, Fly Away

Ladybug ____, fly away!
It's time for you to go and play.

The Picnic Song

Tune: Do Your Ears Hang Low?
I am going on a picnic,
And I am going to take my lunch,
And a lot of snacks to munch, munch, munch.
I have everything I need and something else too,
Not one ant, but two.

USEFUL FACTS AND OTHER INFORMATION

Caterpillar Facts

- Caterpillars are baby insects or the larva of a butterfly.
- There are 112,000 butterflies, each with its own caterpillar.
- Caterpillars are fussy eaters, and each type only eats certain plants.
- Caterpillars have many enemies and protect themselves using camouflage, a hasty odor, squawking loudly, or spinning cocoons.
- Caterpillars cannot see well but they can tell the difference between light and dark.
- Caterpillars molt up to six times before they spin a cocoon.
- Inside a cocoon, a caterpillar's body breaks down and rebuilds itself.

Dragonfly Facts

- There are 5000 types of dragonflies.
- A dragonfly has a head that swivels around to see in all directions.
- The dragonfly has eyes that can see 42 feet.
- Dragonflies can fly 35 miles an hour and even hover like a helicopter.
- Dragonflies cannot fly if it is too cold.
- Dragonflies eat flies, gnats, mosquitoes, and bees.
- Birds, frogs, and fish eat dragonflies.
- A dragonfly nymph molts into a dragonfly at sunset.

Ladybug Facts

There are more than 5,000 different kinds of ladybugs, including:

- red with black spots,
- black with red spots,
- yellow with black spots, and
- red with yellow and black spots.

- Ladybugs are not dangerous but they do bite.
- Animals and birds won't eat ladybugs because they taste terrible.
- Ladybugs eat aphids, which attack alfalfa, wheat, and roses.
- Female ladybug eats about 70 aphids each day, males about 40.
- Ladybugs are now bred and put in orange groves.
- Ladybugs are slow fliers and usually walk.
- Ladybugs clean their faces after eating.
- Ladybugs find shelter and rest in the winter.

PATTERNS

Camel

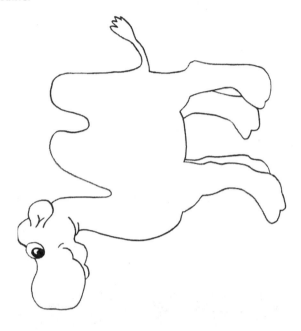

The publisher grants permission for this page to be photocopied for distribution for the teacher's classroom use only.
© Gryphon House, Inc. 800.638.0928. www.gryphonhouse.com.

SONGS AND POEMS

Aloha, Goodbye

Tune: Good Night, Ladies
Aloha, _____
Aloha, _____
Aloha, _____
We're sad to say goodbye.

Aloha Means Hello

Tune: The Farmer in the Dell
Aloha means hello.
Aloha means hello.
Aloha means hello and bye.
Aloha means hello.

Desert Land

_____ in the desert land
Move across the hot, hot sand.

I Am a Rock...

Tune: I'm a Little Teapot
I am a rock out on the beach
Down in the water where you can reach.
The waves go in and waves go out,
The smoother it makes me all about.

I am a rock that you dig up.
I might have a secret that you'll love.
I might have a fossil that you see
Of something that lived before you and me.

I'm a Camel in the Sand

Tune: I'm a Little Teapot
I'm a camel in the sand.
I carry people across the land.
I can have one hump or maybe two,
And sit when there's work that I won't do.

In the Desert Sun

Tune: Do Your Ears Hang Low?
In the desert sun, it is very hot all day
So when it's night, the animals want to play.
There is lots of sand and a cactus too.
Animals like rabbits, snakes, and lizards just to
*   name a few.*

Slithery and Slinky

Tune: Do Your Ears Hang Low

*If you're slithery and slinky
And you slide along the rocks,
You have no legs and arms so…
You don't need shoes or socks.
If you eat your food whole
Without a plate or bowl,
Then you are a snake.*

Snake, Snake

*Snake, snake,
On the land, on the lake,
If you have ____ on you,
Slither over and line up too.*

USEFUL FACTS AND OTHER INFORMATION

Camel Facts

- Camels are mammals; they grow to be about 7 feet high and weigh 1600 lbs.
- Dromedary camels have one hump and live in the deserts of North Africa and the Middle East.
- Bactrian camels have two humps and live in the rocky deserts and steppes of Asia, which can be very hot and very cold.
- Camels can go without water for up to three or four days.
- The camel's hump is fat, not water.
- Camels' eyes have bushy eyebrows and two rows of eyelashes to protect their eyes from the sand.
- Camels eat dates, grass, wheat, and oats. In the wild, camels eat thorny plants.

Desert Facts

- Creatures that live in the desert include camels, ants, Gila monsters, jack rabbits, lizards, ostriches, roadrunners, and snakes.
- Cactus plants grow in the desert.
- Deserts are places where there is less than 10 inches of rainfall in a year.
- The temperature in a desert can be as hot as 126 degrees and as cold as 25 degrees
- Desert nomads are people who herd camels, goats, or sheep and live in tents. They move from place to place looking for food and water.
- An oasis is a small green patch of land in a desert with water.

Snake Facts

- There are about 2,700 different kinds of snakes.
- Snakes move by side winding, concertina movement, wriggling, and creeping.
- Snakes hibernate in winter in caves and underground.
- Snakes can smell with their forked tongues; the smells are passed to a special sense organ.
- Snakes kill either with poisons from their fangs, or wrap themselves around victims and squeeze them.
- Snakes do not chew; they eat victims while they are still alive. They swallow their victims whole.
- To swallow their victims, the snakes' ligaments in their jawbones work like rubber bands.
- Snake have long backbones with many ribs. Their complicated joints allow them to move in almost any direction.
- Snakes do not have ears but hear through vibrations.

WEEK EIGHT: LAZY SUMMER DAYS

PATTERNS

Frog
T-shirt

Dandelion, Dandelion

First you are yellow,
Then you are gray.
Dandelion, dandelion,
Blow away.

Dandelions in the Grass

Tune: London Bridge
Dandelions in the grass,
In the grass, in the grass.
Dandelions in the grass,
Make a wish.

Wish and blow the wish away,
Wish away, wish away.
Wish and blow the wish away,
It may come true.

Hands Up High

Hands up high,
Hands down low,
Snap your fingers as you go.

If, Then

If your shirt is blue,
Then tie your shoe.

If your shirt is red,
Then pat your head.

If your shirt is green,
Then make the meanest face seen.

If your shirt is black,
Then touch your back.

If your shirt is white,
Then hide your face out of sight.

If your shirt is yellow,
Then wave hello.

If your shirt is pink,
Then pretend to drink.

My Hands Can Clap

Tune: The Farmer in the Dell
My hands can clap.
My hands can clap.
Hands can do so many things.
My hands can clap.

Additional verses:
...snap...
...wave...
...roll...
...talk...
...pound...

Ten Little Books

Tune: Ten Little Indians
One little, two little, three little books,
Four little, five little, six little books,
Seven little, eight little, nine little books,
All for us to read.

USEFUL FACTS AND OTHER INFORMATION

Dandelion Facts

- Each yellow flower is made up of numerous florets.
- All the little yellow florets together are called a flower head (each can have up to 200 flowers).
- Dandelion seeds are very light, and can blow in the wind for miles.
- Dandelions open and close for three to four days before closing for good.
- Dandelions were brought from England.
- Young, tender leaves can be put into salads; large leaves can be boiled and eaten. The flowers are sometimes made into wine, and the roots into coffee.

Indices

Children's Books Index

Rhymes Index

Snack Index

Song Index

General Index

Children's Books Index

Rhymes Index

A

Airplane, 274, 368
Alligator in the Bay, 249
Aloha, Goodbye, 286
Animals, Animals, 100, 317
April Showers, 208
Are You Mad? 26

B

Bag, Bag, 224, 345
The Bat Says, 64, 303
Bear Poem, 17, 297–298
Before Your Snack, 115
Bunnies Hopping, 345
Butterfly, Fly Away, 282, 372

C

The Cake Rhyme, 137, 323
Cars Go Fast, 251
Caterpillar Went to Play, 284, 372
Chameleon, Where Will You Go? 215, 345
Cherry, Cherry in the Tree, 150
The Cow Says Moo, 275

D

Dance, Dance, Dance, 107, 317
Dandelion, Dandelion, 291, 376
The Days Song, 90
Desert Land, 285, 374
Dinosaur, 43
Don't Let Me Down, 81
Dots, 135, 324
Dragonfly in the Air, 283, 372
Dragonfly, Way Up High, 283, 372

E

Earth Day Helper, 203, 345
Elephant Moves, 33

F

Five Crows, 78, 311
Five Little Birds, 148
Five Little Kites, 187, 336
Five Little Snowmen, 126, 324
Flashlight, Flashlight, 66
Flowers Don't Eat Cheeseburgers, 220
Flowers Growing One by One, 220
Fly Away, 91, 312
For What It's Worth, 203, 346

G

G Is for Gorilla, 304
Gingerbread Man, 102, 318
Giraffe and Mouse, 266, 366
Go, Team, Go! 140, 324
Going on a Picnic, 280, 372

H

Halloween Witch, 49
Hands Up High, 290, 376
Help Clean Up Our Room Today, 28
Hop, Hop, Hop, 346
Hopping High, Hopping Low, 143, 324
Hot Dogs on the Grill, 257
How Airplanes Fly, 274, 368
Humpty Dumpty Sat on the Ground, 346

I

I Am Big, 84
I Have a Little Snow Friend, 126
I Like Winter, 122, 325
I Stay Healthy, 169
I'm a Camel in the Sand, 289
I'm a Little Duck, 208
I'm a Little Seed, 217
I'm a Little Tree Changing All the Time, 202
I'm a Zebra, 267
Ice Cream, Oh So Sweet, 254, 362
If You Have Blue on Your Shoe, 82, 312
If You Take a Little Red, 204
If Your Paper Clip Is Blue, 216, 346
If, Then, 294, 377
Imagine This, 75
Is There a Monster Here? 59

K

Kites, Kites, 187

L

Ladybug, Fly Away, 281, 373
Leaf, Leaf on the Tree, 55
Leprechaun, Sneak Way, 175
Let Me See, 61
Letter Y, 219
Lion on the Savannah, 268, 367
Listen as I Ring the Bell, 110
Little Miss Muffet, 65
Little Pig, 222, 348
Little Popcorn, 42
Little Scarecrow, 78, 313

M

Merry-Go-Round and Round, 362
Milk, Yogurt, Ice Cream, Cheese, 196
The Mitten Rhyme, 127, 325
Moo, Moo, Brown Cow, 276
Moving Vans, 77
Mud, Mud, Mud, 222
My Hand Can Be a Turkey, 74, 313
My Hands Can Clap, 290
My Trick, 85, 313

N

N Is for No, 76
Name a Word …, 51
Name Something Special About You, 84
New Year, 118, 325
The Nine Rhyme, 183, 337
The Number Rhyme, 202, 348
Number Three, 205

O

O Is for Oatmeal, 51, 304
The O Rhyme, 139
One Little Dolphin, 262, 363
Out in Space, 270, 368

Snack Index

Song Index

A

All About Me and You, 18, 297
Aloha Means Hello, 286, 374
Aloha, Goodbye, 374
Alphabet Song, 14, 185, 247
The Ambulance Song, 170, 331
April Showers, 345

B

The Backwards Song, 237, 353
Baseball Outside, 258, 361
Bats, 64, 303
Berries, Berries, 278, 370
The Bike Song, 232, 353
The Black Song, 61, 303
The Blanket Song, 146, 323
Blue Song, 25, 298
Brown Is the Color of My Teddy Bear, 81, 311
Brush Your Teeth, 171, 331
The Bumble Bee Song, 244, 353
Bunnies Hopping, 211
Butterfly, Butterfly, 372
Butterfly, Fly Around, 282, 372

C

Cartons of Milk, 196, 335
The Cat Song, 250, 354
The Chicka Alphabet, 190, 335
Christmas carols, 97
The Color Song, 12, 247, 298, 354
The Colors of Spring, 192, 335
Cooperation, 88, 311
Country Mouse, City Mouse, 98, 317
The Cow Says Moo, 370
The Cowboy Song, 189, 335
Crayons, 24, 298
Criss Cross Your Shoelace, 82, 311
The Crocodile Song, 249, 354

D

The D Song, 107, 317
Dandelions in the Grass, 291, 376
The Days of the Week, 144, 323
The Days Song, 311
Did You Ever See a Seashell? 259, 363
Dinosaur Roar, 43, 303
Does Your Trunk Hang Low? 33, 298
The Dog Song, 239, 354
Dolphin in the Sea, 262, 363
Down in the Kingdom, 177, 335
The Dreidel Song, 94, 318

E

Early in the Morning, 179, 335
The Exercise Song, 233, 354

F

The Family in the House, 311
Family, Family, 71, 311
Feelings Are Okay, 26, 298
Five Little Birds, 331
Five Little Ducks, 207
Five Little Monkeys Jumping on the Bed, 207
Five-Minute Warning by Sue Fleischmann, 299
The Flower Song, 178, 336
Flowers Don't Eat Cheeseburgers, 345
Flowers Growing One by One, 346
For He's a Very Good Artist, 188, 336
The Four Seasons, 238, 354
Frosty the Snowman, 126
The Fruit Song, 193, 336

G

G Is for Gorilla, 58
G, G, the Letter G, 58, 304
Gallop Around, 245, 354
Giraffes at the Zoo, 266, 366
Going to the Fair, 255, 361
Goldie Is Mad, 84, 312
Good Night, Girls and Boys, 130, 324
Gray Squirrel, 38, 299
Great Big Tiger, 269, 366
The Green Song, 184, 336

H

H Is for Hugs, 27, 299
Happy Birthday, 16, 256
Happy Valentine's Day, 156, 331
Hi, Ho, the Hospital, 170, 331
Hola Means Hello, 236, 355
Homes, 100, 318
Honey Bee Hokey Pokey, 355
Hop, Hop, Hop, 211
Hot Dogs on the Grill, 362
How Many Crows? 78, 312

I

I Am a Cow, 276, 370
I Am a Pirate, 264, 363
I Am a Rock, 374
I Am Big, 312
I Am Kind to My Friends, 119, 324
I Am Special, 18, 299
I Am Very Brave, 73, 312
I Can Be Helpful, 28, 299
I Can Do Whatever I Try, 141, 324
I Eat Corn for Breakfast, 279, 370
I Eat Healthy Foods, 169, 331
I Have a Little Snow Friend, 325
I Like Two, 99, 318
I Like You, 101, 318
I Live on Earth, as You Can See, 203, 347
I Thank You for All You Do, 86, 312
I Think I Can, 31, 299
I'm a Camel in the Sand, 374
I'm a Ladybug, 281, 372
I'm a Little Artist, 188, 336
I'm a Little Cardinal, 148, 332
I'm a Little Caterpillar, 284, 372
I'm a Little Chameleon, 215, 347
I'm a Little Cowpoke, 189
I'm a Little Duck, 347
I'm a Little Earthworm, 221, 347
I'm a Little Kite, 187, 337
I'm a Little Penguin, 131, 325
I'm a Little Potato, 186, 337
I'm a Little Seed, 347
I'm a Little Snowflake, 125, 325
I'm a Little Sponge, 79, 312
I'm a Little Tree Changing All the Time, 347
I'm a Mail Carrier, 162, 332
I'm a Weather Person, 153, 332
I'm a Zebra, 366
I'm Going on a Picnic, 280, 372

W

Y

Z

General Index

A

B